NETWORK SECURITY ESSENTIALS

WIRELESS COMMUNICATIONS AND NETWORKS

A comprehensive, state-of-the art survey. Covers fundamental wireless communications topics, including antennas and propagation, signal encoding techniques, spread spectrum, and error correction techniques. Examines satellite, cellular, wireless local loop networks and wireless LANs, including Bluetooth and 802.11. Covers Mobile IP and WAP. ISBN 0-13-040864-6

LOCAL AND METROPOLITAN AREA NETWORKS, SIXTH EDITION

An in-depth presentation of the technology and architecture of local and metropolitan area networks. Covers topology, transmission media, medium access control, standards, internetworking, and network management. Provides an up-to-date coverage of LAN/MAN systems, including Fast Ethernet, Fibre Channel, and wireless LANs, plus LAN QoS. **Received the 2001 TAA award for long-term excellence in a Computer Science Textbook.** ISBN 0-13-012939-9

ISDN AND BROADBAND ISDN, WITH FRAME RELAY AND ATM: FOURTH EDITION

An in-depth presentation of the technology and architecture of integrated services digital networks (ISDN). Covers the integrated digital network (IDN), xDSL, ISDN services and architecture, signaling system no. 7 (SS7) and provides detailed coverage of the ITU-T protocol standards. Also provides detailed coverage of protocols and congestion control strategies for both frame relay and ATM. ISBN 0-13-973744-8

BUSINESS DATA COMMUNICATIONS, FOURTH EDITION

A comprehensive presentation of data communications and telecommunications from a business perspective. Covers voice, data, image, and video communications and applications technology and includes a number of case studies. ISBN 0-13-088263-1

CRYPTOGRAPHY AND NETWORK SECURITY, THIRD EDITION

A tutorial and survey on network security technology. Each of the basic building blocks of network security, including conventional and public-key cryptography, authentication, and digital signatures, are covered. The book covers important network security tools and applications, including S/MIME IP Security, Kerberos, SSL/TLS, SET, and X509v3. In addition, methods for countering hackers and viruses are explored. **Second edition received the TAA award for the best Computer Science and Engineering Textbook of 1999.** ISBN 0-13-091429-0

Prentice Hall   www.prenhall.com/stallings   telephone: 800-526-0485

NETWORK SECURITY ESSENTIALS

Applications and Standards

SECOND EDITION

William Stallings

Pearson Education International

070051
005 A
5TA

Vice President and Editorial Director, ECS: *Marcia J. Horton*
Publisher: *Alan R. Apt*
Project Manager: *Jake Warde*
Associate Editor: *Toni D. Holm*
Editorial Assistant: *Patrick Lindner*
Vice President and Director of Production and Manufacturing, ESM: *David W. Riccardi*
Executive Managing Editor: *Vince O'Brien*
Assistant Managing Editor: *Camille Trentacoste*
Production Editor: *Rose Kernan*
Director of Creative Services: *Paul Belfanti*
Creative Director: *Carole Anson*
Art Director: *Jon Boylan*
Art Editor: *Greg Dulles*
Cover Designer: *Bruce Kenselaar*
Cover Image: *BZB/Getty Images, Inc.*
Manufacturing Manager: *Trudy Pisciotti*
Manufacturing Buyer: *Lisa McDowell*
Senior Marketing Manager: *Pamela Shaffer*

Printed in the United States of America

10 9 8 7 6 5 4 3 2

ISBN 0-13-120271-5

Pearson Education LTD.
Pearson Education Australia Pty. Limited
Pearson Education Singapore, Pte. Ltd.
Pearson Education North Asia Ltd.
Pearson Education Canada, Ltd.
Pearson Educacíon de Mexico, S.A. de C.V.
Pearson Education—Japan
Pearson Education Malaysia, Pte. Ltd.
Pearson Education, Upper Saddle River, NJ

To Antigone—
never dull,
never boring,
always a Sage

CONTENTS

CHAPTER 1   INTRODUCTION 1

1.1   The OSI Security Architecture 4
1.2   Security Attacks 5
1.3   Security Services 9
1.4   Security Mechanisms 13
1.5   A Model for Network Security 13
1.6   Internet Standards and the Internet Society 17
1.7   Outline of This Book 21
1.8   Recommended Reading 21
1.9   Internet and Web Resources 22

PART ONE   CRYPTOGRAPHY 25

**CHAPTER 2   SYMMETRIC ENCRYPTION
                      AND MESSAGE CONFIDENTIALITY 27**

2.1   Symmetric Encryption Principles 28
2.2   Symmetric Encryption Algorithms 34
2.3   Cipher Block Modes of Operation 44
2.4   Location of Encryption Devices 47
2.5   Key Distribution 49
2.6   Recommended Reading and Web Sites 51
2.7   Key Terms, Review Questions, and Problems 51

**CHAPTER 3   PUBLIC-KEY CRYPTOGRAPHY
                      AND MESSAGE AUTHENTICATION 53**

3.1   Approaches to Message Authentication 54
3.2   Secure Hash Functions and HMAC 58
3.3   Public-Key Cryptography Principles 68
3.4   Public-Key Cryptography Algorithms 72
3.5   Digital Signatures 78
3.6   Key Management 79
3.7   Recommended Reading and Web Sites 81
3.8   Key Terms, Review Questions, and Problems 82

PART TWO NETWORK SECURITY APPLICATIONS 85

CHAPTER 4   AUTHENTICATION APPLICATIONS 87

4.1   Kerberos 88
4.2   X.509 Authentication Service 105
4.3   Recommended Reading and Web Sites 114
4.4   Key Terms, Review Questions, and Problems 115
Appendix 4A   Kerberos Encryption Techniques 117

CHAPTER 5   ELECTRONIC MAIL SECURITY 121

5.1   Pretty Good Privacy 122
5.2   S/MIME 141
5.3   Recommended Web Sites 158
5.4   Key Terms, Review Questions, and Problems 158
Appendix 5A   Data Compression Using Zip 159
Appendix 5B   RADIX-64 Conversion 162
Appendix 5C   PGP Random Number Generation 164

CHAPTER 6   IP SECURITY 167

6.1   IP Security Overview 168
6.2   IP Security Architecture 171
6.3   Authentication Header 177
6.4   Encapsulating Security Payload 182
6.5   Combining Security Associations 187
6.6   Key Management 190
6.7   Recommended Reading and Web Sites 201
6.8   Key Terms, Review Questions, and Problems 202
Appendix 6A   Internetworking and Internet Protocols 203

CHAPTER 7   WEB SECURITY 213

7.1   Web Security Considerations 214
7.2   Secure Socket Layer and Transport Layer Security 217
7.3   Secure Electronic Transaction 234
7.4   Recommended Reading and Web Sites 246
7.5   Key Terms, Review Questions, and Problems 246

CHAPTER 8   NETWORK MANAGEMENT SECURITY 249

     8.1   Basic Concepts of SNMP 250
     8.2   SNMPv1 Community Facility 258
     8.3   SNMPv3 261
     8.4   Recommended Reading and Web Sites 286
     8.5   Key Terms, Review Questions, and Problems 286

PART THREE   SYSTEM SECURITY   291

CHAPTER 9   INTRUDERS 293

     9.1   Intruders 294
     9.2   Intrusion Detection 297
     9.3   Password Management 309
     9.4   Recommended Reading and Web Sites 319
     9.5   Key Terms, Review Questions, and Problems 320
     Appendix 9A   The Base-Rate Fallacy 322

CHAPTER 10 MALICIOUS SOFTWARE 325

     10.1   Viruses and Related Threats 326
     10.2   Virus Countermeasures 337
     10.3   Recommended Reading and Web Site 341
     10.4   Key Terms, Review Questions, and Problems 342

CHAPTER 11 FIREWALLS 343

     11.1   Firewall Design Principles 344
     11.2   Trusted Systems 356
     11.3   Recommended Reading and Web Site 362
     11.4   Key Terms, Review Questions, and Problems 362

APPENDICES

APPENDIX A STANDARDS CITED IN THIS BOOK 365

     A.1   ANSI Standards 365
     A.2   Internet RFGs 365
     A.3   ITU-T Recommendations 366
     A.4   NIST Federal Information Processing Standards 367

APPENDIX B SOME ASPECTS OF NUMBER THEORY 369

    B.1   Prime and Relatively Prime Numbers 370
    B.2   Modular Arithmetic 372

GLOSSARY 375

REFERENCES 381

INDEX 389

PREFACE

"The tie, if I might suggest it, sir, a shade more tightly knotted. One aims at the perfect butterfly effect. If you will permit me—"
"What does it matter, Jeeves, at a time like this? Do you realize that Mr. Little's domestic happiness is hanging in the scale?"
"There is no time, sir, at which ties do not matter."

—*Very Good, Jeeves!* P. G. Wodehouse

In this age of universal electronic connectivity, of viruses and hackers, of electronic eavesdropping and electronic fraud, there is indeed no time at which security does not matter. Two trends have come together to make the topic of this book of vital interest. First, the explosive growth in computer systems and their interconnections via networks has increased the dependence of both organizations and individuals on the information stored and communicated using these systems. This, in turn, has led to a heightened awareness of the need to protect data and resources from disclosure, to guarantee the authenticity of data and messages, and to protect systems from network-based attacks. Second, the disciplines of cryptography and network security have matured, leading to the development of practical, readily available applications to enforce network security.

OBJECTIVES

It is the purpose of this book to provide a practical survey of network security applications and standards. The emphasis is on applications that are widely used on the Internet and for corporate networks, and on standards, especially Internet standards, that have been widely deployed.

INTENDED AUDIENCE

The book is intended for both an academic and a professional audience. As a textbook, it is intended as a one-semester undergraduate course on network security for computer science, computer engineering, and electrical engineering majors. The book also serves as a basic reference volume and is suitable for self-study.

PLAN OF THE BOOK

The book is organized in three parts:

Part One. **Cryptography:** A concise survey of the cryptographic algorithms and protocols underlying network security applications, including encryption, hash functions, digital signatures, and key exchange

Part Two. **Network Security Applications:** Covers important network security tools and applications, including Kerberos, X.509v3 certificates, PGP, S/MIME, IP Security, SSL/TLS, SET, and SNMPv3

Part Three. **System Security:** Looks at system-level security issues, including the threat of and countermeasures for intruders and viruses, and the use of firewalls and trusted systems.

In addition, the book includes an extensive glossary, a list of frequently used acronyms, and a bibliography. Each chapter includes homework problems, review questions, a list of key words, suggestions for further reading, and recommended Web sites.

A more detailed, chapter-by-chapter summary of each part appears at the beginning of that part.

INTERNET SERVICES FOR INSTRUCTORS AND STUDENTS

There is a Web page for this book that provides support for students and instructors. The page includes links to relevant sites, transparency masters of the figures and tables in the book in PDF (Adobe Acrobat) format, and sign-up information for the book's Internet mailing list. The Web page is at WilliamStallings.com/NetSec2e.html. An Internet mailing list has been set up so that instructors using this book can exchange information, suggestions, and questions with each other and with the author. As soon as typos or other errors are discovered, an errata list for this book will be available at WilliamStallings.com. In addition, the Computer Science Student Resource site, at WilliamStallings.com/StudentSupport.html, provides documents, information, and useful links for computer science students and professionals.

PROJECTS FOR TEACHING NETWORK SECURITY

For many instructors, an important component of a cryptography or security course is a project or set of projects by which the student gets hands-on experience to reinforce concepts from the text. This book provides an unparalleled degree of support for including a projects component in the course. The instructor's manual not only includes guidance on how to assign and structure the projects, but also includes a set of suggested projects that covers a broad range of topics from the text:

- **Research Projects:** A series of research assignments that instruct the student to research a particular topic on the Internet and write a report
- **Programming Projects:** A series of programming projects that cover a broad range of topics and that can be implemented in any suitable language on any platform
- **Reading/Report Assignments:** A list of papers in the literature, one for each chapter, that can be assigned for the student to read and then write a short report

See Appendix B for details.

RELATIONSHIP TO CRYPTOGRAPHY AND NETWORK SECURITY, THIRD EDITION

This book is a spin-off from *Cryptography and Network Security, Third Edition* (CNS3e). CNS3e provides a substantial treatment of cryptography, including detailed analysis of algorithms and significant mathematical component, all of which covers almost 400 pages. *Network Security Essentials: Applications and Standards* (NSE2e) provides instead a concise overview of these topics in Chapters 2 and 3. NSE2e includes all of the remaining material of CNS3e. NSE2e also covers SNMP security, which is not covered in CNS3e. Thus, NSE2e is intended for college courses and professional readers where the interest is primarily in the application of network security, without the need or desire to delve deeply into cryptographic theory and principles.

CHAPTER 1

INTRODUCTION

1.1   The OSI Security Architecture

1.2   Security Attacks
        Passive Attacks
        Active Attacks

1.3   Security Services
        Authentication
        Access Control
        Data Confidentiality
        Data Integrity
        Nonrepudiation
        Availability Service

1.4   Security Mechanisms

1.5   A Model for Network Security

1.6   Internet Standards and the Internet Society
        The Internet Organizations and RFC Publication
        The Standardization Process
        Internet Standards Categories
        Other RFC Types

1.7   Outline of This Book

1.8   Recommended Reading

1.9   Internet and Web Resources
        Web Sites for This Book
        Other Web Sites
        USENET Newsgroups

The combination of space, time, and strength that must be considered as the basic elements of this theory of defense makes this a fairly complicated matter. Consequently, it is not easy to find a fixed point of departure.

—On War, Carl Von Clausewitz

The art of war teaches us to rely not on the likelihood of the enemy's not coming, but on our own readiness to receive him; not on the chance of his not attacking, but rather on the fact that we have made our position unassailable.

—The Art of War, Sun Tzu

The requirements of **information security** within an organization have undergone two major changes in the last several decades. Before the widespread use of data processing equipment, the security of information felt to be valuable to an organization was provided primarily by physical and administrative means. An example of the former is the use of rugged filing cabinets with a combination lock for storing sensitive documents. An example of the latter is personnel screening procedures used during the hiring process.

With the introduction of the computer, the need for automated tools for protecting files and other information stored on the computer became evident. This is especially the case for a shared system, such as a time-sharing system, and the need is even more acute for systems that can be accessed over a public telephone network, data network, or the Internet. The generic name for the collection of tools designed to protect data and to thwart hackers is **computer security**.

The second major change that affected security is the introduction of distributed systems and the use of networks and communications facilities for carrying data between terminal user and computer and between computer and computer. Network security measures are needed to protect data during their transmission. In fact, the term **network security** is somewhat misleading, because virtually all business, government, and academic organizations interconnect their data processing equipment with a collection of interconnected networks. Such a collection is often referred to as an internet,[1] and the term **internet security** is used.

There are no clear boundaries between these two forms of security. For example, one of the most publicized types of attack on information systems is the computer virus. A virus may be introduced into a system physically when it arrives on a diskette and is subsequently loaded onto a computer. Viruses may also arrive over an internet. In either case, once the virus is resident on a computer system, internal computer security tools are needed to detect and recover from the virus.

---

[1]We use the term *internet*, with a lowercase "i," to refer to any interconnected collection of network. A corporate intranet is an example of an internet. The Internet with a capital "I" may be one of the facilities used by an organization to construct its internet.

This book focuses on internet security, which consists of measures to deter, prevent, detect, and correct security violations that involve the transmission of information. That is a broad statement that covers a host of possibilities. To give you a feel for the areas covered in this book, consider the following examples of security violations:

1. User A transmits a file to user B. The file contains sensitive information (e.g., payroll records) that is to be protected from disclosure. User C, who is not authorized to read the file, is able to monitor the transmission and capture a copy of the file during its transmission.

2. A network manager, D, transmits a message to a computer, E, under its management. The message instructs computer E to update an authorization file to include the identities of a number of new users who are to be given access to that computer. User F intercepts the message, alters its contents to add or delete entries, and then forwards the message to E, which accepts the message as coming from manager D and updates its authorization file accordingly.

3. Rather than intercept a message, user F constructs its own message with the desired entries and transmits that message to E as if it had come from manager D. Computer E accepts the message as coming from manager D and updates its authorization file accordingly.

4. An employee is fired without warning. The personnel manager sends a message to a server system to invalidate the employee's account. When the invalidation is accomplished, the server is to post a notice to the employee's file as confirmation of the action. The employee is able to intercept the message and delay it long enough to make a final access to the server to retrieve sensitive information. The message is then forwarded, the action taken, and the confirmation posted. The employee's action may go unnoticed for some considerable time.

5. A message is sent from a customer to a stockbroker with instructions for various transactions. Subsequently, the investments lose value and the customer denies sending the message.

Although this list by no means exhausts the possible types of security violations, it illustrates the range of concerns of network security.

Internetwork security is both fascinating and complex. Some of the reasons follow:

1. Security involving communications and networks is not as simple as it might first appear to the novice. The requirements seem to be straightforward; indeed, most of the major requirements for security services can be given self-explanatory one-word labels: confidentiality, authentication, nonrepudiation, integrity. But the mechanisms used to meet those requirements can be quite complex, and understanding them may involve rather subtle reasoning.

2. In developing a particular security mechanism or algorithm, one must always consider potential attacks on those security features. In many cases, successful attacks are designed by looking at the problem in a completely different way, therefore exploiting an unexpected weakness in the mechanism.

3. Because of point 2, the procedures used to provide particular services are often counterintuitive: It is not obvious from the statement of a particular

requirement that such elaborate measures are needed. It is only when the various countermeasures are considered that the measures used make sense.

4. Having designed various security mechanisms, it is necessary to decide where to use them. This is true both in terms of physical placement (e.g., at what points in a network are certain security mechanisms needed) and in a logical sense [e.g., at what layer or layers of an architecture such as TCP/IP (Transmission Control Protocol/Internet Protocol) should mechanisms be placed].

5. Security mechanisms usually involve more than a particular algorithm or protocol. They usually also require that participants be in possession of some secret information (e.g., an encryption key), which raises questions about the creation, distribution, and protection of that secret information. There is also a reliance on communications protocols whose behavior may complicate the task of developing the security mechanism. For example, if the proper functioning of the security mechanism requires setting time limits on the transit time of a message from sender to receiver, then any protocol or network that introduces variable, unpredictable delays may render such time limits meaningless.

Thus, there is much to consider. This chapter provides a general overview of the subject matter that structures the material in the remainder of the book. We begin with a general discussion of network security services and mechanisms and of the types of attacks they are designed for. Then we develop a general overall model within which the security services and mechanisms can be viewed.

1.1 THE OSI SECURITY ARCHITECTURE

To assess effectively the security needs of an organization and to evaluate and choose various security products and policies, the manager responsible for security needs some systematic way of defining the requirements for security and characterizing the approaches to satisfying those requirements. This is difficult enough in a centralized data processing environment; with the use of local area and wide area networks, the problems are compounded.

ITU-T[2] Recommendation X.800, *Security Architecture for OSI*, defines such a systematic approach. The OSI security architecture is useful to managers as a way of organizing the task of providing security. Furthermore, because this architecture was developed as an international standard, computer and communications vendors have developed security features for their products and services that relate to this structured definition of services and mechanisms.

For our purposes, the OSI security architecture provides a useful, if abstract, overview of many of the concepts that this book deals with. The OSI security architecture focuses on security attacks, mechanisms, and services. These can be defined briefly as follows:

---

[2]The International Telecommunication Union (ITU) Telecommunication Standardization Sector (ITU-T) is a United Nations–sponsored agency that develops standards, called Recommendations, relating to telecommunications and to open systems interconnection (OSI).

Table 1.1   Threats and Attacks (RFC 2828)

Threat   A potential for violation of security, which exists when there is a circumstance, capability, action, or event that could breach security and cause harm. That is, a threat is a possible danger that might exploit a vulnerability.
Attack   An assault on system security that derives from an intelligent threat; that is, an intelligent act that is a deliberate attempt (especially in the sense of a method or technique) to evade security services and violate the security policy of a system.

- **Security attack:** Any action that compromises the security of information owned by an organization.
- **Security mechanism:** A mechanism that is designed to detect, prevent, or recover from a security attack.
- **Security service:** A service that enhances the security of the data processing systems and the information transfers of an organization. The services are intended to counter security attacks, and they make use of one or more security mechanisms to provide the service.

In the literature, the terms *threat* and *attack* are commonly used to mean more or less the same thing. Table 1.1 provides definitions taken from RFC 2828, *Internet Security Glossary*.

1.2 SECURITY ATTACKS

A useful means of classifying security attacks, used both in X.800 and RFC 2828, is in terms of *passive attacks* and *active attacks*. A passive attack attempts to learn or make use of information from the system but does not affect system resources. An active attack attempts to alter system resources or affect their operation.

Passive Attacks

Passive attacks are in the nature of eavesdropping on, or monitoring of, transmissions. The goal of the opponent is to obtain information that is being transmitted. Two types of passive attacks are release of message contents and traffic analysis.

The **release of message contents** is easily understood (Figure 1.1a). A telephone conversation, an electronic mail message, and a transferred file may contain sensitive or confidential information. We would like to prevent an opponent from learning the contents of these transmissions.

A second type of passive attack, **traffic analysis**, is subtler (Figure 1.1b). Suppose that we had a way of masking the contents of messages or other information traffic so that opponents, even if they captured the message, could not extract the information from the message. The common technique for masking contents is

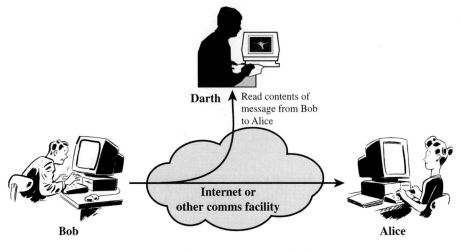

(a) Release of message contents

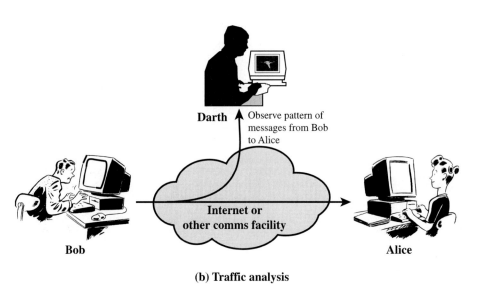

(b) Traffic analysis

Figure 1.1 Passive Attacks

encryption. If we had encryption protection in place, an opponent might still be able to observe the pattern of these messages. The opponent could determine the location and identity of communicating hosts and could observe the frequency and length of messages being exchanged. This information might be useful in guessing the nature of the communication that was taking place.

Passive attacks are very difficult to detect because they do not involve any alteration of the data. Typically, the message traffic is sent and received in an apparently normal fashion and neither the sender nor receiver is aware that a third party has read the messages or observed the traffic pattern. However, it is feasible to pre-

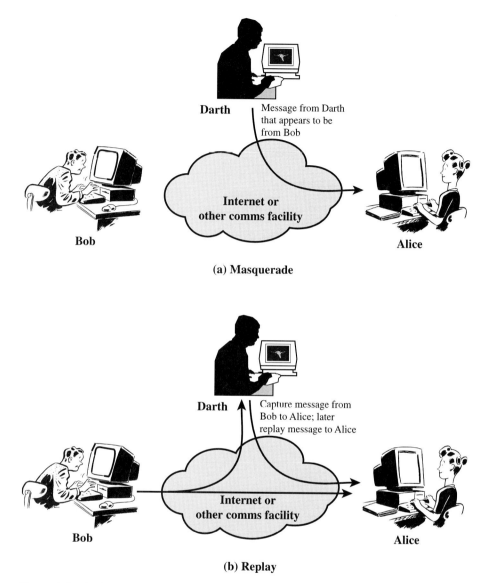

(a) Masquerade

(b) Replay

Figure 1.2   Active Attacks

vent the success of these attacks, usually by means of encryption. Thus, the emphasis in dealing with passive attacks is on prevention rather than detection.

Active Attacks

Active attacks involve some modification of the data stream or the creation of a false stream and can be subdivided into four categories: masquerade, replay, modification of messages, and denial of service.

A **masquerade** takes place when one entity pretends to be a different entity (Figure 1.2a). A masquerade attack usually includes one of the other forms of active

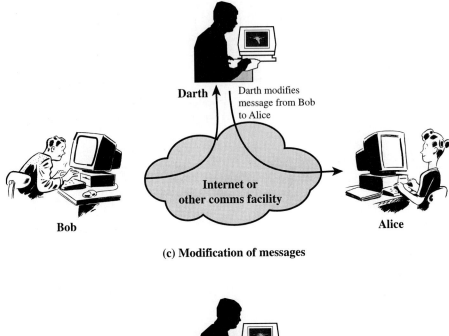

(c) Modification of messages

(d) Denial of service

Figure 1.2 Active Attacks *(continued)*

attack. For example, authentication sequences can be captured and replayed after a valid authentication sequence has taken place, thus enabling an authorized entity with few privileges to obtain extra privileges by impersonating an entity that has those privileges.

Replay involves the passive capture of a data unit and its subsequent retransmission to produce an unauthorized effect (Figure 1.2b).

Modification of messages simply means that some portion of a legitimate message is altered, or that messages are delayed or reordered, to produce an unauthorized effect (Figure 1.2c). For example, a message meaning "Allow John Smith to read confidential file *accounts*" is modified to mean "Allow Fred Brown to read confidential file *accounts.*"

The **denial of service** prevents or inhibits the normal use or management of communications facilities (Figure 1.2d). This attack may have a specific target; for example, an entity may suppress all messages directed to a particular destination (e.g., the security audit service). Another form of service denial is the disruption of an entire network, either by disabling the network or by overloading it with messages so as to degrade performance.

Active attacks present the opposite characteristics of passive attacks. Whereas passive attacks are difficult to detect, measures are available to prevent their success. On the other hand, it is quite difficult to prevent active attacks absolutely, because to do so would require physical protection of all communications facilities and paths at all times. Instead, the goal is to detect them and to recover from any disruption or delays caused by them. Because the detection has a deterrent effect, it may also contribute to prevention.

1.3   SECURITY SERVICES

X.800 defines a security service as a service provided by a protocol layer of communicating open systems, which ensures adequate security of the systems or of data transfers. Perhaps a clearer definition is found in RFC 2828, which provides the following definition: a processing or communication service that is provided by a system to give a specific kind of protection to system resources; security services implement security policies and are implemented by security mechanisms.

X.800 divides these services into five categories and fourteen specific services (Table 1.2). We look at each category in turn.[3]

Authentication

The authentication service is concerned with assuring that a communication is authentic. In the case of a single message, such as a warning or alarm signal, the function of the authentication service is to assure the recipient that the message is from the source that it claims to be from. In the case of an ongoing interaction, such as the connection of a terminal to a host, two aspects are involved. First, at the time of connection initiation, the service assures that the two entities are authentic; that is, that each is the entity that it claims to be. Second, the service must assure that the connection is not interfered with in such a way that a third party can masquerade as one of the two legitimate parties for the purposes of unauthorized transmission or reception.

---

[3]There is no universal agreement about many of the terms used in the security literature. For example, the term *integrity* is sometimes used to refer to all aspects of information security. The term *authentication* is sometimes used to refer both to verification of identity and to the various functions listed under integrity in this chapter. Our usage here agrees with both X.800 and RFC 2828.

Table 1.2   Security Services (X.800)

AUTHENTICATION

The assurance that the communicating entity is the one that it claims to be.

Peer Entity Authentication
Used in association with a logical connection to provide confidence in the identity of the entities connected.

Data-Origin Authentication
In a connectionless transfer, provides assurance that the source of received data is as claimed.

ACCESS CONTROL

The prevention of unauthorized use of a resource (i.e., this service controls who can have access to a resource, under what conditions access can occur, and what those accessing the resource are allowed to do).

DATA CONFIDENTIALITY

The protection of data from unauthorized disclosure.

Connection Confidentiality
The protection of all user data on a connection.

Connectionless Confidentiality
The protection of all user data in a single data block

Selective-Field Confidentiality
The confidentiality of selected fields within the user data on a connection or in a single data block.

Traffic-Flow Confidentiality
The protection of the information that might be derived from observation of traffic flows.

DATA INTEGRITY

The assurance that data received are exactly as sent by an authorized entity (i.e., contain no modification, insertion, deletion, or replay).

Connection Integrity with Recovery
Provides for the integrity of all user data on a connection and detects any modification, insertion, deletion, or replay of any data within an entire data sequence, with recovery attempted.

Connection Integrity without Recovery
As above, but provides only detection without recovery.

Selective-Field Connection Integrity
Provides for the integrity of selected fields within the user data of a data block transferred over a connection and takes the form of determination of whether the selected fields have been modified, inserted, deleted, or replayed.

Connectionless Integrity
Provides for the integrity of a single connectionless data block and may take the form of detection of data modification. Additionally, a limited form of replay detection may be provided.

Selective-Field Connectionless Integrity
Provides for the integrity of selected fields within a single connectionless data block; takes the form of determination of whether the selected fields have been modified.

NONREPUDIATION

Provides protection against denial by one of the entities involved in a communication of having participated in all or part of the communication.

Nonrepudiation, Origin
Proof that the message was sent by the specified party.

Nonrepudiation, Destination
Proof that the message was received by the specified party.

Two specific authentication services are defined in the standard:

- **Peer entity authentication:** Provides for the corroboration of the identity of a peer entity in an association. It is provided for use at the establishment of, or at times during the data transfer phase of, a connection. It attempts to provide confidence that an entity is not performing either a masquerade or an unauthorized replay of a previous connection.
- **Data origin authentication:** Provides for the corroboration of the source of a data unit. It does not provide protection against the duplication or modification of data units. This type of service supports applications like electronic mail where there are no prior interactions between the communicating entities.

Access Control

In the context of network security, access control is the ability to limit and control the access to host systems and applications via communications links. To achieve this, each entity trying to gain access must first be identified, or authenticated, so that access rights can be tailored to the individual.

Data Confidentiality

Confidentiality is the protection of transmitted data from passive attacks. With respect to the content of a data transmission, several levels of protection can be identified. The broadest service protects all user data transmitted between two users over a period of time. For example, when a TCP connection is set up between two systems, this broad protection prevents the release of any user data transmitted over the TCP connection. Narrower forms of this service can also be defined, including the protection of a single message or even specific fields within a message. These refinements are less useful than the broad approach and may even be more complex and expensive to implement.

The other aspect of confidentiality is the protection of traffic flow from analysis. This requires that an attacker not be able to observe the source and destination, frequency, length, or other characteristics of the traffic on a communications facility.

Data Integrity

As with confidentiality, integrity can apply to a stream of messages, a single message, or selected fields within a message. Again, the most useful and straightforward approach is total stream protection.

A connection-oriented integrity service, one that deals with a stream of messages, assures that messages are received as sent, with no duplication, insertion, modification, reordering, or replays. The destruction of data is also covered under this service. Thus, the connection-oriented integrity service addresses both message stream modification and denial of service. On the other hand, a connectionless integrity service, one that deals with individual messages only without regard to any larger context, generally provides protection against message modification only.

We can make a distinction between the service with and without recovery. Because the integrity service relates to active attacks, we are concerned with detection rather than prevention. If a violation of integrity is detected, then the service may simply report this violation, and some other portion of software or human intervention is required to recover from the violation. Alternatively, there are mechanisms available to recover from the loss of integrity of data, as we will review subsequently. The incorporation of automated recovery mechanisms is, in general, the more attractive alternative.

Nonrepudiation

Nonrepudiation prevents either sender or receiver from denying a transmitted message. Thus, when a message is sent, the receiver can prove that the alleged sender in fact sent the message. Similarly, when a message is received, the sender can prove that the alleged receiver in fact received the message.

Availability Service

Both X.800 and RFC 2828 define availability to be the property of a system or a system resource being accessible and usable upon demand by an authorized system entity, according to performance specifications for the system (i.e., a system is available if it provides services according to the system design whenever users request them). A variety of attacks can result in the loss of or reduction in availability. Some of these attacks are amenable to automated countermeasures, such as authentication and encryption, whereas others require some sort of physical action to prevent or recover from loss of availability of elements of a distributed system.

Table 1.3   Relationship between Security Services and Attacks

Service	Attack					
	Release of message contents	Traffic analysis	Masquerade	Replay	Modification of messages	Denial of Service
Peer entity authentication			Y			
Data origin authentication			Y			
Access control			Y			
Confidentiality	Y					
Traffic flow confidentiality		Y				
Data integrity				Y	Y	
Nonrepudiation						
Availability						Y

X.800 treats availability as a property to be associated with various security services. However, it makes sense to call out specifically an availability service. An availability service is one that protects a system to ensure its availability. This service addresses the security concerns raised by denial-of-service attacks. It depends on proper management and control of system resources and thus depends on access control service and other security services.

Table 1.3 indicates the relationship between security services and security mechanisms.

1.4 SECURITY MECHANISMS

Table 1.4 lists the security mechanisms defined in X.800. As can be seen, the mechanisms are divided into those that are implemented in a specific protocol layer and those that are not specific to any particular protocol layer or security service. These mechanisms will be covered in the appropriate places in the book and so we do not elaborate now, except to comment on the definition of encipherment. X.800 distinguishes between reversible encipherment mechanisms and irreversible encipherment mechanisms. A reversible encipherment mechanism is simply an encryption algorithm that allows data to be encrypted and subsequently decrypted. Irreversible encipherment mechanisms include hash algorithms and message authentication codes, which are used in digital signature and message authentication applications.

Table 1.5, based on one in X.800, indicates the relationship between security services and security mechanisms.

1.5 A MODEL FOR NETWORK SECURITY

A model for much of what we will be discussing is captured, in very general terms, in Figure 1.3. A message is to be transferred from one party to another across some sort of internet. The two parties, who are the *principals* in this transaction, must cooperate for the exchange to take place. A logical information channel is established by defining a route through the internet from source to destination and by the cooperative use of communication protocols (e.g., TCP/IP) by the two principals.

Security aspects come into play when it is necessary or desirable to protect the information transmission from an opponent who may present a threat to confidentiality, authenticity, and so on. All the techniques for providing security have two components:

- A security-related transformation on the information to be sent. Examples include the encryption of the message, which scrambles the message so that it is unreadable by the opponent, and the addition of a code based on the contents of the message, which can be used to verify the identity of the sender.
- Some secret information shared by the two principals and, it is hoped, unknown to the opponent. An example is an encryption key used in conjunction

Table 1.4 Security Mechanisms (X.800)

SPECIFIC SECURITY MECHANISMS May be incorporated into the appropriate protocol layer in order to provide some of the OSI security services. **Encipherment** The use of mathematical algorithms to transform data into a form that is not readily intelligible. The transformation and subsequent recovery of the data depend on an algorithm and zero or more encryption keys. **Digital Signature** Data appended to, or a cryptographic transformation of, a data unit that allows a recipient of the data unit to prove the source and integrity of the data unit and protect against forgery (e.g., by the recipient). **Access Control** A variety of mechanisms that enforce access rights to resources. **Data Integrity** A variety of mechanisms used to assure the integrity of a data unit or stream of data units. **Authentication Exchange** A mechanism intended to ensure the identity of an entity by means of information exchange. **Traffic Padding** The insertion of bits into gaps in a data stream to frustrate traffic analysis attempts.	**Routing Control** Enables selection of particular physically secure routes for certain data and allows routing changes, especially when a breach of security is suspected. **Notarization** The use of a trusted third party to assure certain properties of a data exchange. **PERVASIVE SECURITY MECHANISMS** Mechanisms that are not specific to any particular OSI security service or protocol layer. **Trusted Functionality** That which is perceived to be correct with respect to some criteria (e.g., as established by a security policy). **Security Label** The marking bound to a resource (which may be a data unit) that names or designates the security attributes of that resource. **Event Detection** Detection of security-relevant events. **Security Audit Trail** Data collected and potentially used to facilitate a security audit, which is an independent review and examination of system records and activities. **Security Recovery** Deals with requests from mechanisms, such as event handling and management functions, and takes recovery actions.

with the transformation to scramble the message before transmission and unscramble it on reception.[4]

A trusted third party may be needed to achieve secure transmission. For example, a third party may be responsible for distributing the secret information to the two principals while keeping it from any opponent. Or a third party may be

---

[4]Chapter 3 discusses a form of encryption, known as public-key encryption, in which only one of the two principals needs to have the secret information.

Table 1.5 Relationship betwe

Service	Enciph-erment	Digital signature	Access control	Data integrity	cation exchange	Traffic padding	Routing control	Notari-zation
Peer entity authentication	Y	Y			Y			
Data origin authentication	Y	Y						
Access control			Y					
Confidentiality	Y						Y	
Traffic flow confidentiality	Y					Y	Y	
Data integrity	Y	Y		Y				
Nonrepudiation		Y		Y				Y
Availability				Y	Y			

needed to arbitrate disputes between the two principals concerning the authenticity of a message transmission.

This general model shows that there are four basic tasks in designing a particular security service:

1. Design an algorithm for performing the security-related transformation. The algorithm should be such that an opponent cannot defeat its purpose.
2. Generate the secret information to be used with the algorithm.
3. Develop methods for the distribution and sharing of the secret information.
4. Specify a protocol to be used by the two principals that makes use of the security algorithm and the secret information to achieve a particular security service.

Part Two of this book concentrates on the types of security mechanisms and services that fit into the model shown in Figure 1.3. However, there are other security-related situations of interest that do not neatly fit this model but that are considered in this book. A general model of these other situations is illustrated by Figure 1.4, which reflects a concern for protecting an information system from unwanted access. Most readers are familiar with the concerns caused by the existence of hackers, who attempt to penetrate systems that can be accessed over a network. The hacker can be someone who, with no malign intent, simply gets satisfaction from breaking and entering a computer system. Or, the intruder can be a disgruntled employee who wishes to do damage, or a criminal who seeks to exploit computer assets for financial gain (e.g., obtaining credit card numbers or performing illegal money transfers).

Another type of unwanted access is the placement in a computer system of logic that exploits vulnerabilities in the system and that can affect application pro-

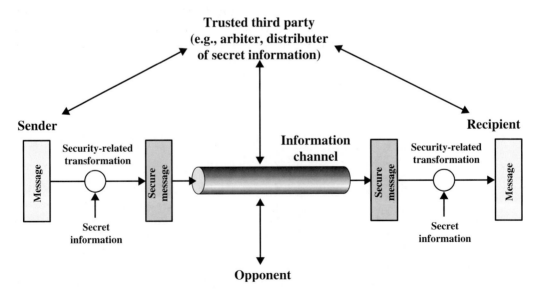

Figure 1.3 Model for Network Security

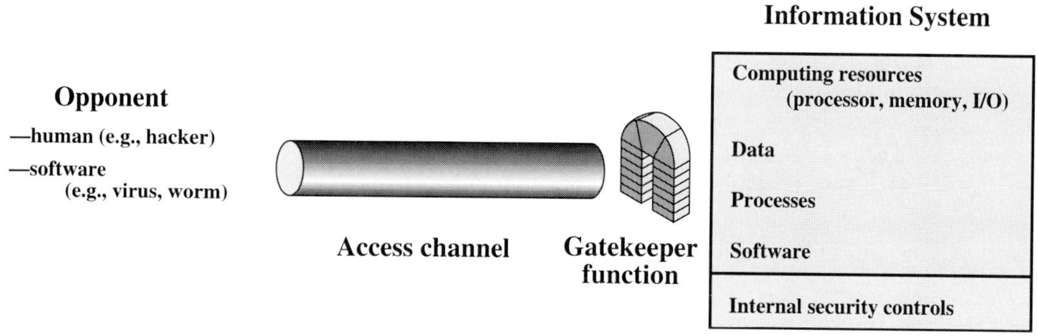

Information System

Figure 1.4 Network Access Security Model

grams as well as utility programs, such as editors and compilers. Programs can present two kinds of threats:

- **Information access threats** intercept or modify data on behalf of users who should not have access to that data.
- **Service threats** exploit service flaws in computers to inhibit use by legitimate users.

Viruses and worms are two examples of software attacks. Such attacks can be introduced into a system by means of a disk that contains the unwanted logic concealed in otherwise useful software. They can also be inserted into a system across a network; this latter mechanism is of more concern in network security.

The security mechanisms needed to cope with unwanted access fall into two broad categories (see Figure 1.4). The first category might be termed a gatekeeper function. It includes password-based login procedures that are designed to deny access to all but authorized users and screening logic that is designed to detect and reject worms, viruses, and other similar attacks. Once either an unwanted user or unwanted software gains access, the second line of defense consists of a variety of internal controls that monitor activity and analyze stored information in an attempt to detect the presence of unwanted intruders. These issues are explored in Part Three.

1.6 INTERNET STANDARDS AND THE INTERNET SOCIETY

Many of the protocols that make up the TCP/IP protocol suite have been standardized or are in the process of standardization. By universal agreement, an organization known as the Internet Society is responsible for the development and publication of these standards. The Internet Society is a professional membership organization that oversees a number of boards and task forces involved in Internet development and standardization.

This section provides a brief description of the way in which standards for the TCP/IP protocol suite are developed.

The Internet Organizations and RFC Publication

The Internet Society is the coordinating committee for Internet design, engineering, and management. Areas covered include the operation of the Internet itself and the standardization of protocols used by end systems on the Internet for interoperability. Three organizations under the Internet Society are responsible for the actual work of standards development and publication:

- **Internet Architecture Board (IAB):** Responsible for defining the overall architecture of the Internet, providing guidance and broad direction to the IETF
- **Internet Engineering Task Force (IETF):** The protocol engineering and development arm of the Internet
- **Internet Engineering Steering Group (IESG):** Responsible for technical management of IETF activities and the Internet standards process

Working groups chartered by the IETF carry out the actual development of new standards and protocols for the Internet. Membership in a working group is voluntary; any interested party may participate. During the development of a specification, a working group will make a draft version of the document available as an Internet Draft, which is placed in the IETF's "Internet Drafts" online directory. The document may remain as an Internet Draft for up to six months, and interested parties may review and comment on the draft. During that time, the IESG may approve publication of the draft as an RFC (Request for Comment). If the draft has not progressed to the status of an RFC during the six-month period, it is withdrawn from the directory. The working group may subsequently publish a revised version of the draft.

The IETF is responsible for publishing the RFCs, with approval of the IESG. The RFCs are the working notes of the Internet research and development community. A document in this series may be on essentially any topic related to computer communications and may be anything from a meeting report to the specification of a standard.

The work of the IETF is divided into eight areas, each with an area director and each composed of numerous working groups. Table 1.6 shows the IETF areas and their focus.

The Standardization Process

The decision of which RFCs become Internet standards is made by the IESG, on the recommendation of the IETF. To become a standard, a specification must meet the following criteria:

- Be stable and well understood
- Be technically competent
- Have multiple, independent, and interoperable implementations with substantial operational experience
- Enjoy significant public support
- Be recognizably useful in some or all parts of the Internet

Table 1.6 IETF Areas

IETF Area	Theme	Example Working Groups
General	IETF process and procedures	Policy framework Process for organization of Internet standards
Applications	Internet applications	Web-related protocols (HTTP) EDI-Internet integration LDAP
Internet	Internet infrastructure	IPv6 PPP extensions
Operations and management	Standards and definitions for network operations	SNMPv3 Remote network monitoring
Routing	Protocols and management for routing information	Multicast routing OSPF QoS routing
Security	Security protocols and technologies	Kerberos IPSec X.509 S/MIME TLS
Transport	Transport-layer protocols	Differentiated services IP telephony NFS RSVP
User services	Methods to improve the quality of information available to users of the Internet	Responsible use of the Internet User services FYI documents

The key difference between these criteria and those used for international standards from ITU is the emphasis here on operational experience.

The left-hand side of Figure 1.5 shows the series of steps, called the *standards track*, that a specification goes through to become a standard; this process is defined in RFC 2026. The steps involve increasing amounts of scrutiny and testing. At each step, the IETF must make a recommendation for advancement of the protocol, and the IESG must ratify it. The process begins when the IESG approves the publication of an Internet Draft document as an RFC with the status of Proposed Standard.

The white boxes in Figure 1.5 represent temporary states, which should be occupied for the minimum practical time. However, a document must remain a Proposed Standard for at least six months and a Draft Standard for at least four months to allow time for review and comment. The gray boxes represent long-term states that may be occupied for years.

For a specification to be advanced to Draft Standard status, there must be at least two independent and interoperable implementations from which adequate operational experience has been obtained.

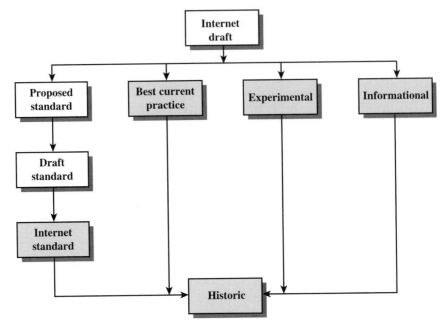

Figure 1.5   Internet RFC Publication Process

After significant implementation and operational experience has been obtained, a specification may be elevated to Internet Standard. At this point, the specification is assigned an STD number as well as an RFC number.

Finally, when a protocol becomes obsolete, it is assigned to the Historic state.

Internet Standards Categories

All Internet standards fall into one of two categories:

- **Technical specification (TS):** A TS defines a protocol, service, procedure, convention, or format. Most Internet standards are TSs.
- **Applicability statement (AS):** An AS specifies how, and under what circumstances, one or more TSs may be applied to support a particular Internet capability. An AS identifies one or more TSs that are relevant to the capability, and may specify values or ranges for particular parameters associated with a TS or functional subsets of a TS that are relevant for the capability.

Other RFC Types

There are numerous RFCs that are not destined to become Internet standards. Some RFCs standardize the results of community deliberations about statements of principle or conclusions about what is the best way to perform some operations or IETF process function. Such RFCs are designated as Best Current Practice (BCP). Approval of BCPs follows essentially the same process for approval of Proposed Standards. Unlike standards-track documents, there is not a three-stage process for BCPs; a BCP goes from Internet draft status to approved BCP in one step.

A protocol or other specification that is not considered ready for standardization may be published as an Experimental RFC. After further work, the specification may be resubmitted. If the specification is generally stable, has resolved known design choices, is believed to be well understood, has received significant community review, and appears to enjoy enough community interest to be considered valuable, then the RFC will be designated a Proposed Standard.

Finally, an Informational Specification is published for the general information of the Internet community.

1.7 OUTLINE OF THIS BOOK

This chapter serves as an introduction to the entire book. The remainder of the book is organized into three parts:

Part One: Provides a concise survey of the cryptographic algorithms and protocols underlying network security applications, including encryption, hash functions, digital signatures, and key exchange.

Part Two: Examines the use of cryptographic algorithms and security protocols to provide security over networks and the Internet. Topics covered include user authentication, e-mail, IP security, and Web security.

Part Three: Deals with security facilities designed to protect a computer system from security threats, including intruders, viruses, and worms. This part also looks at firewall technology.

Many of the cryptographic algorithms and network security protocols and applications described in this book have been specified as standards. The most important of these are Internet Standards, defined in Internet RFCs (Request for Comments), and Federal Information Processing Standards (FIPS), issued by the National Institute of Standards and Technology (NIST). Appendix A lists the standards cited in this book.

1.8 RECOMMENDED READING

[PFLE97] provides a good introduction to both computer and network security. Another excellent survey is [NICH99]. [SCHN00] is valuable reading for any practitioner in the field of computer or network security: It discusses the limitations of technology, and cryptography in particular, in providing security, and the need to consider the hardware, the software implementation, the networks, and the people involved in providing and attacking security.

NICH99 Nichols, R. ed. *ICSA Guide to Cryptography.* New York: McGraw-Hill, 1999.

PFLE97 Pfleeger, C. *Security in Computing.* Upper Saddle River, NJ: Prentice Hall, 1997.

SCHN00 Schneier, B. *Secrets and Lies: Digital Security in a Networked World.* New York: Wiley 2000.

1.9   INTERNET AND WEB RESOURCES

There are a number of resources available on the Internet and the Web to support this book and to help one keep up with developments in this field.

Web Sites for This Book

A special Web page has been set up for this book at

WilliamStallings.com/NetSec2e.html

The site includes the following:

- **Useful Web sites:** There are links to other relevant Web sites, organized by chapter, including the sites listed in this section and throughout this book.
- **Errata sheet:** An errata list for this book will be maintained and updated as needed. Please e-mail any errors that you spot to me. Errata sheets for my other books are at WilliamStallings.com.
- **Figures:** All of the figures in this book in PDF (Adobe Acrobat) format.
- **Tables:** All of the tables in this book in PDF format.
- **Slides:** A set of PowerPoint slides, organized by chapter.
- **Internet mailing list:** The site includes sign-up information for the book's Internet mailing list.
- **Network security courses:** There are links to home pages for courses based on this book; these pages may be useful to other instructors in providing ideas about how to structure their course.

I also maintain the Computer Science Student Resource Site, at

WilliamStallings.com/StudentSupport.html

The purpose of this site is to provide documents, information, and links for computer science students and professionals. Links and documents are organized into four categories:

- **Math:** Includes a basic math refresher, a queuing analysis primer, a number system primer, and links to numerous math sites
- **How-to:** Advice and guidance for solving homework problems, writing technical reports, and preparing technical presentations
- **Research resources:** Links to important collections of papers, technical reports, and bibliographies
- **Miscellaneous:** A variety of other useful documents and links

Other Web Sites

There are numerous Web sites that provide information related to the topics of this book. In subsequent chapters, pointers to specific Web sites can be found in the *Recommended Reading and Web Sites* section. Because the addresses for Web sites tend to change frequently, I have not included these in the book. For all of the Web sites listed in the book, the appropriate link can be found at this book's Web site. Other links not mentioned in this book will be added to the Web site over time.

The following Web sites are of general interest related to cryptography and network security:

- **COAST:** Comprehensive set of links related to cryptography and network security
- **IETF Security Area:** Material related to Internet security standardization efforts
- **Computer and Network Security Reference Index:** A good index to vendor and commercial products, frequently asked questions (FAQs), newsgroup archives, papers, and other Web sites
- **The Cryptography FAQ:** Lengthy and worthwhile FAQ covering all aspects of cryptography
- **Tom Dunigan's Security Page:** An excellent list of pointers to cryptography and network security Web sites
- **IEEE Technical Committee on Security and Privacy:** Copies of their newsletter, information on IEEE-related activities
- **Computer Security Resource Center:** Maintained by the National Institute of Standards and Technology (NIST); contains a broad range of information on security threats, technology, and standards

USENET Newsgroups

A number of USENET newsgroups are devoted to some aspect of network security or cryptography. As with virtually all USENET groups, there is a high noise-to-signal ratio, but it is worth experimenting to see if any meet your needs. The most relevant are as follows:

- **sci.crypt.research:** The best group to follow. This is a moderated newsgroup that deals with research topics; postings must have some relationship to the technical aspects of cryptology.
- **sci.crypt:** A general discussion of cryptology and related topics.
- **sci.crypt.random-numbers:** A discussion of cryptographic strength randomness.
- **alt.security:** A general discussion of security topics.
- **comp.security.misc:** A general discussion of computer security topics.
- **comp.security.firewalls:** A discussion of firewall products and technology.
- **comp.security.announce:** News, announcements from CERT.
- **comp.risks:** A discussion of risks to the public from computers and users.
- **comp.virus:** A moderated discussion of computer viruses.

PART ONE

Cryptography

By far the most important automated tool for network and communications security is encryption. Two forms of encryption are in common use: conventional, or symmetric, encryption and public-key, or asymmetric, encryption. Part One provides a survey of the basic principles of symmetric and public-key cryptography, looks at widely used algorithms, and discusses the basic applicability of the two approaches

CHAPTER 2 SYMMETRIC ENCRYPTION AND MESSAGE CONFIDENTIALITY

Chapter 2 focuses on symmetric encryption, with an emphasis on the most widely used encryption techniques, the Data Encryption Standard (DES) and its follow-on, the triple-key version of DES, and the Advanced Encryption Standard (AES). Beyond questions dealing with the actual construction of a symmetric encryption algorithm, a number of design issues relate to the use of symmetric encryption to provide confidentiality. The chapter includes a discussion of encryption of long messages, end-to-end versus link encryption, and key distribution techniques.

CHAPTER 3 PUBLIC-KEY CRYPTOGRAPHY AND MESSAGE AUTHENTICATION

Of equal importance to confidentiality as a security measure is authentication. At a minimum, message authentication assures that a message comes from the alleged source. In addition, authentication can include protection against modification, delay, replay, and reordering. Chapter 3 begins with an analysis of the requirements for authentication and then provides a presentation of approaches to authentication. A key element of authentication schemes is the use of an authenticator, usually either a message authentication code (MAC) or a hash function. Design considerations for both of these types of algorithms are examined, and several specific examples are analyzed.

After symmetric encryption, the other major form of encryption is public-key encryption, which has revolutionized communications security. Chapter 3 introduces public-key encryption. The RSA algorithm is examined in detail, and the issue of key management is reconsidered. The chapter also covers the widely used Diffie-Hellman key exchange technique. In addition, the chapter defines the digital signatures and examines its application.

CHAPTER 2

SYMMETRIC ENCRYPTION AND MESSAGE CONFIDENTIALITY

2.1 Symmetric Encryption Principles

    Cryptography
    Cryptanalysis
    Feistel Cipher Structure

2.2 Symmetric Encryption Algorithms

    Data Encryption Standard
    Triple DES
    Advanced Encryption Standard
    Other Symmetric Block Ciphers

2.3 Cipher Block Modes of Operation

    Cipher Block Chaining Mode
    Cipher Feedback Mode

2.4 Location of Encryption Devices

2.5 Key Distribution

2.6 Recommended Reading and Web Sites

2.7 Key Terms, Review Questions, and Problems

    Key Terms
    Review Questions
    Problems

All the afternoon Mungo had been working on Stern's code, principally with the aid of the latest messages which he had copied down at the Nevin Square drop. Stern was very confident. He must be well aware London Central knew about that drop. It was obvious that they didn't care how often Mungo read their messages, so confident were they in the impenetrability of the code.

—*Talking to Strange Men*, **Ruth Rendell**

Amongst the tribes of Central Australia every man, woman, and child has a secret or sacred name which is bestowed by the older men upon him or her soon after birth, and which is known to none but the fully initiated members of the group. This secret name is never mentioned except upon the most solemn occasions; to utter it in the hearing of men of another group would be a most serious breach of tribal custom. When mentioned at all, the name is spoken only in a whisper, and not until the most elaborate precautions have been taken that it shall be heard by no one but members of the group. The native thinks that a stranger knowing his secret name would have special power to work him ill by means of magic.

—*The Golden Bough*, **Sir James George Frazer**

Symmetric encryption, also referred to as conventional encryption, secret-key, or single-key encryption, was the only type of encryption in use prior to the development of public-key encryption in the late 1970s.[1] It remains by far the most widely used of the two types of encryption.

This chapter begins with a look at a general model for the symmetric encryption process; this will enable us to understand the context within which the algorithms are used. Then we look at three important encryption algorithms: DES, triple DES, and AES. We then examine the application of these algorithms to achieve confidentiality.

2.1 SYMMETRIC ENCRYPTION PRINCIPLES

A symmetric encryption scheme has five ingredients (Figure 2.1):

* **Plaintext:** This is the original message or data that is fed into the algorithm as input.
* **Encryption algorithm:** The encryption algorithm performs various substitutions and transformations on the plaintext.
* **Secret key:** The secret key is also input to the algorithm. The exact substitutions and transformations performed by the algorithm depend on the key.

---

[1]Public-key encryption was first described in the open literature in 1976; the National Security Agency (NSA) claims to have discovered it some years earlier.

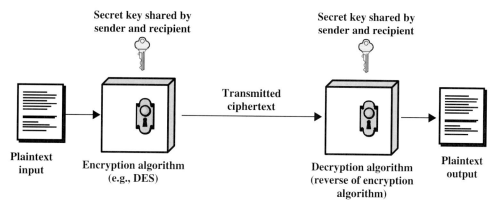

Figure 2.1 Simplified Model of Conventional Encryption

- **Ciphertext:** This is the scrambled message produced as output. It depends on the plaintext and the secret key. For a given message, two different keys will produce two different ciphertexts.
- **Decryption algorithm:** This is essentially the encryption algorithm run in reverse. It takes the ciphertext and the same secret key and produces the original plaintext.

There are two requirements for secure use of symmetric encryption:

1. We need a strong encryption algorithm. At a minimum, we would like the algorithm to be such that an opponent who knows the algorithm and has access to one or more ciphertexts would be unable to decipher the ciphertext or figure out the key. This requirement is usually stated in a stronger form: The opponent should be unable to decrypt ciphertext or discover the key even if he or she is in possession of a number of ciphertexts together with the plaintext that produced each ciphertext.

2. Sender and receiver must have obtained copies of the secret key in a secure fashion and must keep the key secure. If someone can discover the key and knows the algorithm, all communication using this key is readable.

It is important to note that the security of symmetric encryption depends on the secrecy of the key, not the secrecy of the algorithm. That is, it is assumed that it is impractical to decrypt a message on the basis of the ciphertext *plus* knowledge of the encryption/decryption algorithm. In other words, we do not need to keep the algorithm secret; we need to keep only the key secret.

This feature of symmetric encryption is what makes it feasible for widespread use. The fact that the algorithm need not be kept secret means that manufacturers can and have developed low-cost chip implementations of data encryption algorithms. These chips are widely available and incorporated into a number of products. With the use of symmetric encryption, the principal security problem is maintaining the secrecy of the key.

Cryptography

Cryptographic systems are generically classified along three independent dimensions:

1. **The type of operations used for transforming plaintext to ciphertext.** All encryption algorithms are based on two general principles: substitution, in which each element in the plaintext (bit, letter, group of bits or letters) is mapped into another element, and transposition, in which elements in the plaintext are rearranged. The fundamental requirement is that no information be lost (that is, that all operations be reversible). Most systems, referred to as product systems, involve multiple stages of substitutions and transpositions.
2. **The number of keys used.** If both sender and receiver use the same key, the system is referred to as symmetric, single-key, secret-key, or conventional encryption. If the sender and receiver each uses a different key, the system is referred to as asymmetric, two-key, or public-key encryption.
3. **The way in which the plaintext is processed.** A *block cipher* processes the input one block of elements at a time, producing an output block for each input block. A *stream cipher* processes the input elements continuously, producing output one element at a time, as it goes along.

Cryptanalysis

The process of attempting to discover the plaintext or key is known as *cryptanalysis*. The strategy used by the cryptanalyst depends on the nature of the encryption scheme and the information available to the cryptanalyst.

Table 2.1 summarizes the various types of cryptanalytic attacks, based on the amount of information known to the cryptanalyst. The most difficult problem is presented when all that is available is the *ciphertext only*. In some cases, not even the encryption algorithm is known, but in general we can assume that the opponent does know the algorithm used for encryption. One possible attack under these circumstances is the brute-force approach of trying all possible keys. If the key space is very large, this becomes impractical. Thus, the opponent must rely on an analysis of the ciphertext itself, generally applying various statistical tests to it. To use this approach, the opponent must have some general idea of the type of plaintext that is concealed, such as English or French text, an EXE file, a Java source listing, an accounting file, and so on.

The ciphertext-only attack is the easiest to defend against because the opponent has the least amount of information to work with. In many cases, however, the analyst has more information. The analyst may be able to capture one or more plaintext messages as well as their encryptions. Or the analyst may know that certain plaintext patterns will appear in a message. For example, a file that is encoded in the Postscript format always begins with the same pattern, or there may be a standardized header or banner to an electronic funds transfer message, and so on. All these are examples of *known plaintext*. With this knowledge, the analyst may be able to deduce the key on the basis of the way in which the known plaintext is transformed.

Closely related to the known-plaintext attack is what might be referred to as a probable-word attack. If the opponent is working with the encryption of some general prose message, he or she may have little knowledge of what is in the message.

However, if the opponent is after some very specific information, then parts of the message may be known. For example, if an entire accounting file is being transmitted, the opponent may know the placement of certain key words in the header of the file. As another example, the source code for a program developed by a corporation might include a copyright statement in some standardized position.

If the analyst is able somehow to get the source system to insert into the system a message chosen by the analyst, then a *chosen-plaintext* attack is possible. In general, if the analyst is able to choose the messages to encrypt, the analyst may deliberately pick patterns that can be expected to reveal the structure of the key.

Table 2.1 lists two other types of attack: chosen ciphertext and chosen text. These are less commonly employed as cryptanalytic techniques but are nevertheless possible avenues of attack.

Only relatively weak algorithms fail to withstand a ciphertext-only attack. Generally, an encryption algorithm is designed to withstand a known-plaintext attack.

An encryption scheme is **computationally secure** if the ciphertext generated by the scheme meets one or both of the following criteria:

- The cost of breaking the cipher exceeds the value of the encrypted information.
- The time required to break the cipher exceeds the useful lifetime of the information.

The rub is that it is very difficult to estimate the amount of effort required to cryptanalyze ciphertext successfully. However, assuming there are no inherent

Table 2.1 Types of Attacks on Encrypted Messages

Type of Attack	Known to Cryptanalyst
Ciphertext only	• Encryption algorithm • Ciphertext to be decoded
Known plaintext	• Encryption algorithm • Ciphertext to be decoded • One or more plaintext-ciphertext pairs formed with the secret key
Chosen plaintext	• Encryption algorithm • Ciphertext to be decoded • Plaintext message chosen by cryptanalyst, together with its corresponding ciphertext generated with the secret key
Chosen ciphertext	• Encryption algorithm • Ciphertext to be decoded • Purported ciphertext chosen by cryptanalyst, together with its corresponding decrypted plaintext generated with the secret key
Chosen text	• Encryption algorithm • Ciphertext to be decoded • Plaintext message chosen by cryptanalyst, together with its corresponding ciphertext generated with the secret key • Purported ciphertext chosen by cryptanalyst, together with its corresponding decrypted plaintext generated with the secret key

Table 2.2 Average Time Required for Exhaustive Key Search

Key Size (bits)	Number of Alternative Keys	Time Required at 1 Encryption/μs	Time Required at 10^6 Encryptions/μs
32	$2^{32} = 4.3 \times 10^9$	2^{31} μs = 35.8 minutes	2.15 milliseconds
56	$2^{56} = 7.2 \times 10^{16}$	2^{55} μs = 1142 years	10.01 hours
128	$2^{128} = 3.4 \times 10^{38}$	2^{127} μs = 5.4×10^{24} years	5.4×10^{18} years
168	$2^{168} = 3.7 \times 10^{50}$	2^{167} μs = 5.9×10^{36} years	5.9×10^{30} years
26 characters (permutation)	$26! = 4 \times 10^{26}$	2×10^{26} μs = 6.4×10^{12} years	6.4×10^6 years

mathematical weaknesses in the algorithm, then a brute-force approach is indicated, and here we can make some reasonable estimates about costs and time.

A brute-force approach involves trying every possible key until an intelligible translation of the ciphertext into plaintext is obtained. On average, half of all possible keys must be tried to achieve success. Table 2.2 shows how much time is involved for various key sizes. The 56-bit key size is used with the DES (Data Encryption Standard) algorithm. For each key size, the results are shown assuming that it takes 1 μs to perform a single decryption, which is a reasonable order of magnitude for today's machines. With the use of massively parallel organizations of microprocessors, it may be possible to achieve processing rates many orders of magnitude greater. The final column of Table 2.2 considers the results for a system that can process 1 million keys per microsecond. As you can see, at this performance level, DES can no longer be considered computationally secure.

Feistel Cipher Structure

Most symmetric block encryption algorithms, including DES, have a structure first described by Horst Feistel of IBM in 1973 [FEIS73] and shown in Figure 2.2. The inputs to the encryption algorithm are a plaintext block of length $2w$ bits and a key K. The plaintext block is divided into two halves, L_0 and R_0. The two halves of the data pass through n rounds of processing and then combine to produce the ciphertext block. Each round i has as inputs L_{i-1} and R_{i-1}, derived from the previous round, as well as a subkey K_i, derived from the overall K. In general, the subkeys K_i are different from K and from each other and are generated from the key by a subkey generation algorithm.

All rounds have the same structure. A substitution is performed on the left half of the data. This is done by applying a *round function* F to the right half of the data and then taking the exclusive-OR (XOR) of the output of that function and the left half of the data. The round function has the same general structure for each round but is parameterized by the round subkey K_i. Following this substitution, a permutation is performed that consists of the interchange of the two halves of the data.

The exact realization of a Feistel network depends on the choice of the following parameters and design features:

- **Block size:** Larger block sizes mean greater security (all other things being equal) but reduced encryption/decryption speed. A block size of 64 bits is a reasonable tradeoff and is nearly universal in block cipher design.
- **Key size:** Larger key size means greater security but may decrease encryption/decryption speed. The most common key length in modern algorithms is 128 bits.

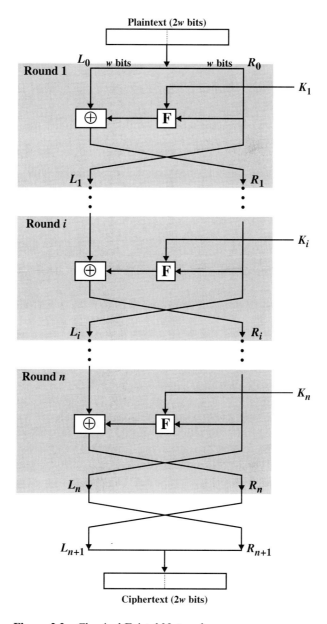

Figure 2.2 Classical Feistel Network

- **Number of rounds:** The essence of the Feistel cipher is that a single round offers inadequate security but that multiple rounds offer increasing security. A typical size is 16 rounds.
- **Subkey generation algorithm:** Greater complexity in this algorithm should lead to greater difficulty of cryptanalysis.
- **Round function:** Again, greater complexity generally means greater resistance to cryptanalysis.

There are two other considerations in the design of a Feistel cipher:

- **Fast software encryption/decryption:** In many cases, encryption is embedded in applications or utility functions in such a way as to preclude a hardware implementation. Accordingly, the speed of execution of the algorithm becomes a concern.
- **Ease of analysis:** Although we would like to make our algorithm as difficult as possible to cryptanalyze, there is great benefit in making the algorithm easy to analyze. That is, if the algorithm can be concisely and clearly explained, it is easier to analyze that algorithm for cryptanalytic vulnerabilities and therefore develop a higher level of assurance as to its strength. DES, for example, does not have an easily analyzed functionality.

Decryption with a Feistel cipher is essentially the same as the encryption process. The rule is as follows: Use the ciphertext as input to the algorithm, but use the subkeys K_i in reverse order. That is, use K_n in the first round, K_{n-1} in the second round, and so on until K_1 is used in the last round. This is a nice feature because it means we need not implement two different algorithms, one for encryption and one for decryption.

2.2 SYMMETRIC ENCRYPTION ALGORITHMS

The most commonly used symmetric encryption algorithms are block ciphers. A block cipher processes the plaintext input in fixed-size blocks and produces a block of ciphertext of equal size for each plaintext block. This section focuses on the three most important symmetric block ciphers: the Data Encryption Standard (DES) and triple DES (3DES), and the Advanced Encryption Standard (AES). We then provide a brief overview of some other popular symmetric encryption algorithms.

Data Encryption Standard

The most widely used encryption scheme is based on the Data Encryption Standard (DES) adopted in 1977 by the National Bureau of Standards, now the National Institute of Standards and Technology (NIST), as Federal Information Processing

Standard 46 (FIPS PUB 46). The algorithm itself is referred to as the Data Encryption Algorithm (DEA).[2]

Description of the Algorithm

The plaintext is 64 bits in length and the key is 56 bits in length; longer plaintext amounts are processed in 64-bit blocks. The DES structure is a minor variation of the Feistel network shown in Figure 2.2. There are sixteen rounds of processing. From the original 56-bit key, sixteen subkeys are generated, one of which is used for each round.

The process of decryption with DES is essentially the same as the encryption process. The rule is as follows: Use the ciphertext as input to the DES algorithm, but use the subkeys K_i in reverse order. That is, use K_{16} on the first iteration, K_{15} on the second iteration, and so on until K_1 is used on the 16th and last iteration.

The Strength of DES

Concerns about the strength of DES fall into two categories: concerns about the algorithm itself and concerns about the use of a 56-bit key. The first concern refers to the possibility that cryptanalysis is possible by exploiting the characteristics of the DES algorithm. Over the years, there have been numerous attempts to find and exploit weaknesses in the algorithm, making DES the most-studied encryption algorithm in existence. Despite numerous approaches, no one has so far succeeded in discovering a fatal weakness in DES.[3]

A more serious concern is key length. With a key length of 56 bits, there are 2^{56} possible keys, which is approximately 7.2×10^{16} keys. Thus, on the face of it, a brute-force attack appears impractical. Assuming that, on average, half the key space has to be searched, a single machine performing one DES encryption per microsecond would take more than a thousand years (see Table 2.2) to break the cipher.

However, the assumption of one encryption per microsecond is overly conservative. DES finally and definitively proved insecure in July 1998, when the Electronic Frontier Foundation (EFF) announced that it had broken a DES encryption using a special-purpose "DES cracker" machine that was built for less than $250,000. The attack took less than three days. The EFF has published a detailed description of the machine, enabling others to build their own cracker [EFF98]. And, of course, hardware prices will continue to drop as speeds increase, making DES virtually worthless.

It is important to note that there is more to a key-search attack than simply running through all possible keys. Unless known plaintext is provided, the analyst must be able to recognize plaintext as plaintext. If the message is just plain text in

---

[2]The terminology is a bit confusing. Until recently, the terms *DES* and *DEA* could be used interchangeably. However, the most recent edition of the DES document includes a specification of the DEA described here plus the triple DEA (3DES) described subsequently. Both DEA and 3DES are part of the Data Encryption Standard. Further, until the recent adoption of the official term *3DES*, the triple DEA algorithm was typically referred to as *triple DES* and written as 3DES. For the sake of convenience, we will use 3DES.

[3]At least, no one has publicly acknowledged such a discovery.

English, then the result pops out easily, although the task of recognizing English would have to be automated. If the text message has been compressed before encryption, then recognition is more difficult. And if the message is some more general type of data, such as a numerical file, and this has been compressed, the problem becomes even more difficult to automate. Thus, to supplement the brute-force approach, some degree of knowledge about the expected plaintext is needed, and some means of automatically distinguishing plaintext from garble is also needed. The EFF approach addresses this issue as well and introduces some automated techniques that would be effective in many contexts.

A final point: If the only form of attack that could be made on an encryption algorithm is brute force, then the way to counter such attacks is obvious: Use longer keys. To get some idea of the size of key required, let us use the EFF cracker as a basis for our estimates. The EFF cracker was a prototype, and we can assume that with today's technology, a faster machine is cost effective. If we assume that a cracker can perform one million decryptions per μs, which is the rate used in Table 2.2, then a DES code would take about 10 hours to crack. This is a speed-up of approximately a factor of 7 compared to the EFF result. Using this rate, Figure 2.3 shows how long it would take to crack a DES-style algorithm as a function of key size. For example, for a 128-bit key, which is common among contemporary algorithms, it would take over 10^{18} years to break the code using the EFF cracker. Even

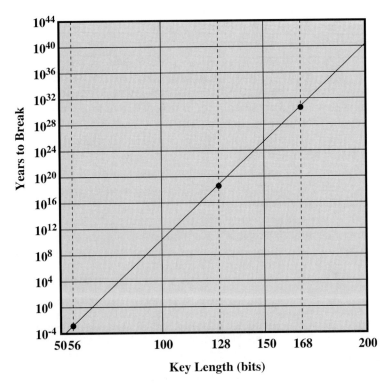

Figure 2.3 Time to Break a Code (assuming 10^6 decryptions/μs)

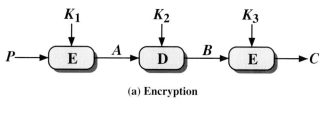

(a) Encryption

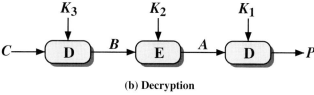

(b) Decryption

Figure 2.4   Triple DES

if we managed to speed up the cracker by a factor of 1 trillion (10^{12}), it would still take over 1 million years to break the code. So a 128-bit key is guaranteed to result in an algorithm that is unbreakable by brute force.

Triple DES

Triple DES (3DES) was first standardized for use in financial applications in ANSI standard X9.17 in 1985. 3DES was incorporated as part of the Data Encryption Standard in 1999, with the publication of FIPS PUB 46-3.

3DES uses three keys and three executions of the DES algorithm. The function follows an encrypt-decrypt-encrypt (EDE) sequence (Figure 2.4a):

$$C = E_{K_3}[D_{K_2}[E_{K_1}[P]]]$$

where

$$
\begin{aligned}
C &= \text{ciphertext} \\
P &= \text{plaintext} \\
E_K[X] &= \text{encryption of } X \text{ using key } K \\
D_K[Y] &= \text{decryption of } Y \text{ using key } K
\end{aligned}
$$

Decryption is simply the same operation with the keys reversed (Figure 2.4b):

$$P = D_{K_1}[E_{K_2}[D_{K_3}[C]]]$$

There is no cryptographic significance to the use of decryption for the second stage of 3DES encryption. Its only advantage is that it allows users of 3DES to decrypt data encrypted by users of the older single DES:

$$C = E_{K_1}[D_{K_1}[E_{K_1}[P]]] = E_{K_1}[P]$$

With three distinct keys, 3DES has an effective key length of 168 bits. FIPS 46-3 also allows for the use of two keys, with $K_1 = K_3$; this provides for a key length of 112 bits. FIPS 46-3 includes the following guidelines for 3DES:

- 3DES is the FIPS approved symmetric encryption algorithm of choice.
- The original DES, which uses a single 56-bit key, is permitted under the standard for legacy systems only. New procurements should support 3DES.
- Government organizations with legacy DES systems are encouraged to transition to 3DES.
- It is anticipated that 3DES and the Advanced Encryption Standard (AES) will coexist as FIPS-approved algorithms, allowing for a gradual transition to AES.

It is easy to see that 3DES is a formidable algorithm. Because the underlying cryptographic algorithm is DEA, 3DES can claim the same resistance to cryptanalysis based on the algorithm as is claimed for DEA. Further, with a 168-bit key length, brute-force attacks are effectively impossible.

Ultimately, AES is intended to replace 3DES, but this process will take a number of years. NIST anticipates that 3DES will remain an approved algorithm (for U.S. government use) for the foreseeable future.

Advanced Encryption Standard

3DES has two attractions that assure its widespread use over the next few years. First, with its 168-bit key length, it overcomes the vulnerability to brute-force attack of DEA. Second, the underlying encryption algorithm in 3DES is the same as in DEA. This algorithm has been subjected to more scrutiny than any other encryption algorithm over a longer period of time, and no effective cryptanalytic attack based on the algorithm rather than brute force has been found. Accordingly, there is a high level of confidence that 3DES is very resistant to cryptanalysis. If security were the only consideration, then 3DES would be an appropriate choice for a standardized encryption algorithm for decades to come.

The principal drawback of 3DES is that the algorithm is relatively sluggish in software. The original DEA was designed for mid-1970s hardware implementation and does not produce efficient software code. 3DES, which has three times as many rounds as DEA, is correspondingly slower. A secondary drawback is that both DEA and 3DES use a 64-bit block size. For reasons of both efficiency and security, a larger block size is desirable.

Because of these drawbacks, 3DES is not a reasonable candidate for long-term use. As a replacement, NIST in 1997 issued a call for proposals for a new Advanced Encryption Standard (AES), which should have a security strength equal to or better than 3DES and significantly improved efficiency. In addition to these general requirements, NIST specified that AES must be a symmetric block cipher with a block length of 128 bits and support for key lengths of 128, 192, and 256 bits. Evaluation criteria include security, computational efficiency, memory requirements, hardware and software suitability, and flexibility.

In a first round of evaluation, 15 proposed algorithms were accepted. A second round narrowed the field to 5 algorithms. NIST completed its evaluation process and published a final standard (FIPS PUB 197) in November of 2001. NIST selected Rijndael as the proposed AES algorithm. The two researchers who developed and submitted Rijndael for the AES are both cryptographers from Belgium: Dr. Joan Daemen and Dr. Vincent Rijmen.

Overview of the Algorithm

AES uses a block length of 128 bits and a key length that can be 128, 192, or 256 bits. In the description of this section, we assume a key length of 128 bits, which is likely to be the one most commonly implemented.

Figure 2.5 shows the overall structure of AES. The input to the encryption and decryption algorithms is a single 128-bit block. In FIPS PUB 197, this block is depicted as a square matrix of bytes. This block is copied into the **State** array, which is modified at each stage of encryption or decryption. After the final stage, **State** is copied to an output matrix. Similarly, the 128-bit key is depicted as a square matrix of bytes. This key is then expanded into an array of key schedule words; each word is four bytes and the total key schedule is 44 words for the 128-bit key. The ordering of bytes within a matrix is by column. So, for example, the first four bytes of a 128-bit plaintext input to the encryption cipher occupy the first column of the **in** matrix, the second four bytes occupy the second column, and so on. Similarly, the first four bytes of the expanded key, which form a word, occupy the first column of the **w** matrix.

The following comments give some insight into AES:

1. One noteworthy feature of this structure is that it is not a Feistel structure. Recall that in the classic Feistel structure, half of the data block is used to modify the other half of the data block, and then the halves are swapped. AES does not use a Feistel structure but processes the entire data block in parallel during each round using substitutions and permutation.

2. The key that is provided as input is expanded into an array of forty-four 32-bit words, $\mathbf{w}[i]$. Four distinct words (128 bits) serve as a round key for each round.

3. Four different stages are used, one of permutation and three of substitution:
   - **Substitute bytes:** Uses a table, referred to as an S-box[4], to perform a byte-by-byte substitution of the block
   - **Shift rows:** A simple permutation that is performed row by row
   - **Mix columns:** A substitution that alters each byte in a column as a function of all of the bytes in the column
   - **Add round key:** A simple bitwise XOR of the current block with a portion of the expanded key

---

[4]The term *S-box*, or substitution box, is commonly used in the description of symmetric ciphers to refer to a table used for a table-lookup type of substitution mechanism.

4. The structure is quite simple. For both encryption and decryption, the cipher begins with an Add Round Key stage, followed by nine rounds that each includes all four stages, followed by a tenth round of three stages. Figure 2.6 depicts the structure of a full encryption round.

5. Only the Add Round Key stage makes use of the key. For this reason, the cipher begins and ends with an Add Round Key stage. Any other stage,

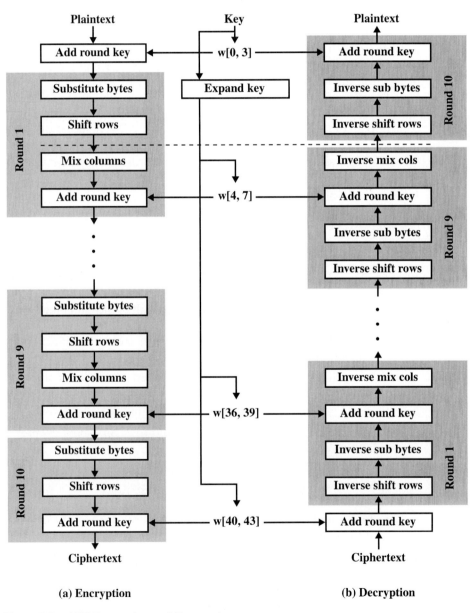

Figure 2.5   AES Encryption and Decryption

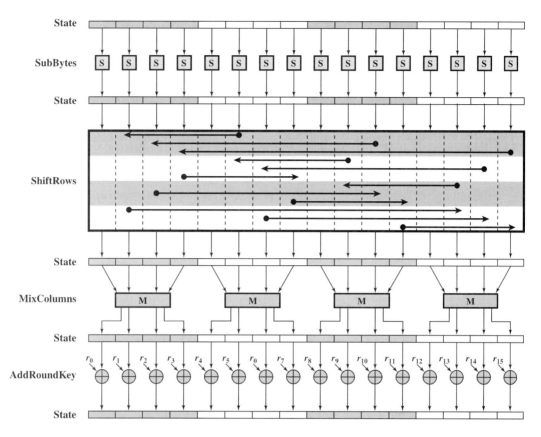

Figure 2.6 AES Encryption Round

applied at the beginning or end, is reversible without knowledge of the key and so would add no security.

6. The Add Round Key stage by itself would not be formidable. The other three stages together scramble the bits, but by themselves would provide no security because they do not use the key. We can view the cipher as alternating operations of XOR encryption (Add Round Key) of a block, followed by scrambling of the block (the other three stages), followed by XOR encryption, and so on. This scheme is both efficient and highly secure.

7. Each stage is easily reversible. For the Substitute Byte, Shift Row, and Mix Columns stages, an inverse function is used in the decryption algorithm. For the Add Round Key stage, the inverse is achieved by XORing the same round key to the block, using the result that $A \oplus A \oplus B = B$.

8. As with most block ciphers, the decryption algorithm makes use of the expanded key in reverse order. However, the decryption algorithm is not identical to the encryption algorithm. This is a consequence of the particular structure of AES.

9. Once it is established that all four stages are reversible, it is easy to verify that decryption does recover the plaintext. Figure 2.5 lays out encryption and decryp-

tion going in opposite vertical directions. At each horizontal point (e.g., the dashed line in the figure), **State** is the same for both encryption and decryption.

10. The final round of both encryption and decryption consists of only three stages. Again, this is a consequence of the particular structure of AES and is required to make the cipher reversible.

Other Symmetric Block Ciphers

Rather than totally reinventing the wheel, virtually all contemporary symmetric block encryption algorithms use the basic Feistel block structure. The reason is that this structure is well understood, and this makes it easier to determine the cryptographic strength of a new algorithm. If an entirely different structure were used, the new structure may have some subtle weakness not immediately apparent to the designer. In this section we look at some of the other ciphers, in addition to DES and 3DES, that have gained commercial acceptance. Some of the principal characteristics are compared in Table 2.3.

IDEA

The International Data Encryption Algorithm (IDEA) is a symmetric block cipher developed by Xuejia Lai and James Massey of the Swiss Federal Institute of Technology in 1991 [LAI91]. IDEA uses a 128-bit key. IDEA differs markedly from DES both in the round function and in the subkey generation function. For the round function, IDEA does not use S-boxes. Rather, IDEA relies on three different mathematical operations: XOR, binary addition of 16-bit integers, and binary multiplication of 16-bit integers. These functions are combined in such a way as to produce a complex transformation that is very difficult to analyze and hence very difficult to cryptanalyze. The subkey generation algorithm relies solely on the use of circular shifts but uses these in a complex way to generate a total of six subkeys for each of the eight rounds of IDEA.

Because IDEA was one of the earliest of the proposed 128-bit replacements for DES, it has undergone considerable scrutiny and so far appears to be highly resistant to cryptanalysis. IDEA is used in Pretty Good Privacy (PGP) as one alternative and is also used in a number of commercial products.

Table 2.3   Conventional Encryption Algorithms

Algorithm	Key Size (bits)	Block Size (bits)	Number of Rounds	Applications
DES	56	64	16	SET, Kerberos
Triple DES	112 or 168	64	48	Financial key management, PGP, S/MIME
AES	128, 192, or 256	128	10, 12, or 14	Intended to replace DES and 3DES
IDEA	128	64	8	PGP
Blowfish	Variable to 448	64	16	Various software packages
RC5	Variable to 2048	64	Variable to 255	Various software packages

Blowfish

Blowfish was developed in 1993 by Bruce Schneier [SCHN93, SCHN94], an independent consultant and cryptographer, and quickly became one of the most popular alternatives to DES. Blowfish was designed to be easy to implement and to have a high execution speed. It is also a very compact algorithm that can run in less than 5K of memory. An interesting feature of Blowfish is that the key length is variable and can be as long as 448 bits. In practice, 128-bit keys are used. Blowfish uses 16 rounds.

Blowfish uses S-boxes and the XOR function, as does DES, but also uses binary addition. Unlike DES, which uses fixed S-boxes, Blowfish uses dynamic S-boxes that are generated as a function of the key. In Blowfish, the subkeys and the S-boxes are generated by repeated application of the Blowfish algorithm itself to the key. A total of 521 executions of the Blowfish encryption algorithm is required to produce the subkeys and S-boxes. Accordingly, Blowfish is not suitable for applications in which the secret key changes frequently.

Blowfish is one of the most formidable symmetric encryption algorithms so far implemented, because both the subkeys and the S-boxes are produced by a process of repeated applications of Blowfish itself, which thoroughly mangles the bits and makes cryptanalysis very difficult. So far, there have been a few published papers on Blowfish cryptanalysis, but no practical weaknesses have been found.

Blowfish is used in a number of commercial applications.

RC5

RC5 was developed in 1994 by Ron Rivest [RIVE94, RIVE95], one of the inventors of the public-key algorithm RSA. RC5 is defined in RFC 2040 and was designed to have the following characteristics:

- **Suitable for hardware or software:** RC5 uses only primitive computational operations commonly found on microprocessors.
- **Fast:** To achieve this, RC5 is a simple algorithm and is word oriented. The basic operations work on full words of data at a time.
- **Adaptable to processors of different word lengths:** The number of bits in a word is a parameter of RC5; different word lengths yield different algorithms.
- **Variable number of rounds:** The number of rounds is a second parameter of RC5. This parameter allows a tradeoff between higher speed and higher security.
- **Variable-length key:** The key length is a third parameter of RC5. Again, this allows a tradeoff between speed and security.
- **Simple:** RC5's simple structure is easy to implement and eases the task of determining the strength of the algorithm.
- **Low memory requirement:** A low memory requirement makes RC5 suitable for smart cards and other devices with restricted memory.
- **High security:** RC5 is intended to provide high security with suitable parameters.
- **Data-dependent rotations:** RC5 incorporates rotations (circular bit shifts) whose amount is data dependent. This appears to strengthen the algorithm against cryptanalysis.

RC5 is used in a number of products from RSA Data Security, Inc.

2.3 CIPHER BLOCK MODES OF OPERATION

A symmetric block cipher processes one block of data at a time. In the case of DES and 3DES, the block length is 64 bits. For longer amounts of plaintext, it is necessary to break the plaintext into 64-bit blocks (padding the last block if necessary). The simplest way to proceed is what is known as electronic codebook (ECB) mode, in which plaintext is handled 64 bits at a time and each block of plaintext is encrypted using the same key. The term *codebook* is used because, for a given key, there is a unique ciphertext for every 64-bit block of plaintext. Therefore, one can imagine a gigantic codebook in which there is an entry for every possible 64-bit plaintext pattern showing its corresponding ciphertext.

With ECB, if the same 64-bit block of plaintext appears more than once in the message, it always produces the same ciphertext. Because of this, for lengthy messages, the ECB mode may not be secure. If the message is highly structured, it may be possible for a cryptanalyst to exploit these regularities. For example, if it is known that the message always starts out with certain predefined fields, then the cryptanalyst may have a number of known plaintext-ciphertext pairs to work with. If the message has repetitive elements, with a period of repetition a multiple of 64 bits, then these elements can be identified by the analyst. This may help in the analysis or may provide an opportunity for substituting or rearranging blocks.

To overcome the security deficiencies of ECB, we would like a technique in which the same plaintext block, if repeated, produces different ciphertext blocks. In this section, we look at two common alternatives, defined in FIPS PUB 81.

Cipher Block Chaining Mode

In the cipher block chaining (CBC) mode (Figure 2.7), the input to the encryption algorithm is the XOR of the current plaintext block and the preceding ciphertext block; the same key is used for each block. In effect, we have chained together the processing of the sequence of plaintext blocks. The input to the encryption function for each plaintext block bears no fixed relationship to the plaintext block. Therefore, repeating patterns of 64 bits are not exposed.

For decryption, each cipher block is passed through the decryption algorithm. The result is XORed with the preceding ciphertext block to produce the plaintext block. To see that this works, we can write

$$C_i = E_K[C_{i-1} \oplus P_i]$$

where $E_K[X]$ is the encryption of plaintext X using key K, and $\oplus$ is the exclusive-OR operation. Then

$$D_K[C_i] = D_K[E_K(C_{i-1} \oplus P_i)]$$

$$D_K[C_i] = (C_{i-1} \oplus P_i)$$

$$C_{i-1} \oplus D_K[C_i] = C_{i-1} \oplus C_{i-1} \oplus P_i = P_i$$

which verifies Figure 2.7b.

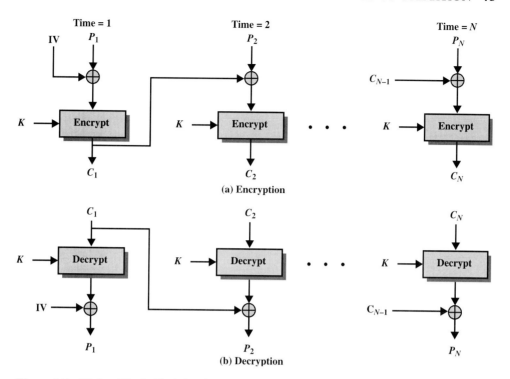

Figure 2.7 Cipher Block Chaining (CBC) Mode

To produce the first block of ciphertext, an initialization vector (IV) is XORed with the first block of plaintext. On decryption, the IV is XORed with the output of the decryption algorithm to recover the first block of plaintext.

The IV must be known to both the sender and receiver. For maximum security, the IV should be protected as well as the key. This could be done by sending the IV using ECB encryption. One reason for protecting the IV is as follows: If an opponent is able to fool the receiver into using a different value for IV, then the opponent is able to invert selected bits in the first block of plaintext. To see this, consider the following:

$$C_1 = E_K(IV \oplus P_1)$$
$$P_1 = IV \oplus D_K(C_1)$$

Now use the notation that $X[j]$ denotes the jth bit of the 64-bit quantity X. Then

$$P_1[j] = IV[j] \oplus D_K(C_1)[j]$$

Then, using the properties of XOR, we can state

$$P_1[j]' = IV[j]' \oplus D_K(C_1)[j]$$

where the prime notation denotes bit complementation. This means that if an opponent can predictably change bits in IV, the corresponding bits of the received value of P_1 can be changed.

CBC is widely used in security applications, as we shall see in Part Two.

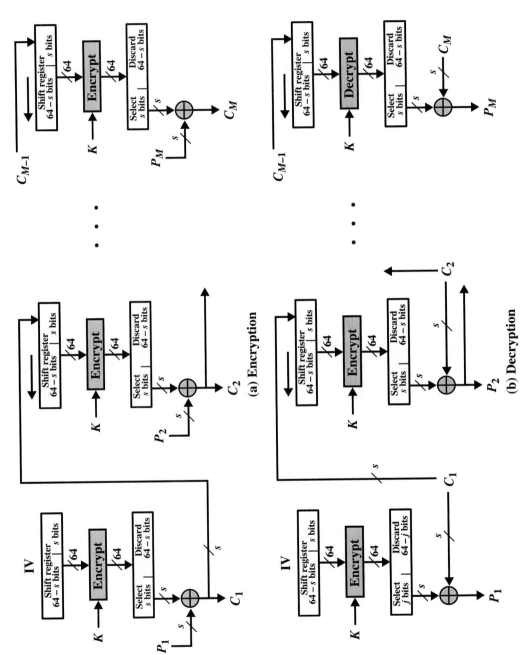

Figure 2.8 *s*-bit Cipher Feedback (CFB) Mode

Cipher Feedback Mode

It is possible to convert any block cipher into a stream cipher by using the cipher feedback (CFB) mode. A stream cipher eliminates the need to pad a message to be an integral number of blocks. It also can operate in real time. Thus, if a character stream is being transmitted, each character can be encrypted and transmitted immediately using a character-oriented stream cipher.

One desirable property of a stream cipher is that the ciphertext be of the same length as the plaintext. Thus, if 8-bit characters are being transmitted, each character should be encrypted using 8 bits. If more than 8 bits are used, transmission capacity is wasted.

Figure 2.8 depicts the CFB scheme. In the figure, it is assumed that the unit of transmission is s bits; a common value is $s = 8$. As with CBC, the units of plaintext are chained together, so that the ciphertext of any plaintext unit is a function of all the preceding plaintext.

First, consider encryption. The input to the encryption function is a 64-bit shift register that is initially set to some initialization vector (IV). The leftmost (most significant) s bits of the output of the encryption function are XORed with the first unit of plaintext P_1 to produce the first unit of ciphertext C_1, which is then transmitted. In addition, the contents of the shift register are shifted left by s bits and C_1 is placed in the rightmost (least significant) s bits of the shift register. This process continues until all plaintext units have been encrypted.

For decryption, the same scheme is used, except that the received ciphertext unit is XORed with the output of the encryption function to produce the plaintext unit. Note that it is the *encryption* function that is used, not the decryption function. This is easily explained. Let $S_s(X)$ be defined as the most significant s bits of X. Then

$$C_1 = P_1 \oplus S_s(E(IV))$$

Therefore,

$$P_1 = C_1 \oplus S_s(E(IV))$$

The same reasoning holds for subsequent steps in the process.

2.4 LOCATION OF ENCRYPTION DEVICES

The most powerful, and most common, approach to countering the threats to network security is encryption. In using encryption, we need to decide what to encrypt and where the encryption gear should be located. There are two fundamental alternatives: link encryption and end-to-end encryption; these are illustrated in use over a packet-switching network in Figure 2.9.

With link encryption, each vulnerable communications link is equipped on both ends with an encryption device. Thus, all traffic over all communications links is secured. Although this requires a lot of encryption devices in a large network, it provides a high level of security. One disadvantage of this approach is that the message must be decrypted each time it enters a packet switch; this is necessary because the switch must read the address (virtual circuit number) in the packet header to route the packet. Thus, the message is vulnerable at each switch. If this is a public packet-switching network, the user has no control over the security of the nodes.

With end-to-end encryption, the encryption process is carried out at the two end systems. The source host or terminal encrypts the data. The data, in encrypted form, are then transmitted unaltered across the network to the destination terminal or host. The destination shares a key with the source and so is able to decrypt the data. This approach would seem to secure the transmission against attacks on the network links or switches. There is, however, still a weak spot.

Consider the following situation. A host connects to an X.25 packet-switching network, sets up a virtual circuit to another host, and is prepared to transfer data to that other host using end-to-end encryption. Data are transmitted over such a network in the form of packets, consisting of a header and some user data. What part of each packet will the host encrypt? Suppose that the host encrypts the entire packet, including the header. This will not work because, remember, only the other host can perform the decryption. The packet-switching node will receive an encrypted packet and be unable to read the header. Therefore, it will not be able to route the packet. It follows that the host may only encrypt the user data portion of the packet and must leave the header in the clear, so that it can be read by the network.

Thus, with end-to-end encryption, the user data are secure. However, the traffic pattern is not, because packet headers are transmitted in the clear. To achieve greater security, both link and end-to-end encryption are needed, as is shown in Figure 2.9.

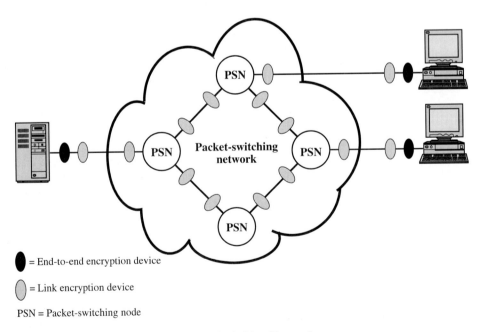

= End-to-end encryption device

= Link encryption device

PSN = Packet-switching node

Figure 2.9 Encryption across a Packet-Switching Network

To summarize, when both forms are employed, the host encrypts the user data portion of a packet using an end-to-end encryption key. The entire packet is then encrypted using a link encryption key. As the packet traverses the network, each switch decrypts the packet using a link encryption key to read the header and then encrypts the entire packet again for sending it out on the next link. Now the entire packet is secure except for the time that the packet is actually in the memory of a packet switch, at which time the packet header is in the clear.

2.5 KEY DISTRIBUTION

For symmetric encryption to work, the two parties to a secure exchange must have the same key, and that key must be protected from access by others. Furthermore, frequent key changes are usually desirable to limit the amount of data compromised if an attacker learns the key. Therefore, the strength of any cryptographic system rests with the key distribution technique, a term that refers to the means of delivering a key to two parties that wish to exchange data, without allowing others to see the key. Key distribution can be achieved in a number of ways. For two parties A and B,

1. A key could be selected by A and physically delivered to B.
2. A third party could select the key and physically deliver it to A and B.
3. If A and B have previously and recently used a key, one party could transmit the new key to the other, encrypted using the old key.
4. If A and B each have an encrypted connection to a third party C, C could deliver a key on the encrypted links to A and B.

Options 1 and 2 call for manual delivery of a key. For link encryption, this is a reasonable requirement, because each link encryption device is only going to be exchanging data with its partner on the other end of the link. However, for end-to-end encryption, manual delivery is awkward. In a distributed system, any given host or terminal may need to engage in exchanges with many other hosts and terminals over time. Thus, each device needs a number of keys, supplied dynamically. The problem is especially difficult in a wide area distributed system.

Option 3 is a possibility for either link encryption or end-to-end encryption, but if an attacker ever succeeds in gaining access to one key, then all subsequent keys are revealed. Even if frequent changes are made to the link encryption keys, these should be done manually. To provide keys for end-to-end encryption, option 4 is preferable.

Figure 2.10 illustrates an implementation that satisfies option 4 for end-to-end encryption. In the figure, link encryption is ignored. This can be added, or not, as required. For this scheme, two kinds of keys are identified:

- **Session key:** When two end systems (hosts, terminals, etc.) wish to communicate, they establish a logical connection (e.g., virtual circuit). For the duration of that logical connection, all user data are encrypted with a one-time

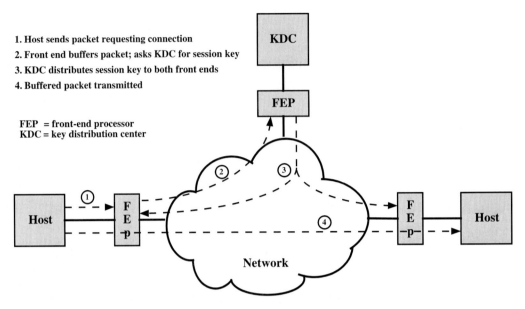

1. Host sends packet requesting connection
2. Front end buffers packet; asks KDC for session key
3. KDC distributes session key to both front ends
4. Buffered packet transmitted

FEP = front-end processor
KDC = key distribution center

Figure 2.10   Automatic Key Distribution for Connection-Oriented Protocol

session key. At the conclusion of the session, or connection, the session key is destroyed.

- **Permanent key:** A permanent key is a key used between entities for the purpose of distributing session keys.

The configuration consists of the following elements:

- **Key distribution center:** The key distribution center (KDC) determines which systems are allowed to communicate with each other. When permission is granted for two systems to establish a connection, the key distribution center provides a one-time session key for that connection.
- **Front-end processor:** The front-end processor (FEP) performs end-to-end encryption and obtains session keys on behalf of its host or terminal.

The steps involved in establishing a connection are shown in Figure 2.10. When one host wishes to set up a connection to another host, it transmits a connection-request packet (step 1). The front-end processor saves that packet and applies to the KDC for permission to establish the connection (step 2). The communication between the FEP and the KDC is encrypted using a master key shared only by the FEP and the KDC. If the KDC approves the connection request, it generates the session key and delivers it to the two appropriate front-end processors, using a unique permanent key for each front end (step 3). The requesting front-end processor can now release the connection request packet, and a connection is set up between the two end systems (step 4). All user data exchanged between the two end systems are encrypted by their respective front-end processors using the one-time session key.

The automated key distribution approach provides the flexibility and dynamic characteristics needed to allow a number of terminal users to access a number of hosts and for the hosts to exchange data with each other.

Another approach to key distribution uses public-key encryption, which is discussed in Chapter 3.

2.6 RECOMMENDED READING AND WEB SITES

The topics in this chapter are covered in greater detail in [STAL03]. For coverage of cryptographic algorithms, [SCHN96] is an essential reference work; it contains descriptions of virtually every cryptographic algorithm and protocol published in the last 15 years. Another worthwhile and detailed survey is [MENE97]. A more in-depth treatment, with rigorous mathematical discussion, is [STIN02].

MENE97   Menezes, A.; Oorshcot, P.; and Vanstone, S. *Handbook of Applied Cryptography.* Boca Raton, FL: CRC Press, 1997.
SCHN96   Schneier, B. *Applied Cryptography.* New York: Wiley, 1996.
STAL03   Stallings, W. *Cryptography and Network Security: Principles and Practice,* 3rd Edition. Upper Saddle River, NJ: Prentice Hall, 2003.
STIN02   Stinson, D. *Cryptography: Theory and Practice.* Boca Raton, FL: CRC Press, 2002.

Recommended Web sites:

- **AES home page:** NIST's page on AES. Contains the standard plus a number of other relevant documents.
- **The Rijndael page:** Maintained by the developers of Rijndael. Contains documents, links to implementations, and other relevant links.

2.7 KEY TERMS, REVIEW QUESTIONS, AND PROBLEMS

Key Terms

Advanced Encryption Standard (AES)	cryptanalysis	key distribution
block cipher	cryptography Data Encryption Standard (DES)	link encryption
brute-force attack	decryption	plaintext
cipher block chaining (CBC) mode	electronic codebook (ECB) mode	session key
cipher feedback (CFB) mode	encryption	stream cipher
ciphertext	end-to-end encryption	subkey
	Feistel cipher	symmetric encryption
		triple DES (3DES)

Review Questions

2.1 What are the essential ingredients of a symmetric cipher?

2.2 What are the two basic functions used in encryption algorithms?

2.3 How many keys are required for two people to communicate via a symmetric cipher?

2.4 What is the difference between a block cipher and a stream cipher?

2.5 What are the two general approaches to attacking a cipher?

2.6 Why do some block cipher modes of operation only use encryption while others use both encryption and decryption?

2.7 What is triple encryption?

2.8 Why is the middle portion of 3DES a decryption rather than an encryption?

2.9 What is the difference between link and end-to-end encryption?

2.10 List ways in which secret keys can be distributed to two communicating parties.

2.11 What is the difference between a session key and a master key?

2.12 What is a key distribution center?

Problems

2.1 Show that Feistel decryption is the inverse of Feistel encryption.

2.2 With the ECB mode, if there is an error in a block of the transmitted ciphertext, only the corresponding plaintext block is affected. However, in the CBC mode, this error propagates. For example, an error in the transmitted C_1 (Figure 2.7) obviously corrupts P_1 and P_2.

    a. Are any blocks beyond P_2 affected?

    b. Suppose that there is a bit error in the source version of P_1. Through how many ciphertext blocks is this error propagated? What is the effect at the receiver?

2.3 If a bit error occurs in the transmission of a ciphertext character in 8-bit CFB mode, how far does the error propagate?

2.4 Key distribution schemes using an access control center and/or a key distribution center have central points vulnerable to attack. Discuss the security implications of such centralization.

2.5 Suppose that someone suggests the following way to confirm that the two of you are both in possession of the same secret key. You create a random bit string the length of the key, XOR it with the key, and send the result over the channel. Your partner XORs the incoming block with the key (which should be the same as your key) and sends it back. You check and if what you receive is your original random string, you have verified that your partner has the same secret key, yet neither of you has ever transmitted the key. Is there a flaw in this scheme?

CHAPTER 3

PUBLIC-KEY CRYPTOGRAPHY AND MESSAGE AUTHENTICATION

3.1 Approaches to Message Authentication
    Authentication Using Conventional Encryption
    Message Authentication without Message Encryption

3.2 Secure Hash Functions and HMAC
    Hash Function Requirements
    Simple Hash Functions
    The SHA-1 Secure Hash Function
    Other Secure Hash Functions
    HMAC

3.3 Public-Key Cryptography Principles
    Public-Key Encryption Structure
    Applications for Public-Key Cryptosystems
    Requirements for Public-Key Cryptography

3.4 Public-Key Cryptography Algorithms
    The RSA Public-Key Encryption Algorithm
    Diffie-Hellman Key Exchange
    Other Public-Key Cryptography Algorithms

3.5 Digital Signatures

3.6 Key Management
    Public-Key Certificates
    Public-Key Distribution of Secret Keys

3.7 Recommended Reading and Web Sites

3.8 Key Terms, Review Questions, and Problems
    Key Terms
    Review Questions
    Problems

Every Egyptian received two names, which were known respectively as the true name and the good name, or the great name and the little name; and while the good or little name was made public, the true or great name appears to have been carefully concealed.

—*The Golden Bough*, Sir James George Frazer

To guard against the baneful influence exerted by strangers is therefore an elementary dictate of savage prudence. Hence before strangers are allowed to enter a district, or at least before they are permitted to mingle freely with the inhabitants, certain ceremonies are often performed by the natives of the country for the purpose of disarming the strangers of their magical powers, or of disinfecting, so to speak, the tainted atmosphere by which they are supposed to be surrounded.

—*The Golden Bough*, Sir James George Frazer

In addition to message confidentiality, message authentication is an important network security function. This chapter examines three aspects of message authentication. First, we look at the use of message authentication codes and hash functions to provide message authentication. Then we look at public-key encryption principles and two specific public-key algorithms. These algorithms are useful in the exchange of conventional encryption keys. Then we look at the use of public-key encryption to produce digital signatures, which provides an enhanced form of message authentication. Finally, we revisit the issue of key management.

3.1 APPROACHES TO MESSAGE AUTHENTICATION

Encryption protects against passive attack (eavesdropping). A different requirement is to protect against active attack (falsification of data and transactions). Protection against such attacks is known as message authentication.

A message, file, document, or other collection of data is said to be authentic when it is genuine and came from its alleged source. Message authentication is a procedure that allows communicating parties to verify that received messages are authentic. The two important aspects are to verify that the contents of the message have not been altered and that the source is authentic. We may also wish to verify a message's timeliness (it has not been artificially delayed and replayed) and sequence relative to other messages flowing between two parties.

Authentication Using Conventional Encryption

It is possible to perform authentication simply by the use of conventional encryption. If we assume that only the sender and receiver share a key (which is as it should be), then only the genuine sender would be able to encrypt a message successfully for the other participant. Furthermore, if the message includes an error-detection code and a sequence number, the receiver is assured that no alterations have been made and that sequencing is proper. If the message also includes a timestamp, the receiver is assured that the message has not been delayed beyond that normally expected for network transit.

Message Authentication without Message Encryption

In this section, we examine several approaches to message authentication that do not rely on encryption. In all of these approaches, an authentication tag is generated and appended to each message for transmission. The message itself is not encrypted and can be read at the destination independent of the authentication function at the destination.

Because the approaches discussed in this section do not encrypt the message, message confidentiality is not provided. Because conventional encryption will provide authentication, and because it is widely used with readily available products, why not simply use such an approach, which provides both confidentiality and authentication? [DAVI89] suggests three situations in which message authentication without confidentiality is preferable:

1. There are a number of applications in which the same message is broadcast to a number of destinations. For example, notification to users that the network is now unavailable or an alarm signal in a control center. It is cheaper and more reliable to have only one destination responsible for monitoring authenticity. Thus, the message must be broadcast in plaintext with an associated message authentication tag. The responsible system performs authentication. If a violation occurs, the other destination systems are alerted by a general alarm.

2. Another possible scenario is an exchange in which one side has a heavy load and cannot afford the time to decrypt all incoming messages. Authentication is carried out on a selective basis, messages being chosen at random for checking.

3. Authentication of a computer program in plaintext is an attractive service. The computer program can be executed without having to decrypt it every time, which would be wasteful of processor resources. However, if a message authentication tag were attached to the program, it could be checked whenever assurance is required of the integrity of the program.

Thus, there is a place for both authentication and encryption in meeting security requirements.

Message Authentication Code

One authentication technique involves the use of a secret key to generate a small block of data, known as a message authentication code, that is appended to the message. This technique assumes that two communicating parties, say A and B, share a common secret key K_{AB}. When A has a message to send to B, it calculates the message authentication code as a function of the message and the key: $MAC_M = F(K_{AB}, M)$. The message plus code are transmitted to the intended recipient. The recipient performs the same calculation on the received message, using the same

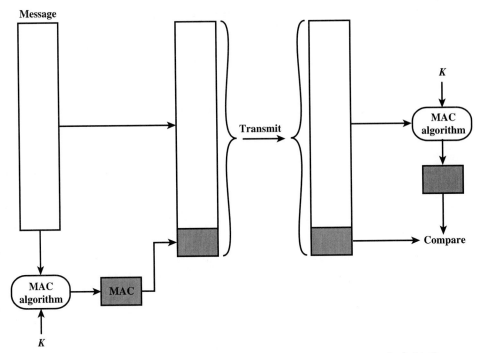

Figure 3.1 Message Authentication Using a Message Authentication Code (MAC)

secret key, to generate a new message authentication code. The received code is compared to the calculated code (Figure 3.1). If we assume that only the receiver and the sender know the identity of the secret key, and if the received code matches the calculated code, then

1. The receiver is assured that the message has not been altered. If an attacker alters the message but does not alter the code, then the receiver's calculation of the code will differ from the received code. Because the attacker is assumed not to know the secret key, the attacker cannot alter the code to correspond to the alterations in the message.
2. The receiver is assured that the message is from the alleged sender. Because no one else knows the secret key, no one else could prepare a message with a proper code.
3. If the message includes a sequence number (such as is used with X.25, HDLC, and TCP), then the receiver can be assured of the proper sequence, because an attacker cannot successfully alter the sequence number.

A number of algorithms could be used to generate the code. The NIST specification, FIPS PUB 113, recommends the use of DES. DES is used to generate an encrypted version of the message, and the last number of bits of ciphertext are used as the code. A 16- or 32-bit code is typical.

The process just described is similar to encryption. One difference is that the authentication algorithm need not be reversible, as it must for decryption. It turns out that because of the mathematical properties of the authentication function, it is less vulnerable to being broken than encryption.

One-Way Hash Function

An alternative to the message authentication code is the one-way hash function. As with the message authentication code, a hash function accepts a variable-size message M as input and produces a fixed-size message digest $H(M)$ as output. Unlike the MAC, a hash function does not also take a secret key as input. To authenticate a message, the message digest is sent with the message in such a way that the message digest is authentic.

Figure 3.2 illustrates three ways in which the message can be authenticated. The message digest can be encrypted using conventional encryption (part a); if it is assumed that only the sender and receiver share the encryption key, then authenticity is assured. The message can also be encrypted using public-key encryption (part b); this is explained in Section 3.5. The public-key approach has two advantages: It provides a digital signature as well as message authentication; and it does not require the distribution of keys to communicating parties.

These two approaches have an advantage over approaches that encrypt the entire message in that less computation is required. Nevertheless, there has been interest in developing a technique that avoids encryption altogether. Several reasons for this interest are pointed out in [TSUD92]:

- Encryption software is quite slow. Even though the amount of data to be encrypted per message is small, there may be a steady stream of messages into and out of a system.

- Encryption hardware costs are nonnegligible. Low-cost chip implementations of DES are available, but the cost adds up if all nodes in a network must have this capability.

- Encryption hardware is optimized toward large data sizes. For small blocks of data, a high proportion of the time is spent in initialization/invocation overhead.

- Encryption algorithms may be covered by patents. Some encryption algorithms, such as the RSA public-key algorithm, are patented and must be licensed, adding a cost.

- Encryption algorithms may be subject to export control. This is true of DES.

Figure 3.2c shows a technique that uses a hash function but no encryption for message authentication. This technique assumes that two communicating parties, say A and B, share a common secret value S_{AB}. When A has a message to send to B, it calculates the hash function over the concatenation of the secret value and the message: $MD_M = H(S_{AB}\|M)$.[1] It then sends $[M\|MD_M]$ to B. Because B possesses S_{AB}, it can recompute $H(S_{AB}\|M)$ and verify MD_M. Because the secret value itself is not sent, it is not possible for an attacker to modify an intercepted message. As long as the secret value remains secret, it is also not possible for an attacker to generate a false message.

---

[1] $\|$ denotes concatenation.

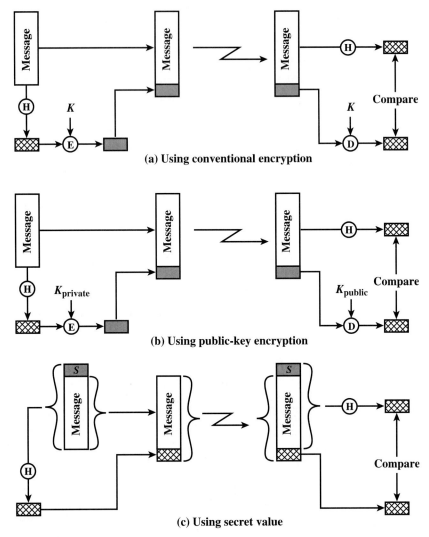

(a) Using conventional encryption

(b) Using public-key encryption

(c) Using secret value

Figure 3.2 Message Authentication Using a One-Way Hash Function

A variation on the third technique, called HMAC, is the one adopted for IP security (described in Chapter 6); it has also been specified for SNMPv3 (Chapter 8).

3.2 SECURE HASH FUNCTIONS AND HMAC

The one-way hash function, or secure hash function, is important not only in message authentication but in digital signatures. In this section, we begin with a discussion of requirements for a secure hash function. Then we look at one of the most important hash functions, SHA-1.

Hash Function Requirements

The purpose of a hash function is to produce a "fingerprint" of a file, message, or other block of data. To be useful for message authentication, a hash function H must have the following properties:

1. H can be applied to a block of data of any size.
2. H produces a fixed-length output.
3. $H(x)$ is relatively easy to compute for any given x, making both hardware and software implementations practical.
4. For any given value h, it is computationally infeasible to find x such that $H(x) = h$. This is sometimes referred to in the literature as the **one-way** property.
5. For any given block x, it is computationally infeasible to find $y \neq x$ with $H(y) = H(x)$. This is sometimes referred to as **weak collision resistance**.
6. It is computationally infeasible to find any pair (x, y) such that $H(x) = H(y)$. This is sometimes referred to as **strong collision resistance**.[2]

The first three properties are requirements for the practical application of a hash function to message authentication. The fourth property is the "one-way" property: It is easy to generate a code given a message, but virtually impossible to generate a message given a code. This property is important if the authentication technique involves the use of a secret value (Figure 3.2c). The secret value itself is not sent; however, if the hash function is not one way, an attacker can easily discover the secret value: If the attacker can observe or intercept a transmission, the attacker obtains the message M and the hash code $MD_M = H(S_{AB}||M)$. The attacker then inverts the hash function to obtain $S_{AB}||M = H^{-1}(MD_M)$. Because the attacker now has both M and $S_{AB}||M$, it is a trivial matter to recover S_{AB}.

The fifth property guarantees that it is impossible to find an alternative message with the same hash value as a given message. This prevents forgery when an encrypted hash code is used (Figures 3.2a and b). If this property were not true, an attacker would be capable of the following sequence: First, observe or intercept a message plus its encrypted hash code; second, generate an unencrypted hash code from the message; third, generate an alternate message with the same hash code.

A hash function that satisfies the first five properties in the preceding list is referred to as a weak hash function. If the sixth property is also satisfied, then it is referred to as a strong hash function. The sixth property protects against a sophisticated class of attack known as the birthday attack.

In addition to providing authentication, a message digest also provides data integrity. It performs the same function as a frame check sequence: If any bits in the message are accidentally altered in transit, the message digest will be in error.

---

[2]Unfortunately, these terms are not used consistently. Alternate terms used in the literature include *one-way hash function* (properties 4 and 5); *collision-resistant hash function* (properties 4, 5, and 6); *weak one-way hash function* (properties 4 and 5); *strong one-way hash function* (properties 4, 5, and 6). The reader must take care in reading the literature to determine the meaning of the particular terms used.

Simple Hash Functions

All hash functions operate using the following general principles. The input (message, file, etc.) is viewed as a sequence of n-bit blocks. The input is processed one block at a time in an iterative fashion to produce an n-bit hash function.

One of the simplest hash functions is the bit-by-bit exclusive-OR (XOR) of every block. This can be expressed as follows:

$$C_i = b_{i1} \oplus b_{i2} \oplus \ldots \oplus b_{im}$$

where

$C_i = i$th bit of the hash code, $1 \leq i \leq n$
m = number of n-bit blocks in the input
$b_{ij} = i$th bit in jth block
$\oplus$ = XOR operation

Figure 3.3 illustrates this operation; it produces a simple parity for each bit position and is known as a longitudinal redundancy check. It is reasonably effective for random data as a data integrity check. Each n-bit hash value is equally likely. Thus, the probability that a data error will result in an unchanged hash value is 2^{-n}. With more predictably formatted data, the function is less effective. For example, in most normal text files, the high-order bit of each octet is always zero. So if a 128-bit hash value is used, instead of an effectiveness of 2^{-128}, the hash function on this type of data has an effectiveness of 2^{-112}.

A simple way to improve matters is to perform a one-bit circular shift, or rotation, on the hash value after each block is processed. The procedure can be summarized as follows:

1. Initially set the n-bit hash value to zero.
2. Process each successive n-bit block of data as follows:
   a. Rotate the current hash value to the left by one bit.
   b. XOR the block into the hash value.

This has the effect of "randomizing" the input more completely and overcoming any regularities that appear in the input.

	bit 1	bit 2	• • •	bit n
Block 1	b_{11}	b_{21}		b_{n1}
Block 2	b_{12}	b_{22}		b_{n2}
	• • •	• • •	• • •	• • •
Block m	b_{1m}	b_{2m}		b_{nm}
Hash code	C_1	C_2		C_n

Figure 3.3 Simple Hash Function Using Bitwise XOR

Although the second procedure provides a good measure of data integrity, it is virtually useless for data security when an encrypted hash code is used with a plaintext message, as in Figures 3.2a and b. Given a message, it is an easy matter to produce a new message that yields that hash code: Simply prepare the desired alternate message and then append an n-bit block that forces the new message plus block to yield the desired hash code.

Although a simple XOR or rotated XOR (RXOR) is insufficient if only the hash code is encrypted, you may still feel that such a simple function could be useful when the message as well as the hash code are encrypted. But one must be careful. A technique originally proposed by the National Bureau of Standards used the simple XOR applied to 64-bit blocks of the message and then an encryption of the entire message that used the cipher block chaining (CBC) mode. We can define the scheme as follows: Given a message consisting of a sequence of 64-bit blocks $X_1, X_2, \ldots, X_N$, define the hash code C as the block-by-block XOR or all blocks and append the hash code as the final block:

$$C = X_{N+1} = X_1 \oplus X_2 \oplus \ldots \oplus X_N$$

Next, encrypt the entire message plus hash code, using CBC mode to produce the encrypted message $Y_1, Y_2, \ldots, Y_{N+1}$. [JUEN85] points out several ways in which the ciphertext of this message can be manipulated in such a way that it is not detectable by the hash code. For example, by the definition of CBC (Figure 2.7), we have

$$X_1 \quad = \text{IV} \oplus \text{D}_K(Y_1)$$
$$X_i \quad = Y_{i-1} \oplus \text{D}_K(Y_i)$$
$$X_{N+1} = Y_N \oplus \text{D}_K(Y_{N+1})$$

But X_{N+1} is the hash code:

$$X_{N+1} = X_1 \oplus X_2 \oplus \ldots \oplus X_N$$
$$= (\text{IV} \oplus \text{D}_K(Y_1)) \oplus (Y_1 \oplus \text{D}_K(Y_2)) \oplus \ldots \oplus (Y_{N-1} \oplus \text{D}_K(Y_N))$$

Because the terms in the preceding equation can be XORed in any order, it follows that the hash code would not change if the ciphertext blocks were permuted.

The SHA-1 Secure Hash Function

The Secure Hash Algorithm (SHA) was developed by the National Institute of Standards and Technology (NIST) and published as a federal information processing standard (FIPS PUB 180) in 1993; a revised version was issued as FIPS PUB 180-1 in 1995 and is generally referred to as SHA-1.

The algorithm takes as input a message with a maximum length of less than 2^{64} bits and produces as output a 160-bit message digest. The input is processed in 512-bit blocks. Figure 3.4 depicts the overall processing of a message to produce a digest. The processing consists of the following steps:

Step 1: Append padding bits. The message is padded so that its length is congruent to 448 modulo 512 (length = 448 mod 512). That is, the length of the padded mes-

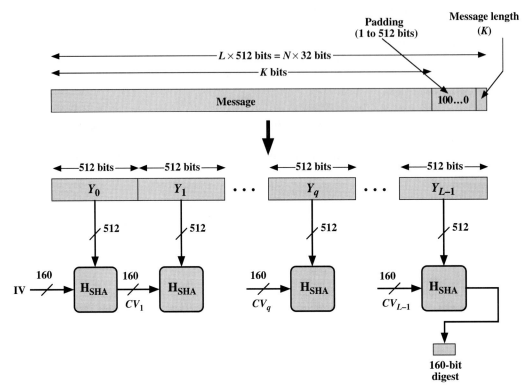

Figure 3.4 Message Digest Generation Using SHA-1

sage is 64 bits less than a multiple of 512 bits. Padding is always added, even if the message is already of the desired length. Thus, the number of padding bits is in the range of 1 to 512. The padding consists of a single 1-bit followed by the necessary number of 0-bits.

Step 2: Append length. A block of 64 bits is appended to the message. This block is treated as an unsigned 64-bit integer (most significant byte first) and contains the length of the original message (before the padding). The inclusion of a length value makes more difficult a kind of attack known as a padding attack [TSUD92].

The outcome of the first two steps yields a message that is an integer multiple of 512 bits in length. In Figure 3.4, the expanded message is represented as the sequence of 512-bit blocks $Y_0, Y_1, \ldots, Y_{L-1}$, so that the total length of the expanded message is $L \times 512$ bits. Equivalently, the result is a multiple of 16 32-bit words. Let $M[0 \ldots N-1]$ denote the words of the resulting message, with N an integer multiple of 16. Thus, $N = L \times 16$.

Step 3: Initialize MD buffer. A 160-bit buffer is used to hold intermediate and final results of the hash function. The buffer can be represented as five 32-bit registers (A, B, C, D, E). These registers are initialized to the following 32-bit integers (hexadecimal values):

$$A = 67452301$$
$$B = EFCDAB89$$
$$C = 98BADCFE$$
$$D = 10325476$$
$$E = C3D2E1F0$$

Step 4: Process message in 512-bit (16-word) blocks. The heart of the algorithm is a module, known as a **compression function**, that consists of four rounds of processing of 20 steps each. The logic is illustrated in Figure 3.5. The four rounds have a similar structure, but each uses a different primitive logical function, which we refer to as f_1, f_2, f_3, and f_4.

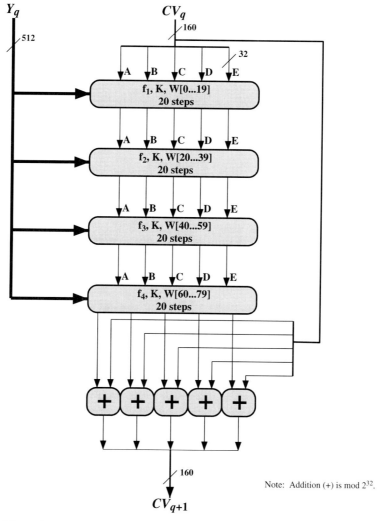

Figure 3.5   SHA-1 Processing of a Single 512-Bit Block (SHA-1 Compression Function)

Each round takes as input the current 512-bit block being processed (Y_q) and the 160-bit buffer value ABCDE and updates the contents of the buffer. Each round also makes use of an additive constant K_t, where $0 \le t \le 79$ indicates one of the 80 steps across five rounds. In fact, only four distinct constants are used. The values, in hexadecimal and decimal, are as follows:

Step Number	Hexadecimal	Take Integer Part of:
$0 \le t \le 19$	$K_t = $ 5A827999	$[2^{30} \times \sqrt{2}]$
$20 \le t \le 39$	$K_t = $ 6ED9EBA1	$[2^{30} \times \sqrt{3}]$
$40 \le t \le 59$	$K_t = $ 8F1BBCDC	$[2^{30} \times \sqrt{5}]$
$60 \le t \le 79$	$K_t = $ CA62C1D6	$[2^{30} \times \sqrt{10}]$

The output of the fourth round (eightieth step) is added to the input to the first round (CV_q) to produce CV_{q+1}. The addition is done independently for each of the five words in the buffer with each of the corresponding words in CV_q, using addition modulo 2^{32}.

Step 5: Output. After all L 512-bit blocks have been processed, the output from the Lth stage is the 160-bit message digest.

The SHA-1 algorithm has the property that every bit of the hash code is a function of every bit of the input. The complex repetition of the basic function f_t produces results that are well mixed; that is, it is unlikely that two messages chosen at random, even if they exhibit similar regularities, will have the same hash code. Unless there is some hidden weakness in SHA-1, which has not so far been published, the difficulty of coming up with two messages having the same message digest is on the order of 2^{80} operations, while the difficulty of finding a message with a given digest is on the order of 2^{160} operations.

Other Secure Hash Functions

As was the case with symmetric block ciphers, designers of secure hash functions have been reluctant to depart from a proven structure. DES is based on the Feistel cipher. Virtually all important subsequent block ciphers follow the Feistel design because the design can be adapted to resist newly discovered cryptanalytic threats. If, instead, an entirely new design were used for a symmetric block cipher, there would be concern that the structure itself opened up new avenues of attack not yet thought of. Similarly, most important modern hash functions follow the basic structure of Figure 3.4, referred to as an iterated hash function and initially proposed by Merkle [MERK79, MERK89]. The motivation for this iterative structure stems from the observation by Merkle [MERK89] and Damgard [DAMG89] that if the compression function is collision resistant, then so is the resultant iterated hash function. Therefore, the structure can be used to produce a secure hash function to operate on a message of any length. The problem of designing a secure hash function reduces to that of designing a collision-resistant compression function that operates on inputs of some fixed size. This has proved to be a fundamentally sound approach, and newer designs simply refine the structure and add to the hash code length.

In this section we look at two other secure hash functions that, in addition to SHA-1, have gained commercial acceptance. Some of the principal characteristics are compared in Table 3.1.

MD5 Message Digest Algorithm

The MD5 message-digest algorithm (RFC 1321) was developed by Ron Rivest. Until the last few years, when both brute-force and cryptanalytic concerns have arisen, MD5 was the most widely used secure hash algorithm. The algorithm takes as input a message of arbitrary length and produces as output a 128-bit message digest. The input is processed in 512-bit blocks.

As processor speeds have increased, the security of a 128-bit hash code has become questionable. It can be shown that the difficulty of coming up with two messages having the same message digest is on the order of 2^{64} operations, whereas the difficulty of finding a message with a given digest is on the order of 2^{128} operations. The former figure is too small for security. Further, a number of cryptanalytic attacks have been developed that suggest the vulnerability of MD5 to cryptanalysis [BERS92, BOER93, DOBB96a].

RIPEMD-160

The RIPEMD-160 message-digest algorithm [DOBB96b, BOSS97] was developed under the European RACE Integrity Primitives Evaluation (RIPE) project, by a group of researchers that launched partially successful attacks on MD4 and MD5. The group originally developed a 128-bit version of RIPEM. After the end of the RIPE project, H. Dobbertin (who was not a part of the RIPE project) found attacks on two rounds of RIPEMD, and later on MD4 and MD5. Because of these attacks, some members of the RIPE consortium decided to upgrade RIPEMD. The design work was done by them and by Dobbertin.

RIPEMD-160 is quite similar in structure to SHA-1. The algorithm takes as input a message of arbitrary length and produces as output a 160-bit message digest. The input is processed in 512-bit blocks.

Table 3.1   A Comparison of Secure Hash Functions

	MD5	SHA-1	RIPEMD-160
Digest length	128 bits	160 bits	160 bits
Basic unit of processing	512 bits	512 bits	512 bits
Number of steps	64 (4 rounds of 16)	80 (4 rounds of 20)	160 (5 paired rounds of 16)
Maximum message size	∞	$2^{64} - 1$ bits	∞
Primitive logical functions	4	4	5
Additive constants used	64	4	9

HMAC

In recent years, there has been increased interest in developing a MAC derived from a cryptographic hash code, such as SHA-1. The motivations for this interest are as follows:

- Cryptographic hash functions generally execute faster in software than conventional encryption algorithms such as DES.
- Library code for cryptographic hash functions is widely available.
- There are no export restrictions from the United States or other countries for cryptographic hash functions, whereas conventional encryption algorithms, even when used for MACs, are restricted.

A hash function such as SHA-1 was not designed for use as a MAC and cannot be used directly for that purpose because it does not rely on a secret key. There have been a number of proposals for the incorporation of a secret key into an existing hash algorithm. The approach that has received the most support is HMAC [BELL96a, BELL96b]. HMAC has been issued as RFC 2104, has been chosen as the mandatory-to-implement MAC for IP Security, and is used in other Internet protocols, such as Transport Layer Security (TLS, soon to replace Secure Sockets Layer) and Secure Electronic Transaction (SET).

HMAC Design Objectives

RFC 2104 lists the following design objectives for HMAC:

- To use, without modifications, available hash functions. In particular, hash functions that perform well in software, and for which code is freely and widely available
- To allow for easy replaceability of the embedded hash function in case faster or more secure hash functions are found or required
- To preserve the original performance of the hash function without incurring a significant degradation
- To use and handle keys in a simple way
- To have a well-understood cryptographic analysis of the strength of the authentication mechanism based on reasonable assumptions on the embedded hash function

The first two objectives are important to the acceptability of HMAC. HMAC treats the hash function as a "black box." This has two benefits. First, an existing implementation of a hash function can be used as a module in implementing HMAC. In this way, the bulk of the HMAC code is prepackaged and ready to use without modification. Second, if it is ever desired to replace a given hash function in an HMAC implementation, all that is required is to remove the existing hash function module and drop in the new module. This could be done if a faster hash function were desired. More important, if the security of the embedded hash function were compromised, the security of HMAC could be retained simply by replacing the embedded hash function with a more secure one.

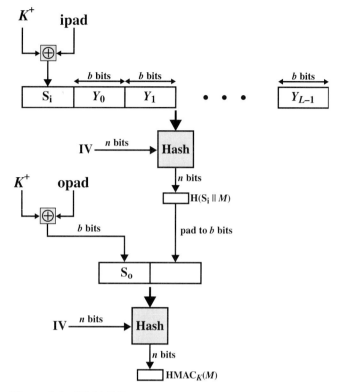

Figure 3.6   HMAC Structure

The last design objective in the preceding list is, in fact, the main advantage of HMAC over other proposed hash-based schemes. HMAC can be proven secure provided that the embedded hash function has some reasonable cryptographic strengths. We return to this point later in this section, but first we examine the structure of HMAC.

HMAC Algorithm

Figure 3.6 illustrates the overall operation of HMAC. Define the following terms:

H = embedded hash function (e.g., SHA-1)
M = message input to HMAC (including the padding specified in the embedded hash function)
Y_i = ith block of M, $0 \leq i \leq (L - 1)$
L = number of blocks in M
b = number of bits in a block
n = length of hash code produced by embedded hash function
K = secret key; if key length is greater than b, the key is input to the hash function to produce an n-bit key; recommended length is $\geq n$
K^+ = K padded with zeros on the left so that the result is b bits in length
ipad   = 00110110 (36 in hexadecimal) repeated $b/8$ times
opad   = 01011100 (5C in hexadecimal) repeated $b/8$ times

Then HMAC can be expressed as follows:

$$\text{HMAC}_K(M) = \text{H}[(K^+ \oplus \text{opad}) \,\|\, \text{H}[(K^+ \oplus \text{ipad}) \,\|\, M]]$$

In words,

1. Append zeros to the left end of K to create a b-bit string K^+ (e.g., if K is of length 160 bits and $b = 512$, then K will be appended with 44 zero bytes 0x00).
2. XOR (bitwise exclusive-OR) K^+ with ipad to produce the b-bit block S_i.
3. Append M to S_i.
4. Apply H to the stream generated in step 3.
5. XOR K^+ with opad to produce the b-bit block S_o.
6. Append the hash result from step 4 to S_o.
7. Apply H to the stream generated in step 6 and output the result.

Note that the XOR with ipad results in flipping one-half of the bits of K. Similarly, the XOR with opad results in flipping one-half of the bits of K, but a different set of bits. In effect, by passing S_i and S_o through the hash algorithm, we have pseudorandomly generated two keys from K.

HMAC should execute in approximately the same time as the embedded hash function for long messages. HMAC adds three executions of the basic hash function (for S_i, S_o, and the block produced from the inner hash).

3.3 PUBLIC-KEY CRYPTOGRAPHY PRINCIPLES

Of equal importance to conventional encryption is public-key encryption, which finds use in message authentication and key distribution. This section looks first at the basic concept of public-key encryption and takes a preliminary look at key distribution issues. Section 3.4 examines the two most important public-key algorithms: RSA and Diffie-Hellman. Section 3.5 introduces digital signatures.

Public-Key Encryption Structure

Public-key encryption, first publicly proposed by Diffie and Hellman in 1976 [DIFF76], is the first truly revolutionary advance in encryption in literally thousands of years. For one thing, public-key algorithms are based on mathematical functions rather than on simple operations on bit patterns. More important, public-key cryptography is asymmetric, involving the use of two separate keys, in contrast to the symmetric conventional encryption, which uses only one key. The use of two keys has profound consequences in the areas of confidentiality, key distribution, and authentication.

Before proceeding, we should first mention several common misconceptions concerning public-key encryption. One is that public-key encryption is more secure from cryptanalysis than conventional encryption. In fact, the security of any encryption scheme depends on (1) the length of the key and (2) the computational work involved in breaking a cipher. There is nothing in principle about either conventional or public-key encryption that makes one superior to another from the point of view of resisting cryptanalysis. A second misconception is that public-key encryption is a general-purpose technique that has made conventional encryption obsolete. On the contrary, because of the computational overhead of current public-key encryption schemes, there seems no foreseeable likelihood that conventional encryption will be abandoned. Finally, there is a feeling that key distribution is trivial when using public-key encryption, compared to the rather cumbersome handshaking involved with key distribution centers for conventional encryption. In fact, some form of protocol is needed, often involving a central agent, and the procedures involved are no simpler or any more efficient than those required for conventional encryption.

A public-key encryption scheme has six ingredients (Figure 3.7a):

- **Plaintext:** This is the readable message or data that is fed into the algorithm as input.
- **Encryption algorithm:** The encryption algorithm performs various transformations on the plaintext.
- **Public and private key:** This is a pair of keys that have been selected so that if one is used for encryption, the other is used for decryption. The exact transformations performed by the encryption algorithm depend on the public or private key that is provided as input.
- **Ciphertext:** This is the scrambled message produced as output. It depends on the plaintext and the key. For a given message, two different keys will produce two different ciphertexts.
- **Decryption algorithm:** This algorithm accepts the ciphertext and the matching key and produces the original plaintext.

As the names suggest, the public key of the pair is made public for others to use, while the private key is known only to its owner. A general-purpose public-key cryptographic algorithm relies on one key for encryption and a different but related key for decryption.

The essential steps are the following:

1. Each user generates a pair of keys to be used for the encryption and decryption of messages.
2. Each user places one of the two keys in a public register or other accessible file. This is the public key. The companion key is kept private. As Figure 3.7a suggests, each user maintains a collection of public keys obtained from others.
3. If Bob wishes to send a private message to Alice, Bob encrypts the message using Alice's public key.
4. When Alice receives the message, she decrypts it using her private key. No other recipient can decrypt the message because only Alice knows Alice's private key.

With this approach, all participants have access to public keys, and private keys are generated locally by each participant and therefore need never be distributed.

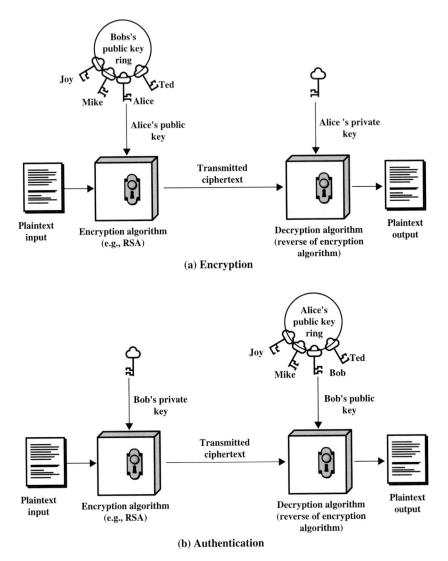

Figure 3.7   Public-Key Cryptography

As long as a user protects his or her private key, incoming communication is secure. At any time, a user can change the private key and publish the companion public key to replace the old public key.

The key used in conventional encryption is typically referred to as a **secret key**. The two keys used for public-key encryption are referred to as the **public key** and the **private key**. Invariably, the private key is kept secret, but it is referred to as a private key rather than a secret key to avoid confusion with conventional encryption.

Applications for Public-Key Cryptosystems

Before proceeding, we need to clarify one aspect of public-key cryptosystems that is otherwise likely to lead to confusion. Public-key systems are characterized by the use of a cryptographic type of algorithm with two keys, one held private and one available publicly. Depending on the application, the sender uses either the sender's private key or the receiver's public key, or both, to perform some type of cryptographic function. In broad terms, we can classify the use of public-key cryptosystems into three categories:

- **Encryption/decryption:** The sender encrypts a message with the recipient's public key.
- **Digital signature:** The sender "signs" a message with its private key. Signing is achieved by a cryptographic algorithm applied to the message or to a small block of data that is a function of the message.
- **Key exchange:** Two sides cooperate to exchange a session key. Several different approaches are possible, involving the private key(s) of one or both parties.

Some algorithms are suitable for all three applications, whereas others can be used only for one or two of these applications. Table 3.2 indicates the applications supported by the algorithms discussed in this chapter, RSA and Diffie Hellman. The table also includes the Digital Signature Standard (DSS) and elliptic-curve cryptography, also mentioned later in this chapter.

Requirements for Public-Key Cryptography

The cryptosystem illustrated in Figure 3.7 depends on a cryptographic algorithm based on two related keys. Diffie and Hellman postulated this system without demonstrating that such algorithms exist. However, they did lay out the conditions that such algorithms must fulfill [DIFF76]:

1. It is computationally easy for a party B to generate a pair (public key KU_b, private key KR_b).
2. It is computationally easy for a sender A, knowing the public key and the message to be encrypted, M, to generate the corresponding ciphertext:

$$C = E_{KU_b}(M)$$

3. It is computationally easy for the receiver B to decrypt the resulting ciphertext using the private key to recover the original message:

$$M = D_{KR_b}(C) = D_{KR_b}[E_{KU_b}(M)]$$

4. It is computationally infeasible for an opponent, knowing the public key, KU_b, to determine the private key, KR_b.

Table 3.2 Applications for Public-Key Cryptosystems

Algorithm	Encryption/Decryption	Digital Signature	Key Exchange
RSA	Yes	Yes	Yes
Diffie-Hellman	No	No	Yes
DSS	No	Yes	No
Elliptic Curve	Yes	Yes	Yes

5. It is computationally infeasible for an opponent, knowing the public key, KU_b, and a ciphertext, C, to recover the original message, M.

We can add a sixth requirement that, although useful, is not necessary for all public-key applications:

6. Either of the two related keys can be used for encryption, with the other used for decryption.

$$M = D_{KR_b} [E_{KU_b} (M)] = D_{KU_b} [E_{KR_b} (M)]$$

3.4 PUBLIC-KEY CRYPTOGRAPHY ALGORITHMS

The two most widely used public-key algorithms are RSA and Diffie-Hellman. We look at both of these in this section and then briefly introduce two other algorithms.[3]

The RSA Public-Key Encryption Algorithm

One of the first public-key schemes was developed in 1977 by Ron Rivest, Adi Shamir, and Len Adleman at MIT and first published in 1978 [RIVE78]. The RSA scheme has since that time reigned supreme as the most widely accepted and implemented approach to public-key encryption. RSA is a block cipher in which the plaintext and ciphertext are integers between 0 and $n - 1$ for some n.

Encryption and decryption are of the following form, for some plaintext block M and ciphertext block C:

$$C = M^e \bmod n$$
$$M = C^d \bmod n = (M^e)^d \bmod n = M^{ed} \bmod n$$

Both sender and receiver must know the values of n and e, and only the receiver knows the value of d. This is a public-key encryption algorithm with a public key of $KU = \{e, n\}$ and a private key of $KR = \{d, n\}$. For this algorithm to be satisfactory for public-key encryption, the following requirements must be met:

1. It is possible to find values of e, d, n such that $M^{ed} = M \bmod n$ for all $M < n$.
2. It is relatively easy to calculate M^e and C^d for all values of $M < n$.
3. It is infeasible to determine d given e and n.

The first two requirements are easily met. The third requirement can be met for a large values of e and n.

Figure 3.8 summarizes the RSA algorithm. Begin by selecting two prime numbers, p and q, and calculating their product n, which is the modulus for encryption and decryption. Next, we need the quantity $\phi(n)$, referred to as the Euler totient of n, which is the number of positive integers less than n and relatively prime to n. Then select an integer e that is relatively prime to $\phi(n)$ [i.e., the greatest common

---

[3]This section uses some elementary concepts from number theory. For a review, see Appendix B.

Key Generation

Select p, q	p and q both prime, $p \neq q$
Calculate $n = p \times q$	
Calculate $\phi(n) = (p-1)(q-1)$	
Select integer e	$\gcd(\phi(n), e) = 1;\ \ 1 < e < \phi(n)$
Calculate d	$de \bmod \phi(n) = 1$
Public key	$KU = \{e, n\}$
Private key	$KR = \{d, n\}$

Encryption

Plaintext:	$M < n$
Ciphertext:	$C = M^e\ (\bmod\ n)$

Decryption

Ciphertext:	C
Plaintext:	$M = C^d\ (\bmod\ n)$

Figure 3.8 The RSA Algorithm

divisor of e and $\phi(n)$ is 1]. Finally, calculate d as the multiplicative inverse of e, modulo $\phi(n)$. It can be shown that d and e have the desired properties.

Suppose that user A has published its public key and that user B wishes to send the message M to A. Then B calculates $C = M^e\ (\bmod\ n)$ and transmits C. On receipt of this ciphertext, user A decrypts by calculating $M = C^d\ (\bmod\ n)$.

An example, from [SING99], is shown in Figure 3.9. For this example, the keys were generated as follows:

1. Select two prime numbers, $p = 17$ and $q = 11$.
2. Calculate $n = pq = 17 \times 11 = 187$.
3. Calculate $\phi(n) = (p - 1)(q - 1) = 16 \times 10 = 160$.
4. Select e such that e is relatively prime to $\phi(n) = 160$ and less than $\phi(n)$; we choose $e = 7$.
5. Determine d such that $de \bmod 160 = 1$ and $d < 160$. The correct value is $d = 23$, because $23 \times 7 = 161 = 10 \times 160 + 1$.

The resulting keys are public key $KU = \{7, 187\}$ and private key $KR = \{23, 187\}$. The example shows the use of these keys for a plaintext input of $M = 88$. For encryption, we need to calculate $C = 88^7 \mod 187$. Exploiting the properties of modular arithmetic, we can do this is follows:

$$88^7 \mod 187 = [(88^4 \mod 187) \times (88^2 \mod 187) \times (88^1 \mod 187)] \mod 187$$
$$88^1 \mod 187 = 88$$
$$88^2 \mod 187 = 7744 \mod 187 = 77$$
$$88^4 \mod 187 = 59{,}969{,}536 \mod 187 = 132$$
$$88^7 \mod 187 = (88 \times 77 \times 132) \mod 187 = 894{,}432 \mod 187 = 11$$

For decryption, we calculate $M = 11^{23} \mod 187$:

$$11^{23} \mod 187 = [(11^1 \mod 187) \times (11^2 \mod 187) \times (11^4 \mod 187) \times$$
$$(11^8 \mod 187) \times (11^8 \mod 187)] \mod 187$$
$$11^1 \mod 187 = 11$$
$$11^2 \mod 187 = 121$$
$$11^4 \mod 187 = 14{,}641 \mod 187 = 55$$
$$11^8 \mod 187 = 214{,}358{,}881 \mod 187 = 33$$
$$11^{23} \mod 187 = (11 \times 121 \times 55 \times 33 \times 33) \mod 187 = 79{,}720{,}245 \mod 187$$
$$= 88$$

There are two possible approaches to defeating the RSA algorithm. The first is the brute-force approach: Try all possible private keys. Thus, the larger the number of bits in e and d, the more secure the algorithm. However, because the calculations involved, both in key generation and in encryption/decryption, are complex, the larger the size of the key, the slower the system will run.

Most discussions of the cryptanalysis of RSA have focused on the task of factoring n into its two prime factors. For a large n with large prime factors, factoring is a hard problem, but not as hard as it used to be. A striking illustration of this occurred in 1977; the three inventors of RSA challenged *Scientific American* readers to decode a cipher they printed in Martin Gardner's "Mathematical Games" column [GARD77]. They offered a $100 reward for the return of a plaintext sentence, an event they predicted might not occur for some 40 quadrillion years. In April of 1994, a group working over the Internet and using over 1600 computers claimed the prize after only eight months of work [LEUT94]. This challenge used a public-key

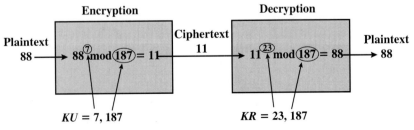

Figure 3.9 Example of RSA Algorithm

size (length of n) of 129 decimal digits, or around 428 bits. This result does not invalidate the use of RSA; it simply means that larger key sizes must be used. Currently, a 1024-bit key size (about 300 decimal digits) is considered strong enough for virtually all applications.

Diffie-Hellman Key Exchange

The first published public-key algorithm appeared in the seminal paper by Diffie and Hellman that defined public-key cryptography [DIFF76] and is generally referred to as Diffie-Hellman key exchange. A number of commercial products employ this key exchange technique.

The purpose of the algorithm is to enable two users to exchange a secret key securely that can then be used for subsequent encryption of messages. The algorithm itself is limited to the exchange of the keys.

The Diffie-Hellman algorithm depends for its effectiveness on the difficulty of computing discrete logarithms. Briefly, we can define the discrete logarithm in the following way. First, we define a primitive root of a prime number p as one whose powers generate all the integers from 1 to $p - 1$. That is, if a is a primitive root of the prime number p, then the numbers

$$a \bmod p, a^2 \bmod p, \ldots, a^{p-1} \bmod p$$

are distinct and consist of the integers from 1 through $p - 1$ in some permutation. For any integer b less than p and a primitive root a of prime number p, one can find a unique exponent i such that

$$b = a^i \bmod p \qquad\qquad \text{where } 0 \leq i \leq (p - 1)$$

The exponent i is referred to as the discrete logarithm, or index, of b for the base a, mod p. This value is denoted as $\text{ind}_{a,p}(b)$.

With this background we can define the Diffie-Hellman key exchange, which is summarized in Figure 3.10. For this scheme, there are two publicly known numbers: a prime number q and an integer α that is a primitive root of q. Suppose the users A and B wish to exchange a key. User A selects a random integer $X_A < q$ and computes $Y_A = \alpha^{X_A} \bmod q$. Similarly, user B independently selects a random integer $X_B < q$ and computes $Y_B = \alpha^{X_B} \bmod q$. Each side keeps the X value private and makes the Y value available publicly to the other side. User A computes the key as $K = (Y_B)^{X_A} \bmod q$ and user B computes the key as $K = (Y_A)^{X_B} \bmod q$. These two calculations produce identical results:

$$
\begin{aligned}
K &= (Y_B)^{X_A} \bmod q \\
&= (\alpha^{X_B} \bmod q)^{X_A} \bmod q \\
&= (\alpha^{X_B})^{X_A} \bmod q \\
&= \alpha^{X_B X_A} \bmod q \\
&= (\alpha^{X_A})^{X_B} \bmod q \\
&= (\alpha^{X_A} \bmod q)^{X_B} \bmod q \\
&= (Y_A)^{X_B} \bmod q
\end{aligned}
$$

Global Public Elements

q	prime number
α	$\alpha < q$ and α a primitive root of q

User A Key Generation

Select private X_A	$X_A < q$
Calculate public Y_A	$Y_A = \alpha^{X_A} \bmod q$

User B Key Generation

Select private X_B	$X_B < q$
Calculate public Y_B	$Y_B = \alpha^{X_B} \bmod q$

Generation of Secret Key by User A

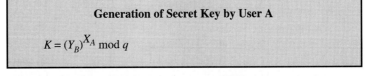
$$K = (Y_B)^{X_A} \bmod q$$

Generation of Secret Key by User B

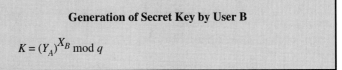
$$K = (Y_A)^{X_B} \bmod q$$

Figure 3.10 The Diffie-Hellman Key Exchange Algorithm

Thus, the two sides have exchanged a secret key. Furthermore, because X_A and X_B are private, an opponent only has the following ingredients to work with: q, a, Y_A, and Y_B. Thus, the opponent is forced to take a discrete logarithm to determine the key. For example, attacking the secret key of user B, the opponent must compute

$$X_B = \mathrm{ind}_{\alpha,q}(Y_B)$$

The opponent can then calculate the key K in the same manner as user B calculates it.

The security of the Diffie-Hellman key exchange lies in the fact that, while it is relatively easy to calculate exponentials modulo a prime, it is very difficult to calculate discrete logarithms. For large primes, the latter task is considered infeasible.

For example, select the prime number $q = 71$ and a primitive root of 71, in this case $\alpha = 7$. A and B select private keys $X_A = 5$ and $X_B = 12$, respectively. Each computes its public key:

$$Y_A = 7^5 \bmod 71 = 51$$
$$Y_B = 7^{12} \bmod 71 = 4$$

After they exchange public keys, each can compute the common secret key:

$$K = (Y_B)^{X_A} \bmod 71 = 4^5 \bmod 71 = 30$$
$$K = (Y_A)^{X_B} \bmod 71 = 51^{12} \bmod 71 = 30$$

From {51, 4}, an attacker cannot easily compute 30.

Figure 3.11 shows a simple protocol that makes use of the Diffie-Hellman calculation. Suppose that user A wishes to set up a connection with user B and use a secret key to encrypt messages on that connection. User A can generate a one-time private key X_A, calculate Y_A, and send that to user B. User B responds by generating a private value X_B, calculating Y_B, and sending Y_B to user A. Both users can now calculate the key. The necessary public values q and α would need to be known ahead of time. Alternatively, user A could pick values for q and α and include those in the first message.

As an example of another use of the Diffie-Hellman algorithm, suppose that a group of users (e.g., all users on a LAN) each generate a long-lasting private value X_A and calculate a public value Y_A. These public values, together with global public values for q and α, are stored in some central directory. At any time, user B can access user A's public value, calculate a secret key, and use that to send an encrypted message to user A. If the central directory is trusted, then this form of communication provides both confidentiality and a degree of authentication. Because only A and B can determine the key, no other user can read the message

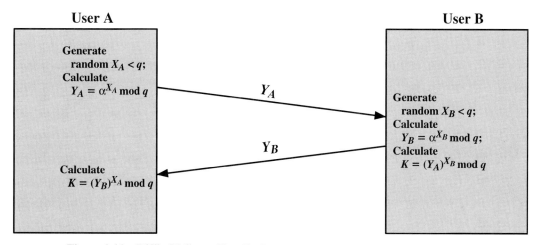

Figure 3.11 Diffie-Hellman Key Exchange

(confidentiality). Recipient A knows that only user B could have created a message using this key (authentication). However, the technique does not protect against replay attacks.

Other Public-Key Cryptography Algorithms

Two other public-key algorithms have found commercial acceptance: DSS and elliptic-curve cryptography.

Digital Signature Standard

The National Institute of Standards and Technology (NIST) has published Federal Information Processing Standard FIPS PUB 186, known as the Digital Signature Standard (DSS). The DSS makes use of the SHA-1 and presents a new digital signature technique, the Digital Signature Algorithm (DSA). The DSS was originally proposed in 1991 and revised in 1993 in response to public feedback concerning the security of the scheme. There was a further minor revision in 1996. The DSS uses an algorithm that is designed to provide only the digital signature function. Unlike RSA, it cannot be used for encryption or key exchange.

Elliptic-Curve Cryptography

The vast majority of the products and standards that use public-key cryptography for encryption and digital signatures use RSA. The bit length for secure RSA use has increased over recent years, and this has put a heavier processing load on applications using RSA. This burden has ramifications, especially for electronic commerce sites that conduct large numbers of secure transactions. Recently, a competing system has begun to challenge RSA: elliptic curve cryptography (ECC). Already, ECC is showing up in standardization efforts, including the IEEE P1363 Standard for Public-Key Cryptography.

The principal attraction of ECC compared to RSA is that it appears to offer equal security for a far smaller bit size, thereby reducing processing overhead. On the other hand, although the theory of ECC has been around for some time, it is only recently that products have begun to appear and that there has been sustained cryptanalytic interest in probing for weaknesses. Thus, the confidence level in ECC is not yet as high as that in RSA.

ECC is fundamentally more difficult to explain than either RSA or Diffie-Hellman, and a full mathematical description is beyond the scope of this book. The technique is based on the use of a mathematical construct known as the elliptic curve.

3.5 DIGITAL SIGNATURES

Public-key encryption can be used in another way, as illustrated in Figure 3.7b. Suppose that Bob wants to send a message to Alice and, although it is not important that the message be kept secret, he wants Alice to be certain that the message is indeed from him. In this case Bob uses his own private key to encrypt the message. When Alice receives the ciphertext, she finds that she can decrypt it with Bob's public key, thus proving that the message must have been encrypted by Bob. No one else has Bob's private key and therefore no one else could have created a cipher-text that could be decrypted with Bob's public key. Therefore, the entire encrypted message serves as a **digital signature**. In addition, it is impossible to alter the message without access to Bob's private key, so the message is authenticated both in terms of source and in terms of data integrity.

In the preceding scheme, the entire message is encrypted, which, although validating both author and contents, requires a great deal of storage. Each document must be kept in plaintext to be used for practical purposes. A copy also must be stored in ciphertext so that the origin and contents can be verified in case of a dispute. A more efficient way of achieving the same results is to encrypt a small block of bits that is a function of the document. Such a block, called an authenticator, must have the property that it is infeasible to change the document without changing the authenticator. If the authenticator is encrypted with the sender's private key, it serves as a signature that verifies origin, content, and sequencing. A secure hash code such as SHA-1 can serve this function. Figure 3.2b illustrates this scenario.

It is important to emphasize that the encryption process just described does not provide confidentiality. That is, the message being sent is safe from alteration but not safe from eavesdropping. This is obvious in the case of a signature based on a portion of the message, because the rest of the message is transmitted in the clear. Even in the case of complete encryption, there is no protection of confidentiality because any observer can decrypt the message by using the sender's public key.

3.6 KEY MANAGEMENT

One of the major roles of public-key encryption is to address the problem of key distribution. There are actually two distinct aspects to the use of public-key encryption in this regard:

- The distribution of public keys
- The use of public-key encryption to distribute secret keys

We examine each of these areas in turn.

Public-Key Certificates

On the face of it, the point of public-key encryption is that the public key is public. Thus, if there is some broadly accepted public-key algorithm, such as RSA, any participant can send his or her public key to any other participant or broadcast the key to the community at large. Although this approach is convenient, it has a major weakness. Anyone can forge such a public announcement. That is, some user could pretend to be user A and send a public key to another participant or broadcast such a public key. Until such time as user A discovers the forgery and alerts other participants, the forger is able to read all encrypted messages intended for A and can use the forged keys for authentication.

The solution to this problem is the public-key certificate. In essence, a certificate consists of a public key plus a User ID of the key owner, with the whole block

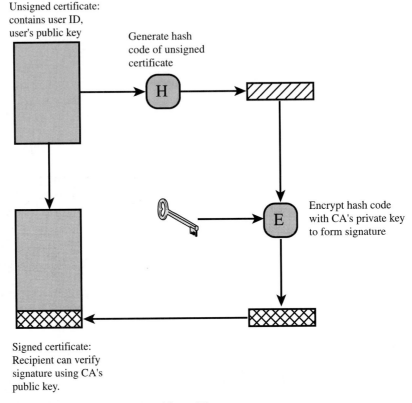

Figure 3.12   Public-Key Certificate Use

signed by a trusted third party. Typically, the third party is a certificate authority (CA) that is trusted by the user community, such as a government agency or a financial institution. A user can present his or her public key to the authority in a secure manner and obtain a certificate. The user can then publish the certificate. Anyone needing this user's public key can obtain the certificate and verify that it is valid by way of the attached trusted signature. Figure 3.12 illustrates the process.

One scheme has become universally accepted for formatting public-key certificates: the X.509 standard. X.509 certificates are used in most network security applications, including IP security, secure sockets layer (SSL), secure electronic transactions (SET), and S/MIME, all of which are discussed in Part Two. X.509 is examined in detail in Chapter 4.

Public-Key Distribution of Secret Keys

With conventional encryption, a fundamental requirement for two parties to communicate securely is that they share a secret key. Suppose Bob wants to create a messaging application that will enable him to exchange e-mail securely with anyone who has access to the Internet or to some other network that the two of them share. Suppose Bob wants to do this using conventional encryption. With conventional encryption, Bob and his correspondent, say, Alice, must come up with a way to share a unique secret key that no one else knows. How are they going to do that? If Alice is in the next room from Bob, Bob could generate a key and write it down on a piece of paper or store it on a diskette and hand it to Alice. But if Alice is on the other side of the continent or the world, what can Bob do? He could encrypt this key using conventional encryption and e-mail it to Alice, but this means that Bob and Alice must share a secret key to encrypt this new secret key. Furthermore, Bob and everyone else who uses this new e-mail package faces the same problem with every potential correspondent: Each pair of correspondents must share a unique secret key.

One approach is the use of Diffie-Hellman key exchange. This approach is indeed widely used. However, it suffers the drawback that, in its simplest form, Diffie-Hellman provides no authentication of the two communicating partners.

A powerful alternative is the use of public-key certificates. When Bob wishes to communicate with Alice, Bob can do the following:

1. Prepare a message.
2. Encrypt that message using conventional encryption with a one-time conventional session key.
3. Encrypt the session key using public-key encryption with Alice's public key.
4. Attach the encrypted session key to the message and send it to Alice.

Only Alice is capable of decrypting the session key and therefore of recovering the original message. If Bob obtained Alice's public key by means of Alice's public-key certificate, then Bob is assured that it is a valid key.

3.7 RECOMMENDED READING AND WEB SITES

Solid treatments of hash functions and message authentication codes are found in [STIN02] and [MENE97].

The recommended treatments of encryption provided in Chapter 2 cover public-key as well as conventional encryption. [DIFF88] describes in detail the several attempts to devise secure two-key cryptoalgorithms and the gradual evolution of a variety of protocols based on them. A good book-length treatment of public-key cryptography is [SALO96]. [CORM01] provides a concise but complete and readable summary of all of the algorithms relevant to the verification, computation, and cryptanalysis of RSA.

CORM01   Cormen, T.; Leiserson, C.; Rivest, R.; and Stein, C. *Introduction to Algorithms.* Cambridge, MA: MIT Press, 2001.

DIFF88   Diffie, W. "The First Ten Years of Public-Key Cryptography." *Proceedings of the IEEE,* May 1988. Reprinted in [SIMM92].

MENE97   Menezes, A.; Oorshcot, P.; and Vanstone, S. *Handbook of Applied Cryptography.* Boca Raton, FL: CRC Press, 1997.

SALO96   Salomaa, A. *Public-Key Cryptography.* New York: Springer-Verlag, 1996.

SIMM92   Simmons, G., ed. *Contemporary Cryptology: The Science of Information Integrity.* Piscataway, NJ: IEEE Press, 1992.

STIN02   Stinson, D. *Cryptography: Theory and Practice.* Boca Raton, FL: CRC Press, 2002.

Recommended Web sites:

- **RSA Laboratories:** Extensive collection of technical material on RSA and other topics in cryptography
- **NIST Secure Hashing Page:** SHA FIPS and related documents

3.8 KEY TERMS, REVIEW QUESTIONS, AND PROBLEMS

Key Terms

Diffie-Hellman key exchange	MD5	public-key certificate
digital signature	message authentication	public-key encryption
Digital Signature Standard	message authentication code	RIPEMD-160
(DSS)	(MAC)	RSA
elliptic-curve cryptography	message digest	secret key
(ECC)	one-way hash function	secure hash function
HMAC	private key	SHA-1
key exchange	public key	

Review Questions

3.1 List three approaches to message authentication.

3.2 What is a message authentication code?

3.3 Briefly describe the three schemes illustrated in Figure 3.2.

3.4 What properties must a hash function have to be useful for message authentication?

3.5 In the context of a hash function, what is a compression function?

3.6 What are the principal ingredients of a public-key cryptosystem?

3.7 List and briefly define three uses of a public-key cryptosystem.

3.8 What is the difference between a private key and a secret key?

3.9 What is a digital signature?

3.10 What is a public-key certificate?

3.12 How can public-key encryption be used to distribute a secret key?

Problems

3.1 One of the most widely used MACs, referred to as the Data Authentication Algorithm, is based on DES. The algorithm is both a FIPS publication (FIPS PUB 113) and an ANSI standard (X9.17). The algorithm can be defined as using the cipher block chaining (CBC) mode of operation of DES with an initialization vector of zero (Figure 2.7). The data (e.g., message, record, file, or program) to be authenticated are grouped into contiguous 64-bit blocks: $P_1, P_2, \ldots, P_N$. If necessary, the final block is padded on the right with 0s to form a full 64-bit block. The MAC consists of either the entire ciphertext block C_N or the leftmost M bits of the block, with $16 \leq M \leq 64$. Show that the same result can be produced using the cipher feedback mode.

3.2 Consider a 32-bit hash function defined as the concatenation of two 16-bit functions: XOR and RXOR, defined in Section 3.1 as "two simple hash functions."

    a. Will this checksum detect all errors caused by an odd number of error bits? Explain.

    b. Will this checksum detect all errors caused by an even number of error bits? If not, characterize the error patterns that will cause the checksum to fail.

    c. Comment on the effectiveness of this function for use as a hash function for authentication.

3.3 It is possible to use a hash function to construct a block cipher with a structure similar to DES. Because a hash function is one way and a block cipher must be reversible (to decrypt), how is it possible?

3.4 Prior to the discovery of any specific public-key schemes, such as RSA, an existence proof was developed whose purpose was to demonstrate that public-key encryption is possible in theory. Consider the functions $f_1(x_1) = z_1$; $f_2(x_2, y_2) = z_2$; $f_3(x_3, y_3) = z_3$, where all values are integers with $1 \le x_i, y_i, z_i \le N$. Function f_1 can be represented by a vector M1 of length N, in which the kth entry is the value of $f_1(k)$. Similarly, f_2 and f_3 can be represented by $N \times N$ matrices M2 and M3. The intent is to represent the encryption/decryption process by table look-ups for tables with very large values of N. Such tables would be impractically huge but could , in principle, be constructed. The scheme works as follows: construct M1 with a random permutation of all integers between 1 and N; that is, each integer appears exactly once in M1. Construct M2 so that each row contains a random permutation of the first N integers. Finally, fill in M3 to satisfy the following condition:

$$f_3(f_2(f_1(k),p),k) = p \qquad\qquad \text{for all } k, p \text{ with } 1 \le k, p \le N$$

In words,

1. M1 takes an input k and produces an output x.

2. M2 takes inputs x and p giving output z.

3. M3 takes inputs z and k and produces p.

    The three tables, once constructed, are made public.

    a. It should be clear that it is possible to construct M3 to satisfy the preceding condition. As an example, fill in M3 for the following simple case:

$$
\text{M1} = \begin{array}{|c|} \hline 5 \\ \hline 4 \\ \hline 2 \\ \hline 3 \\ \hline 1 \\ \hline \end{array}
\qquad
\text{M2} = \begin{array}{|c|c|c|c|c|} \hline 5 & 2 & 3 & 4 & 1 \\ \hline 4 & 2 & 5 & 1 & 3 \\ \hline 1 & 3 & 2 & 4 & 5 \\ \hline 3 & 1 & 4 & 2 & 5 \\ \hline 2 & 5 & 3 & 4 & 1 \\ \hline \end{array}
\qquad
\text{M3} = \begin{array}{|c|c|c|c|c|} \hline & & & & \\ \hline & & & & \\ \hline & & & & \\ \hline & & & & \\ \hline & & & & \\ \hline \end{array}
$$

    Convention: The ith element of M1 corresponds to $k = i$. The ith row of M2 corresponds to $x = i$; the jth column of M2 corresponds to $p = j$. The ith row of M3 corresponds to $z = i$; the jth column of M3 corresponds to $k = j$.

    b. Describe the use of this set of tables to perform encryption and decryption between two users.

    c. Argue that this is a secure scheme.

3.5 Perform encryption and decryption using the RSA algorithm, as in Figure 3.9, for the following:

    a. $p = 3$; $q = 11$, $e = 7$; $M = 5$

    b. $p = 5$; $q = 11$, $e = 3$; $M = 9$

    c. $p = 7$; $q = 11$, $e = 17$; $M = 8$

     d. $p = 11$; $q = 13$, $e = 11$; $M = 7$

     e. $p = 17$; $q = 31$, $e = 7$; $M = 2$. *Hint:* Decryption is not as hard as you think; use some finesse.

3.6 In a public-key system using RSA, you intercept the ciphertext $C = 10$ sent to a user whose public key is $e = 5$, $n = 35$. What is the plaintext M?

3.7 In an RSA system, the public key of a given user is $e = 31$, $n = 3599$. What is the private key of this user?

3.8 Suppose we have a set of blocks encoded with the RSA algorithm and we don't have the private key. Assume $n = pq$, e is the public key. Suppose also someone tells us they know one of the plaintext blocks has a common factor with n. Does this help us in any way?

3.9 Show how RSA can be represented by matrices M1, M2, and M3 of Problem 3.4.

3.10 Consider the following scheme:

     1. Pick an odd number, E.

     2. Pick two prime numbers, P and Q, where $(P - 1)(Q - 1) - 1$ is evenly divisible by E.

     3. Multiply P and Q to get N.

     4. Calculate $D = \dfrac{(P - 1)(Q - 1)(E - 1) + 1}{E}$.

     Is this scheme equivalent to RSA? Show why or why not.

3.11 Consider using RSA with a known key to construct a one-way hash function. Then process a message consisting of a sequence of blocks as follows: Encrypt the first block, XOR the result with the second block and encrypt again, and so on. Show that this scheme is not secure by solving the following problem. Given a two-block message B1, B2, and its hash

$$\text{RSAH(B1,B2)} = \text{RSA(RSA(B1)} \oplus \text{B2)}$$

     Given an arbitrary block C1, choose C2 so that RSAH(C1, C2) = RSAH(B1, B2).

3.12 Consider a Diffie-Hellman scheme with a common prime $q = 11$ and a primitive root $\alpha = 2$.

     a. If user A has public key $Y_A = 9$, what is A's private key X_A?

     b. If user B has public key $Y_B = 3$, what is the shared secret key K?

PART TWO

Network Security Applications

Part Two surveys important network security tools and applications. These can be used across a single network, a corporate intranet, or the Internet.

CHAPTER 4   AUTHENTICATION APPLICATIONS

Chapter 4 is a survey of two of the most important authentication specifications in current use. Kerberos is an authentication protocol based on symmetric encryption that has received widespread support and is used in a variety of systems. X.509 specifies an authentication algorithm and defines a certificate facility. The latter enables users to obtain certificates of public keys so that a community of users can have confidence in the validity of the public keys. This facility is employed as a building block in a number applications.

CHAPTER 5   ELECTRONIC MAIL SECURITY

The most heavily used distributed application is electronic mail, and there is increasing interest in providing authentication and confidentiality services as part of an electronic mail facility. Chapter 5 looks at the two approaches likely to dominate electronic mail security in the near future. Pretty Good Privacy (PGP) is a widely used scheme that does not depend on any organization or authority. Thus, it is as well suited to individual, personal use as it is to incorporation in network configurations operated by organizations. S/MIME (Secure/Multipurpose Internet Mail Extension) was developed specifically to be an Internet Standard.

CHAPTER 6   IP SECURITY

The Internet Protocol (IP) is the central element in the Internet and private intranets. Security at the IP level, accordingly, is important to the design of any internetwork-based security scheme. Chapter 6 looks at the IP security scheme that has been developed to operate both with the current IP and the emerging next-generation IP, known as IPv6.

CHAPTER 7   WEB SECURITY

The explosive growth in the use of the World Wide Web for electronic commerce and to disseminate information has generated the need for strong Web-based security. Chapter 7 provides a survey of this important new security area and looks at two key standards: Secure Sockets Layer (SSL) and Secure Electronic Transaction (SET).

CHAPTER 8   NETWORK MANAGEMENT SECURITY

With the increasing use of network management systems to control multivendor networks, there is increasing demand for accompanying security capabilities. Chapter 8 focuses on the most widely used multivendor network management scheme, the Simple Network Management Protocol (SNMP). Version 1 of SNMP has only a rudimentary password-based authentication facility. SNMPv2 provides additional functionality, and SNMPv3 provides a full-blown security facility for confidentiality and authentication, which can be used in conjunction with SNMPv1 or SNMPv2.

CHAPTER 4

AUTHENTICATION APPLICATIONS

4.1 Kerberos

Motivation
Kerberos Version 4
Kerberos Version 5

4.2 X.509 Authentication Service

Certificates
Authentication Procedures
X.509 Version 3

4.3 Recommended Reading and Web Sites

4.4 Key Terms, Review Questions, and Problems

Key Terms
Review Questions
Problems

Appendix 4A Kerberos Encryption Techniques

Password-to-Key Transformation
Propagating Cipher Block Chaining Mode

We cannot enter into alliance with neighboring princes until we are acquainted with their designs.

—The Art of War, **Sun Tzu**

T his chapter examines some of the authentication functions that have been developed to support application-level authentication and digital signatures.

We begin by looking at one of the earliest and also one of the most widely used services, which is known as Kerberos. Next, we examine the X.509 directory authentication service. This standard is important as part of the directory service that it supports, but is also a basic building block used in other standards, such as S/MIME, discussed in Chapter 5.

4.1 KERBEROS

Kerberos[1] is an authentication service developed as part of Project Athena at MIT. The problem that Kerberos addresses is this: Assume an open distributed environment in which users at workstations wish to access services on servers distributed throughout the network. We would like for servers to be able to restrict access to authorized users and to be able to authenticate requests for service. In this environment, a workstation cannot be trusted to identify its users correctly to network services. In particular, the following three threats exist:

- A user may gain access to a particular workstation and pretend to be another user operating from that workstation.
- A user may alter the network address of a workstation so that the requests sent from the altered workstation appear to come from the impersonated workstation.
- A user may eavesdrop on exchanges and use a replay attack to gain entrance to a server or to disrupt operations.

In any of these cases, an unauthorized user may be able to gain access to services and data that he or she is not authorized to access. Rather than building in elaborate authentication protocols at each server, Kerberos provides a centralized authentication server whose function is to authenticate users to servers and servers

---

[1]"In Greek mythology, a many headed dog, commonly three, perhaps with a serpent's tail, the guardian of the entrance of Hades." From *Dictionary of Subjects and Symbols in Art*, by James Hall, Harper & Row, 1979. Just as the Greek Kerberos has three heads, the modern Kerberos was intended to have three components to guard a network's gate: authentication, accounting, and audit. The last two heads were never implemented.

to users. Unlike most other authentication schemes described in this book, Kerberos relies exclusively on symmetric encryption, making no use of public-key encryption.

Two versions of Kerberos are in common use. Version 4 [MILL88, STEI88] is still widely used. Version 5 [KOHL94] corrects some of the security deficiencies of version 4 and has been issued as a proposed Internet Standard (RFC 1510).[2]

We begin this section with a brief discussion of the motivation for the Kerberos approach. Then, because of the complexity of Kerberos, it is best to start with a description of the authentication protocol used in version 4. This enables us to see the essence of the Kerberos strategy without considering some of the details required to handle subtle security threats. Finally, we examine version 5.

Motivation

If a set of users is provided with dedicated personal computers that have no network connections, then a user's resources and files can be protected by physically securing each personal computer. When these users instead are served by a centralized time-sharing system, the time-sharing operating system must provide the security. The operating system can enforce access control policies based on user identity and use the logon procedure to identify users.

Today, neither of these scenarios is typical. More common is a distributed architecture consisting of dedicated user workstations (clients) and distributed or centralized servers. In this environment, three approaches to security can be envisioned:

1. Rely on each individual client workstation to assure the identity of its user or users and rely on each server to enforce a security policy based on user identification (ID).
2. Require that client systems authenticate themselves to servers, but trust the client system concerning the identity of its user.
3. Require the user to prove identity for each service invoked. Also require that servers prove their identity to clients.

In a small, closed environment, in which all systems are owned and operated by a single organization, the first or perhaps the second strategy may suffice.[3] But in a more open environment, in which network connections to other machines are supported, the third approach is needed to protect user information and resources housed at the server. This third approach is supported by Kerberos. Kerberos assumes a distributed client/server architecture and employs one or more Kerberos servers to provide an authentication service.

The first published report on Kerberos [STEI88] listed the following requirements for Kerberos:

- **Secure:** A network eavesdropper should not be able to obtain the necessary information to impersonate a user. More generally, Kerberos should be strong enough that a potential opponent does not find it to be the weak link.

---

[2]Versions 1 through 3 were internal development versions. Version 4 is the "original" Kerberos.
[3]However, even a closed environment faces the threat of attack by a disgruntled employee.

- **Reliable:** For all services that rely on Kerberos for access control, lack of availability of the Kerberos service means lack of availability of the supported services. Hence, Kerberos should be highly reliable and should employ a distributed server architecture, with one system able to back up another.
- **Transparent:** Ideally, the user should not be aware that authentication is taking place, beyond the requirement to enter a password.
- **Scalable:** The system should be capable of supporting large numbers of clients and servers. This suggests a modular, distributed architecture.

To support these requirements, the overall scheme of Kerberos is that of a trusted third-party authentication service. It is trusted in the sense that clients and servers trust Kerberos to mediate their mutual authentication. Assuming the Kerberos protocol is well designed, then the authentication service is secure if the Kerberos server itself is secure.[4]

Kerberos Version 4

Version 4 of Kerberos makes use of DES, in a rather elaborate protocol, to provide the authentication service. Viewing the protocol as a whole, it is difficult to see the need for the many elements contained therein. Therefore, we adopt a strategy used by Bill Bryant of Project Athena [BRYA88] and build up to the full protocol by looking first at several hypothetical dialogues. Each successive dialogue adds additional complexity to counter security vulnerabilities revealed in the preceding dialogue.

After examining the protocol, we look at some other aspects of version 4.

A Simple Authentication Dialogue

In an unprotected network environment, any client can apply to any server for service. The obvious security risk is that of impersonation. An opponent can pretend to be another client and obtain unauthorized privileges on server machines. To counter this threat, servers must be able to confirm the identities of clients who request service. Each server can be required to undertake this task for each client/server interaction, but in an open environment, this places a substantial burden on each server.

An alternative is to use an authentication server (AS) that knows the passwords of all users and stores these in a centralized database. In addition, the AS shares a unique secret key with each server. These keys have been distributed physically or in some other secure manner. Consider the following hypothetical dialogue:[5]

---

[4]Remember that the security of the Kerberos server should not automatically be assumed but must be guarded carefully (e.g., in a locked room). It is well to remember the fate of the Greek Kerberos, whom Hercules was ordered by Eurystheus to capture as his Twelfth Labor: "Hercules found the great dog on its chain and seized it by the throat. At once the three heads tried to attack, and Kerberos lashed about with his powerful tail. Hercules hung on grimly, and Kerberos relaxed into unconsciousness. Eurystheus may have been surprised to see Hercules alive—when he saw the three slavering heads and the huge dog they belonged to he was frightened out of his wits, and leapt back into the safety of his great bronze jar." From *The Hamlyn Concise Dictionary of Greek and Roman Mythology*, by Michael Stapleton, Hamlyn, 1982.

[5]The portion to the left of the colon indicates the sender and receiver; the portion to the right indicates the contents of the message; the symbol || indicates concatenation.

(1) C → AS: $ID_C \| P_C \| ID_V$

(2) AS → C: *Ticket*

(3) C → V: $ID_C \| Ticket$

      $Ticket = E_{K_v}[ID_C \| AD_C \| ID_v]$

where

$$
\begin{aligned}
C &= \text{client} \\
AS &= \text{authentication server} \\
V &= \text{server} \\
ID_C &= \text{identifier of user on C} \\
ID_V &= \text{identifier of V} \\
P_C &= \text{password of user on C} \\
AD_C &= \text{network address of C} \\
K_v &= \text{secret encryption key shared by AS and V} \\
\| &= \text{concatenation}
\end{aligned}
$$

In this scenario, the user logs on to a workstation and requests access to server V. The client module C in the user's workstation requests the user's password and then sends a message to the AS that includes the user's ID, the server's ID, and the user's password. The AS checks its database to see if the user has supplied the proper password for this user ID and whether this user is permitted access to server V. If both tests are passed, the AS accepts the user as authentic and must now convince the server that this user is authentic. To do so, the AS creates a ticket that contains the user's ID and network address and the server's ID. This ticket is encrypted using the secret key shared by the AS and this server. This ticket is then sent back to C. Because the ticket is encrypted, it cannot be altered by C or by an opponent.

With this ticket, C can now apply to V for service. C sends a message to V containing C's ID and the ticket. V decrypts the ticket and verifies that the user ID in the ticket is the same as the unencrypted user ID in the message. If these two match, the server considers the user authenticated and grants the requested service.

Each of the ingredients of message (3) is significant. The ticket is encrypted to prevent alteration or forgery. The server's ID (ID_V) is included in the ticket so that the server can verify that it has decrypted the ticket properly. ID_C is included in the ticket to indicate that this ticket has been issued on behalf of C. Finally, AD_C serves to counter the following threat. An opponent could capture the ticket transmitted in message (2), then use the name ID_C and transmit a message of form (3) from another workstation. The server would receive a valid ticket that matches the user ID and grant access to the user on that other workstation. To prevent this attack, the AS includes in the ticket the network address from which the original request came. Now the ticket is valid only if it is transmitted from the same workstation that initially requested the ticket.

A More Secure Authentication Dialogue

Although the foregoing scenario solves some of the problems of authentication in an open network environment, problems remain. Two in particular stand out. First, we would like to minimize the number of times that a user has to enter a password. Suppose each ticket can be used only once. If user C logs on to a workstation in the morning and wishes to check his or her mail at a mail server, C must supply a password to get a ticket for the mail server. If C wishes to check the mail several times during the day, each attempt requires reentering the password. We can improve matters by saying that tickets are reusable. For a single logon session, the workstation can store the mail server ticket after it is received and use it on behalf of the user for multiple accesses to the mail server.

However, under this scheme it remains the case that a user would need a new ticket for every different service. If a user wished to access a print server, a mail server, a file server, and so on, the first instance of each access would require a new ticket and hence require the user to enter the password.

The second problem is that the earlier scenario involved a plaintext transmission of the password [message (1)]. An eavesdropper could capture the password and use any service accessible to the victim.

To solve these additional problems, we introduce a scheme for avoiding plaintext passwords and a new server, known as the ticket-granting server (TGS). The new but still hypothetical scenario is as follows:

Once per user logon session:

    (1) C $\rightarrow$ AS: $ID_C \, \| \, ID_{tgs}$

    (2) AS $\rightarrow$ C: $E_{K_c}[Ticket_{tgs}]$

Once per type of service:

    (3) C $\rightarrow$ TGS: $ID_C \, \| \, ID_V \, \| \, Ticket_{tgs}$

    (4) TGS $\rightarrow$ C: $Ticket_v$

Once per service session:

    (5) C $\rightarrow$ V: $ID_C \, \| \, Ticket_v$

$Ticket_{tgs} = E_{K_{tgs}}[ID_C \, \| \, AD_C \, \| \, ID_{tgs} \, \| \, TS_1 \, \| \, Lifetime_1]$

$Ticket_v \; = E_{K_v}[ID_C \, \| \, AD_C \, \| \, ID_v \, \| \, TS_2 \, \| \, Lifetime_2]$

The new service, TGS, issues tickets to users who have been authenticated to AS. Thus, the user first requests a ticket-granting ticket ($Ticket_{tgs}$) from the AS. This ticket is saved by the client module in the user workstation. Each time the user requires access to a new service, the client applies to the TGS, using the ticket to authenticate itself. The TGS then grants a ticket for the particular service. The client saves each service-granting ticket and uses it to authenticate its user to a server each time a particular service is requested. Let us look at the details of this scheme:

1. The client requests a ticket-granting ticket on behalf of the user by sending its user's ID to the AS, together with the TGS ID, indicating a request to use the TGS service.
2. The AS responds with a ticket that is encrypted with a key that is derived from the user's password. When this response arrives at the client, the client prompts the user for his or her password, generates the key, and attempts to decrypt the incoming message. If the correct password is supplied, the ticket is successfully recovered.

Because only the correct user should know the password, only the correct user can recover the ticket. Thus, we have used the password to obtain credentials from Kerberos without having to transmit the password in plaintext. The ticket itself consists of the ID and network address of the user, and the ID of the TGS. This corresponds to the first scenario. The idea is that this ticket can be used by the client to request multiple service-granting tickets. So the ticket-granting ticket is to be reusable. However, we do not wish an opponent to be able to capture the ticket and use it. Consider the following scenario: An opponent captures the ticket and waits until the user has logged off his or her workstation. Then the opponent either gains access to that workstation or configures his workstation with the same network address as that of the victim. The opponent would be able to reuse the ticket to spoof the TGS. To counter this, the ticket includes a timestamp, indicating the date and time at which the ticket was issued, and a lifetime, indicating the length of time for which the ticket is valid (e.g., eight hours). Thus, the client now has a reusable ticket and need not bother the user for a password for each new service request. Finally, note that the ticket-granting ticket is encrypted with a secret key known only to the AS and the TGS. This prevents alteration of the ticket. The ticket is reencrypted with a key based on the user's password. This assures that the ticket can be recovered only by the correct user, providing the authentication.

Now that the client has a ticket-granting ticket, access to any server can be obtained with steps 3 and 4:

3. The client requests a service-granting ticket on behalf of the user. For this purpose, the client transmits a message to the TGS containing the user's ID, the ID of the desired service, and the ticket-granting ticket.

4. The TGS decrypts the incoming ticket and verifies the success of the decryption by the presence of its ID. It checks to make sure that the lifetime has not expired. Then it compares the user ID and network address with the incoming information to authenticate the user. If the user is permitted access to V, the TGS issues a ticket to grant access to the requested service.

The service-granting ticket has the same structure as the ticket-granting ticket. Indeed, because the TGS is a server, we would expect that the same elements are needed to authenticate a client to the TGS and to authenticate a client to an application server. Again, the ticket contains a timestamp and lifetime. If the user wants access to the same service at a later time, the client can simply use the previously acquired service-granting ticket and need not bother the user for a password. Note that the ticket is encrypted with a secret key (K_v) known only to the TGS and the server, preventing alteration.

Finally, with a particular service-granting ticket, the client can gain access to the corresponding service with step 5:

5. The client requests access to a service on behalf of the user. For this purpose, the client transmits a message to the server containing the user's ID and the service-granting ticket. The server authenticates by using the contents of the ticket.

This new scenario satisfies the two requirements of only one password query per user session and protection of the user password.

The Version 4 Authentication Dialogue

Although the foregoing scenario enhances security compared to the first attempt, two additional problems remain. The heart of the first problem is the lifetime associated with the ticket-granting ticket. If this lifetime is very short (e.g., minutes), then the user will be repeatedly asked for a password. If the lifetime is long (e.g., hours), then an opponent has a greater opportunity for replay. An opponent could eavesdrop on the network and capture a copy of the ticket-granting ticket and then wait for the legitimate user to log out. Then the opponent could forge the legitimate user's network address and send the message of step (3) to the TGS. This would give the opponent unlimited access to the resources and files available to the legitimate user.

Similarly, if an opponent captures a service-granting ticket and uses it before it expires, the opponent has access to the corresponding service.

Thus, we arrive at an additional requirement. A network service (the TGS or an application service) must be able to prove that the person using a ticket is the same person to whom that ticket was issued.

The second problem is that there may be a requirement for servers to authenticate themselves to users. Without such authentication, an opponent could sabotage the configuration so that messages to a server were directed to another location. The false server would then be in a position to act as a real server and capture any information from the user and deny the true service to the user.

We examine these problems in turn and refer to Table 4.1, which shows the actual Kerberos protocol.

First, consider the problem of captured ticket-granting tickets and the need to determine that the ticket presenter is the same as the client for whom the ticket was issued. The threat is that an opponent will steal the ticket and use it before it expires. To get around this problem, let us have the AS provide both the client and the TGS with a secret piece of information in a secure manner. Then the client can prove its identity to the TGS by revealing the secret information, again in a secure manner. An efficient way of accomplishing this is to use an encryption key as the secure information; this is referred to as a session key in Kerberos.

Table 4.1a shows the technique for distributing the session key. As before, the client sends a message to the AS requesting access to the TGS. The AS responds with a message, encrypted with a key derived from the user's password (K_c), that contains the ticket. The encrypted message also contains a copy of the session key, $K_{c,tgs}$, where the subscripts indicate that this is a session key for C and TGS. Because this session key is inside the message encrypted with K_c, only the user's client can read it. The same session key is included in the ticket, which can be read only by the TGS. Thus, the session key has been securely delivered to both C and the TGS.

Before proceeding, note that several additional pieces of information have been added to this first phase of the dialogue. Message (1) includes a timestamp, so that the AS knows that the message is timely. Message (2) includes several elements of the ticket in a form accessible to C. This enables C to confirm that this ticket is for the TGS and to learn its expiration time.

Armed with the ticket and the session key, C is ready to approach the TGS. As before, C sends the TGS a message that includes the ticket plus the ID of the requested service [message (3) in Table 4.1b]. In addition, C transmits an authenti-

Table 4.1 Summary of Kerberos Version 4 Message Exchanges

> **(a) Authentication Service Exchange: to obtain ticket-granting ticket**
>
> **(1) C → AS:** $ID_c \,\|\, ID_{tgs} \,\|\, TS_1$
> **(2) AS → C:** $E_{K_c} [K_{c,tgs} \,\|\, ID_{tgs} \,\|\, TS_2 \,\|\, Lifetime_2 \,\|\, Ticket_{tgs}]$
>
> $Ticket_{tgs} = E_{K_{tgs}} [K_{c,tgs} \,\|\, ID_C \,\|\, AD_C \,\|\, ID_{tgs} \,\|\, TS_2 \,\|\, Lifetime_2]$
>
> **(b) Ticket-Granting Service Exchange: to obtain service-granting ticket**
>
> **(3) C → TGS:** $ID_v \,\|\, Ticket_{tgs} \,\|\, Authenticator_c$
> **(4) TGS → C:** $E_{K_{c,tgs}} [K_{c,v} \,\|\, ID_v \,\|\, TS_4 \,\|\, Ticket_v]$
>
> $Ticket_{tgs} = E_{K_{tgs}} [K_{c,tgs} \,\|\, ID_C \,\|\, AD_C \,\|\, ID_{tgs} \,\|\, TS_2 \,\|\, Lifetime_2]$
> $Ticket_v = E_{K_v} [K_{c,v} \,\|\, ID_C \,\|\, AD_C \,\|\, ID_v \,\|\, TS_4 \,\|\, Lifetime_4]$
> $Authenticator_c = E_{K_{c,tgs}} [ID_C \,\|\, AD_C \,\|\, TS_3]$
>
> **(c) Client/Server Authentication Exchange: to obtain service**
>
> **(5) C → V:** $Ticket_v \,\|\, Authenticator_c$
> **(6) V → C:** $E_{K_{c,v}} [TS_5 + 1]$ (for mutual authentication)
>
> $Ticket_v = E_{K_v} [K_{c,v} \,\|\, ID_C \,\|\, AD_C \,\|\, ID_v \,\|\, TS_4 \,\|\, Lifetime_4]$
> $Authenticator_c = E_{K_{c,v}} [ID_C \,\|\, AD_C \,\|\, TS_5]$

cator, which includes the ID and address of C's user and a timestamp. Unlike the ticket, which is reusable, the authenticator is intended for use only once and has a very short lifetime. The TGS can decrypt the ticket with the key that it shares with the AS. This ticket indicates that user C has been provided with the session key $K_{c,tgs}$. In effect, the ticket says, "Anyone who uses $K_{c,tgs}$ must be C." The TGS uses the session key to decrypt the authenticator. The TGS can then check the name and address from the authenticator with that of the ticket and with the network address of the incoming message. If all match, then the TGS is assured that the sender of the ticket is indeed the ticket's real owner. In effect, the authenticator says, "At time TS_3, I hereby use $K_{c,tgs}$." Note that the ticket does not prove anyone's identity but is a way to distribute keys securely. It is the authenticator that proves the client's identity. Because the authenticator can be used only once and has a short lifetime, the threat of an opponent stealing both the ticket and the authenticator for presentation later is countered.

The reply from the TGS, in message (4), follows the form of message (2). The message is encrypted with the session key shared by the TGS and C and includes a session key to be shared between C and the server V, the ID of V, and the timestamp of the ticket. The ticket itself includes the same session key.

C now has a reusable service-granting ticket for V. When C presents this ticket, as shown in message (5), it also sends an authenticator. The server can decrypt the ticket, recover the session key, and decrypt the authenticator.

If mutual authentication is required, the server can reply as shown in message (6) of Table 4.1. The server returns the value of the timestamp from the authenticator, incremented by 1, and encrypted in the session key. C can decrypt this message to recover the incremented timestamp. Because the message was encrypted by the session key, C is assured that it could have been created only by V. The contents of the message assures C that this is not a replay of an old reply.

Finally, at the conclusion of this process, the client and server share a secret key. This key can be used to encrypt future messages between the two or to exchange a new random session key for that purpose.

Table 4.2 summarizes the justification for each of the elements in the Kerberos protocol, and Figure 4.1 provides a simplified overview of the action.

Table 4.2   Rationale for the Elements of the Kerberos Version 4 Protocol

(a) Authentication Service Exchange	
Message (1)	Client requests ticket-granting ticket
ID_C:	Tells AS identity of user from this client
ID_{tgs}:	Tells AS that user requests access to TGS
TS_1:	Allows AS to verify that client's clock is synchronized with that of AS
Message (2)	AS returns ticket-granting ticket
E_{K_c}:	Encryption is based on user's password, enabling AS and client to verify password, and protecting contents of message (2)
$K_{c,tgs}$:	Copy of session key accessible to client; created by AS to permit secure exchange between client and TGS without requiring them to share a permanent key
ID_{tgs}:	Confirms that this ticket is for the TGS
TS_2:	Informs client of time this ticket was issued
$Lifetime_2$:	Informs client of the lifetime of this ticket
$Ticket_{tgs}$:	Ticket to be used by client to access TGS
(b) Ticket-Granting Service Exchange	
Message (3)	Client requests service-granting ticket
ID_V:	Tells TGS that user requests access to server V
$Ticket_{tgs}$:	Assures TGS that this user has been authenticated by AS
$Authenticator_c$:	Generated by client to validate ticket
Message (4)	TGS returns service-granting ticket
$E_{K_{c,tgs}}$:	Key shared only by C and TGS; protects contents of message (4)
$K_{c,tgs}$:	Copy of session key accessible to client; created by TGS to permit secure exchange between client and server without requiring them to share a permanent key
ID_V:	Confirms that this ticket is for server V
TS_4:	Informs client of time this ticket was issued
$Ticket_V$:	Ticket to be used by client to access server V
$Ticket_{tgs}$:	Reusable so that user does not have to reenter password
$E_{K_{tgs}}$:	Ticket is encrypted with key known only to AS and TGS, to prevent tampering
$K_{c,tgs}$:	Copy of session key accessible to TGS; used to decrypt authenticator, thereby authenticating ticket
ID_C:	Indicates the rightful owner of this ticket
AD_C:	Prevents use of ticket from workstation other than one that initially requested the ticket
ID_{tgs}:	Assures server that it has decrypted ticket properly
TS_2:	Informs TGS of time this ticket was issued
$Lifetime_2$:	Prevents replay after ticket has expired
$Authenticator_c$:	Assures TGS that the ticket presenter is the same as the client for whom the ticket was issued; has very short lifetime to prevent replay

Table 4.2 *Continued*

(b) Ticket-Granting Service Exchange, *continued*	
$E_{K_{c,tgs}}$:	Authenticator is encrypted with key known only to client and TGS, to prevent tampering
ID_C:	Must match ID in ticket to authenticate ticket
AD_C:	Must match address in ticket to authenticate ticket
TS_2:	Informs TGS of time this authenticator was generated
(c) Client/Server Authentication Exchange	
Message (5)	Client requests service
$Ticket_V$:	Assures server that this user has been authenticated by AS
$Authenticator_c$:	Generated by client to validate ticket
Message (6)	Optional authentication of server to client
$E_{K_{c,v}}$:	Assures C that this message is from V
$TS_5 + 1$:	Assures C that this is not a replay of an old reply
$Ticket_v$:	Reusable so that client does not need to request a new ticket from TGS for each access to the same server
E_{K_v}:	Ticket is encrypted with key known only to TGS and server, to prevent tampering
$K_{c,v}$:	Copy of session key accessible to client; used to decrypt authenticator, thereby authenticating ticket
ID_C:	Indicates the rightful owner of this ticket
AD_C:	Prevents use of ticket from workstation other than one that initially requested the ticket
ID_V:	Assures server that it has decrypted ticket properly
TS_4:	Informs server of time this ticket was issued
$Lifetime_4$:	Prevents replay after ticket has expired
$Authenticator_c$:	Assures server that the ticket presenter is the same as the client for whom the ticket was issued; has very short lifetime to prevent replay
$E_{K_{c,v}}$:	Authenticator is encrypted with key known only to client and server, to prevent tampering
ID_C:	Must match ID in ticket to authenticate ticket
AD_c:	Must match address in ticket to authenticate ticket
TS_5:	Informs server of time this authenticator was generated

Kerberos Realms and Multiple Kerberi

A full-service Kerberos environment consisting of a Kerberos server, a number of clients, and a number of application servers requires the following:

1. The Kerberos server must have the user ID (UID) and hashed password of all participating users in its database. All users are registered with the Kerberos server.
2. The Kerberos server must share a secret key with each server. All servers are registered with the Kerberos server.

Such an environment is referred to as a **realm**. Networks of clients and servers under different administrative organizations typically constitute different realms. That is, it generally is not practical, or does not conform to administrative policy, to have users and servers in one administrative domain registered with a

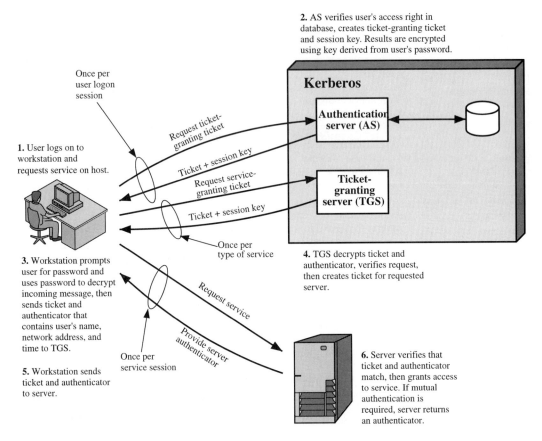

Figure 4.1   Overview of Kerberos

Kerberos server elsewhere. However, users in one realm may need access to servers in other realms, and some servers may be willing to provide service to users from other realms, provided that those users are authenticated.

Kerberos provides a mechanism for supporting such interrealm authentication. For two realms to support inter-realm authentication, a third requirement is added:

3. The Kerberos server in each interoperating realm shares a secret key with the server in the other realm. The two Kerberos servers are registered with each other.

The scheme requires that the Kerberos server in one realm trust the Kerberos server in the other realm to authenticate its users. Furthermore, the participating servers in the second realm must also be willing to trust the Kerberos server in the first realm.

With these ground rules in place, we can describe the mechanism as follows (Figure 4.2): A user wishing service on a server in another realm needs a ticket for that server. The user's client follows the usual procedures to gain access to the local

TGS and then requests a ticket-granting ticket for a remote TGS (TGS in another realm). The client can then apply to the remote TGS for a service-granting ticket for the desired server in the realm of the remote TGS.

The details of the exchanges illustrated in Figure 4.2 are as follows (compare Table 4.1):

(1) C → AS: $ID_c \parallel ID_{tgs} \parallel TS_1$

(2) AS → C: $E_{K_c} [K_{c,tgs} \parallel ID_{tgs} \parallel TS_2 \parallel Lifetime_2 \parallel Ticket_{tgs}]$

(3) C → TGS: $ID_{tgsrem} \parallel Ticket_{tgs} \parallel Authenticator_c$

(4) TGS → C: $E_{K_{c,tgs}} [K_{c,tgsrem} \parallel ID_{tgsrem} \parallel TS_4 \parallel Ticket_{tgsrem}]$

(5) C → TGS$_{rem}$: $ID_{vrem} \parallel Ticket_{tgsrem} \parallel Authenticator_c$

(6) TGS$_{rem}$ → C: $E_{K_{c,tgsrem}} [K_{c,vrem} \parallel ID_{vrem} \parallel TS_6 \parallel Ticket_{vrem}]$

(7) C → V$_{rem}$: $Ticket_{vrem} \parallel Authenticator_c$

The ticket presented to the remote server (V$_{rem}$) indicates the realm in which the user was originally authenticated. The server chooses whether to honor the remote request.

One problem presented by the foregoing approach is that it does not scale well to many realms. If there are N realms, then there must be $N(N-1)/2$ secure key exchanges so that each Kerberos realm can interoperate with all other Kerberos realms.

Kerberos Version 5

Version 5 of Kerberos is specified in RFC 1510 and provides a number of improvements over version 4 [KOHL94]. To begin, we provide an overview of the changes from version 4 to version 5 and then look at the version 5 protocol.

Differences between Versions 4 and 5

Version 5 is intended to address the limitations of version 4 in two areas: environmental shortcomings and technical deficiencies. Let us briefly summarize the improvements in each area.[6]

Version 4 of Kerberos was developed for use within the Project Athena environment and, accordingly, did not fully address the need to be of general purpose. This led to the following **environmental shortcomings**:

1. **Encryption system dependence:** Version 4 requires the use of DES. Export restriction on DES as well as doubts about the strength of DES are thus of concern. In version 5, ciphertext is tagged with an encryption type identifier so that any encryption technique may be used. Encryption keys are tagged with a type and a length, allowing the same key to be used in different algorithms and allowing the specification of different variations on a given algorithm.

2. **Internet protocol dependence:** Version 4 requires the use of Internet Protocol (IP) addresses. Other address types, such as the ISO network address, are not

---

[6]The following discussion follows the presentation in [KOHL94].

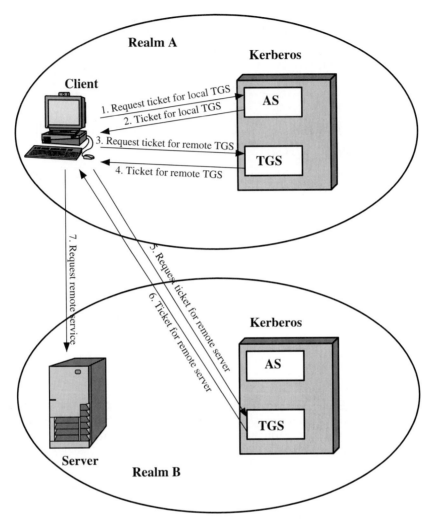

Figure 4.2 Request for Service in Another Realm

accommodated. Version 5 network addresses are tagged with type and length, allowing any network address type to be used.

3. **Message byte ordering:** In version 4, the sender of a message employs a byte ordering of its own choosing and tags the message to indicate least significant byte in lowest address or most significant byte in lowest address. This techniques works but does not follow established conventions. In version 5, all message structures are defined using Abstract Syntax Notation One (ASN.1) and Basic Encoding Rules (BER), which provide an unambiguous byte ordering.

4. **Ticket lifetime:** Lifetime values in version 4 are encoded in an 8-bit quantity in units of five minutes. Thus, the maximum lifetime that can be expressed is $2^8 \times 5 = 1280$ minutes, or a little over 21 hours. This may be inadequate for some applications (e.g., a long-running simulation that requires valid Kerberos

credentials throughout execution). In version 5, tickets include an explicit start time and end time, allowing tickets with arbitrary lifetimes.

5. **Authentication forwarding:** Version 4 does not allow credentials issued to one client to be forwarded to some other host and used by some other client. This capability would enable a client to access a server and have that server access another server on behalf of the client. For example, a client issues a request to a print server that then accesses the client's file from a file server, using the client's credentials for access. Version 5 provides this capability.

6. **Interrealm authentication:** In version 4, interoperability among N realms requires on the order of N^2 Kerberos-to-Kerberos relationships, as described earlier. Version 5 supports a method that requires fewer relationships, as described shortly.

Apart from these environmental limitations, there are **technical deficiencies** in the version 4 protocol itself. Most of these deficiencies were documented in [BELL90], and version 5 attempts to address these. The deficiencies are the following:

1. **Double encryption:** Note in Table 4.1 [messages (2) and (4)] that tickets provided to clients are encrypted twice, once with the secret key of the target server and then again with a secret key known to the client. The second encryption is not necessary and is computationally wasteful.

2. **PCBC encryption:** Encryption in version 4 makes use of a nonstandard mode of DES known as propagating block chaining (PCBC).[7] It has been demonstrated that this mode is vulnerable to an attack involving the interchange of ciphertext blocks [KOHL89]. PCBC was intended to provide an integrity check as part of the encryption operation. Version 5 provides explicit integrity mechanisms, allowing the standard CBC mode to be used for encryption.

3. **Session keys:** Each ticket includes a session key that is used by the client to encrypt the authenticator sent to the service associated with that ticket. In addition, the session key may subsequently be used by the client and the server to protect messages passed during that session. However, because the same ticket may be used repeatedly to gain service from a particular server, there is the risk that an opponent will replay messages from an old session to the client or the server. In version 5, it is possible for a client and server to negotiate a subsession key, which is to be used only for that one connection. A new access by the client would result in the use of a new subsession key.

4. **Password attacks:** Both versions are vulnerable to a password attack. The message from the AS to the client includes material encrypted with a key based on the client's password.[8] An opponent can capture this message and attempt to decrypt it by trying various passwords. If the result of a test decryption is of the proper form, then the opponent has discovered the client's password and may subsequently use it to gain authentication credentials from Kerberos. This is the same type of password attack described in Chapter 9, with the same

---

[7]This is described in Appendix 4A.
[8]Appendix 4A describes the mapping of passwords to encryption keys.

Table 4.3 Summary of Kerberos Version 5 Message Exchanges

(a) Authentication Service Exchange: to obtain ticket-granting ticket

(1) C → AS: Options $\| ID_c \| Realm_c \| ID_{tgs} \| Times \| Nonce_1$

(2) AS → C: $Realm_c \| ID_C \| Ticket_{tgs} \| E_{Kc}[K_{c,tgs} \| Times \| Nonce_1 \| Realm_{tgs} \| ID_{tgs}]$

$Ticket_{tgs} = E_{K_{tgs}} [Flags \| K_{c,tgs} \| Realm_c \| ID_C \| AD_C \| Times]$

(b) Ticket-Granting Service Exchange: to obtain service-granting ticket

(3) C → TGS: Options $\| ID_v \| Times \| Nonce_2 \| Ticket_{tgs} \| Authenticator_c$

(4) TGS → C: $Realm_c \| ID_C \| Ticket_v \| E_{Kc,tgs}[K_{c,v} \| Times \| Nonce_2 \| Realm_v \| ID_V]$

$Ticket_{tgs} = E_{K_{tgs}} [Flags \| K_{c,tgs} \| Realm_c \| ID_C \| AD_C \| Times]$

$Ticket_v = E_{K_v} [Flags \| K_{c,v} \| Realm_c \| ID_C \| AD_C \| Times]$

$Authenticator_c = E_{Kc,tgs} [ID_C \| Realm_c \| TS_1]$

(c) Client/Server Authentication Exchange: to obtain service

(5) C → V: Options $\| Ticket_v \| Authenticator_c$

(6) V → C: $E_{Kc,v} [TS_2 \| Subkey \| Seq\#]$

$Ticket_v = E_{K_v} [Flags \| K_{c,v} \| Realm_c \| ID_C \| AD_C \| Times]$

$Authenticator_c = E_{Kc,v} [ID_C \| Realm_c \| TS_2 \| Subkey \| Seq\#]$

---

kinds of countermeasures being applicable. Version 5 does provide a mechanism known as preauthentication, which should make password attacks more difficult, but it does not prevent them.

The Version 5 Authentication Dialogue

Table 4.3 summarizes the basic version 5 dialogue. This is best explained by comparison with version 4 (Table 4.1).

First, consider the **authentication service exchange**. Message (1) is a client request for a ticket-granting ticket. As before, it includes the ID of the user and the TGS. The following new elements are added:

- **Realm:** Indicates realm of user
- **Options:** Used to request that certain flags be set in the returned ticket
- **Times:** Used by the client to request the following time settings in the ticket:
  - from: the desired start time for the requested ticket
  - till: the requested expiration time for the requested ticket
  - rtime: requested renew-till time
- **Nonce:** A random value to be repeated in message (2) to assure that the response is fresh and has not been replayed by an opponent

Message (2) returns a ticket-granting ticket, identifying information for the client, and a block encrypted using the encryption key based on the user's password. This block includes the session key to be used between the client and the TGS, times specified in message (1), the nonce from message (1), and TGS identifying information. The ticket itself includes the session key, identifying information for the client, the requested time values, and flags that reflect the status of this ticket and the requested options. These flags introduce significant new functionality to version 5. For now, we defer a discussion of these flags and concentrate on the overall structure of the version 5 protocol.

Let us now compare the **ticket-granting service exchange** for versions 4 and 5. We see that message (3) for both versions includes an authenticator, a ticket, and the name of the requested service. In addition, version 5 includes requested times and options for the ticket and a nonce, all with functions similar to those of message (1). The authenticator itself is essentially the same as the one used in version 4.

Message (4) has the same structure as message (2), returning a ticket plus information needed by the client, the latter encrypted with the session key now shared by the client and the TGS.

Finally, for the **client/server authentication exchange**, several new features appear in version 5. In message (5), the client may request as an option that mutual authentication is required. The authenticator includes several new fields as follows:

- **Subkey:** The client's choice for an encryption key to be used to protect this specific application session. If this field is omitted, the session key from the ticket ($K_{c,v}$) is used.
- **Sequence number:** An optional field that specifies the starting sequence number to be used by the server for messages sent to the client during this session. Messages may be sequence numbered to detect replays.

If mutual authentication is required, the server responds with message (6). This message includes the timestamp from the authenticator. Note that in version 4, the timestamp was incremented by one. This is not necessary in version 5 because the nature of the format of messages is such that it is not possible for an opponent to create message (6) without knowledge of the appropriate encryption keys. The subkey field, if present, overrides the subkey field, if present, in message (5). The optional sequence number field specifies the starting sequence number to be used by the client.

Ticket Flags

The flags field included in tickets in version 5 supports expanded functionality compared to that available in version 4. Table 4.4 summarizes the flags that may be included in a ticket.

The INITIAL flag indicates that this ticket was issued by the AS, not by the TGS. When a client requests a service-granting ticket from the TGS, it presents a ticket-granting ticket obtained from the AS. In version 4, this was the only way to obtain a service-granting ticket. Version 5 provides the additional capability that the client can get a service-granting ticket directly from the AS. The utility of this is as follows: A server, such as a password-changing server, may wish to know that the client's password was recently tested.

The PRE-AUTHENT flag, if set, indicates that when the AS received the initial request [message (1)], it authenticated the client before issuing a ticket. The exact form of this preauthentication is left unspecified. As an example, the MIT implementation

Table 4.4 Kerberos Version 5 Flags

INITIAL	This ticket was issued using the AS protocol, and not issued based on a ticket-granting ticket.
PRE-AUTHENT	During initial authentication, the client was authenticated by the KDC before a ticket was issued.
HW-AUTHENT	The protocol employed for initial authentication required the use of hardware expected to be possessed solely by the named client.
RENEWABLE	Tells TGS that this ticket can be used to obtain a replacement ticket that expires at a later date.
MAY-POSTDATE	Tells TGS that a postdated ticket may be issued based on this ticket-granting ticket.
POSTDATED	Indicates that this ticket has been postdated; the end server can check the authtime field to see when the original authentication occurred.
INVALID	This ticket is invalid and must be validated by the KDC before use.
PROXIABLE	Tells TGS that a new service-granting ticket with a different network address may be issued based on the presented ticket.
PROXY	Indicates that this ticket is a proxy.
FORWARDABLE	Tells TGS that a new ticket-granting ticket with a different network address may be issued based on this ticket-granting ticket.
FORWARDED	Indicates that this ticket has either been forwarded or was issued based on authentication involving a forwarded ticket-granting ticket.

of version 5 has encrypted timestamp preauthentication, enabled by default. When a user wants to get a ticket, it has to send to the AS a preauthentication block containing a random confounder, a version number, and a timestamp, encrypted in the client's password-based key. The AS decrypts the block and will not send a ticket-granting ticket back unless the timestamp in the preauthentication block is within the allowable time skew (time interval to account for clock drift and network delays). Another possibility is the use of a smart card that generates continually changing passwords that are included in the preauthenticated messages. The passwords generated by the card can be based on a user's password but be transformed by the card so that, in effect, arbitrary passwords are used. This prevents an attack based on easily guessed passwords. If a smart card or similar device was used, this is indicated by the HW-AUTHENT flag.

When a ticket has a long lifetime, there is the potential for it to be stolen and used by an opponent for a considerable period. If a short lifetime is used to lessen the threat, then overhead is involved in acquiring new tickets. In the case of a ticket-granting ticket, the client would either have to store the user's secret key, which is clearly risky, or repeatedly ask the user for a password. A compromise scheme is the use of renewable tickets. A ticket with the RENEWABLE flag set includes two expiration times: one for this specific ticket and one that is the latest permissible value for an expiration time. A client can have the ticket renewed by presenting it to the TGS with a requested new expiration time. If the new time is within the limit of the latest permissible value, the TGS can issue a new ticket with a new session time and a later specific expiration time. The advantage of this mechanism is that the TGS may refuse to renew a ticket reported as stolen.

A client may request that the AS provide a ticket-granting ticket with the MAY-POSTDATE flag set. The client can then use this ticket to request a ticket that is flagged as POSTDATED and INVALID from the TGS. Subsequently, the client may submit the postdated ticket for validation. This scheme can be useful for running a long batch job on a server that requires a ticket periodically. The client can obtain a number of tickets for this session at once, with spread-out time values. All but the first ticket are initially invalid. When the execution reaches a point in time when a new ticket is required, the client can get the appropriate ticket validated. With this approach, the client does not have to repeatedly use its ticket-granting ticket to obtain a service-granting ticket.

In version 5 it is possible for a server to act as a proxy on behalf of a client, in effect adopting the credentials and privileges of the client to request a service from another server. If a client wishes to use this mechanism, it requests a ticket-granting ticket with the PROXIABLE flag set. When this ticket is presented to the TGS, the TGS is permitted to issue a service-granting ticket with a different network address; this latter ticket will have its PROXY flag set. An application receiving such a ticket may accept it or require additional authentication to provide an audit trail.

The proxy concept is a limited case of the more powerful forwarding procedure. If a ticket is set with the FORWARDABLE flag, a TGS can issue to the requestor a ticket-granting ticket with a different network address and the FORWARDED flag set. This ticket can then be presented to a remote TGS. This capability allows a client to gain access to a server on another realm without requiring that each Kerberos maintain a secret key with Kerberos servers in every other realm. For example, realms could be structured hierarchically. Then a client could walk up the tree to a common node and then back down to reach a target realm. Each step of the walk would involve forwarding a ticket-granting ticket to the next TGS in the path.

4.2 X.509 AUTHENTICATION SERVICE

ITU-T recommendation X.509 is part of the X.500 series of recommendations that define a directory service. The directory is, in effect, a server or distributed set of servers that maintains a database of information about users. The information includes a mapping from user name to network address, as well as other attributes and information about the users.

X.509 defines a framework for the provision of authentication services by the X.500 directory to its users. The directory may serve as a repository of public-key certificates. Each certificate contains the public key of a user and is signed with the private key of a trusted certification authority. In addition, X.509 defines alternative authentication protocols based on the use of public-key certificates.

X.509 is an important standard because the certificate structure and authentication protocols defined in X.509 are used in a variety contexts. For example, the X.509 certificate format is used in S/MIME (Chapter 5), IP Security (Chapter 6), and SSL/TLS and SET (Chapter 7).

X.509 was initially issued in 1988. The standard was subsequently revised to address some of the security concerns documented in [IANS90] and [MITC90]; a revised recommendation was issued in 1993. A third version was issued in 1995 and revised in 2000.

X.509 is based on the use of public-key cryptography and digital signatures. The standard does not dictate the use of a specific algorithm but recommends RSA. The digital signature scheme is assumed to require the use of a hash function. Again, the standard does not dictate a specific hash algorithm. The 1988 recommendation included the description of a recommended hash algorithm; this algorithm has since been shown to be insecure and was dropped from the 1993 recommendation.

Certificates

The heart of the X.509 scheme is the public-key certificate associated with each user. These user certificates are assumed to be created by some trusted certification authority (CA) and placed in the directory by the CA or by the user. The directory server itself is not responsible for the creation of public keys or for the certification function; it merely provides an easily accessible location for users to obtain certificates.

Figure 4.3a shows the general format of a certificate, which includes the following elements:

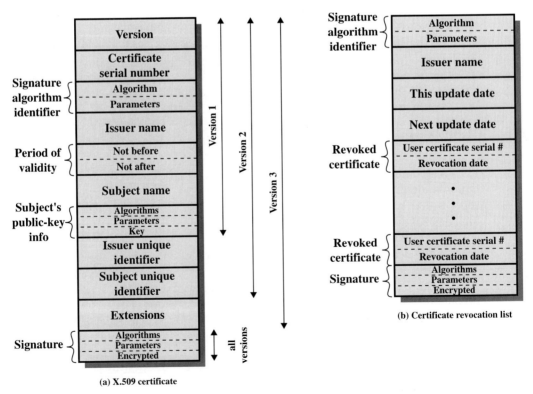

(a) X.509 certificate

(b) Certificate revocation list

Figure 4.3 X.509 Formats

- **Version:** Differentiates among successive versions of the certificate format; the default is version 1. If the Issuer Unique Identifier or Subject Unique Identifier are present, the value must be version 2. If one or more extensions are present, the version must be version 3.
- **Serial number:** An integer value, unique within the issuing CA, that is unambiguously associated with this certificate.
- **Signature algorithm identifier:** The algorithm used to sign the certificate, together with any associated parameters. Because this information is repeated in the Signature field at the end of the certificate, this field has little, if any, utility.
- **Issuer name:** X.500 name of the CA that created and signed this certificate.
- **Period of validity:** Consists of two dates: the first and last on which the certificate is valid.
- **Subject name:** The name of the user to whom this certificate refers. That is, this certificate certifies the public key of the subject who holds the corresponding private key.
- **Subject's public-key information:** The public key of the subject, plus an identifier of the algorithm for which this key is to be used, together with any associated parameters.
- **Issuer unique identifier:** An optional bit string field used to identify uniquely the issuing CA in the event the X.500 name has been reused for different entities.
- **Subject unique identifier:** An optional bit string field used to identify uniquely the subject in the event the X.500 name has been reused for different entities.
- **Extensions:** A set of one or more extension fields. Extensions were added in version 3 and are discussed later in this section.
- **Signature:** Covers all of the other fields of the certificate; it contains the hash code of the other fields, encrypted with the CA's private key. This field includes the signature algorithm identifier.

The unique identifier fields were added in version 2 to handle the possible reuse of subject and/or issuer names over time. These fields are rarely used.

The standard uses the following notation to define a certificate:

$$CA<<A>> = CA \{V, SN, AI, CA, T_A, A, Ap\}$$

where

$Y<<X>>$ = the certificate of user X issued by certification authority Y
$Y \{I\}$ = the signing of I by Y. It consists of I with an encrypted hash code appended

The CA signs the certificate with its private key. If the corresponding public key is known to a user, then that user can verify that a certificate signed by the CA is valid. This is the typical digital signature approach illustrated in Figure 3.2c.

Obtaining a User's Certificate

User certificates generated by a CA have the following characteristics:

- Any user with access to the public key of the CA can verify the user public key that was certified.
- No party other than the certification authority can modify the certificate without this being detected.

Because certificates are unforgeable, they can be placed in a directory without the need for the directory to make special efforts to protect them.

If all users subscribe to the same CA, then there is a common trust of that CA. All user certificates can be placed in the directory for access by all users. In addition, a user can transmit his or her certificate directly to other users. In either case, once B is in possession of A's certificate, B has confidence that messages it encrypts with A's public key will be secure from eavesdropping and that messages signed with A's private key are unforgeable.

If there is a large community of users, it may not be practical for all users to subscribe to the same CA. Because it is the CA that signs certificates, each participating user must have a copy of the CA's own public key to verify signatures. This public key must be provided to each user in an absolutely secure (with respect to integrity and authenticity) way so that the user has confidence in the associated certificates. Thus, with many users, it may be more practical for there to be a number of CAs, each of which securely provides its public key to some fraction of the users.

Now suppose that A has obtained a certificate from certification authority X_1 and B has obtained a certificate from CA X_2. If A does not securely know the public key of X_2, then B's certificate, issued by X_2, is useless to A. A can read B's certificate, but A cannot verify the signature. However, if the two CAs have securely exchanged their own public keys, the following procedure will enable A to obtain B's public key:

1. A obtains, from the directory, the certificate of X_2 signed by X_1. Because A securely knows X_1's public key, A can obtain X_2's public key from its certificate and verify it by means of X_1's signature on the certificate.
2. A then goes back to the directory and obtains the certificate of B signed by X_2. Because A now has a trusted copy of X_2's public key, A can verify the signature and securely obtain B's public key.

A has used a chain of certificates to obtain B's public key. In the notation of X.509, this chain is expressed as

$$X_1 << X_2 >> X_2 << B >>$$

In the same fashion, B can obtain A's public key with the reverse chain:

$$X_2 << X_1 >> X_1 << A >>$$

This scheme need not be limited to a chain of two certificates. An arbitrarily long path of CAs can be followed to produce a chain. A chain with N elements would be expressed as

$$X_1 << X_2 >> X_2 << X_3 >> \ldots X_N << B >>$$

In this case, each pair of CAs in the chain (X_i, X_{i+1}) must have created certificates for each other.

All these certificates of CAs by CAs need to appear in the directory, and the user needs to know how they are linked to follow a path to another user's public-key certificate. X.509 suggests that CAs be arranged in a hierarchy so that navigation is straightforward.

Figure 4.4, taken from X.509, is an example of such a hierarchy. The connected circles indicate the hierarchical relationship among the CAs; the associated boxes indicate certificates maintained in the directory for each CA entry. The directory entry for each CA includes two types of certificates:

- **Forward certificates:** Certificates of X generated by other CAs
- **Reverse certificates:** Certificates generated by X that are the certificates of other CAs

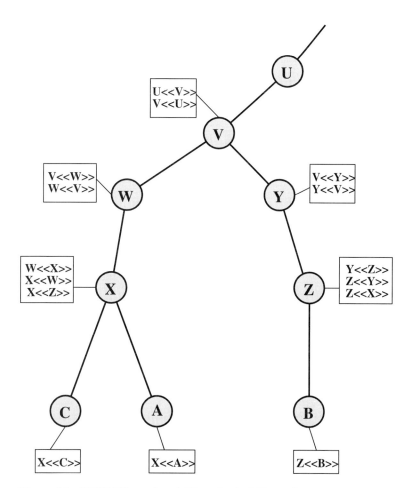

Figure 4.4   X.509 Hierarchy: A Hypothetical Example

In this example, user A can acquire the following certificates from the directory to establish a certification path to B:

$$X<<W>>\ W<<V>>\ V<<Y>>\ Y<<Z>>\ Z<<B>>$$

When A has obtained these certificates, it can unwrap the certification path in sequence to recover a trusted copy of B's public key. Using this public key, A can send encrypted messages to B. If A wishes to receive encrypted messages back from B, or to sign messages sent to B, then B will require A's public key, which can be obtained from the following certification path:

$$Z<<Y>>\ Y<<V>>\ V<<W>>\ W<<X>>\ X<<A>>$$

B can obtain this set of certificates from the directory, or A can provide them as part of its initial message to B.

Revocation of Certificates

Recall from Figure 4.3 that each certificate includes a period of validity, much like a credit card. Typically, a new certificate is issued just before the expiration of the old one. In addition, it may be desirable on occasion to revoke a certificate before it expires, for one of the following reasons:

1. The user's private key is assumed to be compromised.
2. The user is no longer certified by this CA.
3. The CA's certificate is assumed to be compromised.

Each CA must maintain a list consisting of all revoked but not expired certificates issued by that CA, including both those issued to users and to other CAs. These lists should also be posted on the directory.

Each certificate revocation list (CRL) posted to the directory is signed by the issuer and includes (Figure 4.3b) the issuer's name, the date the list was created, the date the next CRL is scheduled to be issued, and an entry for each revoked certificate. Each entry consists of the serial number of a certificate and revocation date for that certificate. Because serial numbers are unique within a CA, the serial number is sufficient to identify the certificate.

When a user receives a certificate in a message, the user must determine whether the certificate has been revoked. The user could check the directory each time a certificate is received. To avoid the delays (and possible costs) associated with directory searches, it is likely that the user would maintain a local cache of certificates and lists or revoked certificates.

Authentication Procedures

X.509 also includes three alternative authentication procedures that are intended for use across a variety of applications. All these procedures make use of public-key signatures. It is assumed that the two parties know each other's public key, either by obtaining each other's certificates from the directory or because the certificate is included in the initial message from each side.

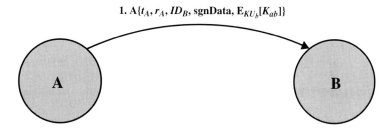

(a) One-way authentication

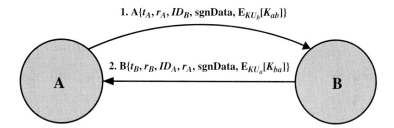

(b) Two-way authentication

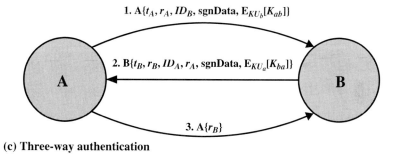

(c) Three-way authentication

Figure 4.5 X.509 Strong Authentication Procedures

Figure 4.5 illustrates the three procedures.

One-Way Authentication

One way authentication involves a single transfer of information from one user (A) to another (B), and establishes the following:

1. The identity of A and that the message was generated by A
2. That the message was intended for B
3. The integrity and originality (it has not been sent multiple times) of the message

Note that only the identity of the initiating entity is verified in this process, not that of the responding entity.

At a minimum, the message includes a timestamp t_A, a nonce r_A, and the identity of B and is signed with A's private key. The timestamp consists of an optional generation time and an expiration time. This prevents delayed delivery of messages. The nonce can be used to detect replay attacks. The nonce value must be unique within the expiration time of the message. Thus, B can store the nonce until it expires and reject any new messages with the same nonce.

For pure authentication, the message is used simply to present credentials to B. The message may also include information to be conveyed. This information, sgnData, is included within the scope of the signature, guaranteeing its authenticity and integrity. The message may also be used to convey a session key to B, encrypted with B's public key.

Two-Way Authentication

In addition to the three elements just listed, two-way authentication establishes the following elements:

4. The identity of B and that the reply message was generated by B
5. That the message was intended for A
6. The integrity and originality of the reply

Two-way authentication thus permits both parties in a communication to verify the identity of the other.

The reply message includes the nonce from A, to validate the reply. It also includes a timestamp and nonce generated by B. As before, the message may include signed additional information and a session key encrypted with A's public key.

Three-Way Authentication

In three-way authentication, a final message from A to B is included, which contains a signed copy of the nonce r_B. The intent of this design is that timestamps need not be checked: Because both nonces are echoed back by the other side, each side can check the returned nonce to detect replay attacks. This approach is needed when synchronized clocks are not available.

X.509 Version 3

The X.509 version 2 format does not convey all of the information that recent design and implementation experience has shown to be needed. [FORD95] lists the following requirements not satisfied by version 2:

1. The Subject field is inadequate to convey the identity of a key owner to a public-key user. X.509 names may be relatively short and lacking in obvious identification details that may be needed by the user.
2. The Subject field is also inadequate for many applications, which typically recognize entities by an Internet e-mail address, a URL, or some other Internet-related identification.
3. There is a need to indicate security policy information. This enables a security application or function, such as IPSec, to relate an X.509 certificate to a given policy.

4. There is a need to limit the damage that can result from a faulty or malicious CA by setting constraints on the applicability of a particular certificate.

5. It is important to be able to identify separately different keys used by the same owner at different times. This feature supports key life cycle management, in particular the ability to update key pairs for users and CAs on a regular basis or under exceptional circumstances.

Rather than continue to add fields to a fixed format, standards developers felt that a more flexible approach was needed. Thus, version 3 includes a number of optional extensions that may be added to the version 2 format. Each extension consists of an extension identifier, a criticality indicator, and an extension value. The criticality indicator indicates whether an extension can be safely ignored. If the indicator has a value of TRUE and an implementation does not recognize the extension, it must treat the certificate as invalid.

The certificate extensions fall into three main categories: key and policy information, subject and issuer attributes, and certification path constraints.

Key and Policy Information

These extensions convey additional information about the subject and issuer keys, plus indicators of certificate policy. A certificate policy is a named set of rules that indicates the applicability of a certificate to a particular community and/or class of application with common security requirements. For example, a policy might be applicable to the authentication of electronic data interchange (EDI) transactions for the trading of goods within a given price range.

This area includes the following:

*   **Authority key identifier:** Identifies the public key to be used to verify the signature on this certificate or CRL. Enables distinct keys of the same CA to be differentiated. One use of this field is to handle CA key pair updating.

*   **Subject key identifier:** Identifies the public key being certified. Useful for subject key pair updating. Also, a subject may have multiple key pairs and, correspondingly, different certificates for different purposes (e.g., digital signature and encryption key agreement).

*   **Key usage:** Indicates a restriction imposed as to the purposes for which, and the policies under which, the certified public key may be used. May indicate one or more of the following: digital signature, nonrepudiation, key encryption, data encryption, key agreement, CA signature verification on certificates, CA signature verification on CRLs.

*   **Private-key usage period:** Indicates the period of use of the private key corresponding to the public key. Typically, the private key is used over a different period from the validity of the public key. For example, with digital signature keys, the usage period for the signing private key is typically shorter than that for the verifying public key.

*   **Certificate policies:** Certificates may be used in environments where multiple policies apply. This extension lists policies that the certificate is recognized as supporting, together with optional qualifier information.

- **Policy mappings:** Used only in certificates for CAs issued by other CAs. Policy mappings allow an issuing CA to indicate that one or more of that issuer's policies can be considered equivalent to another policy used in the subject CA's domain.

Certificate Subject and Issuer Attributes

These extensions support alternative names, in alternative formats, for a certificate subject or certificate issuer and can convey additional information about the certificate subject, to increase a certificate user's confidence that the certificate subject is a particular person or entity. For example, information such as postal address, position within a corporation, or picture image may be required.

The extension fields in this area include the following:

- **Subject alternative name:** Contains one or more alternative names, using any of a variety of forms. This field is important for supporting certain applications, such as electronic mail, EDI, and IPSec, which may employ their own name forms.
- **Issuer alternative name:** Contains one or more alternative names, using any of a variety of forms.
- **Subject directory attributes:** Conveys any desired X.500 directory attribute values for the subject of this certificate.

Certification Path Constraints

These extensions allow constraint specifications to be included in certificates issued for CAs by other CAs. The constraints may restrict the types of certificates that can be issued by the subject CA or that may occur subsequently in a certification chain.

The extension fields in this area include the following:

- **Basic constraints:** Indicates if the subject may act as a CA. If so, a certification path length constraint may be specified.
- **Name constraints:** Indicates a name space within which all subject names in subsequent certificates in a certification path must be located.
- **Policy constraints:** Specifies constraints that may require explicit certificate policy identification or inhibit policy mapping for the remainder of the certification path.

4.3 RECOMMENDED READING AND WEB SITES

A painless way to get a grasp of Kerberos concepts is found in [BRYA88]. One of the best treatments of Kerberos is [KOHL94]. [TUNG99] describes Kerberos from a user's point of view.

BRYA88 Bryant, W. *Designing an Authentication System: A Dialogue in Four Scenes.* Project Athena document, February 1988. Available at http://web.mit.edu/kerberos/www/dialogue.html.

KOHL94 Kohl, J.; Neuman, B.; and Ts'o, T. "The Evolution of the Kerberos Authentication Service." in Brazier, F., and Johansen, D. *Distributed Open Systems.* Los Alamitos, CA: IEEE Computer Society Press, 1994. Available at http://web.mit.edu/kerberos/www/papers.html.

TUNG99 Tung, B. *Kerberos: A Network Authentication System.* Reading, MA: Addison-Wesley, 1999.

Recommended Web sites:

- **MIT Kerberos Site:** Information about Kerberos, including the FAQ, papers and documents, and pointers to commercial product sites
- **USC/ISI Kerberos Page:** Another good source of Kerberos material
- **Public-Key Infrastructure Working Group:** IETF group developing standards based on X.509v3
- **Verisign:** A leading commercial vendor of X.509-related products; white papers and other worthwhile material at this site

4.4 KEY TERMS, REVIEW QUESTIONS, AND PROBLEMS

Key Terms

authentication	nonce	sequence number
authentication server	propagating cipher block	subkey
Kerberos	chaining (PCBC) mode	ticket
Kerberos realm	public-key certificate	ticket-granting server (TGS)
lifetime	realm	X.509 certificate

Review Questions

4.1 What problem was Kerberos designed to address?

4.2 What are three threats associated with user authentication over a network or Internet?

4.3 List three approaches to secure user authentication in a distributed environment.

4.4 What four requirements were defined for Kerberos?

4.5 What entities constitute a full-service Kerberos environment?

4.6 In the context of Kerberos, what is a realm?

4.7 What are the principal differences between version 4 and version 5 of Kerberos?

4.8 What is the purpose of the X.509 standard?

4.9 What is a chain of certificates?

4.10 How is an X.509 certificate revoked?

Problems

4.1   Show that a random error in one block of ciphertext is propagated to all subsequent blocks of plaintext in PCBC mode (Figure 4.7).

4.2   Suppose that, in PCBC mode, blocks Ci and Ci11 are interchanged during transmission. Show that this affects only the decrypted blocks Pi and Pi11 but not subsequent blocks.

4.3   The original three-way authentication procedure for X.509 illustrated in Figure 4.5c contains a security flaw. The essence of the protocol is as follows:

$$A \rightarrow B: \quad A \{t_A, r_A, ID_B\}$$
$$B \rightarrow A: \quad B \{t_B, r_B, ID_A, r_A\}$$
$$A \rightarrow B: \quad A \{r_B\}$$

The text of X.509 states that checking timestamps t_A and t_B is optional for three-way authentication. But consider the following example. Suppose A and B have used the preceding protocol on some previous occasion, an1d opponent C has intercepted the preceding three messages. In addition, suppose that timestamps are not used and are all set to 0. Finally, suppose C wishes to impersonate A to B. C initially sends the first captured message to B:

$$C \rightarrow B: \quad A \{0, r_A, ID_B\}$$

B responds, thinking it is talking to A but is actually talking to C:

$$B \rightarrow C: \quad B \{0, r'_B, ID_A, r_A\}$$

C meanwhile causes A to initiate authentication with C, by some means. As a result, A sends C the following:

$$A \rightarrow C: \quad A \{0, r'_A, ID_C\}$$

C responds to A, using the same nonce provided to C by B.

$$C \rightarrow A: \quad C \{0, r'_B, A, r'_A\}$$

A responds with

$$A \rightarrow C: \quad A \{r'_B\}$$

This is exactly what C needs to convince B that it is talking to A, so C now repeats the incoming message back out to B.

$$C \rightarrow B: \quad A \{r'_B\}$$

So B will believe it is talking to A whereas it is actually talking to C. Suggest a simple solution to this problem that does not involve the use of timestamps.

4.4   The 1988 version of X.509 lists properties that RSA keys must satisfy to be secure, given current knowledge about the difficulty of factoring large numbers. The discussion concludes with a constraint on the public exponent and the modulus n:

It must be ensured that $e > \log_2(n)$ to prevent attack by taking the eth root mod n to disclose the plaintext.

Although the constraint is correct, the reason given for requiring it is incorrect. What is wrong with the reason given and what is the correct reason?

APPENDIX 4A KERBEROS ENCRYPTION TECHNIQUES

Kerberos includes an encryption library that supports various encryption-related operations.

Password-to-Key Transformation

In Kerberos, passwords are limited to the use of the characters that can be represented in a 7-bit ASCII format. This password, of arbitrary length, is converted into an encryption key that is stored in the Kerberos database. Figure 4.6 illustrates the procedure.

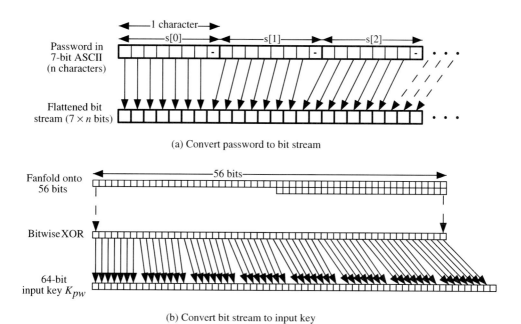

(a) Convert password to bit stream

(b) Convert bit stream to input key

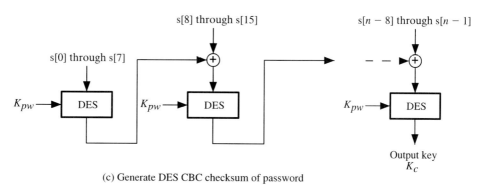

(c) Generate DES CBC checksum of password

Figure 4.6 Generation of Encryption Key from Password

First, the character string, s, is packed into a bit string, b, such that the first character is stored in the first 7 bits, the second character in the second 7 bits, and so on. This can be expressed as

$$b[0] = \text{bit } 0 \text{ of } s[0]$$
$$\vdots$$
$$b[6] = \text{bit } 6 \text{ of } s[0]$$
$$b[7] = \text{bit } 0 \text{ of } s[1]$$
$$\vdots$$
$$b[7i + m] = \text{bit } m \text{ of } s[i] \qquad 0 \le m \le 6$$

Next, the bit string is compacted to 56 bits by aligning the bits in "fanfold" fashion and performing a bitwise XOR. For example, if the bit string is of length 59, then

$$b[55] = b[55] \oplus b[56]$$
$$b[54] = b[54] \oplus b[57]$$
$$b[53] = b[53] \oplus b[58]$$

This creates a 56-bit DES key. To conform to the expected 64-bit key format, the string is treated as a sequence of eight 7-bit blocks and is mapped into eight 8-bit blocks to form an input key K_{pw}.

Finally, the original password is encrypted using the cipher block chaining (CBC) mode of DES with key K_{pw}. The last 64-bit block returned from this process, known as the CBC checksum, is the output key associated with this password.

The entire algorithm can be viewed as a hash function that maps an arbitrary password into a 64-bit hash code.

Propagating Cipher Block Chaining Mode

Recall from Chapter 2 that, in the CBC mode of DES, the input to the DES algorithm at each stage consists of the XOR of the current plaintext block and the preceding ciphertext block, with the same key used for each block (Figure 3.12). The advantage of this mode over the electronic codebook (ECB) mode, in which each plaintext block is independently encrypted, is this: With CBC, the same plaintext block, if repeated, produces different ciphertext blocks.

CBC has the property that if an error occurs in transmission of ciphertext block C_I, then this error propagates to the recovered plaintext blocks P_I and P_{I+1}.

Version 4 of Kerberos uses an extension to CBC, called the propagating CBC (PCBC) mode [MEYE82]. This mode has the property that an error in one ciphertext block is propagated to all subsequent decrypted blocks of the message, rendering each block useless. Thus, data encryption and integrity are combined in one operation.

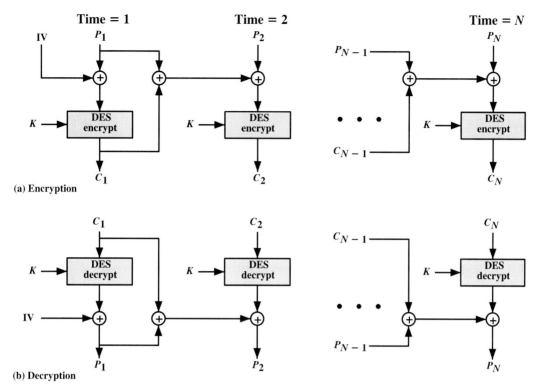

Figure 4.7   Propagating Cipher Block Chaining (PCBC) Mode

PCBC is illustrated in Figure 4.7. In this scheme, the input to the encryption algorithm is the XOR of the current plaintext block, the preceding cipher text block, and the preceding plaintext block:

$$C_n = E_K[C_{n-1} \oplus P_{n-1} \oplus P_n]$$

On decryption, each ciphertext block is passed through the decryption algorithm. Then the output is XORed with the preceding ciphertext block and the preceding plaintext block. We can demonstrate that this scheme works, as follows:

$$D_K[C_n] = D_K[E_K[C_{n-1} \oplus P_{n-1} \oplus P_n]]$$
$$= C_{n-1} \oplus P_{n-1} \oplus P_n$$

$$C_{n-1} \oplus P_{n-1} \oplus D_K[C_n] = P_n$$

CHAPTER 5

ELECTRONIC MAIL SECURITY

5.1 Pretty Good Privacy

Notation
Operational Description
Cryptographic Keys and Key Rings
Public-Key Management

5.2 S/MIME

RFC 822
Multipurpose Internet Mail Extensions
S/MIME Functionality
S/MIME Messages
S/MIME Certificate Processing
Enhanced Security Services

5.3 Recommended Web Sites

5.4 Key Terms, Review Questions, and Problems

Key Terms
Review Questions
Problems

Appendix 5A   Data Compression Using Zip

Compression Algorithm
Decompression Algorithm

Appendix 5B   RADIX-64 Conversion

Appendix 5C   PGP Random Number Generation

True Random Numbers
Pseudorandom Numbers

Despite the refusal of VADM Poindexter and LtCol North to appear, the Board's access to other sources of information filled much of this gap. The FBI provided documents taken from the files of the National Security Advisor and relevant NSC staff members, including messages from the PROF system between VADM Poindexter and LtCol North. The PROF messages were conversations by computer, written at the time events occurred and presumed by the writers to be protected from disclosure. In this sense, they provide a first-hand, contemporaneous account of events.

**—The Tower Commission Report
to President Reagan on the Iran-Contra Affair, 1987**

*Bless the man who made it,
And pray that he ain't dead.
He could've made a million
If he'd sold it to the feds,
But he was hot for freedom;
He gave it out for free.
Now every common citizen's got PGP.*

**—From the song "P.G.P."
by Leslie Fish**

In virtually all distributed environments, electronic mail is the most heavily used network-based application. It is also the only distributed application that is widely used across all architectures and vendor platforms. Users expect to be able to, and do, send mail to others who are connected directly or indirectly to the Internet, regardless of host operating system or communications suite.

With the explosively growing reliance on electronic mail for every conceivable purpose, there grows a demand for authentication and confidentiality services. Two schemes stand out as approaches that enjoy widespread use: Pretty Good Privacy (PGP) and S/MIME. Both are examined in this chapter.

5.1 PRETTY GOOD PRIVACY

PGP is a remarkable phenomenon. Largely the effort of a single person, Phil Zimmermann, PGP provides a confidentiality and authentication service that can be used for electronic mail and file storage applications. In essence, Zimmermann has done the following:

1. Selected the best available cryptographic algorithms as building blocks
2. Integrated these algorithms into a general-purpose application that is independent of operating system and processor and that is based on a small set of easy-to-use commands

3. Made the package and its documentation, including the source code, freely available via the Internet, bulletin boards, and commercial networks such as AOL (America On Line).

4. Entered into an agreement with a company (Viacrypt, now Network Associates) to provide a fully compatible, low-cost commercial version of PGP

PGP has grown explosively and is now widely used. A number of reasons can be cited for this growth:

1. It is available free worldwide in versions that run on a variety of platforms, including Windows, UNIX, Macintosh, and many more. In addition, the commercial version satisfies users who want a product that comes with vendor support.

2. It is based on algorithms that have survived extensive public review and are considered extremely secure. Specifically, the package includes RSA, DSS, and Diffie-Hellman for public-key encryption; CAST-128, IDEA, and 3DES for symmetric encryption; and SHA-1 for hash coding.

3. It has a wide range of applicability, from corporations that wish to select and enforce a standardized scheme for encrypting files and messages to individuals who wish to communicate securely with others worldwide over the Internet and other networks.

4. It was not developed by, nor is it controlled by, any governmental or standards organization. For those with an instinctive distrust of "the establishment," this makes PGP attractive.

5. PGP is now on an Internet standards track (RFC 3156). Nevertheless, PGP still has an aura of an antiestablishment endeavor.

We begin with an overall look at the operation of PGP. Next, we examine how cryptographic keys are created and stored. Then, we address the vital issue of public key management.

Notation

Most of the notation used in this chapter has been used before, but a few terms are new. It is perhaps best to summarize those at the beginning. The following symbols are used:

$$
\begin{aligned}
K_s &= \text{session key used in symmetric encryption scheme} \\
KR_a &= \text{private key of user A, used in public-key encryption scheme} \\
KU_a &= \text{public key of user A, used in public-key encryption scheme} \\
EP &= \text{public-key encryption} \\
DP &= \text{public-key decryption} \\
EC &= \text{symmetric encryption} \\
DC &= \text{symmetric decryption} \\
H &= \text{hash function} \\
\| &= \text{concatenation} \\
Z &= \text{compression using ZIP algorithm} \\
R64 &= \text{conversion to radix 64 ASCII format}
\end{aligned}
$$

The PGP documentation often uses the term *secret key* to refer to a key paired with a public key in a public-key encryption scheme. As was mentioned earlier, this practice risks confusion with a secret key used for symmetric encryption. Hence, we will use the term *private key* instead.

Operational Description

The actual operation of PGP, as opposed to the management of keys, consists of five services: authentication, confidentiality, compression, e-mail compatibility, and segmentation (Table 5.1). We examine each of these in turn.

Authentication

Figure 5.1a illustrates the digital signature service provided by PGP. This is the digital signature scheme discussed in Chapter 3 and illustrated in Figure 3.2c. The sequence is as follows:

1. The sender creates a message.
2. SHA-1 is used to generate a 160-bit hash code of the message.
3. The hash code is encrypted with RSA using the sender's private key, and the result is prepended to the message.
4. The receiver uses RSA with the sender's public key to decrypt and recover the hash code.
5. The receiver generates a new hash code for the message and compares it with the decrypted hash code. If the two match, the message is accepted as authentic.

Table 5.1   Summary of PGP Services

Function	Algorithms Used	Description
Digital signature	DSS/SHA or RSA/SHA	A hash code of a message is created using SHA-1. This message digest is encrypted using DSS or RSA with the sender's private key, and included with the message.
Message encryption	CAST or IDEA or Three-Key Triple DES with Diffie-Hellman or RSA	A message is encrypted using CAST-128 or IDEA or 3DES with a one-time session key generated by the sender. The session key is encrypted using Diffie-Hellman or RSA with the recipient's public key, and included with the message.
Compression	ZIP	A message may be compressed, for storage or transmission, using ZIP.
E-mail compatibility	Radix 64 conversion	To provide transparency for e-mail applications, an encrypted message may be converted to an ASCII string using radix 64 conversion.
Segmentation	—	To accommodate maximum message size limitations, PGP performs segmentation and reassembly.

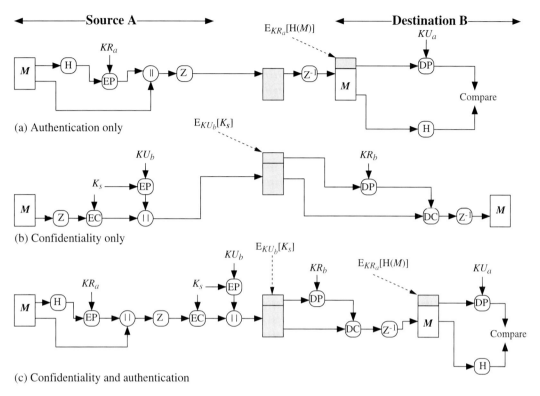

Figure 5.1 PGP Cryptographic Functions

The combination of SHA-1 and RSA provides an effective digital signature scheme. Because of the strength of RSA, the recipient is assured that only the possessor of the matching private key can generate the signature. Because of the strength of SHA-1, the recipient is assured that no one else could generate a new message that matches the hash code and, hence, the signature of the original message.

As an alternative, signatures can be generated using DSS/SHA-1.

Although signatures normally are found attached to the message or file that they sign, this is not always the case: Detached signatures are supported. A detached signature may be stored and transmitted separately from the message it signs. This is useful in several contexts. A user may wish to maintain a separate signature log of all messages sent or received. A detached signature of an executable program can detect subsequent virus infection. Finally, detached signatures can be used when more than one party must sign a document, such as a legal contract. Each person's signature is independent and therefore is applied only to the document. Otherwise, signatures would have to be nested, with the second signer signing both the document and the first signature, and so on.

Confidentiality

Another basic service provided by PGP is confidentiality, which is provided by encrypting messages to be transmitted or to be stored locally as files. In both cases, the symmetric encryption algorithm CAST-128 may be used. Alternatively, IDEA or 3DES may be used. The 64-bit cipher feedback (CFB) mode is used.

As always, one must address the problem of key distribution. In PGP, each symmetric key is used only once. That is, a new key is generated as a random 128-bit number for each message. Thus, although this is referred to in the documentation as a session key, it is in reality a one-time key. Because it is to be used only once, the session key is bound to the message and transmitted with it. To protect the key, it is encrypted with the receiver's public key. Figure 5.1b illustrates the sequence, which can be described as follows:

1. The sender generates a message and a random 128-bit number to be used as a session key for this message only.
2. The message is encrypted, using CAST-128 (or IDEA or 3DES) with the session key.
3. The session key is encrypted with RSA, using the recipient's public key, and is prepended to the message.
4. The receiver uses RSA with its private key to decrypt and recover the session key.
5. The session key is used to decrypt the message.

As an alternative to the use of RSA for key encryption, PGP provides an option referred to as *Diffie-Hellman*. As was explained in Chapter 3, Diffie-Hellman is a key exchange algorithm. In fact, PGP uses a variant of Diffie-Hellman that does provide encryption/decryption, known as ElGamal.

Several observations may be made. First, to reduce encryption time the combination of symmetric and public-key encryption is used in preference to simply using RSA or ElGamal to encrypt the message directly: CAST-128 and the other symmetric algorithms are substantially faster than RSA or ElGamal. Second, the use of the public-key algorithm solves the session key distribution problem, because only the recipient is able to recover the session key that is bound to the message. Each message is a one-time independent event with its own key. Furthermore, given the store-and-forward nature of electronic mail, the use of handshaking to assure that both sides have the same session key is not practical. Finally, the use of one-time symmetric keys strengthens what is already a strong symmetric encryption approach. Only a small amount of plaintext is encrypted with each key, and there is no relationship among the keys. Thus, to the extent that the public-key algorithm is secure, the entire scheme is secure. To this end, PGP provides the user with a range of key size options from 768 to 3072 bits (the DSS key for signatures is limited to 1024 bits).

Confidentiality and Authentication

As Figure 5.1c illustrates, both services may be used for the same message. First, a signature is generated for the plaintext message and prepended to the message. Then the plaintext message plus signature is encrypted using CAST-128 (or IDEA or 3DES), and the session key is encrypted using RSA (or ElGamal). This sequence is preferable to the opposite: encrypting the message and then generating a signature for the encrypted message. It is generally more convenient to store a signature with a plaintext version of a message. Furthermore, for purposes of third-party verification, if the signature is performed first, a third party need not be concerned with the symmetric key when verifying the signature.

In summary, when both services are used, the sender first signs the message with its own private key, then encrypts the message with a session key, and then encrypts the session key with the recipient's public key.

Compression

As a default, PGP compresses the message after applying the signature but before encryption. This has the benefit of saving space both for e-mail transmission and for file storage.

The placement of the compression algorithm, indicated by Z for compression and Z^{-1} for decompression in Figure 5.1, is critical:

1. The signature is generated before compression for two reasons:
   a. It is preferable to sign an uncompressed message so that one can store only the uncompressed message together with the signature for future verification. If one signed a compressed document, then it would be necessary either to store a compressed version of the message for later verification or to recompress the message when verification is required.
   b. Even if one were willing to generate dynamically a recompressed message for verification, PGP's compression algorithm presents a difficulty. The algorithm is not deterministic; various implementations of the algorithm achieve different tradeoffs in running speed versus compression ratio and, as a result, produce different compressed forms. However, these different compression algorithms are interoperable because any version of the algorithm can correctly decompress the output of any other version. Applying the hash function and signature after compression would constrain all PGP implementations to the same version of the compression algorithm.
2. Message encryption is applied after compression to strengthen cryptographic security. Because the compressed message has less redundancy than the original plaintext, cryptanalysis is more difficult.

The compression algorithm used is ZIP, which is described in Appendix 5A.

E-mail Compatibility

When PGP is used, at least part of the block to be transmitted is encrypted. If only the signature service is used, then the message digest is encrypted (with the sender's private key). If the confidentiality service is used, the message plus signature (if present) are encrypted (with a one-time symmetric key). Thus, part or all of the resulting block consists of a stream of arbitrary 8-bit octets. However, many electronic mail systems only permit the use of blocks consisting of ASCII text. To accommodate this restriction, PGP provides the service of converting the raw 8-bit binary stream to a stream of printable ASCII characters.

The scheme used for this purpose is radix-64 conversion. Each group of three octets of binary data is mapped into four ASCII characters. This format also appends a CRC to detect transmission errors. See Appendix 5B for a description.

The use of radix 64 expands a message by 33%. Fortunately, the session key and signature portions of the message are relatively compact, and the plaintext message has been compressed. In fact, the compression should be more than enough to compensate for the radix-64 expansion. For example, [HELD96] reports an average compression ratio of about 2.0 using ZIP. If we ignore the relatively small signature and key components, the typical overall effect of compression and expansion of a file of length X would be $1.33 \times 0.5 \times X = 0.665 \times X$. Thus, there is still an overall compression of about one-third.

One noteworthy aspect of the radix-64 algorithm is that it blindly converts the input stream to radix-64 format regardless of content, even if the input happens to be ASCII text. Thus, if a message is signed but not encrypted and the conversion is applied to the entire block, the output will be unreadable to the casual observer, which provides a certain level of confidentiality. As an option, PGP can be configured to convert to radix-64 format only the signature portion of signed plaintext messages. This enables the human recipient to read the message without using PGP. PGP would still have to be used to verify the signature.

Figure 5.2 shows the relationship among the four services so far discussed. On transmission, if it is required, a signature is generated using a hash code of the uncompressed plaintext. Then the plaintext, plus signature if present, is compressed. Next, if confidentiality is required, the block (compressed plaintext or compressed signature plus plaintext) is encrypted and prepended with the public-key- encrypted symmetric encryption key. Finally, the entire block is converted to radix-64 format.

On reception, the incoming block is first converted back from radix-64 format to binary. Then, if the message is encrypted, the recipient recovers the session key and decrypts the message. The resulting block is then decompressed. If the message is signed, the recipient recovers the transmitted hash code and compares it to its own calculation of the hash code.

Segmentation and Reassembly

E-mail facilities often are restricted to a maximum message length. For example, many of the facilities accessible through the Internet impose a maximum length of 50,000 octets. Any message longer than that must be broken up into smaller segments, each of which is mailed separately.

To accommodate this restriction, PGP automatically subdivides a message that is too large into segments that are small enough to send via e-mail. The segmentation is done after all of the other processing, including the radix-64 conversion. Thus, the session key component and signature component appear only once, at the beginning of the first segment. At the receiving end, PGP must strip off all e-mail headers and reassemble the entire original block before performing the steps illustrated in Figure 5.2b.

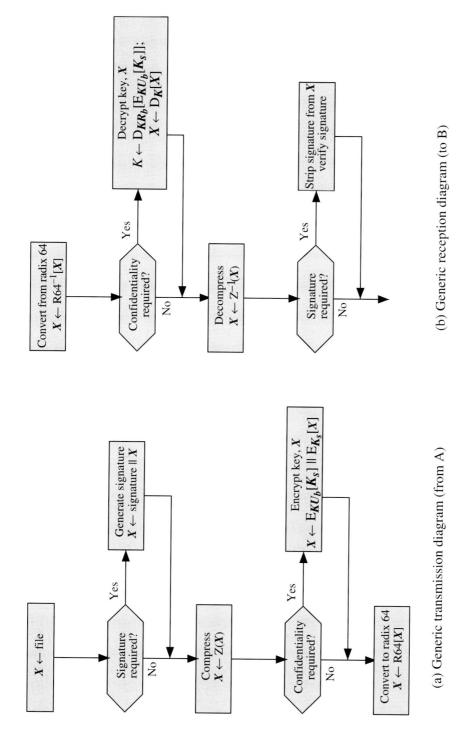

(a) Generic transmission diagram (from A)

(b) Generic reception diagram (to B)

Figure 5.2 Transmission and Reception of PGP Messages

Cryptographic Keys and Key Rings

PGP makes use of four types of keys: one-time session symmetric keys, public keys, private keys, and passphrase-based symmetric keys (explained subsequently). Three separate requirements can be identified with respect to these keys:

1. A means of generating unpredictable session keys is needed.
2. We would like to allow a user to have multiple public-key/private-key pairs. One reason is that the user may wish to change his or her key pair from time to time. When this happens, any messages in the pipeline will be constructed with an obsolete key. Furthermore, recipients will know only the old public key until an update reaches them. In addition to the need to change keys over time, a user may wish to have multiple key pairs at a given time to interact with different groups of correspondents or simply to enhance security by limiting the amount of material encrypted with any one key. The upshot of all this is that there is not a one-to-one correspondence between users and their public keys. Thus, some means is needed for identifying particular keys.
3. Each PGP entity must maintain a file of its own public/private key pairs as well as a file of public keys of correspondents.

We examine each of these requirements in turn.

Session Key Generation

Each session key is associated with a single message and is used only for the purpose of encrypting and decrypting that message. Recall that message encryption/decryption is done with a symmetric encryption algorithm. CAST-128 and IDEA use 128-bit keys; 3DES uses a 168-bit key. For the following discussion, we assume CAST-128.

Random 128-bit numbers are generated using CAST-128 itself. The input to the random number generator consists of a 128-bit key and two 64-bit blocks that are treated as plaintext to be encrypted. Using cipher feedback mode, the CAST-128 encrypter produces two 64-bit cipher text blocks, which are concatenated to form the 128-bit session key. The algorithm that is used is based on the one specified in ANSI X12.17.

The "plaintext" input to the random number generator, consisting of two 64-bit blocks, is itself derived from a stream of 128-bit randomized numbers. These numbers are based on keystroke input from the user. Both the keystroke timing and the actual keys struck are used to generate the randomized stream. Thus, if the user hits arbitrary keys at his or her normal pace, a reasonably "random" input will be generated. This random input is also combined with previous session key output from CAST-128 to form the key input to the generator. The result, given the effective scrambling of CAST-128, is to produce a sequence of session keys that is effectively unpredictable.

Appendix 5C discusses PGP random number generation techniques in more detail.

Key Identifiers

As we have discussed, an encrypted message is accompanied by an encrypted form of the session key that was used. The session key itself is encrypted with the recipient's public key. Hence, only the recipient will be able to recover the session key and therefore recover the message. If each user employed a single public/ private key pair, then the recipient would automatically know which key to use to decrypt the session key: the recipient's unique private key. However, we have stated a requirement that any given user may have multiple public/private key pairs.

How, then, does the recipient know which of its public keys was used to encrypt the session key? One simple solution would be to transmit the public key with the message. The recipient could then verify that this is indeed one of its public keys, and proceed. This scheme would work, but it is unnecessarily wasteful of space. An RSA public key may be hundreds of decimal digits in length. Another solution would be to associate an identifier with each public key that is unique at least within one user. That is, the combination of user ID and key ID would be sufficient to identify a key uniquely. Then only the much shorter key ID would need to be transmitted. This solution, however, raises a management and overhead problem: Key IDs must be assigned and stored so that both sender and recipient could map from key ID to public key. This seems unnecessarily burdensome.

The solution adopted by PGP is to assign a key ID to each public key that is, with very high probability, unique within a user ID. The key ID associated with each public key consists of its least significant 64 bits. That is, the key ID of public key KU_a is $(KU_a \bmod 2^{64})$. This is a sufficient length that the probability of duplicate key IDs is very small.

A key ID is also required for the PGP digital signature. Because a sender may use one of a number of private keys to encrypt the message digest, the recipient must know which public key is intended for use. Accordingly, the digital signature component of a message includes the 64-bit key ID of the required public key. When the message is received, the recipient verifies that the key ID is for a public key that it knows for that sender and then proceeds to verify the signature.

Now that the concept of key ID has been introduced, we can take a more detailed look at the format of a transmitted message, which is shown in Figure 5.3. A message consists of three components: the message component, a signature (optional), and a session key component (optional).

The **message component** includes the actual data to be stored or transmitted, as well as a filename and a timestamp that specifies the time of creation.

The **signature component** includes the following:

- **Timestamp:** The time at which the signature was made.
- **Message digest:** The 160-bit SHA-1 digest, encrypted with the sender's private signature key. The digest is calculated over the signature timestamp concatenated with the data portion of the message component. The inclusion of the signature timestamp in the digest assures against replay types of attacks. The exclusion of the filename and timestamp portions of the message component ensures that detached signatures are exactly the same as attached signatures

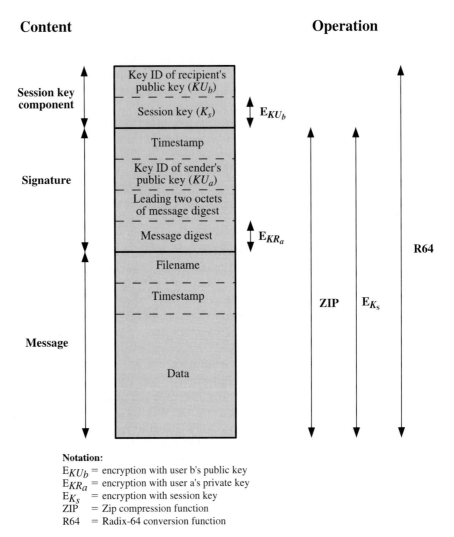

Figure 5.3 General Format of PGP Message (from A to B)

prefixed to the message. Detached signatures are calculated on a separate file that has none of the message component header fields.

- **Leading two octets of message digest:** To enable the recipient to determine if the correct public key was used to decrypt the message digest for authentication, by comparing this plaintext copy of the first two octets with the first two octets of the decrypted digest. These octets also serve as a 16-bit frame check sequence for the message.

- **Key ID of sender's public key:** Identifies the public key that should be used to decrypt the message digest and, hence, identifies the private key that was used to encrypt the message digest.

The message component and optional signature component may be compressed using ZIP and may be encrypted using a session key.

The **session key component** includes the session key and the identifier of the recipient's public key that was used by the sender to encrypt the session key.

The entire block is usually encoded with radix-64 encoding.

Key Rings

We have seen how key IDs are critical to the operation of PGP and that two key IDs are included in any PGP message that provides both confidentiality and authentication. These keys need to be stored and organized in a systematic way for efficient and effective use by all parties. The scheme used in PGP is to provide a pair of data structures at each node, one to store the public/private key pairs owned by that node and one to store the public keys of other users known at this node. These data structures are referred to, respectively, as the private-key ring and the public-key ring.

Figure 5.4 shows the general structure of a **private-key ring**. We can view the ring as a table, in which each row represents one of the public/private key pairs owned by this user. Each row contains the following entries:

- **Timestamp:** The date/time when this key pair was generated.
- **Key ID:** The least significant 64 bits of the public key for this entry.
- **Public key:** The public-key portion of the pair.
- **Private key:** The private-key portion of the pair; this field is encrypted.
- **User ID:** Typically, this will be the user's e-mail address (e.g., stallings@acm. org). However, the user may choose to associate a different name with each pair (e.g., Stallings, WStallings, WilliamStallings, etc.) or to reuse the same User ID more than once.

The private-key ring can be indexed by either User ID or Key ID; later we will see the need for both means of indexing.

Although it is intended that the private-key ring be stored only on the machine of the user that created and owns the key pairs, and that it be accessible only to that user, it makes sense to make the value of the private key as secure as possible. Accordingly, the private key itself is not stored in the key ring. Rather, this key is encrypted using CAST-128 (or IDEA or 3DES). The procedure is as follows:

1. The user selects a passphrase to be used for encrypting private keys.
2. When the system generates a new public/private key pair using RSA, it asks the user for the passphrase. Using SHA-1, a 160-bit hash code is generated from the passphrase, and the passphrase is discarded.
3. The system encrypts the private key using CAST-128 with the 128 bits of the hash code as the key. The hash code is then discarded, and the encrypted private key is stored in the private-key ring.

Subsequently, when a user accesses the private-key ring to retrieve a private key, he or she must supply the passphrase. PGP will retrieve the encrypted pri-

Private-Key Ring

Timestamp	Key ID*	Public Key	Encrypted Private Key	User ID*
• • •	• • •	• • •	• • •	• • •
T_i	$KU_i \bmod 2^{64}$	KU_i	$E_{H(P_i)}[KR_i]$	User i
• • •	• • •	• • •	• • •	• • •

Public-Key Ring

Timestamp	Key ID*	Public Key	Owner Trust	User ID*	Key Legitimacy	Signature(s)	Signature Trust(s)
• • •	• • •	• • •	• • •	• • •	• • •	• • •	• • •
T_i	$KU_i \bmod 2^{64}$	KU_i	trust_flag $_i$	User $_i$	trust_flag $_i$		
• • •	• • •	• • •	• • •	• • •	• • •	• • •	• • •

* = field used to index table

Figure 5.4 General Structure of Private- and Public-Key Rings

vate key, generate the hash code of the passphrase, and decrypt the encrypted private key using CAST-128 with the hash code.

This is a very compact and effective scheme. As in any system based on passwords, the security of this system depends on the security of the password. To avoid the temptation to write it down, the user should use a passphrase that is not easily guessed but that is easily remembered.

Figure 5.4 also shows the general structure of a **public-key ring**. This data structure is used to store public keys of other users that are known to this user. For the moment, let us ignore some fields shown in the table and describe the following fields:

- **Timestamp:** The date/time when this entry was generated.
- **Key ID:** The least significant 64 bits of the public key for this entry.
- **Public Key:** The public key for this entry.
- **User ID:** Identifies the owner of this key. Multiple user IDs may be associated with a single public key.

The public-key ring can be indexed by either User ID or Key ID; we will see the need for both means of indexing later.

We are now in a position to show how these key rings are used in message transmission and reception. For simplicity, we ignore compression and radix-64 conversion in the following discussion. First consider message transmission (Figure 5.5) and assume that the message is to be both signed and encrypted. The sending PGP entity performs the following steps:

1. Signing the message
    a. PGP retrieves the sender's private key from the private-key ring using your_userid as an index. If your_userid was not provided in the command, the first private key on the ring is retrieved.
    b. PGP prompts the user for the passphrase to recover the unencrypted private key.
    c. The signature component of the message is constructed.
2. Encrypting the message
    a. PGP generates a session key and encrypts the message.
    b. PGP retrieves the recipient's public key from the public-key ring using her_userid as an index.
    c. The session key component of the message is constructed.

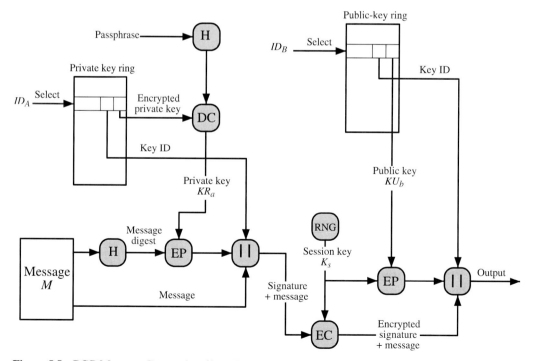

Figure 5.5 PGP Message Generation (from User A to User B; no compression or radix 64 conversion)

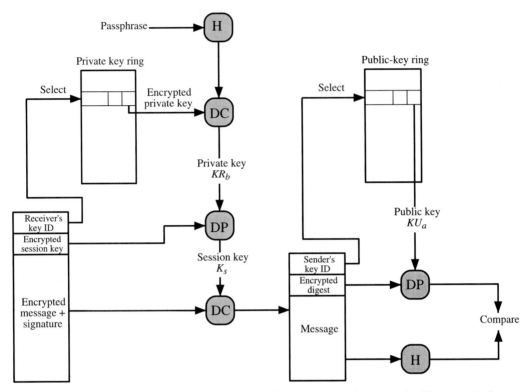

Figure 5.6 PGP Reception (from User A to User B; no compression or radix 64 conversion)

The receiving PGP entity performs the following steps (Figure 5.6):

1. Decrypting the message
   a. PGP retrieves the receiver's private key from the private-key ring, using the Key ID field in the session key component of the message as an index.
   b. PGP prompts the user for the passphrase to recover the unencrypted private key.
   c. PGP then recovers the session key and decrypts the message.
2. Authenticating the message
   a. PGP retrieves the sender's public key from the public-key ring, using the Key ID field in the signature key component of the message as an index.
   b. PGP recovers the transmitted message digest.
   c. PGP computes the message digest for the received message and compares it to the transmitted message digest to authenticate.

Public-Key Management

As can be seen from the discussion so far, PGP contains a clever, efficient, interlocking set of functions and formats to provide an effective confidentiality and authentication service. To complete the system, one final area needs to be addressed, that of public-key management. The PGP documentation captures the importance of this area:

> This whole business of protecting public keys from tampering is the single most difficult problem in practical public key applications. It is the "Achilles heel" of public key cryptography, and a lot of software complexity is tied up in solving this one problem.

PGP provides a structure for solving this problem, with several suggested options that may be used. Because PGP is intended for use in a variety of formal and informal environments, no rigid public-key management scheme is set up, such as we will see in our discussion of S/MIME later in this chapter.

Approaches to Public-Key Management

The essence of the problem is this: User A must build up a public-key ring containing the public keys of other users to interoperate with them using PGP. Suppose that A's key ring contains a public key attributed to B but that the key is, in fact, owned by C. This could happen if, for example, A got the key from a bulletin board system (BBS) that was used by B to post the public key but that has been compromised by C. The result is that two threats now exist. First, C can send messages to A and forge B's signature, so that A will accept the message as coming from B. Second, any encrypted message from A to B can be read by C.

A number of approaches are possible for minimizing the risk that a user's public-key ring contains false public keys. Suppose that A wishes to obtain a reliable public key for B. The following are some approaches that could be used:

1. Physically get the key from B. B could store her public key (KU_b) on a floppy disk and hand it to A. A could then load the key into his system from the floppy disk. This is a very secure method but has obvious practical limitations.

2. Verify a key by telephone. If A can recognize B on the phone, A could call B and ask her to dictate the key, in radix-64 format, over the phone. As a more practical alternative, B could transmit her key in an e-mail message to A. A could have PGP generate a 160-bit SHA-1 digest of the key and display it in hexadecimal format; this is referred to as the "fingerprint" of the key. A could then call B and ask her to dictate the fingerprint over the phone. If the two fingerprints match, the key is verified.

3. Obtain B's public key from a mutual trusted individual D. For this purpose, the introducer, D, creates a signed certificate. The certificate includes B's public key, the time of creation of the key, and a validity period for the key. D generates an SHA-1 digest of this certificate, encrypts it with her private key, and attaches the signature to the certificate. Because only D could have created the signature, no one else can create a false public key and pretend that it is signed by D. The signed certificate could be sent directly to A by B or D, or could be posted on a bulletin board.

4. Obtain B's public key from a trusted certifying authority. Again, a public key certificate is created and signed by the authority. A could then access the authority, providing a user name and receiving a signed certificate.

For cases 3 and 4, A would already have to have a copy of the introducer's public key and trust that this key is valid. Ultimately, it is up to A to assign a level of trust to anyone who is to act as an introducer.

The Use of Trust

Although PGP does not include any specification for establishing certifying authorities or for establishing trust, it does provide a convenient means of using trust, associating trust with public keys, and exploiting trust information.

The basic structure is as follows. Each entry in the public-key ring is a public-key certificate, as described in the preceding subsection. Associated with each such entry is a **key legitimacy field** that indicates the extent to which PGP will trust that this is a valid public key for this user; the higher the level of trust, the stronger is the binding of this user ID to this key. This field is computed by PGP. Also associated with the entry are zero or more signatures that the key ring owner has collected that sign this certificate. In turn, each signature has associated with it a **signature trust field** that indicates the degree to which this PGP user trusts the signer to certify public keys. The key legitimacy field is derived from the collection of signature trust fields in the entry. Finally, each entry defines a public key associated with a particular owner, and an **owner trust field** is included that indicates the degree to which this public key is trusted to sign other public-key certificates; this level of trust is assigned by the user. We can think of the signature trust fields as cached copies of the owner trust field from another entry.

The three fields mentioned in the previous paragraph are each contained in a structure referred to as a trust flag byte. The content of this trust flag for each of these three uses is shown in Table 5.2. Suppose that we are dealing with the public-key ring of user A. We can describe the operation of the trust processing as follows:

1. When A inserts a new public key on the public-key ring, PGP must assign a value to the trust flag that is associated with the owner of this public key. If the owner is A, and therefore this public key also appears in the private-key ring, then a value of *ultimate trust* is automatically assigned to the trust field. Otherwise, PGP asks A for his assessment of the trust to be assigned to the owner of this key, and A must enter the desired level. The user can specify that this owner is unknown, untrusted, marginally trusted, or completely trusted.

2. When the new public key is entered, one or more signatures may be attached to it. More signatures may be added later. When a signature is inserted into the entry, PGP searches the public-key ring to see if the author of this signature is among the known public-key owners. If so, the OWNERTRUST value for this owner is assigned to the SIGTRUST field for this signature. If not, an *unknown user* value is assigned.

3. The value of the key legitimacy field is calculated on the basis of the signature trust fields present in this entry. If at least one signature has a signature trust value of *ultimate*, then the key legitimacy value is set to complete. Otherwise, PGP computes a weighted sum of the trust values. A weight of $1/X$ is given to signatures that are always trusted and $1/Y$ to signatures that are usually trusted, where X and Y are user-configurable parameters. When the total of weights of the introducers of a key/UserID combination reaches 1, the binding is con-

Table 5.2 Contents of Trust Flag Byte

(a) Trust Assigned to Public-Key Owner (appears after key packet; user defined)	(b) Trust Assigned to Public Key/User ID Pair (appears after User ID packet; computed by PGP)	(c) Trust Assigned to Signature (appears after signature packet; cached copy of OWNERTRUST for this signator)
OWNERTRUST Field —undefined trust —unknown user —usually not trusted to sign other keys —usually trusted to sign other keys —always trusted to sign other keys —this key is present in secret key ring (ultimate trust) BUCKSTOP bit —set if this key appears in secret key ring	KEYLEGIT Field —unknown or undefined trust —key ownership not trusted —marginal trust in key ownership —complete trust in key ownership WARNONLY bit —set if user wants only to be warned when key that is not fully validated is used for encryption	SIGTRUST Field —undefined trust —unknown user —usually not trusted to sign other keys —usually trusted to sign other keys —always trusted to sign other keys —this key is present in secret key ring (ultimate trust) CONTIG bit —set if signature leads up a contiguous trusted cetification path back to the ultimately trusted key ring owner

sidered to be trustworthy, and the key legitimacy value is set to complete. Thus, in the absence of ultimate trust, at least X signatures that are always trusted or Y signatures that are usually trusted or some combination is needed.

Periodically, PGP processes the public-key ring to achieve consistency. In essence, this is a top-down process. For each OWNERTRUST field, PGP scans the ring for all signatures authored by that owner and updates the SIGTRUST field to equal the OWNERTRUST field. This process starts with keys for which there is ultimate trust. Then all KEYLEGIT fields are computed on the basis of the attached signatures.

Figure 5.7 provides an example of the way in which signature trust and key legitimacy are related.[1] The figure shows the structure of a public-key ring. The user has acquired a number of public keys, some directly from their owners and some from a third party such as a key server.

The node labeled "You" refers to the entry in the public-key ring corresponding to this user. This key is legitimate and the OWNERTRUST value is ultimate trust. Each other node in the key ring has an OWNERTRUST value of undefined unless some other value is assigned by the user. In this example, this user has specified that it always trusts the following users to sign other keys: D, E, F, L. This user partially trusts users A and B to sign other keys.

So the shading, or lack thereof, of the nodes in Figure 5.7 indicates the level of trust assigned by this user. The tree structure indicates which keys have been

---

[1] Figure provided to the author by Phil Zimmermann.

signed by which other users. If a key is signed by a user whose key is also in this key ring, the arrow joins the signed key to the signatory. If the key is signed by a user whose key is not present in this key ring, the arrow joins the signed key to a question mark, indicating that the signatory is unknown to this user.

Several points are illustrated in Figure 5.7:

1. Note that all keys whose owners are fully or partially trusted by this user have been signed by this user, with the exception of node L. Such a user signature is not always necessary, as the presence of node L indicates, but in practice, most users are likely to sign the keys for most owners that they trust. So, for example, even though E's key is already signed by trusted introducer F, the user chose to sign E's key directly.

2. We assume that two partially trusted signatures are sufficient to certify a key. Hence, the key for user H is deemed legitimate by PGP because it is signed by A and B, both of whom are partially trusted.

3. A key may be determined to be legitimate because it is signed by one fully trusted or two partially trusted signatories, but its user may not be trusted to sign other keys. For example, N's key is legitimate because it is signed by E, whom this user trusts, but N is not trusted to sign other keys because this user has not assigned N that trust value. Therefore, although R's key is signed by N, PGP does not consider R's key legitimate. This situation makes perfect sense. If you wish to send a private message to some individual, it is not nec-

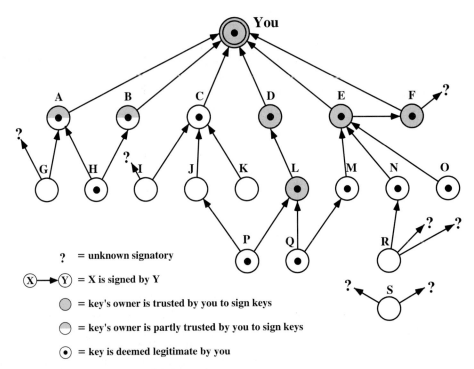

Figure 5.7 PGP Trust Model Example

essary that you trust that individual in any respect. It is only necessary that you are sure that you have the correct public key for that individual.

4. Figure 5.7 also shows an example of a detached "orphan" node S, with two unknown signatures. Such a key may have been acquired from a key server. PGP cannot assume that this key is legitimate simply because it came from a reputable server. The user must declare the key legitimate by signing it or by telling PGP that it is willing to trust fully one of the key's signatories.

A final point: Earlier it was mentioned that multiple user IDs may be associated with a single public key on the public-key ring. This could be because a person has changed names or has been introduced via signature under multiple names, indicating different e-mail addresses for the same person, for example. So we can think of a public key as the root of a tree. A public key has a number of user IDs associating with it, with a number of signatures below each user ID. The binding of a particular user ID to a key depends on the signatures associated with that user ID and that key, whereas the level of trust in this key (for use in signing other keys) is a function of all the dependent signatures.

Revoking Public Keys

A user may wish to revoke his or her current public key either because compromise is suspected or simply to avoid the use of the same key for an extended period. Note that a compromise would require that an opponent somehow had obtained a copy of your unencrypted private key or that the opponent had obtained both the private key from your private-key ring and your passphrase.

The convention for revoking a public key is for the owner to issue a key revocation certificate, signed by the owner. This certificate has the same form as a normal signature certificate but includes an indicator that the purpose of this certificate is to revoke the use of this public key. Note that the corresponding private key must be used to sign a certificate that revokes a public key. The owner should then attempt to disseminate this certificate as widely and as quickly as possible to enable potential correspondents to update their public-key rings.

Note that an opponent who has compromised the private key of an owner can also issue such a certificate. However, this would deny the opponent as well as the legitimate owner the use of the public key, and therefore it seems a much less likely threat than the malicious use of a stolen private key.

5.2 S/MIME

S/MIME (Secure/Multipurpose Internet Mail Extension) is a security enhancement to the MIME Internet e-mail format standard, based on technology from RSA Data Security. Although both PGP and S/MIME are on an IETF standards track, it appears likely that S/MIME will emerge as the industry standard for commercial and organizational use, while PGP will remain the choice for personal e-mail security for many users. S/MIME is defined in a number of documents, most importantly RFCs 2630, 2632, and 2633.

To understand S/MIME, we need first to have a general understanding of the underlying e-mail format that it uses, namely MIME. But to understand the significance of MIME, we need to go back to the traditional e-mail format standard, RFC 822, which is still in common use. Accordingly, this section first provides an introduction to these two earlier standards and then moves on to a discussion of S/MIME.

RFC 822

RFC 822 defines a format for text messages that are sent using electronic mail. It has been the standard for Internet-based text mail message and remains in common use. In the RFC 822 context, messages are viewed as having an envelope and contents. The envelope contains whatever information is needed to accomplish transmission and delivery. The contents compose the object to be delivered to the recipient. The RFC 822 standard applies only to the contents. However, the content standard includes a set of header fields that may be used by the mail system to create the envelope, and the standard is intended to facilitate the acquisition of such information by programs.

The overall structure of a message that conforms to RFC 822 is very simple. A message consists of some number of header lines (*the header*) followed by unrestricted text (*the body*). The header is separated from the body by a blank line. Put differently, a message is ASCII text, and all lines up to the first blank line are assumed to be header lines used by the user agent part of the mail system.

A header line usually consists of a keyword, followed by a colon, followed by the keyword's arguments; the format allows a long line to be broken up into several lines. The most frequently used keywords are *From*, *To*, *Subject*, and *Date*. Here is an example message:

```
Date: Tue, 16 Jan 1998 10:37:17 (EST)
From: "William Stallings" <ws@shore.net>
Subject: The Syntax in RFC 822
To: Smith@Other-host.com
Cc: Jones@Yet-Another-Host.com

Hello. This section begins the actual message body, which is
delimited from the message heading by a blank line.
```

Another field that is commonly found in RFC 822 headers is *Message-ID*. This field contains a unique identifier associated with this message.

Multipurpose Internet Mail Extensions

MIME is an extension to the RFC 822 framework that is intended to address some of the problems and limitations of the use of SMTP (Simple Mail Transfer Protocol) or some other mail transfer protocol and RFC 822 for electronic mail. [MURH98] lists the following limitations of the SMTP/822 scheme:

1. SMTP cannot transmit executable files or other binary objects. A number of schemes are in use for converting binary files into a text form that can be used

by SMTP mail systems, including the popular UNIX UUencode/UUdecode scheme. However, none of these is a standard or even a de facto standard.

2. SMTP cannot transmit text data that includes national language characters because these are represented by 8-bit codes with values of 128 decimal or higher, and SMTP is limited to 7-bit ASCII.

3. SMTP servers may reject mail message over a certain size.

4. SMTP gateways that translate between ASCII and the character code EBCDIC do not use a consistent set of mappings, resulting in translation problems.

5. SMTP gateways to X.400 electronic mail networks cannot handle nontextual data included in X.400 messages.

6. Some SMTP implementations do not adhere completely to the SMTP standards defined in RFC 821. Common problems include
   - Deletion, addition, or reordering of carriage return and linefeed
   - Truncating or wrapping lines longer than 76 characters
   - Removal of trailing white space (tab and space characters)
   - Padding of lines in a message to the same length
   - Conversion of tab characters into multiple space characters

MIME is intended to resolve these problems in a manner that is compatible with existing RFC 822 implementations. The specification is provided in RFCs 2045 through 2049.

Overview

The MIME specification includes the following elements:

1. Five new message header fields are defined, which may be included in an RFC 822 header. These fields provide information about the body of the message.

2. A number of content formats are defined, thus standardizing representations that support multimedia electronic mail.

3. Transfer encodings are defined that enable the conversion of any content format into a form that is protected from alteration by the mail system.

In this subsection, we introduce the five message header fields. The next two subsections deal with content formats and transfer encodings.

The five header fields defined in MIME are as follows:

- **MIME-Version:** Must have the parameter value 1.0. This field indicates that the message conforms to RFCs 2045 and 2046.
- **Content-Type:** Describes the data contained in the body with sufficient detail that the receiving user agent can pick an appropriate agent or mechanism to represent the data to the user or otherwise deal with the data in an appropriate manner.
- **Content-Transfer-Encoding:** Indicates the type of transformation that has been used to represent the body of the message in a way that is acceptable for mail transport.

- **Content-ID:** Used to identify MIME entities uniquely in multiple contexts.
- **Content-Description:** A text description of the object with the body; this is useful when the object is not readable (e.g., audio data).

Any or all of these fields may appear in a normal RFC 822 header. A compliant implementation must support the MIME-Version, Content-Type, and Content-Transfer-Encoding fields; the Content-ID and Content-Description fields are optional and may be ignored by the recipient implementation.

MIME Content Types

The bulk of the MIME specification is concerned with the definition of a variety of content types. This reflects the need to provide standardized ways of dealing with a wide variety of information representations in a multimedia environment.

Table 5.3 lists the content types specified in RFC 2046. There are seven different major types of content and a total of 15 subtypes. In general, a content type declares the general type of data, and the subtype specifies a particular format for that type of data.

Table 5.3   MIME Content Types

Type	Subtype	Description
Text	Plain	Unformatted text; may be ASCII or ISO 8859.
	Enriched	Provides greater format flexibility.
Multipart	Mixed	The different parts are independent but are to be transmitted together. They should be presented to the receiver in the order that they appear in the mail message.
	Parallel	Differs from Mixed only in that no order is defined for delivering the parts to the receiver.
	Alternative	The different parts are alternative versions of the same information. They are ordered in increasing faithfulness to the original, and the recipient's mail system should display the "best" version to the user.
	Digest	Similar to Mixed, but the default type/subtype of each part is message/rfc822.
Message	rfc822	The body is itself an encapsulated message that conforms to RFC 822.
	Partial	Used to allow fragmentation of large mail items, in a way that is transparent to the recipient.
	External-body	Contains a pointer to an object that exists elsewhere.
Image	jpeg	The image is in JPEG format, JFIF encoding.
	gif	The image is in GIF format.
Video	mpeg	MPEG format.
Audio	Basic	Single-channel 8-bit ISDN mu-law encoding at a sample rate of 8 kHz.
Application	PostScript	Adobe Postscript
	Octet-stream	General binary data consisting of 8-bit bytes.

For the **text type** of body, no special software is required to get the full meaning of the text, aside from support of the indicated character set. The primary subtype is *plain text*, which is simply a string of ASCII characters or ISO 8859 characters. The *enriched* subtype allows greater formatting flexibility.

The **multipart type** indicates that the body contains multiple, independent parts. The Content-Type header field includes a parameter, called boundary, that defines the delimiter between body parts. This boundary should not appear in any parts of the message. Each boundary starts on a new line and consists of two hyphens followed by the boundary value. The final boundary, which indicates the end of the last part, also has a suffix of two hyphens. Within each part, there may be an optional ordinary MIME header.

Here is a simple example of a multipart message, containing two parts both consisting of simple text (taken from RFC 2046):

```
From: Nathaniel Borenstein <nsb@bellcore.com>
To: Ned Freed <ned@innosoft.com>
Subject: Sample message
MIME-Version: 1.0
Content-type: multipart/mixed; boundary="simple boundary"

This is the preamble. It is to be ignored, though it is a handy
place for mail composers to include an explanatory note to non-
MIME conformant readers.--simple boundary

This is implicitly typed plain ASCII text. It does NOT end with a
linebreak.--simple boundary
Content-type: text/plain; charset=us-ascii

This is explicitly typed plain ASCII text. It DOES end with a
linebreak.

--simple boundary--
This is the epilogue. It is also to be ignored.
```

There are four subtypes of the multipart type, all of which have the same overall syntax. The **multipart/mixed subtype** is used when there are multiple independent body parts that need to be bundled in a particular order. For the **multipart/parallel subtype**, the order of the parts is not significant. If the recipient's system is appropriate, the multiple parts can be presented in parallel. For example, a picture or text part could be accompanied by a voice commentary that is played while the picture or text is displayed.

For the **multipart/alternative subtype**, the various parts are different representations of the same information. The following is an example:

```
From: Nathaniel Borenstein <nsb@bellcore.com>
To: Ned Freed <ned@innosoft.com>
Subject: Formatted text mail
MIME-Version: 1.0
Content-Type: multipart/alternative; boundary=boundary42
```

```
--boundary42

Content-Type: text/plain; charset=us-ascii

... plain text version of message goes here ....

--boundary42
Content-Type: text/enriched

.... RFC 1896 text/enriched version of same message goes here ...
--boundary42--
```

In this subtype, the body parts are ordered in terms of increasing preference. For this example, if the recipient system is capable of displaying the message in the text/enriched format, this is done; otherwise, the plain text format is used.

The **multipart/digest subtype** is used when each of the body parts is interpreted as an RFC 822 message with headers. This subtype enables the construction of a message whose parts are individual messages. For example, the moderator of a group might collect e-mail messages from participants, bundle these messages, and send them out in one encapsulating MIME message.

The **message type** provides a number of important capabilities in MIME. The **message/rfc822 subtype** indicates that the body is an entire message, including header and body. Despite the name of this subtype, the encapsulated message may be not only a simple RFC 822 message, but any MIME message.

The **message/partial subtype** enables fragmentation of a large message into a number of parts, which must be reassembled at the destination. For this subtype, three parameters are specified in the Content-Type: Message/Partial field: an *id* common to all fragments of the same message, a *sequence number* unique to each fragment, and the *total* number of fragments.

The **message/external-body subtype** indicates that the actual data to be conveyed in this message are not contained in the body. Instead, the body contains the information needed to access the data. As with the other message types, the message/external-body subtype has an outer header and an encapsulated message with its own header. The only necessary field in the outer header is the Content-Type field, which identifies this as a message/external-body subtype. The inner header is the message header for the encapsulated message. The Content-Type field in the outer header must include an access-type parameter, which indicates the method of access, such as FTP (file transfer protocol).

The **application type** refers to other kinds of data, typically either uninterpreted binary data or information to be processed by a mail-based application.

MIME Transfer Encodings

The other major component of the MIME specification, in addition to content type specification, is a definition of transfer encodings for message bodies. The objective is to provide reliable delivery across the largest range of environments.

The MIME standard defines two methods of encoding data. The Content-Transfer-Encoding field can actually take on six values, as listed in Table 5.4. How-

Table 5.4 MIME Transfer Encodings

7bit	The data are all represented by short lines of ASCII characters.
8bit	The lines are short, but there may be non-ASCII characters (octets with the high-order bit set).
binary	Not only may non-ASCII characters be present, but the lines are not necessarily short enough for SMTP transport.
quoted-printable	Encodes the data in such a way that if the data being encoded are mostly ASCII text, the encoded form of the data remains largely recognizable by humans.
base64	Encodes data by mapping 6-bit blocks of input to 8-bit blocks of output, all of which are printable ASCII characters.
x-token	A named nonstandard encoding.

ever, three of these values (7bit, 8bit, and binary) indicate that no encoding has been done but provide some information about the nature of the data. For SMTP transfer, it is safe to use the 7bit form. The 8bit and binary forms may be usable in other mail transport contexts. Another Content-Transfer-Encoding value is x-token, which indicates that some other encoding scheme is used, for which a name is to be supplied. This could be a vendor-specific or application-specific scheme. The two actual encoding schemes defined are quoted-printable and base64. Two schemes are defined to provide a choice between a transfer technique that is essentially human readable and one that is safe for all types of data in a way that is reasonably compact.

The **quoted-printable** transfer encoding is useful when the data consists largely of octets that correspond to printable ASCII characters. In essence, it represents nonsafe characters by the hexadecimal representation of their code and introduces reversible (soft) line breaks to limit message lines to 76 characters.

The **base64 transfer encoding**, also known as radix-64 encoding, is a common one for encoding arbitrary binary data in such a way as to be invulnerable to the processing by mail transport programs. It is also used in PGP and is described in Appendix 5B.

A Multipart Example

Figure 5.8, taken from RFC 2045, is the outline of a complex multipart message. The message has five parts to be displayed serially: two introductory plain text parts, an embedded multipart message, a richtext part, and a closing encapsulated text message in a non-ASCII character set. The embedded multipart message has two parts to be displayed in parallel, a picture and an audio fragment.

Canonical Form

An important concept in MIME and S/MIME is that of canonical form. Canonical form is a format, appropriate to the content type, that is standardized for use between systems. This is in contrast to native form, which is a format that may be peculiar to a particular system. Table 5.5, from RFC 2049, should help clarify this matter.

MIME-Version: 1.0
From: Nathaniel Borenstein <nsb@bellcore.com>
To: Ned Freed <ned@innosoft.com>
Subject: A multipart example
Content-Type: multipart/mixed;
    boundary=unique-boundary-1

This is the preamble area of a multipart message. Mail readers that understand multipart format should ignore this preamble. If you are reading this text, you might want to consider changing to a mail reader that understands how to properly display multipart messages.

--unique-boundary-1

    ...Some text appears here...
[Note that the preceding blank line means no header fields were given and this is text, with charset US ASCII. It could have been done with explicit typing as in the next part.]

--unique-boundary-1
Content-type: text/plain; charset=US-ASCII

This could have been part of the previous part, but illustrates explicit versus implicit typing of body parts.

--unique-boundary-1
Content-Type: multipart/parallel;   boundary=unique-boundary-2

--unique-boundary-2
Content-Type: audio/basic
Content-Transfer-Encoding: base64

    ... base64-encoded 8000 Hz single-channel mu-law-format audio data goes here....

--unique-boundary-2
Content-Type: image/jpeg
Content-Transfer-Encoding: base64

    ... base64-encoded image data goes here.,.,

--unique-boundary-2--

--unique-boundary-1
Content-type: text/enriched

This is <bold><italic>richtext.</italic></bold> <smaller>as defined in RFC 1896</smaller>

Isn't it <bigger><bigger>cool?</bigger></bigger>

--unique-boundary-1
Content-Type: message/rfc822

From: (mailbox in US-ASCII)
To: (address in US-ASCII)
Subject: (subject in US-ASCII)
Content-Type: Text/plain; charset=ISO-8859-1
Content-Transfer-Encoding: Quoted-printable

    ... Additional text in ISO-8859-1 goes here ...

--unique-boundary-1--

Figure 5.8   Example MIME Message Structure

Table 5.5 Native and Canonical Form

Native Form	The body to be transmitted is created in the system's native format. The native character set is used and, where appropriate, local end-of-line conventions are used as well. The body may be a UNIX-style text file, or a Sun raster image, or a VMS indexed file, or audio data in a system-dependent format stored only in memory, or anything else that corresponds to the local model for the representation of some form of information. Fundamentally, the data is created in the "native" form that corresponds to the type specified by the media type.
Canonical Form	The entire body, including "out-of-band" information such as record lengths and possibly file attribute information, is converted to a universal canonical form. The specific media type of the body as well as its associated attributes dictate the nature of the canonical form that is used. Conversion to the proper canonical form may involve character set conversion, transformation of audio data, compression, or various other operations specific to the various media types. If character set conversion is involved, however, care must be taken to understand the semantics of the media type, which may have strong implications for any character set conversion (e.g., with regard to syntactically meaningful characters in a text subtype other than "plain").

S/MIME Functionality

In terms of general functionality, S/MIME is very similar to PGP. Both offer the ability to sign and/or encrypt messages. In this subsection, we briefly summarize S/MIME capability. We then look in more detail at this capability by examining message formats and message preparation.

Functions

S/MIME provides the following functions:

- **Enveloped data:** This consists of encrypted content of any type and encrypted-content encryption keys for one or more recipients.
- **Signed data:** A digital signature is formed by taking the message digest of the content to be signed and then encrypting that with the private key of the signer. The content plus signature are then encoded using base64 encoding. A signed data message can only be viewed by a recipient with S/MIME capability.
- **Clear-signed data:** As with signed data, a digital signature of the content is formed. However, in this case, only the digital signature is encoded using base64. As a result, recipients without S/MIME capability can view the message content, although they cannot verify the signature.
- **Signed and enveloped data:** Signed-only and encrypted-only entities may be nested, so that encrypted data may be signed and signed data or clear-signed data may be encrypted.

Cryptographic Algorithms

Table 5.6 summarizes the cryptographic algorithms used in S/MIME. S/MIME uses the following terminology, taken from RFC 2119 to specify the requirement level:

Table 5.6 Cryptographic Algorithms Used in S/MIME

Function	Requirement
Create a message digest to be used in forming a digital signature.	MUST support SHA-1. Receiver SHOULD support MD5 for backward compatibility.
Encrypt message digest to form digital signature.	Sending and receiving agents MUST support DSS. Sending agents SHOULD support RSA encryption. Receiving agents SHOULD support verification of RSA signatures with key sizes 512 bits to 1024 bits.
Encrypt session key for transmission with message.	Sending and receiving agents MUST support Diffie-Hellman. Sending agent SHOULD support RSA encryption with key sizes 512 bits to 1024 bits. Receiving agent SHOULD support RSA decryption.
Encrypt message for transmission with one-time session key.	Sending agents SHOULD support encryption with tripleDES and RC2/40. Receiving agents MUST support decryption using tripleDES and SHOULD support decryption with RC2/40.

- **MUST:** The definition is an absolute requirement of the specification. An implementation must include this feature or function to be in conformance with the specification.
- **SHOULD:** There may exist valid reasons in particular circumstances to ignore this feature or function, but it is recommended that an implementation include the feature or function.

S/MIME incorporates three public-key algorithms. The Digital Signature Standard (DSS) mentioned in Chapter 3 is the preferred algorithm for digital signature. S/MIME lists Diffie-Hellman as the preferred algorithm for encrypting session keys; in fact, S/MIME uses a variant of Diffie-Hellman that does provide encryption/decryption, known as ElGamal. As an alternative, RSA, described in Chapter 3, can be used for both signatures and session key encryption. These are the same algorithms used in PGP and provide a high level of security. For the hash function used to create the digital signature, the specification requires the 160-bit SHA-1 but recommends receiver support for the 128-bit MD5 for backward compatibility with older versions of S/MIME. As we discussed in Chapter 3, there is justifiable concern about the security of MD5, so SHA-1 is clearly the preferred alternative.

For message encryption, three-key triple DES (tripleDES) is recommended, but compliant implementations must support 40-bit RC2. The latter is a weak encryption algorithm but allows compliance with U.S. export controls.

The S/MIME specification includes a discussion of the procedure for deciding which content encryption algorithm to use. In essence, a sending agent has two decisions to make. First, the sending agent must determine if the receiving agent is capable of decrypting using a given encryption algorithm. Second, if the receiving agent is only capable of accepting weakly encrypted content, the sending agent must decide if it is acceptable to send using weak encryption. To support this decision process, a sending agent may announce its decrypting capabilities in order of preference any message that it sends out. A receiving agent may store that information for future use.

The following rules, in the following order, should be followed by a sending agent:

1. If the sending agent has a list of preferred decrypting capabilities from an intended recipient, it SHOULD choose the first (highest preference) capability on the list that it is capable of using.

2. If the sending agent has no such list of capabilities from an intended recipient but has received one or more messages from the recipient, then the outgoing message SHOULD use the same encryption algorithm as was used on the last signed and encrypted message received from that intended recipient.

3. If the sending agent has no knowledge about the decryption capabilities of the intended recipient and is willing to risk that the recipient may not be able to decrypt the message, then the sending agent SHOULD use tripleDES.

4. If the sending agent has no knowledge about the decryption capabilities of the intended recipient and is not willing to risk that the recipient may not be able to decrypt the message, then the sending agent MUST use RC2/40.

If a message is to be sent to multiple recipients and a common encryption algorithm cannot be selected for all, then the sending agent will need to send two messages. However, in that case, it is important to note that the security of the message is made vulnerable by the transmission of one copy with lower security.

S/MIME Messages

S/MIME makes use of a number of new MIME content types, which are shown in Table 5.7. All of the new application types use the designation PKCS. This refers to a set of public-key cryptography specifications issued by RSA Laboratories and made available for the S/MIME effort.

Table 5.7 S/MIME Content Types

Type	Subtype	smime Parameter	Description
Multipart	Signed		A clear-signed message in two parts: One is the message and the other is the signature.
Application	pkcs7-mime	signedData	A signed S/MIME entity.
	pkcs7-mime	envelopedData	An encrypted S/MIME entity.
	pkcs7-mime	degenerate signedData	An entity containing only public-key certificates.
	pkcs7-signature	—	The content type of the signature subpart of a multipart/signed message.
	pkcs10-mime	—	A certificate registration request message.

We examine each of these in turn after first looking at the general procedures for S/MIME message preparation.

Securing a MIME Entity

S/MIME secures a MIME entity with a signature, encryption, or both. A MIME entity may be an entire message (except for the RFC 822 headers), or if the MIME content type is multipart, then a MIME entity is one or more of the subparts of the message. The MIME entity is prepared according to the normal rules for MIME message preparation. Then the MIME entity plus some security-related data, such as algorithm identifiers and certificates, are processed by S/MIME to produce what is known as a PKCS object. A PKCS object is then treated as message content and wrapped in MIME (provided with appropriate MIME headers). This process should become clear as we look at specific objects and provide examples.

In all cases, the message to be sent is converted to canonical form. In particular, for a given type and subtype, the appropriate canonical form is used for the message content. For a multipart message, the appropriate canonical form is used for each subpart.

The use of transfer encoding requires special attention. For most cases, the result of applying the security algorithm will be to produce an object that is partially or totally represented in arbitrary binary data. This will then be wrapped in an outer MIME message and transfer encoding can be applied at that point, typically base64. However, in the case of a multipart signed message, described in more detail later, the message content in one of the subparts is unchanged by the security process. Unless that content is 7bit, it should be transfer encoded using base64 or quoted-printable, so that there is no danger of altering the content to which the signature was applied.

We now look at each of the S/MIME content types.

EnvelopedData

An application/pkcs7-mime subtype is used for one of four categories of S/MIME processing, each with a unique smime-type parameter. In all cases, the resulting entity, referred to as an *object*, is represented in a form known as Basic Encoding Rules (BER), which is defined in ITU-T Recommendation X.209. The BER format consists of arbitrary octet strings and is therefore binary data. Such an object should be transfer encoded with base64 in the outer MIME message. We first look at envelopedData.

The steps for preparing an envelopedData MIME entity are as follows:

1. Generate a pseudorandom session key for a particular symmetric encryption algorithm (RC2/40 or tripleDES).
2. For each recipient, encrypt the session key with the recipient's public RSA key.
3. For each recipient, prepare a block known as RecipientInfo that contains an identifier of the recipient's public-key certificate,[2] an identifier of the algorithm used to encrypt the session key, and the encrypted session key.

---

[2]This is an X.509 certificate, discussed later in this section.

4. Encrypt the message content with the session key.

The RecipientInfo blocks followed by the encrypted content constitute the envelopedData. This information is then encoded into base64. A sample message (excluding the RFC 822 headers) is the following:

```
Content-Type: application/pkcs7-mime; smime-type=enveloped-data;
     name=smime.p7m
Content-Transfer-Encoding: base64
Content-Disposition: attachment; filename=smime.p7m

rfvbnj756tbBghyHhHUujhJhjH77n8HHGT9HG4VQpfyF467GhIGfHfYT6
7n8HHGghyHhHUujhJh4VQpfyF467GhIGfHfYGTrfvbnjT6jH7756tbB9H
f8HHGTrfvhJhjH776tbB9HG4VQbnj7567GhIGfHfYT6ghyHhHUujpfyF4
0GhIGfHfQbnj756YT64V
```

To recover the encrypted message, the recipient first strips off the base64 encoding. Then the recipient's private key is used to recover the session key. Finally, the message content is decrypted with the session key.

SignedData

The signedData smime-type can actually be used with one or more signers. For clarity, we confine our description to the case of a single digital signature. The steps for preparing a signedData MIME entity are as follows:

1. Select a message digest algorithm (SHA or MD5).
2. Compute the message digest, or hash function, of the content to be signed.
3. Encrypt the message digest with the signer's private key.
4. Prepare a block known as SignerInfo that contains the signer's public-key certificate, an identifier of the message digest algorithm, an identifier of the algorithm used to encrypt the message digest, and the encrypted message digest.

The signedData entity consists of a series of blocks, including a message digest algorithm identifier, the message being signed, and SignerInfo. The signedData entity may also include a set of public-key certificates sufficient to constitute a chain from a recognized root or top-level certification authority to the signer. This information is then encoded into base64. A sample message (excluding the RFC 822 headers) is the following:

```
Content-Type: application/pkcs7-mime; smime-type=signed-data;
     name=smime.p7m
Content-Transfer-Encoding: base64
Content-Disposition: attachment; filename=smime.p7m

567GhIGfHfYT6ghyHhHUujpfyF4f8HHGTrfvhJhjH776tbB9HG4VQbnj7
77n8HHGT9HG4VQpfyF467GhIGfHfYT6rfvbnj756tbBghyHhHUujhJhjH
HUujhJh4VQpfyF467GhIGfHfYGTrfvbnjT6jH7756tbB9H7n8HHGghyHh
6YT64V0GhIGfHfQbnj75
```

To recover the signed message and verify the signature, the recipient first strips off the base64 encoding. Then the signer's public key is used to decrypt the message digest. The recipient independently computes the message digest and compares it to the decrypted message digest to verify the signature.

Clear Signing

Clear signing is achieved using the multipart content type with a signed subtype. As was mentioned, this signing process does not involve transforming the message to be signed, so that the message is sent "in the clear." Thus, recipients with MIME capability but not S/MIME capability are able to read the incoming message.

A multipart/signed message has two parts. The first part can be any MIME type but must be prepared so that it will not be altered during transfer from source to destination. This means that if the first part is not 7bit, then it needs to be encoded using base64 or quoted-printable. Then this part is processed in the same manner as signedData, but in this case an object with signedData format is created that has an empty message content field. This object is a detached signature. It is then transfer encoded using base64 to become the second part of the multipart/signed message. This second part has a MIME content type of application and a subtype of pkcs7-signature. Here is a sample message:

```
Content-Type: multipart/signed;
    protocol="application/pkcs7-signature";
    micalg=sha1; boundary=boundary42


--boundary42
Content-Type: text/plain

This is a clear-signed message.

--boundary42
Content-Type: application/pkcs7-signature; name=smime.p7s
Content-Transfer-Encoding: base64
Content-Disposition: attachment; filename=smime.p7s

ghyHhHUujhJhjH77n8HHGTrfvbnj756tbB9HG4VQpfyF467GhIGfHfYT6
4VQpfyF467GhIGfHfYT6jH77n8HHGghyHhHUujhJh756tbB9HGTrfvbnj
n8HHGTrfvhJhjH776tbB9HG4VQbnj7567GhIGfHfYT6ghyHhHUujpfyF4
7GhIGfHfYT64VQbnj756
--boundary42--
```

The protocol parameter indicates that this is a two-part clear-signed entity. The micalg parameter indicates the type of message digest used. The receiver can verify the signature by taking the message digest of the first part and comparing this to the message digest recovered from the signature in the second part.

Registration Request

Typically, an application or user will apply to a certification authority for a public-key certificate. The application/pkcs10 S/MIME entity is used to transfer a certification request. The certification request includes certificationRequestInfo block, followed by an identifier of the public-key encryption algorithm, followed by the signature of the certificationRequestInfo block, made using the sender's private key. The certificationRequestInfo block includes a name of the certificate subject (the entity whose public key is to be certified) and a bit-string representation of the user's public key.

Certificates-Only Message

A message containing only certificates or a certificate revocation list (CRL) can be sent in response to a registration request. The message is an application/pkcs7-mime type/subtype with an smime-type parameter of degenerate. The steps involved are the same as those for creating a signedData message, except that there is no message content and the signerInfo field is empty.

S/MIME Certificate Processing

S/MIME uses public-key certificates that conform to version 3 of X.509 (see Chapter 4). The key-management scheme used by S/MIME is in some ways a hybrid between a strict X.509 certification hierarchy and PGP's web of trust. As with the PGP model, S/MIME managers and/or users must configure each client with a list of trusted keys and with certificate revocation lists. That is, the responsibility is local for maintaining the certificates needed to verify incoming signatures and to encrypt outgoing messages. On the other hand, the certificates are signed by certification authorities.

User Agent Role

An S/MIME user has several key-management functions to perform:

- **Key generation:** The user of some related administrative utility (e.g., one associated with LAN management) MUST be capable of generating separate Diffie-Hellman and DSS key pairs and SHOULD be capable of generating RSA key pairs. Each key pair MUST be generated from a good source of nondeterministic random input and be protected in a secure fashion. A user agent SHOULD generate RSA key pairs with a length in the range of 768 to 1024 bits and MUST NOT generate a length of less than 512 bits.

- **Registration:** A user's public key must be registered with a certification authority in order to receive an X.509 public-key certificate.

- **Certificate storage and retrieval:** A user requires access to a local list of certificates in order to verify incoming signatures and to encrypt outgoing messages. Such a list could be maintained by the user or by some local administrative entity on behalf of a number of users.

VeriSign Certificates

There are several companies that provide certification authority (CA) services. For example, Nortel has designed an enterprise CA solution and can provide S/MIME support within an organization. There are a number of Internet-based CAs, including VeriSign, GTE, and the U.S. Postal Service. Of these, the most widely used is the VeriSign CA service, a brief description of which we now provide.

VeriSign provides a CA service that is intended to be compatible with S/MIME and a variety of other applications. VeriSign issues X.509 certificates with the product name VeriSign Digital ID. As of early 1998, over 35,000 commercial Web sites were using VeriSign Server Digital IDs, and over a million consumer Digital IDs had been issued to users of Netscape and Microsoft browsers.

The information contained in a Digital ID depends on the type of Digital ID and its use. At a minimum, each Digital ID contains the

- Owner's public key
- Owner's name or alias
- Expiration date of the Digital ID
- Serial number of the Digital ID
- Name of the certification authority that issued the Digital ID
- Digital signature of the certification authority that issued the Digital ID

Digital IDs can also contain other user-supplied information, including

- Address
- E-mail address
- Basic registration information (country, zip code, age, and gender)

VeriSign provides three levels, or classes, of security for public-key certificates, as summarized in Table 5.8. A user requests a certificate online at VeriSign's Web site or other participating Web sites. Class 1 and Class 2 requests are processed online, and in most cases take only a few seconds to approve. Briefly, the following procedures are used:

- For Class 1 Digital IDs, VeriSign confirms the user's e-mail address by sending a PIN and Digital ID pick-up information to the e-mail address provided in the application.
- For Class 2 Digital IDs, VeriSign verifies the information in the application through an automated comparison with a consumer database in addition to performing all of the checking associated with a Class 1 Digital ID. Finally, confirmation is sent to the specified postal address alerting the user that a Digital ID has been issued in his or her name.
- For Class 3 Digital IDs, VeriSign requires a higher level of identity assurance. An individual must prove his or her identity by providing notarized credentials or applying in person.

Enhanced Security Services

As of this writing, three enhanced security services have been proposed in an Internet draft. The details of these may change, and additional services may be added. The three services are as follows:

- **Signed receipts:** A signed receipt may be requested in a SignedData object. Returning a signed receipt provides proof of delivery to the originator of a

Table 5.8 VeriSign Public-Key Certificate Classes

	Summary of Confirmation of Identity	IA Private-Key Protection	Certificate Applicant and Subscriber Private Key Protection	Applications Implemented or Contemplated by Users
Class 1	Automated unambiguous name and e-mail address search	PCA: trustworthy hardware; CA: trustworthy software or trustworthy hardware	Encryption software (PIN protected) recommended but not required	Web browsing and certain e-mail usage
Class 2	Same as Class 1, plus automated enrollment information check plus automated address check	PCA and CA: trustworthy hardware	Encryption software (PIN protected) required	Individual and intra- and intercompany e-mail, on-line subscriptions, password replace-ment, and software validation
Class 3	Same as Class 1, plus personal presence and ID documents plus Class 2 automated ID check for individuals; business records (or filings) for organizations	PCA and CA: trustworthy hardware	Encryption software (PIN protected) required; hardware token recommended but not required	E-banking, corp. database access, personal banking, membership-based on-line services, content integrity services, e-commerce server, software validation; authentica-tion of LRAAs; and strong encryption for certain servers

IA: Issuing Authority
CA: Certification Authority
PCA: VeriSign Public Primary Certification Authority
PIN: Personal Identification Number
LRAA: Local Registration Authority Administrator

message and allows the originator to demonstrate to a third party that the recipient received the message. In essence, the recipient signs the entire orig-inal message plus original (sender's) signature and appends the new signature to form a new S/MIME message.

- **Security labels:** A security label may be included in the authenticated attrib-utes of a SignedData object. A security label is a set of security information regarding the sensitivity of the content that is protected by S/MIME encapsu-lation. The labels may be used for access control, by indicating which users are permitted access to an object. Other uses include priority (secret, confidential, restricted, and so on) or role based, describing which kind of people can see the information (e.g., patient's health-care team, medical billing agents, etc.).
- **Secure mailing lists:** When a user sends a message to multiple recipients, a cer-tain amount of per-recipient processing is required, including the use of each

recipient's public key. The user can be relieved of this work by employing the services of an S/MIME Mail List Agent (MLA). An MLA can take a single incoming message, perform the recipient-specific encryption for each recipient, and forward the message. The originator of a message need only send the message to the MLA, with encryption performed using the MLA's public key.

5.3 RECOMMENDED WEB SITES

Recommended Web sites:

- **PGP Home Page:** PGP Web site by Network Associates, the leading PGP commercial vendor.
- **MIT Distribution Site for PGP:** Leading distributor of freeware PGP. Contains FAQ, other information, and links to other PGP sites.
- **S/MIME Charter:** Latest RFCs and internet drafts for S/MIME.
- **S/MIME Central:** RSA Inc.'s Web site for S/MIME. Includes FAQ and other useful information.

5.4 KEY TERMS, REVIEW QUESTIONS, AND PROBLEMS

Key Terms

detached signature	Pretty Good Privacy (PGP)	S/MIME
electronic mail	radix 64	trust
Multipurpose Internet Mail Extensions (MIME)	session key	ZIP

Review Questions

5.1 What are the five principal services provided by PGP?
5.2 What is the utility of a detached signature?
5.3 Why does PGP generate a signature before applying compression?
5.4 What is R64 conversion?
5.5 Why is R64 conversion useful for an e-mail application?
5.6 Why is the segmentation and reassembly function in PGP needed?
5.7 How does PGP use the concept of trust?
5.8 What is RFC 822?
5.9 What is MIME?
5.10 What is S/MIME?

Problems

5.1 PGP makes use of the cipher feedback (CFB) mode of CAST-128, whereas most symmetric encryption applications (other than key encryption) use the cipher block chaining (CBC) mode. We have

$$\text{CBC: } C_i = E_K[C_{i-1} \oplus P_i]; \qquad P_i = C_{i-1} \oplus D_K[C_i]$$
$$\text{CFB: } C_i = P_i \oplus E_K[C_{i-1}]; \qquad P_i = C_i \oplus E_K[C_{i-1}]$$

These two appear to provide equal security. Suggest a reason why PGP uses the CFB mode.

5.2 The first 16 bits of the message digest in a PGP signature are translated in the clear.

a. To what extent does this compromise the security of the hash algorithm?

b. To what extent does it in fact perform its intended function, namely, to help determine if the correct RSA key was used to decrypt the digest?

5.3 In Figure 5.4, each entry in the public-key ring contains an owner trust field that indicates the degree of trust associated with this public-key owner. Why is that not enough? That is, if this owner is trusted and this is supposed to be the owner's public key, why is not that trust enough to permit PGP to use this public key?

5.4 Consider radix-64 conversion as a form of encryption. In this case, there is no key. But suppose that an opponent knew only that some form of substitution algorithm was being used to encrypt English text. How effective would this algorithm be against cryptanalysis?

5.5 Phil Zimmermann chose IDEA, three-key triple DES, and CAST-128 as symmetric encryption algorithms for PGP. Give reasons why each of the following symmetric encryption algorithms described in this book is suitable or unsuitable for PGP: DES, two-key triple DES, Blowfish, and RC5.

APPENDIX 5A   DATA COMPRESSION USING ZIP

PGP makes use of a compression package called ZIP, written by Jean-lup Gailly, Mark Adler, and Richard Wales. ZIP is a freeware package written in C that runs as a utility on UNIX and some other systems. ZIP is functionally equivalent to PKZIP, a widely available shareware package for Windows systems developed by PKWARE, Inc. The zip algorithm is perhaps the most commonly used cross-platform compression technique; freeware and shareware versions are available for Macintosh and other systems as well as Windows and UNIX systems.

Zip and similar algorithms stem from research by Jacob Ziv and Abraham Lempel. In 1977, they described a technique based on a sliding window buffer that holds the most recently processed text [ZIV77]. This algorithm is generally referred to as LZ77. A version of this algorithm is used in the zip compression scheme (PKZIP, gzip, zipit, etc.).

LZ77 and its variants exploit the fact that words and phrases within a text stream (image patterns in the case of GIF) are likely to be repeated. When a repetition occurs, the repeated sequence can be replaced by a short code. The compression program scans for such repetitions and develops codes on the fly to replace the repeated sequence. Over time, codes are reused to capture new sequences. The algorithm must be defined in such a way that the decompression program is able to deduce the current mapping between codes and sequences of source data.

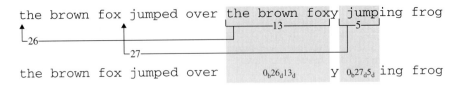

Figure 5.9 Example of LZ77 Scheme

Before looking at the details of LZ77, let us look at a simple example.[3] Consider the nonsense phrase

```
the brown fox jumped over the brown foxy jumping frog
```

which is 53 octets = 424 bits long. The algorithm processes this text from left to right. Initially, each character is mapped into a 9-bit pattern consisting of a binary 1 followed by the 8-bit ASCII representation of the character. As the processing proceeds, the algorithm looks for repeated sequences. When a repetition is encountered, the algorithm continues scanning until the repetition ends. In other words, each time a repetition occurs, the algorithm includes as many characters as possible. The first such sequence encountered is **the brown fox**. This sequence is replaced by a pointer to the prior sequence and the length of the sequence. In this case the prior sequence of **the brown fox** occurs 26 character positions before and the length of the sequence is 13 characters. For this example, assume two options for encoding; an 8-bit pointer and a 4-bit length, or a 12-bit pointer and a 6-bit length; a 2-bit header indicates which option is chosen, with 00 indicating the first option and 01 the second option. Thus, the second occurrence of **the brown fox** is encoded as $<00_b><26_d><13_d>$, or 00 00011010 1101.

The remaining parts of the compressed message are the letter **y**; the sequence $<00_b><27_d><5_d>$, which replaces the sequence consisting of the space character followed by **jump**; and the character sequence **ing frog**.

Figure 5.9 illustrates the compression mapping. The compressed message consists of 35 9-bit characters and two codes, for a total of $35 \times 9 + 2 \times 14 = 343$ bits. This compares with 424 bits in the uncompressed message for a compression ratio of 1.24.

Compression Algorithm

The compression algorithm for LZ77 and its variants makes use of two buffers. A **sliding history buffer** contains the last N characters of source that have been processed, and a **look-ahead buffer** contains the next L characters to be processed (Figure 5.10a). The algorithm attempts to match two or more characters from the beginning of the look-ahead buffer to a string in the sliding history buffer. If no match is found, the first character in the look-ahead buffer is output as a 9-bit

---

[3]Based on an example in [WEIS93].

character and is also shifted into the sliding window, with the oldest character in the sliding window shifted out. If a match is found, the algorithm continues to scan for the longest match. Then the matched string is output as a triplet (indicator, pointer, length). For a K-character string, the K oldest characters in the sliding window are shifted out, and the K characters of the encoded string are shifted into the window.

Figure 5.10b shows the operation of this scheme on our example sequence. The illustration assumes a 39-character sliding window and a 13-character look-ahead buffer. In the upper part of the example, the first 40 characters have been processed and the uncompressed version of the most recent 39 of these characters is in the sliding window. The remaining source is in the look-ahead window. The compression algorithm determines the next match, shifts 5 characters from the look-ahead buffer into the sliding window, and outputs the code for this string. The state of the buffer after these operations is shown in the lower part of the example.

While LZ77 is effective and does adapt to the nature of the current input, it has some drawbacks. The algorithm uses a finite window to look for matches in previous text. For a very long block of text, compared to the size of the window, many potential matches are eliminated. The window size can be increased, but this imposes two penalties: (1) The processing time of the algorithm increases because it must perform a string comparison against the look-ahead buffer for every position in the sliding window, and (2) the <pointer> field must be larger to accommodate the longer jumps.

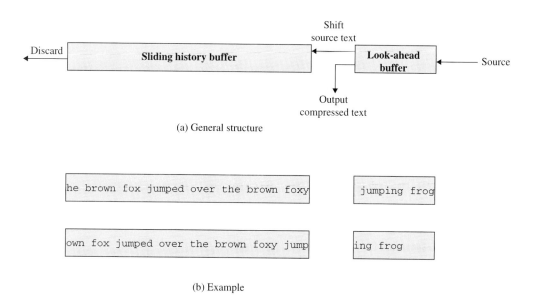

(a) General structure

(b) Example

Figure 5.10   LZ77 Scheme

Decompression Algorithm

Decompression of LZ77-compressed text is simple. The decompression algorithm must save the last N characters of decompressed output. When an encoded string is encountered, the decompression algorithm uses the <pointer> and <length> fields to replace the code with the actual text string.

APPENDIX 5B   RADIX-64 CONVERSION

Both PGP and S/MIME make use of an encoding technique referred to as radix-64 conversion. This technique maps arbitrary binary input into printable character output. The form of encoding has the following relevant characteristics:

1. The range of the function is a character set that is universally representable at all sites, not a specific binary encoding of that character set. Thus, the characters themselves can be encoded into whatever form is needed by a specific system. For example, the character "E" is represented in an ASCII-based system as hexadecimal 45 and in an EBCDIC-based system as hexadecimal C5.
2. The character set consists of 65 printable characters, one of which is used for padding. With $2^6 = 64$ available characters, each character can be used to represent 6 bits of input.
3. No control characters are included in the set. Thus, a message encoded in radix 64 can traverse mail-handling systems that scan the data stream for control characters.
4. The hyphen character ("-") is not used. This character has significance in the RFC 822 format and should therefore be avoided.

Table 5.9   Radix-64 Encoding

6-Bit value	Character encoding	6-Bit value	Character encoding	6-Bit value	Character encoding	6-Bit value	Character encoding
0	A	16	Q	32	g	48	w
1	B	17	R	33	h	49	x
2	C	18	S	34	i	50	y
3	D	19	T	35	j	51	z
4	E	20	U	36	k	52	0
5	F	21	V	37	l	53	1
6	G	22	W	38	m	54	2
7	H	23	X	39	n	55	3
8	I	24	Y	40	o	56	4
9	J	25	Z	41	p	57	5
10	K	26	a	42	q	58	6
11	L	27	b	43	r	59	7
12	M	28	c	44	s	60	8
13	N	29	d	45	t	61	9
14	O	30	e	46	u	62	+
15	P	31	f	47	v	63	/
						(pad)	=

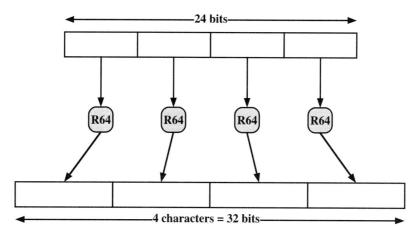

Figure 5.11 Printable Encoding of Binary Data into Radix-64 Format

Table 5.9 shows the mapping of 6-bit input values to characters. The character set consists of the alphanumeric characters plus "+" and "/". The "=" character is used as the padding character.

Figure 5.11 illustrates the simple mapping scheme. Binary input is processed in blocks of 3 octets, or 24 bits. Each set of 6 bits in the 24-bit block is mapped into a character. In the figure, the characters are shown encoded as 8-bit quantities. In this typical case, each 24-bit input is expanded to 32 bits of output.

For example, consider the 24-bit raw text sequence 00100011 01011100 10010001, which can be expressed in hexadecimal as 235C91. We arrange this input in blocks of 6 bits:

001000 110101 110010 010001

The extracted 6-bit decimal values are 8, 53, 50, 17. Looking these up in Table 5.9 yields the radix-64 encoding as the following characters: I1yR. If these characters are stored in 8-bit ASCII format with parity bit set to zero, we have

01001001 00110001 01111001 01010010

In hexadecimal, this is 49317952. To summarize,

Input Data		
Binary representation	00100011 01011100 10010001	
Hexadecimal representation	235C91	
Radix-64 Encoding of Input Data		
Character representation	I1yR	
ASCII code (8 bit, zero parity)	01001001 00110001 01111001 01010010	
Hexadecimal representation	49317952	

APPENDIX 5C   PGP RANDOM NUMBER GENERATION

PGP uses a complex and powerful scheme for generating random numbers and pseudorandom numbers, for a variety of purposes. PGP generates random numbers from the content and timing of user keystrokes, and pseudorandom numbers using an algorithm based on the one in ANSI X9.17. PGP uses these numbers for the following purposes:

- True random numbers:
  - used to generate RSA key pairs
  - provide the initial seed for the pseudorandom number generator
  - provide additional input during pseudorandom number generation
- Pseudorandom numbers:
  - used to generate session keys
  - used to generate initialization vectors (IVs) for use with the session key in CFB mode encryption

True Random Numbers

PGP maintains a 256-byte buffer of random bits. Each time PGP expects a keystroke, it records the time, in 32-bit format, at which it starts waiting. When it receives the keystroke, it records the time the key was pressed and the 8-bit value of the keystroke. The time and keystroke information are used to generate a key, which is, in turn, used to encrypt the current value of the random-bit buffer.

Pseudorandom Numbers

Pseudorandom number generation makes use of a 24-octet seed and produces a 16-octet session key, an 8-octet initialization vector, and a new seed to be used for the next pseudorandom number generation. The algorithm uses the following data structures:

1. Input
   - randseed.bin (24 octets): If this file is empty, it is filled with 24 true random octets.
   - message: The session key and IV that will be used to encrypt a message are themselves a function of that message. This further contributes to the randomness of the key and IV, and if an opponent already knows the plaintext content of the message, there is no apparent need for capturing the one-time session key.
2. Output
   - K (24 octets): The first 16 octets, K[0..15], contain a session key, and the last eight octets, K[16..23], contain an IV.
   - randseed.bin (24 octets): A new seed value is placed in this file.

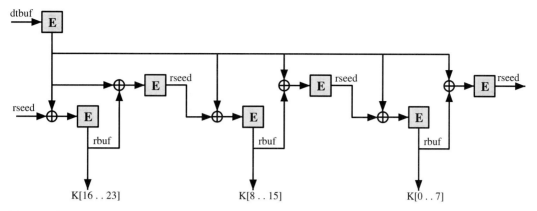

Figure 5.12 PGP Session Key and IV Generation (steps G2 through G8)

3. Internal data structures
    o dtbuf (8 octets): The first 4 octets, dtbuf[0..3], are initialized with the current date/time value. This buffer is equivalent to the DT variable in the X12.17 algorithm.
    o rkey (16 octets): CAST-128 encryption key used at all stages of the algorithm.
    o rseed (8 octets): Equivalent to the X12.17 V_i variable.
    o rbuf (8 octets): A pseudorandom number generated by the algorithm. This buffer is equivalent to the X12.17 R_i variable.
    o K′ (24 octets): Temporary buffer for the new value of randseed.bin.

The algorithm consists of nine steps, G1 through G9. The first and last steps are obfuscation steps, intended to reduce the value of a captured randseed.bin file to an opponent. The remaining steps are essentially equivalent to three iterations of the X12.17 algorithm and are illustrated in Figure 5.12. To summarize,

G1. [Prewash previous seed]
   a. Copy randseed.bin to K[0..23].
   b. Take the hash of the message (this has already been generated if the message is being signed; otherwise the first 4K octets of the message are used). Use the result as a key, use a null IV, and encrypt K in CFB mode; store result back in K.

G2. [Set initial seed]
   a. Set dtbuf[0..3] to the 32-bit local time. Set dtbuf[4..7] to all zeros. Copy rkey ← K[0..15]. Copy rseed ← K[16..23].
   b. Encrypt the 64-bit dtbuf using the 128-bit rkey in ECB mode; store the result back in dtbuf.

G3. **[Prepare to generate random octets]** Set rcount ← 0 and k ← 23. The loop of steps G4–G7 will be executed 24 times (k = 23...0), once for each random octet produced and placed in K. The variable rcount is the number of unused random octets in rbuf. It will count down from 8 to 0 three times to generate the 24 octets.

G4. **[Bytes available?]** If rcount = 0 goto G5 else goto G7. Steps G5 and G6 perform one instance of the X12.17 algorithm to generate a new batch of eight random octets.

G5. **[Generate new random octets]**

    a. rseed ← rseed ⊕ dtbuf

    b. rbuf ← E_{rkey}[rseed] in ECB mode

G6. **[Generate next seed]**

    a. rseed ← rbuf ⊕ dtbuf

    b. rseed ← E_{rkey}[rseed] in ECB mode

    c. Set rcount ← 8

G7. **[Transfer one byte at a time from rbuf to K]**

    a. Set rcount ← rcount − 1

    b. Generate a true random byte b, and set K[k] ← rbuf[rcount] ⊕ b

G8. **[Done?] If k = 0 goto G9 else set k ← k − 1 and goto G4**

G9. **[Postwash seed and return result]**

    a. Generate 24 more bytes by the method of steps G4-G7, except do not XOR in a random byte in G7. Place the result in buffer K′

    b. Encrypt K′ with key K[0..15] and IV K[16..23] in CFB mode; store result in randseed.bin

    c. Return K

It should not be possible to determine the session key from the 24 new octets generated in step G9.a. However, to make sure that the stored randseed.bin file provides no information about the most recent session key, the 24 new octets are encrypted and the result is stored as the new seed.

This elaborate algorithm should provide cryptographically strong pseudo-random numbers.

CHAPTER 6

IP SECURITY

6.1 IP Security Overview
       Applications of IPSec
       Benefits of IPSec
       Routing Applications
6.2 IP Security Architecture
       IPSec Documents
       IPSec Services
       Security Associations
       Transport and Tunnel Modes
6.3 Authentication Header
       Anti-Replay Service
       Integrity Check Value
       Transport and Tunnel Modes
6.4 Encapsulating Security Payload
       ESP Format
       Encryption and Authentication Algorithms
       Padding
       Transport and Tunnel Modes
6.5 Combining Security Associations
       Authentication Plus Confidentiality
       Basic Combinations of Security Associations
6.6 Key Management
       Oakley Key Determination Protocol
       ISAKMP
6.7 Recommended Reading and Web Sites
6.8 Key Terms, Review Questions, and Problems
       Key Terms
       Review Questions
       Problems
Appendix 6A Internetworking and Internet Protocols
       The Role of an Internet Protocol
       IPv4
       IPv6

If a secret piece of news is divulged by a spy before the time is ripe, he must be put to death, together with the man to whom the secret was told.

—*The Art of War*, **Sun Tzu**

The Internet community has developed application-specific security mechanisms in a number of application areas, including electronic mail (S/MIME, PGP), client/server (Kerberos), Web access (Secure Sockets Layer), and others. However, users have some security concerns that cut across protocol layers. For example, an enterprise can run a secure, private TCP/IP network by disallowing links to untrusted sites, encrypting packets that leave the premises, and authenticating packets that enter the premises. By implementing security at the IP level, an organization can ensure secure networking not only for applications that have security mechanisms but for the many security-ignorant applications.

IP-level security encompasses three functional areas: authentication, confidentiality, and key management. The authentication mechanism assures that a received packet was, in fact, transmitted by the party identified as the source in the packet header. In addition, this mechanism assures that the packet has not been altered in transit. The confidentiality facility enables communicating nodes to encrypt messages to prevent eavesdropping by third parties. The key management facility is concerned with the secure exchange of keys.

We begin this chapter with an overview of IP security (IPSec) and an introduction to the IPSec architecture. We then look at each of the three functional areas in detail. The appendix to this chapter reviews internet protocols.

6.1 IP SECURITY OVERVIEW

In 1994, the Internet Architecture Board (IAB) issued a report entitled "Security in the Internet Architecture" (RFC 1636). The report stated the general consensus that the Internet needs more and better security, and it identified key areas for security mechanisms. Among these were the need to secure the network infrastructure from unauthorized monitoring and control of network traffic and the need to secure end-user-to-end-user traffic using authentication and encryption mechanisms.

These concerns are fully justified. As confirmation, the 2001 annual report from the Computer Emergency Response Team (CERT) lists over 52,000 reported security incidents. The most serious types of attacks included IP spoofing, in which intruders create packets with false IP addresses and exploit applications that use authentication based on IP; and various forms of eavesdropping and packet sniffing, in which attackers read transmitted information, including logon information and database contents.

In response to these issues, the IAB included authentication and encryption as necessary security features in the next-generation IP, which has been issued as IPv6.

Fortunately, these security capabilities were designed to be usable both with the current IPv4 and the future IPv6. This means that vendors can begin offering these features now, and many vendors do now have some IPSec capability in their products.

Applications of IPSec

IPSec provides the capability to secure communications across a LAN, across private and public WANs, and across the Internet. Examples of its use include the following:

- **Secure branch office connectivity over the Internet:** A company can build a secure virtual private network over the Internet or over a public WAN. This enables a business to rely heavily on the Internet and reduce its need for private networks, saving costs and network management overhead.
- **Secure remote access over the Internet:** An end user whose system is equipped with IP security protocols can make a local call to an Internet service provider (ISP) and gain secure access to a company network. This reduces the cost of toll charges for traveling employees and telecommuters.
- **Establishing extranet and intranet connectivity with partners:** IPSec can be used to secure communication with other organizations, ensuring authentication and confidentiality and providing a key exchange mechanism.
- **Enhancing electronic commerce security:** Even though some Web and electronic commerce applications have built-in security protocols, the use of IPSec enhances that security.

The principal feature of IPSec that enables it to support these varied applications is that it can encrypt and/or authenticate *all* traffic at the IP level. Thus, all distributed applications, including remote logon, client/server, e-mail, file transfer, Web access, and so on, can be secured.

Figure 6.1 is a typical scenario of IPSec usage. An organization maintains LANs at dispersed locations. Nonsecure IP traffic is conducted on each LAN. For traffic offsite, through some sort of private or public WAN, IPSec protocols are used. These protocols operate in networking devices, such as a router or firewall, that connect each LAN to the outside world. The IPSec networking device will typically encrypt and compress all traffic going into the WAN, and decrypt and decompress traffic coming from the WAN; these operations are transparent to workstations and servers on the LAN. Secure transmission is also possible with individual users who dial into the WAN. Such user workstations must implement the IPSec protocols to provide security.

Benefits of IPSec

[MARK97] lists the following benefits of IPSec:

- When IPSec is implemented in a firewall or router, it provides strong security that can be applied to all traffic crossing the perimeter. Traffic within a company or workgroup does not incur the overhead of security-related processing.

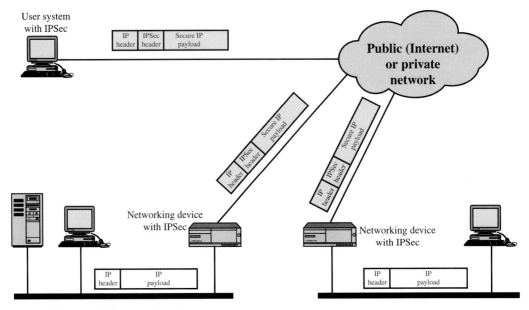

Figure 6.1   An IP Security Scenario

- IPSec in a firewall is resistant to bypass if all traffic from the outside must use IP, and the firewall is the only means of entrance from the Internet into the organization.
- IPSec is below the transport layer (TCP, UDP) and so is transparent to applications. There is no need to change software on a user or server system when IPSec is implemented in the firewall or router. Even if IPSec is implemented in end systems, upper-layer software, including applications, is not affected.
- IPSec can be transparent to end users. There is no need to train users on security mechanisms, issue keying material on a per-user basis, or revoke keying material when users leave the organization.
- IPSec can provide security for individual users if needed. This is useful for off-site workers and for setting up a secure virtual subnetwork within an organization for sensitive applications.

Routing Applications

In addition to supporting end users and protecting premises systems and networks, IPSec can play a vital role in the routing architecture required for internetworking. [HUIT98] lists the following examples of the use of IPSec. IPSec can assure that

- A router advertisement (a new router advertises its presence) comes from an authorized router.
- A neighbor advertisement (a router seeks to establish or maintain a neighbor relationship with a router in another routing domain) comes from an authorized router.

- A redirect message comes from the router to which the initial packet was sent.
- A routing update is not forged.

Without such security measures, an opponent can disrupt communications or divert some traffic. Routing protocols such as OSPF should be run on top of security associations between routers that are defined by IPSec.

6.2 IP SECURITY ARCHITECTURE

The IPSec specification has become quite complex. To get a feel for the overall architecture, we begin with a look at the documents that define IPSec. Then we discuss IPSec services and introduce the concept of security association.

IPSec Documents

The IPSec specification consists of numerous documents. The most important of these, issued in November of 1998, are RFCs 2401, 2402, 2406, and 2408:

- RFC 2401: An overview of a security architecture
- RFC 2402: Description of a packet authentication extension to IPv4 and IPv6
- RFC 2406: Description of a packet encryption extension to IP v4 and IPv6
- RFC 2408: Specification of key management capabilities

Support for these features is mandatory for IPv6 and optional for IPv4. In both cases, the security features are implemented as extension headers that follow the main IP header. The extension header for authentication is known as the Authentication header; that for encryption is known as the Encapsulating Security Payload (ESP) header.

In addition to these four RFCs, a number of additional drafts have been published by the IP Security Protocol Working Group set up by the IETF. The documents are divided into seven groups, as depicted in Figure 6.2 (RFC 2401):

- **Architecture:** Covers the general concepts, security requirements, definitions, and mechanisms defining IPSec technology.
- **Encapsulating Security Payload (ESP):** Covers the packet format and general issues related to the use of the ESP for packet encryption and, optionally, authentication.
- **Authentication Header (AH):** Covers the packet format and general issues related to the use of AH for packet authentication.
- **Encryption Algorithm:** A set of documents that describe how various encryption algorithms are used for ESP.
- **Authentication Algorithm:** A set of documents that describe how various authentication algorithms are used for AH and for the authentication option of ESP.
- **Key Management:** Documents that describe key management schemes.

> • **Domain of Interpretation (DOI):** Contains values needed for the other documents to relate to each other. These include identifiers for approved encryption and authentication algorithms, as well as operational parameters such as key lifetime.

IPSec Services

IPSec provides security services at the IP layer by enabling a system to select required security protocols, determine the algorithm(s) to use for the service(s), and put in place any cryptographic keys required to provide the requested services. Two protocols are used to provide security: an authentication protocol designated by the header of the protocol, Authentication Header (AH); and a combined encryption/authentication protocol designated by the format of the packet for that protocol, Encapsulating Security Payload (ESP). The services are as follows:

- Access control
- Connectionless integrity
- Data origin authentication
- Rejection of replayed packets (a form of partial sequence integrity)

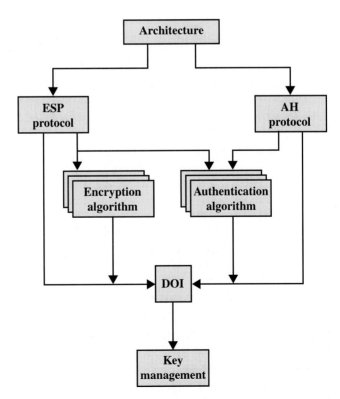

Figure 6.2   IPSec Document Overview

Table 6.1 IPSec Services

	AH	ESP (encryption only)	ESP (encryption plus authentication)
Access control	✔	✔	✔
Connectionless integrity	✔		✔
Data origin authentication	✔		✔
Rejection of replayed packets	✔	✔	✔
Confidentiality		✔	✔
Limited traffic flow confidentiality		✔	✔

- Confidentiality (encryption)
- Limited traffic flow confidentiality

Table 6.1 shows which services are provided by the AH and ESP protocols. For ESP, there are two cases: with and without the authentication option. Both AH and ESP are vehicles for access control, based on the distribution of cryptographic keys and the management of traffic flows relative to these security protocols.

Security Associations

A key concept that appears in both the authentication and confidentiality mechanisms for IP is the security association (SA). An association is a one-way relationship between a sender and a receiver that affords security services to the traffic carried on it. If a peer relationship is needed, for two-way secure exchange, then two security associations are required. Security services are afforded to an SA for the use of AH or ESP, but not both.

A security association is uniquely identified by three parameters:

- **Security Parameters Index (SPI):** A bit string assigned to this SA and having local significance only. The SPI is carried in AH and ESP headers to enable the receiving system to select the SA under which a received packet will be processed.
- **IP Destination Address:** Currently, only unicast addresses are allowed; this is the address of the destination endpoint of the SA, which may be an end user system or a network system such as a firewall or router.
- **Security Protocol Identifier:** This indicates whether the association is an AH or ESP security association.

Hence, in any IP packet,[1] the security association is uniquely identified by the Destination Address in the IPv4 or IPv6 header and the SPI in the enclosed extension header (AH or ESP).

---

[1]In this chapter, the term *IP packet* refers to either an IPv4 datagram or an IPv6 packet.

SA Parameters

In each IPSec implementation, there is a nominal[2] Security Association Database that defines the parameters associated with each SA. A security association is normally defined by the following parameters:

- **Sequence Number Counter:** A 32-bit value used to generate the Sequence Number field in AH or ESP headers, described in Section 6.3 (required for all implementations).
- **Sequence Counter Overflow:** A flag indicating whether overflow of the Sequence Number Counter should generate an auditable event and prevent further transmission of packets on this SA (required for all implementations).
- **Anti-Replay Window:** Used to determine whether an inbound AH or ESP packet is a replay, described in Section 6.3 (required for all implementations).
- **AH Information:** Authentication algorithm, keys, key lifetimes, and related parameters being used with AH (required for AH implementations).
- **ESP Information:** Encryption and authentication algorithm, keys, initialization values, key lifetimes, and related parameters being used with ESP (required for ESP implementations).
- **Lifetime of this Security Association:** A time interval or byte count after which an SA must be replaced with a new SA (and new SPI) or terminated, plus an indication of which of these actions should occur (required for all implementations).
- **IPSec Protocol Mode:** Tunnel, transport, or wildcard (required for all implementations). These modes are discussed later in this section.
- **Path MTU:** Any observed path maximum transmission unit (maximum size of a packet that can be transmitted without fragmentation) and aging variables (required for all implementations).

The key management mechanism that is used to distribute keys is coupled to the authentication and privacy mechanisms only by way of the Security Parameters Index. Hence, authentication and privacy have been specified independent of any specific key management mechanism.

SA Selectors

IPSec provides the user with considerable flexibility in the way in which IPSec services are applied to IP traffic. As we will see later, SAs can be combined in a number of ways to yield the desired user configuration. Furthermore, IPSec provides a high degree of granularity in discriminating between traffic that is afforded IPSec protection and traffic that is allowed to bypass IPSec, in the former case relating IP traffic to specific SAs.

---

[2]Nominal in the sense that the functionality provided by a Security Association Database must be present in any IPSec implementation, but the way in which that functionality is provided is up to the implementer.

The means by which IP traffic is related to specific SAs (or no SA in the case of traffic allowed to bypass IPSec) is the nominal Security Policy Database (SPD). In its simplest form, an SPD contains entries, each of which defines a subset of IP traffic and points to an SA for that traffic. In more complex environments, there may be multiple entries that potentially relate to a single SA or multiple SAs associated with a single SPD entry. The reader is referred to the relevant IPSec documents for a full discussion.

Each SPD entry is defined by a set of IP and upper-layer protocol field values, called *selectors*. In effect, these selectors are used to filter outgoing traffic in order to map it into a particular SA. Outbound processing obeys the following general sequence for each IP packet:

1. Compare the values of the appropriate fields in the packet (the selector fields) against the SPD to find a matching SPD entry, which will point to zero or more SAs.
2. Determine the SA if any for this packet and its associated SPI.
3. Do the required IPSec processing (i.e., AH or ESP processing).

The following selectors determine an SPD entry:

- **Destination IP Address:** This may be a single IP address, an enumerated list or range of addresses, or a wildcard (mask) address. The latter two are required to support more than one destination system sharing the same SA (e.g., behind a firewall).

- **Source IP Address:** This may be a single IP address, an enumerated list or range of addresses, or a wildcard (mask) address. The latter two are required to support more than one source system sharing the same SA (e.g., behind a firewall).

- **UserID:** A user identifier from the operating system. This is not a field in the IP or upper-layer headers but is available if IPSec is running on the same operating system as the user.

- **Data Sensitivity Level:** Used for systems providing information flow security (e.g., Secret or Unclassified).

- **Transport Layer Protocol:** Obtained from the IPv4 Protocol or IPv6 Next Header field. This may be an individual protocol number, a list of protocol numbers, or a range of protocol numbers.

- **IPSec Protocol (AH or ESP or AH/ESP):** If present, this is obtained from the IPv4 Protocol or IPv6 Next Header field.

- **Source and Destination Ports:** These may be individual TCP or UDP port values, an enumerated list of ports, or a wildcard port.

- **IPv6 Class:** Obtained from the IPv6 header. This may be a specific IPv6 Class value or a wildcard value.

- **IPv6 Flow Label:** Obtained from the IPv6 header. This may be a specific IPv6 Flow Label value or a wildcard value.

- **IPv4 Type of Service (TOS):** Obtained from the IPv4 header. This may be a specific IPv4 TOS value or a wildcard value.

Transport and Tunnel Modes

Both AH and ESP support two modes of use: transport and tunnel mode. The operation of these two modes is best understood in the context of a description of AH and ESP, which are covered in Sections 6.3 and 6.4, respectively. Here we provide a brief overview.

Transport Mode

Transport mode provides protection primarily for upper-layer protocols. That is, transport mode protection extends to the payload of an IP packet. Examples include a TCP or UDP segment or an ICMP packet, all of which operate directly above IP in a host protocol stack. Typically, transport mode is used for end-to-end communication between two hosts (e.g., a client and a server, or two workstations). When a host runs AH or ESP over IPv4, the payload is the data that normally follow the IP header. For IPv6, the payload is the data that normally follow both the IP header and any IPv6 extensions headers that are present, with the possible exception of the destination options header, which may be included in the protection.

ESP in transport mode encrypts and optionally authenticates the IP payload but not the IP header. AH in transport mode authenticates the IP payload and selected portions of the IP header.

Tunnel Mode

Tunnel mode provides protection to the entire IP packet. To achieve this, after the AH or ESP fields are added to the IP packet, the entire packet plus security fields is treated as the payload of new "outer" IP packet with a new outer IP header. The entire original, or inner, packet travels through a "tunnel" from one point of an IP network to another; no routers along the way are able to examine the inner IP header. Because the original packet is encapsulated, the new, larger packet may have totally different source and destination addresses, adding to the security. Tunnel mode is used when one or both ends of an SA is a security gateway, such as a firewall or router that implements IPSec. With tunnel mode, a number of hosts on networks behind firewalls may engage in secure communications without implementing IPSec. The unprotected packets generated by such hosts are tunneled through external networks by tunnel mode SAs set up by the IPSec software in the firewall or secure router at the boundary of the local network.

Here is an example of how tunnel mode IPSec operates. Host A on a network generates an IP packet with the destination address of host B on another network. This packet is routed from the originating host to a firewall or secure router at the boundary of A's network. The firewall filters all outgoing packets to determine the need for IPSec processing. If this packet from A to B requires IPSec, the firewall performs IPSec processing and encapsulates the packet with an outer IP header. The source IP address of this outer IP packet is this firewall, and the destination address may be a firewall that forms the boundary to B's local network. This packet is now routed to B's firewall, with intermediate routers examining only the outer IP header. At B's firewall, the outer IP header is stripped off, and the inner packet is delivered to B.

Table 6.2   Tunnel Mode and Transport Mode Functionality

	Transport Mode SA	**Tunnel Mode SA**
AH	Authenticates IP payload and selected portions of IP header and IPv6 extension headers.	Authenticates entire inner IP packet (inner header plus IP payload) plus selected portions of outer IP header and outer IPv6 extension headers.
ESP	Encrypts IP payload and any IPv6 extension headers following the ESP header.	Encrypts inner IP packet.
ESP with Authentication	Encrypts IP payload and any IPv6 extension headers following the ESP header. Authenticates IP payload but not IP header.	Encrypts inner IP packet. Authenticates inner IP packet.

ESP in tunnel mode encrypts and optionally authenticates the entire inner IP packet, including the inner IP header. AH in tunnel mode authenticates the entire inner IP packet and selected portions of the outer IP header.

Table 6.2 summarizes transport and tunnel mode functionality.

6.3 AUTHENTICATION HEADER

The Authentication Header provides support for data integrity and authentication of IP packets. The data integrity feature ensures that undetected modification to a packet's content in transit is not possible. The authentication feature enables an end system or network device to authenticate the user or application and filter traffic accordingly; it also prevents the address spoofing attacks observed in today's Internet. The AH also guards against the replay attack described later in this section.

Authentication is based on the use of a message authentication code (MAC), as described in Chapter 3; hence the two parties must share a secret key.

The Authentication Header consists of the following fields (Figure 6.3):

- **Next Header (8 bits):** Identifies the type of header immediately following this header.
- **Payload Length (8 bits):** Length of Authentication Header in 32-bit words, minus 2. For example, the default length of the authentication data field is 96 bits, or three 32-bit words. With a three-word fixed header, there are a total of six words in the header, and the Payload Length field has a value of 4.
- **Reserved (16 bits):** For future use.
- **Security Parameters Index (32 bits):** Identifies a security association.
- **Sequence Number (32 bits):** A monotonically increasing counter value, discussed later.

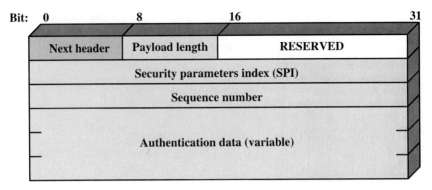

Figure 6.3   IPSec Authentication Header

- **Authentication Data (variable):** A variable-length field (must be an integral number of 32-bit words) that contains the Integrity Check Value (ICV), or MAC, for this packet, discussed later.

Anti-Replay Service

A replay attack is one in which an attacker obtains a copy of an authenticated packet and later transmits it to the intended destination. The receipt of duplicate, authenticated IP packets may disrupt service in some way or may have some other undesired consequence. The Sequence Number field is designed to thwart such attacks. First, we discuss sequence number generation by the sender, and then we look at how it is processed by the recipient.

When a new SA is established, the **sender** initializes a sequence number counter to 0. Each time that a packet is sent on this SA, the sender increments the counter and places the value in the Sequence Number field. Thus, the first value to be used is 1. If anti-replay is enabled (the default), the sender must not allow the sequence number to cycle past $2^{32} - 1$ back to zero. Otherwise, there would be multiple valid packets with the same sequence number. If the limit of $2^{32} - 1$ is reached, the sender should terminate this SA and negotiate a new SA with a new key.

Because IP is a connectionless, unreliable service, the protocol does not guarantee that packets will be delivered in order and does not guarantee that all packets will be delivered. Therefore, the IPSec authentication document dictates that the **receiver** should implement a window of size W, with a default of $W = 64$. The right edge of the window represents the highest sequence number, N, so far received for a valid packet. For any packet with a sequence number in the range from $N - W + 1$ to N that has been correctly received (i.e., properly authenticated), the corresponding slot in the window is marked (Figure 6.4). Inbound processing proceeds as follows when a packet is received:

1. If the received packet falls within the window and is new, the MAC is checked. If the packet is authenticated, the corresponding slot in the window is marked.
2. If the received packet is to the right of the window and is new, the MAC is checked. If the packet is authenticated, the window is advanced so that this

sequence number is the right edge of the window, and the corresponding slot in the window is marked.

3. If the received packet is to the left of the window, or if authentication fails, the packet is discarded; this is an auditable event.

Integrity Check Value

The Authentication Data field holds a value referred to as the Integrity Check Value. The ICV is a message authentication code or a truncated version of a code produced by a MAC algorithm. The current specification dictates that a compliant implementation must support

- HMAC-MD5-96
- HMAC-SHA-1-96

Both of these use the HMAC algorithm, the first with the MD5 hash code and the second with the SHA-1 hash code (all of these algorithms are described in Chapter 3). In both cases, the full HMAC value is calculated but then truncated by using the first 96 bits, which is the default length for the Authentication Data field.

The MAC is calculated over

- IP header fields that either do not change in transit (immutable) or that are predictable in value upon arrival at the endpoint for the AH SA. Fields that may change in transit and whose value on arrival are unpredictable are set to zero for purposes of calculation at both source and destination.
- The AH header other than the Authentication Data field. The Authentication Data field is set to zero for purposes of calculation at both source and destination.
- The entire upper-level protocol data, which is assumed to be immutable in transit (e.g., a TCP segment or an inner IP packet in tunnel mode).

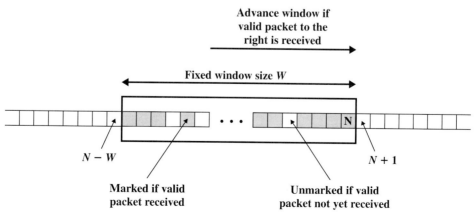

Figure 6.4 Anti-Replay Mechanism

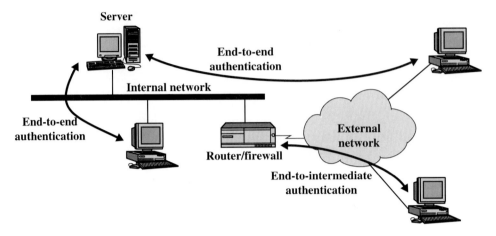

Figure 6.5 End-to-End versus End-to-Intermediate Authentication

For IPv4, examples of immutable fields are Internet Header Length and Source Address. An example of a mutable but predictable field is the Destination Address (with loose or strict source routing). Examples of mutable fields that are zeroed prior to ICV calculation are the Time to Live and Header Checksum fields. Note that both source and destination address fields are protected, so that address spoofing is prevented.

For IPv6, examples in the base header are Version (immutable), Destination Address (mutable but predictable), and Flow Label (mutable and zeroed for calculation).

Transport and Tunnel Modes

Figure 6.5 shows two ways in which the IPSec authentication service can be used. In one case, authentication is provided directly between a server and client workstations; the workstation can be either on the same network as the server or on an external network. As long as the workstation and the server share a protected secret key, the authentication process is secure. This case uses a transport mode SA. In the other case, a remote workstation authenticates itself to the corporate firewall, either for access to the entire internal network or because the requested server does not support the authentication feature. This case uses a tunnel mode SA.

In this subsection, we look at the scope of authentication provided by AH and the authentication header location for the two modes. The considerations are somewhat different for IPv4 and IPv6. Figure 6.6a shows typical IPv4 and IPv6 packets. In this case, the IP payload is a TCP segment; it could also be a data unit for any other protocol that uses IP, such as UDP or ICMP.

For **transport mode AH** using IPv4, the AH is inserted after the original IP header and before the IP payload (e.g., a TCP segment); this is shown in the upper part of Figure 6.6b. Authentication covers the entire packet, excluding mutable fields in the IPv4 header that are set to zero for MAC calculation.

In the context of IPv6, AH is viewed as an end-to-end payload; that is, it is not examined or processed by intermediate routers. Therefore, the AH appears after the IPv6 base header and the hop-by-hop, routing, and fragment extension headers. The destination options extension header could appear before or after the AH header, depending on the semantics desired. Again, authentication covers the entire packet, excluding mutable fields that are set to zero for MAC calculation.

For **tunnel mode AH**, the entire original IP packet is authenticated, and the AH is inserted between the original IP header and a new outer IP header (Figure

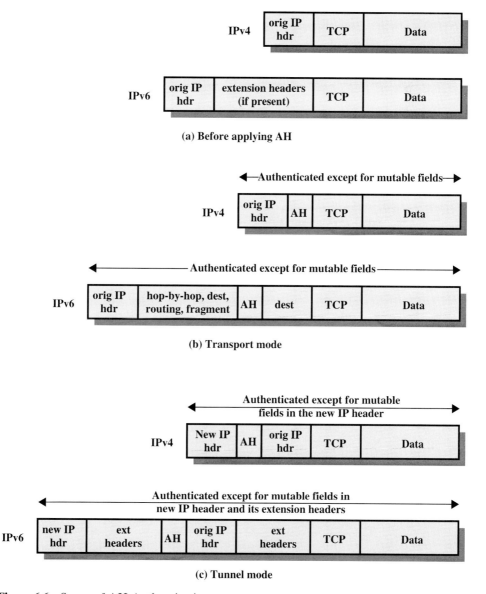

(a) Before applying AH

(b) Transport mode

(c) Tunnel mode

Figure 6.6 Scope of AH Authentication

6.6c). The inner IP header carries the ultimate source and destination addresses, while an outer IP header may contain different IP addresses (e.g., addresses of fire-walls or other security gateways).

With tunnel mode, the entire inner IP packet, including the entire inner IP header, is protected by AH. The outer IP header (and in the case of IPv6, the outer IP extension headers) is protected except for mutable and unpredictable fields.

6.4 ENCAPSULATING SECURITY PAYLOAD

The Encapsulating Security Payload provides confidentiality services, including confidentiality of message contents and limited traffic flow confidentiality. As an optional feature, ESP can also provide the same authentication services as AH.

ESP Format

Figure 6.7 shows the format of an ESP packet. It contains the following fields:

- **Security Parameters Index (32 bits):** Identifies a security association.
- **Sequence Number (32 bits):** A monotonically increasing counter value; this provides an anti-replay function, as discussed for AH.
- **Payload Data (variable):** This is a transport-level segment (transport mode) or IP packet (tunnel mode) that is protected by encryption.
- **Padding (0–255 bytes):** The purpose of this field is discussed later.

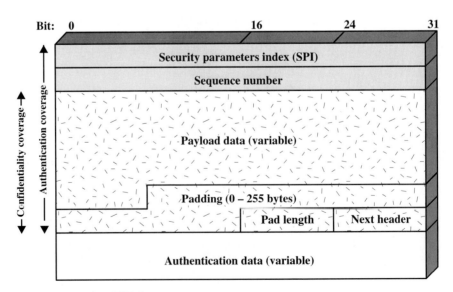

Figure 6.7   IPSec ESP format

- **Pad Length (8 bits):** Indicates the number of pad bytes immediately preceding this field.
- **Next Header (8 bits):** Identifies the type of data contained in the payload data field by identifying the first header in that payload (for example, an extension header in IPv6, or an upper-layer protocol such as TCP).
- **Authentication Data (variable):** A variable-length field (must be an integral number of 32-bit words) that contains the Integrity Check Value computed over the ESP packet minus the Authentication Data field.

Encryption and Authentication Algorithms

The Payload Data, Padding, Pad Length, and Next Header fields are encrypted by the ESP service. If the algorithm used to encrypt the payload requires cryptographic synchronization data, such as an initialization vector (IV), then these data may be carried explicitly at the beginning of the Payload Data field. If included, an IV is usually not encrypted, although it is often referred to as being part of the ciphertext.

The current specification dictates that a compliant implementation must support DES in cipher block chaining (CBC) mode (described in Chapter 2). A number of other algorithms have been assigned identifiers in the DOI document and could therefore easily be used for encryption; these include

- Three-key triple DES
- RC5
- IDEA
- Three-key triple IDEA
- CAST
- Blowfish

Many of these algorithms are described in Chapter 2.

As with AH, ESP supports the use of a MAC with a default length of 96 bits. Also as with AH, the current specification dictates that a compliant implementation must support HMAC-MD5-96 and HMAC-SHA-1-96.

Padding

The Padding field serves several purposes:

- If an encryption algorithm requires the plaintext to be a multiple of some number of bytes (e.g., the multiple of a single block for a block cipher), the Padding field is used to expand the plaintext (consisting of the Payload Data, Padding, Pad Length, and Next Header fields) to the required length.
- The ESP format requires that the Pad Length and Next Header fields be right aligned within a 32-bit word. Equivalently, the ciphertext must be an integer multiple of 32 bits. The Padding field is used to assure this alignment.
- Additional padding may be added to provide partial traffic flow confidentiality by concealing the actual length of the payload.

Transport and Tunnel Modes

Figure 6.8 shows two ways in which the IPSec ESP service can be used. In the upper part of the figure, encryption (and optionally authentication) is provided directly between two hosts. Figure 6.8b shows how tunnel mode operation can be used to set up a *virtual private network.* In this example, an organization has four private networks interconnected across the Internet. Hosts on the internal networks use the Internet for transport of data but do not interact with other Internet-based hosts. By terminating the tunnels at the security gateway to each internal network, the configuration allows the hosts to avoid implementing the security capability. The former technique is support by a transport mode SA, while the latter technique uses a tunnel mode SA.

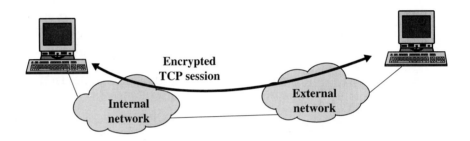

(a) Transport-level security

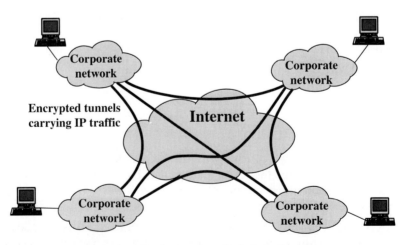

(b) A virtual private network via tunnel mode

Figure 6.8   Transport Mode versus Tunnel Mode Encryption

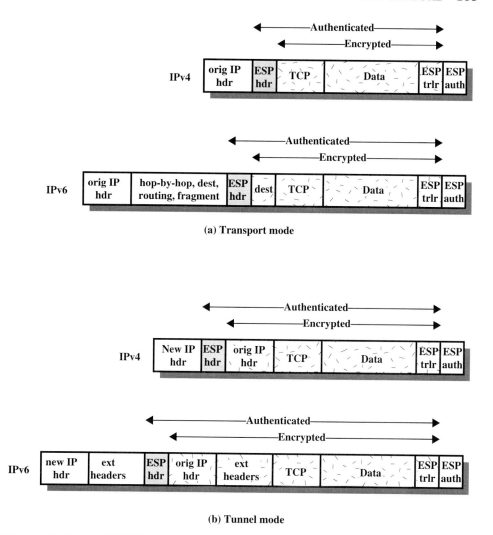

Figure 6.9 Scope of ESP Encryption and Authentication

In this section, we look at the scope of ESP for the two modes. The considerations are somewhat different for IPv4 and IPv6. As with our discussion of AH scope, we will use the packet formats of Figure 6.6a as a starting point.

Transport Mode ESP

Transport mode ESP is used to encrypt and optionally authenticate the data carried by IP (e.g., a TCP segment), as shown in Figure 6.9a. For this mode using IPv4, the ESP header is inserted into the IP packet immediately prior to the transport-layer header (e.g., TCP, UDP, ICMP) and an ESP trailer (Padding, Pad Length, and Next Header fields) is placed after the IP packet; if authentication is selected, the ESP Authentication Data field is added after the ESP trailer. The entire transport-level segment plus the ESP trailer are encrypted. Authentication covers all of the ciphertext plus the ESP header.

In the context of IPv6, ESP is viewed as an end-to-end payload; that is, it is not examined or processed by intermediate routers. Therefore, the ESP header appears after the IPv6 base header and the hop-by-hop, routing, and fragment extension headers. The destination options extension header could appear before or after the ESP header, depending on the semantics desired. For IPv6, encryption covers the entire transport-level segment plus the ESP trailer plus the destination options extension header if it occurs after the ESP header. Again, authentication covers the ciphertext plus the ESP header.

Transport mode operation may be summarized as follows:

1. At the source, the block of data consisting of the ESP trailer plus the entire transport-layer segment is encrypted and the plaintext of this block is replaced with its ciphertext to form the IP packet for transmission. Authentication is added if this option is selected.
2. The packet is then routed to the destination. Each intermediate router needs to examine and process the IP header plus any plaintext IP extension headers but does not need to examine the ciphertext.
3. The destination node examines and processes the IP header plus any plaintext IP extension headers. Then, on the basis of the SPI in the ESP header, the destination node decrypts the remainder of the packet to recover the plaintext transport-layer segment.

Transport mode operation provides confidentiality for any application that uses it, thus avoiding the need to implement confidentiality in every individual application. This mode of operation is also reasonably efficient, adding little to the total length of the IP packet. One drawback to this mode is that it is possible to do traffic analysis on the transmitted packets.

Tunnel Mode ESP

Tunnel mode ESP is used to encrypt an entire IP packet (Figure 6.9b). For this mode, the ESP header is prefixed to the packet and then the packet plus the ESP trailer is encrypted. This method can be used to counter traffic analysis.

Because the IP header contains the destination address and possibly source routing directives and hop-by-hop option information, it is not possible simply to transmit the encrypted IP packet prefixed by the ESP header. Intermediate routers would be unable to process such a packet. Therefore, it is necessary to encapsulate the entire block (ESP header plus ciphertext plus Authentication Data, if present) with a new IP header that will contain sufficient information for routing but not for traffic analysis.

Whereas the transport mode is suitable for protecting connections between hosts that support the ESP feature, the tunnel mode is useful in a configuration that includes a firewall or other sort of security gateway that protects a trusted network from external networks. In this latter case, encryption occurs only between an external host and the security gateway or between two security gateways. This relieves hosts on the internal network of the processing burden of encryption and simplifies the key distribution task by reducing the number of needed keys. Further, it thwarts traffic analysis based on ultimate destination.

Consider a case in which an external host wishes to communicate with a host on an internal network protected by a firewall, and in which ESP is implemented in the external host and the firewalls. The following steps occur for transfer of a transport-layer segment from the external host to the internal host:

1. The source prepares an inner IP packet with a destination address of the target internal host. This packet is prefixed by an ESP header; then the packet and ESP trailer are encrypted and Authentication Data may be added. The resulting block is encapsulated with a new IP header (base header plus optional extensions such as routing and hop-by-hop options for IPv6) whose destination address is the firewall; this forms the outer IP packet.

2. The outer packet is routed to the destination firewall. Each intermediate router needs to examine and process the outer IP header plus any outer IP extension headers but does not need to examine the ciphertext.

3. The destination firewall examines and processes the outer IP header plus any outer IP extension headers. Then, on the basis of the SPI in the ESP header, the destination node decrypts the remainder of the packet to recover the plaintext inner IP packet. This packet is then transmitted in the internal network.

4. The inner packet is routed through zero or more routers in the internal network to the destination host.

6.5 COMBINING SECURITY ASSOCIATIONS

An individual SA can implement either the AH or ESP protocol but not both. Sometimes a particular traffic flow will call for the services provided by both AH and ESP. Further, a particular traffic flow may require IPSec services between hosts and, for that same flow, separate services between security gateways, such as firewalls. In all of these cases, multiple SAs must be employed for the same traffic flow to achieve the desired IPSec services. The term *security association bundle* refers to a sequence of SAs through which traffic must be processed to provide a desired set of IPSec services. The SAs in a bundle may terminate at different endpoints or at the same endpoints.

Security associations may be combined into bundles in two ways:

- **Transport adjacency:** Refers to applying more than one security protocol to the same IP packet, without invoking tunneling. This approach to combining AH and ESP allows for only one level of combination; further nesting yields no added benefit since the processing is performed at one IPsec instance: the (ultimate) destination.

- **Iterated tunneling:** Refers to the application of multiple layers of security protocols effected through IP tunneling. This approach allows for multiple levels of nesting, since each tunnel can originate or terminate at a different IPsec site along the path.

The two approaches can be combined, for example, by having a transport SA between hosts travel part of the way through a tunnel SA between security gateways.

One interesting issue that arises when considering SA bundles is the order in which authentication and encryption may be applied between a given pair of endpoints and the ways of doing so. We examine that issue next. Then we look at combinations of SAs that involve at least one tunnel.

Authentication Plus Confidentiality

Encryption and authentication can be combined in order to transmit an IP packet that has both confidentiality and authentication between hosts. We look at several approaches.

ESP with Authentication Option

This approach is illustrated in Figure 6.9. In this approach, the user first applies ESP to the data to be protected and then appends the authentication data field. There are actually two subcases:

- **Transport mode ESP:** Authentication and encryption apply to the IP payload delivered to the host, but the IP header is not protected.
- **Tunnel mode ESP:** Authentication applies to the entire IP packet delivered to the outer IP destination address (e.g., a firewall), and authentication is performed at that destination. The entire inner IP packet is protected by the privacy mechanism, for delivery to the inner IP destination.

For both cases, authentication applies to the ciphertext rather than the plaintext.

Transport Adjacency

Another way to apply authentication after encryption is to use two bundled transport SAs, with the inner being an ESP SA and the outer being an AH SA. In this case ESP is used without its authentication option. Because the inner SA is a transport SA, encryption is applied to the IP payload. The resulting packet consists of an IP header (and possibly IPv6 header extensions) followed by an ESP. AH is then applied in transport mode, so that authentication covers the ESP plus the original IP header (and extensions) except for mutable fields. The advantage of this approach over simply using a single ESP SA with the ESP authentication option is that the authentication covers more fields, including the source and destination IP addresses. The disadvantage is the overhead of two SAs versus one SA.

Transport-Tunnel Bundle

The use of authentication prior to encryption might be preferable for several reasons. First, because the authentication data are protected by encryption, it is impossible for anyone to intercept the message and alter the authentication data without detection. Second, it may be desirable to store the authentication information with the message at the destination for later reference. It is more convenient to do this if the authentication information applies to the unencrypted message; otherwise the message would have to be reencrypted to verify the authentication information.

One approach to applying authentication before encryption between two hosts is to use a bundle consisting of an inner AH transport SA and an outer ESP tunnel SA. In this case, authentication is applied to the IP payload plus the IP header (and extensions) except for mutable fields. The resulting IP packet is then processed in tunnel mode by ESP; the result is that the entire, authenticated inner packet is encrypted and a new outer IP header (and extensions) is added.

Basic Combinations of Security Associations

The IPSec Architecture document lists four examples of combinations of SAs that must be supported by compliant IPSec hosts (e.g., workstation, server) or security gateways (e.g. firewall, router). These are illustrated in Figure 6.10. The lower part of each case in the figure represents the physical connectivity of the elements; the upper part represents logical connectivity via one or more nested SAs. Each SA can be either AH or ESP. For host-to-host SAs, the mode may be either transport or tunnel; otherwise it must be tunnel mode.

In **Case 1**, all security is provided between end systems that implement IPSec. For any two end systems to communicate via an SA, they must share the appropriate secret keys. The following are among the possible combinations:

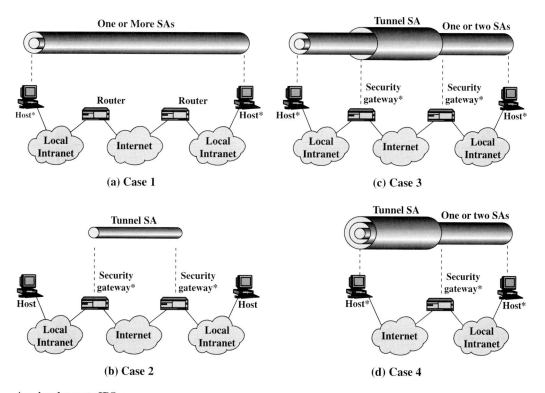

(a) Case 1

(b) Case 2

(c) Case 3

(d) Case 4

* = implements IPSec

Figure 6.10   Basic Combinations of Security Associations

a. AH in transport mode
b. ESP in transport mode
c. AH followed by ESP in transport mode (an ESP SA inside an AH SA)
d. Any one of a, b, or c inside an AH or ESP in tunnel mode

We have already discussed how these various combinations can be used to support authentication, encryption, authentication before encryption, and authentication after encryption.

For **Case 2**, security is provided only between gateways (routers, firewalls, etc.) and no hosts implement IPSec. This case illustrates simple virtual private network support. The security architecture document specifies that only a single tunnel SA is needed for this case. The tunnel could support AH, ESP, or ESP with the authentication option. Nested tunnels are not required because the IPSec services apply to the entire inner packet.

Case 3 builds on Case 2 by adding end-to-end security. The same combinations discussed for cases 1 and 2 are allowed here. The gateway-to-gateway tunnel provides either authentication or confidentiality or both for all traffic between end systems. When the gateway-to-gateway tunnel is ESP, it also provides a limited form of traffic confidentiality. Individual hosts can implement any additional IPSec services required for given applications or given users by means of end-to-end SAs.

Case 4 provides support for a remote host that uses the Internet to reach an organization's firewall and then to gain access to some server or workstation behind the firewall. Only tunnel mode is required between the remote host and the firewall. As in Case 1, one or two SAs may be used between the remote host and the local host.

6.6 KEY MANAGEMENT

The key management portion of IPSec involves the determination and distribution of secret keys. A typical requirement is four keys for communication between two applications: transmit and receive pairs for both AH and ESP. The IPSec Architecture document mandates support for two types of key management:

- **Manual:** A system administrator manually configures each system with its own keys and with the keys of other communicating systems. This is practical for small, relatively static environments.
- **Automated:** An automated system enables the on-demand creation of keys for SAs and facilitates the use of keys in a large distributed system with an evolving configuration.

The default automated key management protocol for IPSec is referred to as ISAKMP/Oakley and consists of the following elements:

- **Oakley Key Determination Protocol:** Oakley is a key exchange protocol based on the Diffie-Hellman algorithm but providing added security. Oakley is generic in that it does not dictate specific formats.

- **Internet Security Association and Key Management Protocol (ISAKMP):** ISAKMP provides a framework for Internet key management and provides the specific protocol support, including formats, for negotiation of security attributes.

ISAKMP by itself does not dictate a specific key exchange algorithm; rather, ISAKMP consists of a set of message types that enable the use of a variety of key exchange algorithms. Oakley is the specific key exchange algorithm mandated for use with the initial version of ISAKMP.

We begin with an overview of Oakley and then look at ISAKMP.

Oakley Key Determination Protocol

Oakley is a refinement of the Diffie-Hellman key exchange algorithm. Recall that Diffie-Hellman involves the following interaction between users A and B. There is prior agreement on two global parameters: q, a large prime number; and α, a primitive root of q. A selects a random integer X_A as its private key, and transmits to B its public key $Y_A = \alpha^{X_A} \bmod q$. Similarly, B selects a random integer X_B as its private key and transmits to A its public key $Y_B = \alpha^{X_B} \bmod q$. Each side can now compute the secret session key:

$$K = (Y_B)^{X_A} \bmod q = (Y_A)^{X_B} \bmod q = \alpha^{X_A X_B} \bmod q$$

The Diffie-Hellman algorithm has two attractive features:

- Secret keys are created only when needed. There is no need to store secret keys for a long period of time, exposing them to increased vulnerability.
- The exchange requires no preexisting infrastructure other than an agreement on the global parameters.

However, there are a number of weaknesses to Diffie-Hellman, as pointed out in [HUIT98]:

- It does not provide any information about the identities of the parties.
- It is subject to a man-in-the-middle attack, in which a third party C impersonates B while communicating with A and impersonates A while communicating with B. Both A and B end up negotiating a key with C, which can then listen to and pass on traffic. The man-in-the-middle attack proceeds as follows:
  1. B sends his public key Y_B in a message addressed to A (see Figure 3.11).
  2. The enemy (E) intercepts this message. E saves B's public key and sends a message to A that has B's User ID but E's public key Y_E. This message is sent in such a way that it appears as though it was sent from B's host system. A receives E's message and stores E's public key with B's User ID. Similarly, E sends a message to B with E's public key, purporting to come from A.
  3. B computes a secret key K_1 based on B's private key and Y_E. A computes a secret key K_2 based on A's private key and Y_E. E computes K_1 using E's secret key X_E and Y_B and computer K_2 using X_E and Y_A.

4. From now on E is able to relay messages from A to B and from B to A, appropriately changing their encipherment en route in such a way that neither A nor B will know that they share their communication with E.

- It is computationally intensive. As a result, it is vulnerable to a clogging attack, in which an opponent requests a high number of keys. The victim spends considerable computing resources doing useless modular exponentiation rather than real work.

Oakley is designed to retain the advantages of Diffie-Hellman while countering its weaknesses.

Features of Oakley

The Oakley algorithm is characterized by five important features:

1. It employs a mechanism known as cookies to thwart clogging attacks.
2. It enables the two parties to negotiate a *group*; this, in essence, specifies the global parameters of the Diffie-Hellman key exchange.
3. It uses nonces to ensure against replay attacks.
4. It enables the exchange of Diffie-Hellman public key values.
5. It authenticates the Diffie-Hellman exchange to thwart man-in-the-middle attacks.

We have already discussed Diffie-Hellman. Let us look the remainder of these elements in turn. First, consider the problem of clogging attacks. In this attack, an opponent forges the source address of a legitimate user and sends a public Diffie-Hellman key to the victim. The victim then performs a modular exponentiation to compute the secret key. Repeated messages of this type can *clog* the victim's system with useless work. The **cookie exchange** requires that each side send a pseudorandom number, the cookie, in the initial message, which the other side acknowledges. This acknowledgment must be repeated in the first message of the Diffie-Hellman key exchange. If the source address was forged, the opponent gets no answer. Thus, an opponent can only force a user to generate acknowledgments and not to perform the Diffie-Hellman calculation.

ISAKMP mandates that cookie generation satisfy three basic requirements:

1. The cookie must depend on the specific parties. This prevents an attacker from obtaining a cookie using a real IP address and UDP port and then using it to swamp the victim with requests from randomly chosen IP addresses or ports.
2. It must not be possible for anyone other than the issuing entity to generate cookies that will be accepted by that entity. This implies that the issuing entity will use local secret information in the generation and subsequent verification of a cookie. It must not be possible to deduce this secret information from any particular cookie. The point of this requirement is that the issuing entity need not save copies of its cookies, which are then more vulnerable to discovery, but can verify an incoming cookie acknowledgment when it needs to.
3. The cookie generation and verification methods must be fast to thwart attacks intended to sabotage processor resources.

The recommended method for creating the cookie is to perform a fast hash (e.g., MD5) over the IP Source and Destination addresses, the UDP Source and Destination ports, and a locally generated secret value.

Oakley supports the use of different **groups** for the Diffie-Hellman key exchange. Each group includes the definition of the two global parameters and the identity of the algorithm. The current specification includes the following groups:

- Modular exponentiation with a 768-bit modulus

$$q = 2^{768} - 2^{704} - 1 + 2^{64} \times (\lfloor 2^{638} \times \pi \rfloor + 149686)$$
$$\alpha = 2$$

- Modular exponentiation with a 1024-bit modulus

$$q = 2^{1024} - 2^{960} - 1 + 2^{64} \times (\lfloor 2^{894} \times \pi \rfloor + 129093)$$
$$\alpha = 2$$

- Modular exponentiation with a 1536-bit modulus
  - Parameters to be determined
- Elliptic curve group over 2^{155}
  - Generator (hexadecimal): X = 7B, Y = 1C8
  - Elliptic curve parameters (hexadecimal): A = 0, Y = 7338F
- Elliptic curve group over 2^{185}
  - Generator (hexadecimal): X = 18, Y = D
  - Elliptic curve parameters (hexadecimal): A = 0, Y = 1EE9

The first three groups are the classic Diffie-Hellman algorithm using modular exponentiation. The last two groups use the elliptic curve analog to Diffie-Hellman.

Oakley employs **nonces** to ensure against replay attacks. Each nonce is a locally generated pseudorandom number. Nonces appear in responses and are encrypted during certain portions of the exchange to secure their use.

Three different **authentication** methods can be used with Oakley:

- **Digital signatures:** The exchange is authenticated by signing a mutually obtainable hash; each party encrypts the hash with its private key. The hash is generated over important parameters, such as user IDs and nonces.
- **Public-key encryption:** The exchange is authenticated by encrypting parameters such as IDs and nonces with the sender's private key.
- **Symmetric-key encryption:** A key derived by some out-of-band mechanism can be used to authenticate the exchange by symmetric encryption of exchange parameters.

Oakley Exchange Example

The Oakley specification includes a number of examples of exchanges that are allowable under the protocol. To give a flavor of Oakley, we present one example, called aggressive key exchange in the specification, so called because only three messages are exchanged.

Figure 6.11 shows the aggressive key exchange protocol. In the first step, the initiator (I) transmits a cookie, the group to be used, and I's public Diffie-Hellman key for this exchange. I also indicates the offered public-key encryption, hash, and authentication algorithms to be used in this exchange. Also included in this message are the identifiers of I and the responder (R) and I's nonce for this exchange. Finally, I appends a signature using I's private key that signs the two identifiers, the nonce, the group, the Diffie-Hellman public key, and the offered algorithms.

When R receives the message, R verifies the signature using I's public signing key. R acknowledges the message by echoing back I's cookie, identifier, and nonce, as well as the group. R also includes in the message a cookie, R's Diffie-Hellman public key, the selected algorithms (which must be among the offered algorithms), R's identifier, and R's nonce for this exchange. Finally, R appends a signature using R's private key that signs the two identifiers, the two nonces, the group, the two Diffie-Hellman public keys, and the selected algorithms.

When I receives the second message, I verifies the signature using R's public key. The nonce values in the message assure that this is not a replay of an old message. To complete the exchange, I must send a message back to R to verify that I has received R's public key.

ISAKMP

ISAKMP defines procedures and packet formats to establish, negotiate, modify, and delete security associations. As part of SA establishment, ISAKMP defines payloads for exchanging key generation and authentication data. These payload formats provide a consistent framework independent of the specific key exchange protocol, encryption algorithm, and authentication mechanism.

ISAKMP Header Format

An ISAKMP message consists of an ISAKMP header followed by one or more payloads. All of this is carried in a transport protocol. The specification dictates that implementations must support the use of UDP for the transport protocol.

Figure 6.12a shows the header format for an ISAKMP message. It consists of the following fields:

- **Initiator Cookie (64 bits):** Cookie of entity that initiated SA establishment, SA notification, or SA deletion.
- **Responder Cookie (64 bits):** Cookie of responding entity; null in first message from initiator.
- **Next Payload (8 bits):** Indicates the type of the first payload in the message; payloads are discussed in the next subsection.
- **Major Version (4 bits):** Indicates major version of ISAKMP in use.
- **Minor Version (4 bits):** Indicates minor version in use.
- **Exchange Type (8 bits):** Indicates the type of exchange; these are discussed later in this section.
- **Flags (8 bits):** Indicates specific options set for this ISAKMP exchange. Two bits so far defined: The Encryption bit is set if all payloads following the

I → R: CKY_I, OK_KEYX, GRP, g^x, EHAO, NIDP, ID_I, ID_R, N_I, $S_{KI}[ID_I \parallel ID_R \parallel N_I \parallel GRP \parallel g^x \parallel EHAO]$

R → I: CKY_R, CKY_I, OK_KEYX, GRP, g^y, EHAS, NIDP, ID_R, ID_I, N_R, N_I, $S_{KR}[ID_R \parallel ID_I \parallel N_R \parallel N_I \parallel GRP \parallel g^y \parallel g^x \parallel EHAS]$

I → R: CKY_I, CKY_R, OK_KEYX, GRP, g^x, EHAS, NIDP, ID_I, ID_R, N_I, N_R, $S_{KI}[ID_I \parallel ID_R \parallel N_I \parallel N_R \parallel GRP \parallel g^x \parallel g^y \parallel EHAS]$

Notation:

I	=	Initiator
R	=	Responder
CKY_I, CKY_R	=	Initiator, responder cookies
OK_KEYX	=	Key exchange message type
GRP	=	Name of Diffie-Hellman group for this exchange
g^x, g^y	=	Public key of initiator, responder; g^{xy} = session key from this exchange
EHAO, EHAS	=	Encryption, hash, authentication functions, offered and selected
NIDP	=	Indicates encryption is not used for remainder of this message
ID_I, ID_R	=	Identifier for initiator, responder
N_I, N_R	=	Random nonce supplied by initiator, responder for this exchange
$S_{KI}[X]$, $S_{KR}[X]$	=	Indicates the signature over X using the private key (signing key) of initiator, responder

Figure 6.11 Example of Aggressive Oakley Key Exchange

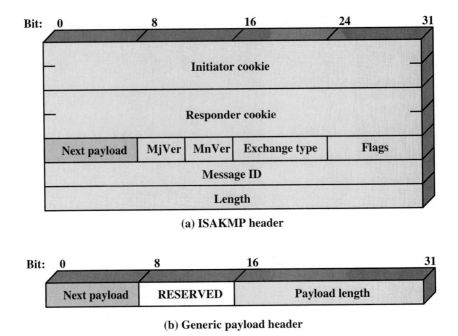

(a) ISAKMP header

(b) Generic payload header

Figure 6.12 ISAKMP Formats

header are encrypted using the encryption algorithm for this SA. The Commit bit is used to ensure that encrypted material is not received prior to completion of SA establishment.

- **Message ID (32 bits):** Unique ID for this message.
- **Length (32 bits):** Length of total message (header plus all payloads) in octets.

ISAKMP Payload Types

All ISAKMP payloads begin with the same generic payload header shown in Figure 6.12b. The Next Payload field has a value of 0 if this is the last payload in the message; otherwise its value is the type of the next payload. The Payload Length field indicates the length in octets of this payload, including the generic payload header.

Table 6.3 summarizes the payload types defined for ISAKMP, and lists the fields, or parameters, that are part of each payload. The **SA payload** is used to begin the establishment of an SA. In this payload, the Domain of Interpretation parameter identifies the DOI under which negotiation is taking place. The IPSec DOI is one example, but ISAKMP can be used in other contexts. The Situation parameter defines the security policy for this negotiation; in essence, the levels of security required for encryption and confidentiality are specified (e.g., sensitivity level, security compartment).

The **Proposal payload** contains information used during SA negotiation. The payload indicates the protocol for this SA (ESP or AH) for which services and mechanisms are being negotiated. The payload also includes the sending entity's SPI

Table 6.3 ISAKMP Payload Types

Type	Parameters	Description
Security Association (SA)	Domain of Interpretation, Situation	Used to negotiate security attributes and indicate the DOI and Situation under which negotiation is taking place.
Proposal (P)	Proposal #, Protocol-ID, SPI Size, # of Transforms, SPI	Used during SA negotiation; indicates protocol to be used and number of transforms.
Transform (T)	Transform #, Transform-ID, SA Attributes	Used during SA negotiation; indicates transform and related SA attributes.
Key Exchange (KE)	Key Exchange Data	Supports a variety of key exchange techniques.
Identification (ID)	ID Type, ID Data	Used to exchange identification information.
Certificate (CERT)	Cert Encoding, Certificate Data	Used to transport certificates and other certificate-related information.
Certificate Request (CR)	# Cert Types, Certificate Types, # Cert Auths, Certificate Authorities	Used to request certificates; indicates the types of certificates requested and the acceptable certificate authorities.
Hash (HASH)	Hash Data	Contains data generated by a hash function.
Signature (SIG)	Signature Data	Contains data generated by a digital signature function.
Nonce (NONCE)	Nonce Data	Contains a nonce.
Notification (N)	DOI, Protocol-ID, SPI Size, Notify Message Type, SPI, Notification Data	Used to transmit notification data, such as an error condition.
Delete (D)	DOI, Protocol-ID, SPI Size, # of SPIs, SPI (one or more)	Indicates an SA that is no longer valid.

and the number of transforms. Each transform is contained in a transform payload. The use of multiple transform payloads enables the initiator to offer several possibilities, of which the responder must choose one or reject the offer.

The **Transform payload** defines a security transform to be used to secure the communications channel for the designated protocol. The Transform # parameter serves to identify this particular payload so that the responder may use it to indicate acceptance of this transform. The Transform-ID and Attributes fields identify a specific transform (e.g., 3DES for ESP, HMAC-SHA-1-96 for AH) with its associated attributes (e.g., hash length).

The **Key Exchange payload** can be used for a variety of key exchange techniques, including Oakley, Diffie-Hellman, and the RSA-based key exchange used by PGP. The Key Exchange data field contains the data required to generate a session key and is dependent on the key exchange algorithm used.

The **Identification payload** is used to determine the identity of communicating peers and may be used for determining authenticity of information. Typically the ID Data field will contain an IPv4 or IPv6 address.

The **Certificate payload** transfers a public-key certificate. The Certificate Encoding field indicates the type of certificate or certificate-related information, which may include the following:

- PKCS #7 wrapped X.509 certificate
- PGP certificate
- DNS signed key
- X.509 certificate—signature
- X.509 certificate—key exchange
- Kerberos tokens
- Certificate Revocation List (CRL)
- Authority Revocation List (ARL)
- SPKI certificate

At any point in an ISAKMP exchange, the sender may include a **Certificate Request** payload to request the certificate of the other communicating entity. The payload may list more than one certificate type that is acceptable and more than one certificate authority that is acceptable.

The **Hash payload** contains data generated by a hash function over some part of the message and/or ISAKMP state. This payload may be used to verify the integrity of the data in a message or to authenticate negotiating entities.

The **Signature payload** contains data generated by a digital signature function over some part of the message and/or ISAKMP state. This payload is used to verify the integrity of the data in a message and may be used for nonrepudiation services.

The **Nonce payload** contains random data used to guarantee liveness during an exchange and protect against replay attacks.

The **Notification payload** contains either error or status information associated with this SA or this SA negotiation. The following ISAKMP error messages have been defined:

Invalid Payload Type	Invalid Protocol ID	Invalid Cert Encoding
DOI Not Supported	Invalid SPI	Invalid Certificate
Situation Not Supported	Invalid Transform ID	Bad Cert Request Syntax
Invalid Cookie	Attributes Not Supported	Invalid Cert Authority
Invalid Major Version	No Proposal Chosen	Invalid Hash Information
Invalid Minor Version	Bad Proposal Syntax	Authentication Failed
Invalid Exchange Type	Payload Malformed	Invalid Signature
Invalid Flags	Invalid Key Information	Address Notification
Invalid Message ID		

The only ISAKMP status message so far defined is Connected. In addition to these ISAKMP notifications, DOI-specific notifications are used. For IPSec, the following additional status messages are defined:

- **Responder-Lifetime:** Communicates the SA lifetime chosen by the responder
- **Replay-Status:** Used for positive confirmation of the responder's election of whether or not the responder will perform anti-replay detection.
- **Initial-Contact:** Informs the other side that this is the first SA being established with the remote system. The receiver of this notification might then delete any existing SA's it has for the sending system under the assumption that the sending system has rebooted and no longer has access to those SAs.

The **Delete payload** indicates one or more SAs that the sender has deleted from its database and that therefore are no longer valid.

ISAKMP Exchanges

ISAKMP provides a framework for message exchange, with the payload types serving as the building blocks. The specification identifies five default exchange types that should be supported; these are summarized in Table 6.4. In the table, SA refers to an SA payload with associated Protocol and Transform payloads.

The **Base Exchange** allows key exchange and authentication material to be transmitted together. This minimizes the number of exchanges at the expense of not providing identity protection. The first two messages provide cookies and establish an SA with agreed protocol and transforms; both sides use a nonce to ensure against replay attacks. The last two messages exchange the key material and user IDs, with the AUTH payload used to authenticate keys, identities, and the nonces from the first two messages.

The **Identity Protection Exchange** expands the Base Exchange to protect the users' identities. The first two messages establish the SA. The next two messages perform key exchange, with nonces for replay protection. Once the session key has been computed, the two parties exchange encrypted messages that contain authentication information, such as digital signatures and optionally certificates validating the public keys.

The **Authentication Only Exchange** is used to perform mutual authentication, without a key exchange. The first two messages establish the SA. In addition,

Table 6.4   ISAKMP Exchange Types

Exchange	Note
(a) Base Exchange	
(1) **I → R:** SA; NONCE	Begin ISAKMP-SA negotiation
(2) **R → I:** SA; NONCE	Basic SA agreed on
(3) **I → R:** KE; ID_I; AUTH	Key generated; Initiator identity verified by responder
(4) **R → I:** KE; ID_R; AUTH	Responder identity verified by initiator; Key generated; SA established
(b) Identity Protection Exchange	
(1) **I → R:** SA	Begin ISAKMP-SA negotiation
(2) **R → I:** SA	Basic SA agreed on
(3) **I → R:** KE; NONCE	Key generated
(4) **R → I:** KE; NONCE	Key generated
(5)* **I → R:** ID_I; AUTH	Initiator identity verified by responder
(6)* **R → I:** ID_R; AUTH	Responder identity verified by initiator; SA established
(c) Authentication Only Exchange	
(1) **I → R:** SA; NONCE	Begin ISAKMP-SA negotiation
(2) **R → I:** SA; NONCE; ID_R; AUTH	Basic SA agreed on; Responder identity verified by initiator
(3) **I → R:** ID_I; AUTH	Initiator identity verified by responder; SA established
(d) Aggressive Exchange	
(1) **I → R:** SA; KE; NONCE; ID_I	Begin ISAKMP-SA negotiation and key exchange
(2) **R → I:** SA; KE; NONCE; ID_R; AUTH	Initiator identity verified by responder; Key generated; Basic SA agreed upon
(3)* **I → R:** AUTH	Responder identity verified by initiator; SA established
(e) Informational Exchange	
(1)* **I → R:** N/D	Error or status notification or deletion

Notation:

I = initiator

R = responder

* = signifies payload encryption after the ISAKMP header

the responder uses the second message to convey its ID and uses authentication to protect the message. The initiator sends the third message to transmit its authenticated ID.

The **Aggressive Exchange** minimizes the number of exchanges at the expense of not providing identity protection. In the first message, the initiator proposes an SA with associated offered protocol and transform options. The initiator also begins the key exchange and provides its ID. In the second message, the responder indicates its acceptance of the SA with a particular protocol and transform, completes the key exchange, and authenticates the transmitted information. In the third message, the initiator transmits an authentication result that covers the previous information, encrypted using the shared secret session key.

The **Informational Exchange** is used for one-way transmittal of information for SA management.

6.7 RECOMMENDED READING AND WEB SITES

IPv6 and IPv4 are covered in more detail in [STAL00]. Good coverage of internetworking and IPv4 can be found in [COME00] and [STEV94]. [HUIT98] is a straightforward technical description of the various RFCs that together make up the IPv6 specification; the book provides a discussion of the purpose of various features and of the operation of the protocol. [MILL98] is another treatment of IPv6, this one emphasizing practical and implementation issues. [CHEN98] provides a good discussion of an IPSec design. [FRAN01] and [DORA99] are more comprehensive treatments of IPSec.

CHEN98   Cheng, P., et al. "A Security Architecture for the Internet Protocol." *IBM Systems Journal*, Number 1, 1998.

COME00   Comer, D. *Internetworking with TCP/IP, Volume I: Principles, Protocols and Architecture.* Upper Saddle River, NJ: Prentice Hall, 2000.

DORA99   Doraswamy, N., and Harkins, D. *IPSec.* Upper Saddle River, NJ: Prentice Hall, 1999.

FRAN01   Frankel, S. *Demystifying the IPSec Puzzle.* Boston: Artech House, 2001.

HUIT98   Huitema, C. *IPv6: The New Internet Protocol.* Upper Saddle River, NJ: Prentice Hall, 1998.

MILL98   Miller, S. *IPv6: The New Internet Protocol.* Upper Saddle River, NJ: Prentice Hall, 1998.

STAL00   Stallings, W. *Data and Computer Communications,* 6th edition. Upper Saddle River, NJ: Prentice Hall, 2000.

STEV94   Stevens, W. *TCP/IP Illustrated, Volume 1: The Protocols.* Reading, MA: Addison-Wesley, 1994.

Recommended Web sites:

- **IP Security Protocol (ipsec) Charter:** Latest RFCs and internet drafts for IPsec

- **IP Security Working Group News:** Working group documents, mail archives, related technical papers, and other useful material

- **IP Security (IPSEC) Resources:** List of companies implementing IPSec, implementation survey, and other useful material

6.8 KEY TERMS, REVIEW QUESTIONS, AND PROBLEMS

Key Terms

antireplay service	IP Security (IPSec)	replay attack
authentication header (AH)	IPv4	security association (SA)
encapsulating security	IPv6	transport mode
payload (ESP)	Oakley key determination	tunnel mode
Internet Security Association	protocol	
and Key Management		
Protocol (ISAKMP)		

Review Questions

6.1 Give examples of applications of IPSec.

6.2 What services are provided by IPSec?

6.3 What parameters identify an SA and what paramters characterize the nature of a particular SA?

6.4 What is the difference between transport mode and tunnel mode?

6.5 What is a replay attack?

6.6 Why does ESP include a padding field?

6.7 What are the basic approaches to bundling SAs?

6.8 What are the roles of the Oakley key determination protocol and ISAKMP in IPSec?

Problems

6.1 In discussing AH processing, it was mentioned that not all of the fields in an IP header are included in MAC calculation.

  a. For each of the fields in the IPv4 header, indicate whether the field is immutable, mutable but predictable, or mutable (zeroed prior to ICV calculation).

  b. Do the same for the IPv6 header.

  c. Do the same for the IPv6 extension headers.

  In each case, justify your decision for each field.

6.2 When tunnel mode is used, a new outer IP header is constructed. For both IPv4 and IPv6, indicate the relationship of each outer IP header field and each extension header in the outer packet to the corresponding field or extension header of the inner IP packet. That is, indicate which outer values are derived from inner values and which are constructed independently of the inner values.

6.3 End-to-end authentication and encryption are desired between two hosts. Draw figures similar to Figures 6.6 and 6.9 that show

  a. Transport adjacency, with encryption applied before authentication

  b. A transport SA bundled inside a tunnel SA, with encryption applied before authentication

  c. A transport SA bundled inside a tunnel SA, with authentication applied before encryption

6.4 The IPSec architecture document states that when two transport mode SAs are bundled to allow both AH and ESP protocols on the same end-to-end flow, only one ordering of security protocols seems appropriate: performing the ESP protocol before performing the AH protocol. Why is this approach recommended rather than authentication before encryption?

6.5 a. Which of the ISAKMP Exchange Types (Table 6.4) corresponds to the aggressive Oakley key exchange (Figure 6.11)?

b. For the Oakley aggressive key exchange, indicate which parameters in each message go in which ISAKMP payload types.

APPENDIX 6A   INTERNETWORKING AND INTERNET PROTOCOLS

This appendix provides an overview of internet protocols. We begin with a summary of the role of an internet protocol in providing internetworking. Then the two main internet protocols, IPv4 and IPv6, are introduced.

The Role of an Internet Protocol

An internet protocol (IP) provides the functionality for interconnecting end systems across multiple networks. For this purpose, IP is implemented in each end system and in routers, which are devices that provide connection between networks. Higher-level data at a source end system are encapsulated in an IP protocol data unit (PDU) for transmission. This PDU is then passed through one or more networks and connecting routers to reach the destination end system.

The router must be able to cope with a variety of differences among networks, including the following:

- **Addressing schemes:** The networks may use different schemes for assigning addresses to devices. For example, an IEEE 802 LAN uses either 16-bit or 48-bit binary addresses for each attached device; an X.25 public packet-switching network uses 12-digit decimal addresses (encoded as 4 bits per digit for a 48-bit address). Some form of global network addressing must be provided, as well as a directory service.

- **Maximum packet sizes:** Packets from one network may have to be broken into smaller pieces to be transmitted on another network, a process known as **fragmentation**. For example, Ethernet imposes a maximum packet size of 1500 bytes; a maximum packet size of 1000 bytes is common on X.25 networks. A packet that is transmitted on an Ethernet system and picked up by a router for retransmission on an X.25 network may have to fragment the incoming packet into two smaller ones.

- **Interfaces:** The hardware and software interfaces to various networks differ. The concept of a router must be independent of these differences.

- **Reliability:** Various network services may provide anything from a reliable end-to-end virtual circuit to an unreliable service. The operation of the routers should not depend on an assumption of network reliability.

The operation of the router, as Figure 6.13 indicates, depends on an internet protocol. In this example, the Internet Protocol (IP) of the TCP/IP protocol suite

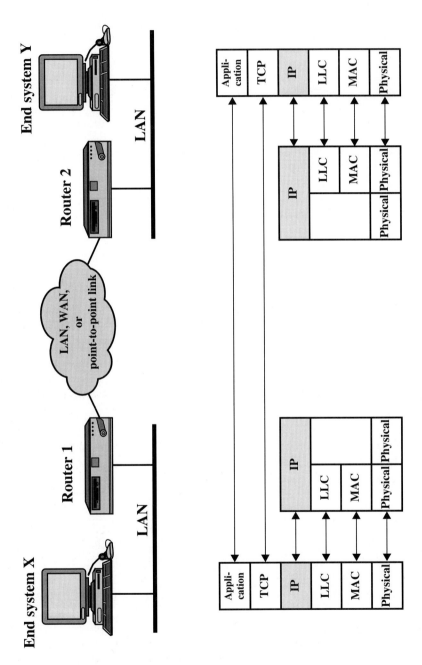

Figure 6.13 Configuration for TCP/IP Example

performs that function. IP must be implemented in all end systems on all networks as well as on the routers. In addition, each end system must have compatible protocols above IP to communicate successfully. The intermediate routers need only have up through IP.

Consider the transfer of a block of data from end system X to end system Y in Figure 6.13. The IP layer at X receives blocks of data to be sent to Y from TCP in X. The IP layer attaches a header that specifies the global internet address of Y. That address is in two parts: network identifier and end system identifier. Let us refer to this block as the IP packet. Next, IP recognizes that the destination (Y) is on another subnetwork. So the first step is to send the packet to a router, in this case router 1. To accomplish this, IP hands its data unit down to LLC with the appropriate addressing information. LLC creates an LLC PDU, which is handed down to the MAC layer. The MAC layer constructs a MAC packet whose header contains the address of router 1.

Next, the packet travels through LAN to router 1. The router removes the packet and LLC headers and trailers and analyzes the IP header to determine the ultimate destination of the data, in this case Y. The router must now make a routing decision. There are two possibilities:

1. The destination end system Y is connected directly to one of the subnetworks to which the router is attached.
2. To reach the destination, one or more additional routers must be traversed.

In this example, the packet must be routed through router 2 before reaching the destination. So router 1 passes the IP packet to router 2 via the intermediate network. For this purpose, the protocols of that network are used. For example, if the intermediate network is an X.25 network, the IP data unit is wrapped in an X.25 packet with appropriate addressing information to reach router 2. When this packet arrives at router 2, the packet header is stripped off. The router determines that this IP packet is destined for Y, which is connected directly to a subnetwork to which the router is attached. The router therefore creates a packet with a destination address of Y and sends it out onto the LAN. The data finally arrive at Y, where the packet, LLC, and internet headers and trailers can be stripped off.

This service offered by IP is an unreliable one. That is, IP does not guarantee that all data will be delivered or that the data that are delivered will arrive in the proper order. It is the responsibility of the next higher layer, in this case TCP, to recover from any errors that occur. This approach provides for a great deal of flexibility. Because delivery is not guaranteed, there is no particular reliability requirement on any of the subnetworks. Thus, the protocol will work with any combination of subnetwork types. Because the sequence of delivery is not guaranteed, successive packets can follow different paths through the internet. This allows the protocol to react to congestion and failure in the internet by changing routes.

IPv4

For decades, the keystone of the TCP/IP protocol architecture has been the Internet Protocol (IP) version 4. Figure 6.14a shows the IP header format, which is a minimum of 20 octets, or 160 bits. The fields are as follows:

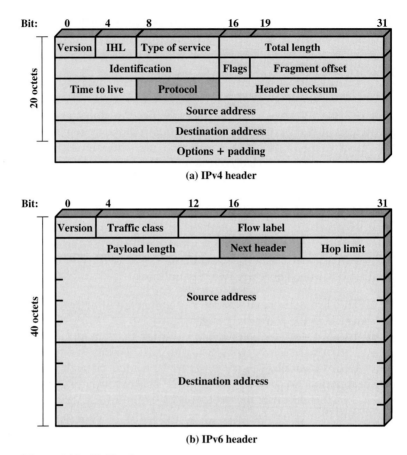

Figure 6.14 IP Headers

- **Version (4 bits):** Indicates version number, to allow evolution of the protocol; the value is 4.
- **Internet Header Length (IHL) (4 bits):** Length of header in 32-bit words. The minimum value is five, for a minimum header length of 20 octets.
- **Type of Service (8 bits):** Provides guidance to end system IP modules and to routers along the packet's path, in terms of the packet's relative priority.
- **Total Length (16 bits):** Total IP packet length, in octets.
- **Identification (16 bits):** A sequence number that, together with the source address, destination address, and user protocol, is intended to identify a packet uniquely. Thus, the identifier should be unique for the packet's source address, destination address, and user protocol for the time during which the packet will remain in the internet.
- **Flags (3 bits):** Only two of the bits are currently defined. When a packet is fragmented, the More bit indicates whether this is the last fragment in the original packet. The Don't Fragment bit prohibits fragmentation when set. This bit may be useful if it is known that the destination does not have the capability

to reassemble fragments. However, if this bit is set, the packet will be discarded if it exceeds the maximum size of an en route subnetwork. Therefore, if the bit is set, it may be advisable to use source routing to avoid subnetworks with small maximum packet size.

- **Fragment Offset (13 bits):** Indicates where in the original packet this fragment belongs, measured in 64-bit units. This implies that fragments other than the last fragment must contain a data field that is a multiple of 64 bits in length.
- **Time to Live (8 bits):** Specifies how long, in seconds, a packet is allowed to remain in the internet. Every router that processes a packet must decrease the TTL by at least one, so the TTL is somewhat similar to a hop count.
- **Protocol (8 bits):** Indicates the next higher level protocol, which is to receive the data field at the destination; thus, this field identifies the type of the next header in the packet after the IP header.
- **Header Checksum (16 bits):** An error-detecting code applied to the header only. Because some header fields may change during transit (e.g., time to live, segmentation-related fields), this is reverified and recomputed at each router. The checksum field is the 16-bit one's complement addition of all 16-bit words in the header. For purposes of computation, the checksum field is itself initialized to a value of zero.
- **Source Address (32 bits):** Coded to allow a variable allocation of bits to specify the network and the end system attached to the specified network (7 and 24 bits, 14 and 16 bits, or 21 and 8 bits).
- **Destination Address (32 bits):** Same characteristics as source address.
- **Options (variable):** Encodes the options requested by the sending user; these may include security label, source routing, record routing, and timestamping.
- **Padding (variable):** Used to ensure that the packet header is a multiple of 32 bits in length.

IPv6

In 1995, the Internet Engineering Task Force (IETF), which develops protocol standards for the Internet, issued a specification for a next-generation IP, known then as IPng. This specification was turned into a standard in 1996 known as IPv6. IPv6 provides a number of functional enhancements over the existing IP (known as IPv4), designed to accommodate the higher speeds of today's networks and the mix of data streams, including graphic and video, that are becoming more prevalent. But the driving force behind the development of the new protocol was the need for more addresses. IPv4 uses a 32-bit address to specify a source or destination. With the explosive growth of the Internet and of private networks attached to the Internet, this address length became insufficient to accommodate all systems needing addresses. As Figure 6.14b shows, IPv6 includes 128-bit source and destination address fields. Ultimately, all installations using TCP/IP are expected to migrate from the current IP to IPv6, but this process will take many years, if not decades.

IPv6 Header

The IPv6 header has a fixed length of 40 octets, consisting of the following fields (Figure 6.14b):

- **Version (4 bits):** Internet Protocol version number; the value is 6.
- **Traffic Class (8 bits):** Available for use by originating nodes and/or forwarding routers to identify and distinguish between different classes or priorities of IPv6 packets. The use of this field is still under study.
- **Flow Label (20 bits):** May be used by a host to label those packets for which it is requesting special handling by routers within a network. Flow labeling may assist resource reservation and real-time traffic processing.
- **Payload Length (16 bits):** Length of the remainder of the IPv6 packet following the header, in octets. In other words, this is the total length of all of the extension headers plus the transport-level PDU.
- **Next Header (8 bits):** Identifies the type of header immediately following the IPv6 header; this will either be an IPv6 extension header or a higher-layer header, such as TCP or UDP.
- **Hop Limit (8 bits):** The remaining number of allowable hops for this packet. The hop limit is set to some desired maximum value by the source and decremented by 1 by each node that forwards the packet. The packet is discarded if Hop Limit is decremented to zero.
- **Source Address (128 bits):** The address of the originator of the packet.
- **Destination Address (128 bits):** The address of the intended recipient of the packet. This may not in fact be the intended ultimate destination if a Routing extension header is present, as explained later.

Although the IPv6 header is longer than the mandatory portion of the IPv4 header (40 octets versus 20 octets), it contains fewer fields (8 versus 12). Thus, routers have less processing to do per header, which should speed up routing.

IPv6 Extension Headers

An IPv6 packet includes the IPv6 header, just discussed, and zero or more extension headers. Outside of IPSec, the following extension headers have been defined:

- **Hop-by-Hop Options Header:** Defines special options that require hop-by-hop processing
- **Routing Header:** Provides extended routing, similar to IPv4 source routing
- **Fragment Header:** Contains fragmentation and reassembly information
- **Authentication Header:** Provides packet integrity and authentication
- **Encapsulating Security Payload Header:** Provides privacy
- **Destination Options Header:** Contains optional information to be examined by the destination node

The IPv6 standard recommends that, when multiple extension headers are used, the IPv6 headers appear in the following order:

1. IPv6 header: Mandatory, must always appear first
2. Hop-by-Hop Options header

3. Destination Options header: For options to be processed by the first destination that appears in the IPv6 Destination Address field plus subsequent destinations listed in the Routing header
4. Routing header
5. Fragment header
6. Authentication header
7. Encapsulating Security Payload header
8. Destination Options header: For options to be processed only by the final destination of the packet

Figure 6.15 shows an example of an IPv6 packet that includes an instance of each nonsecurity header. Note that the IPv6 header and each extension header include a Next Header field. This field identifies the type of the immediately following header. If the next header is an extension header, then this field contains the type identifier of that header. Otherwise, this field contains the protocol identifier of the upper-layer protocol using IPv6 (typically a transport-level protocol), using the same values as the IPv4 Protocol field. In the figure, the upper-layer protocol is TCP, so

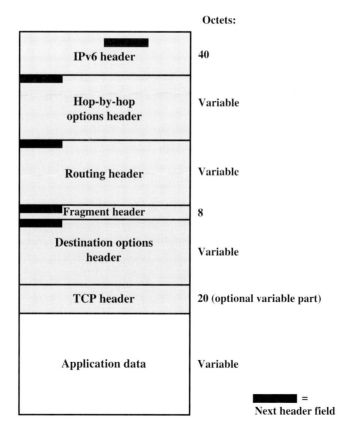

Figure 6.15 Ipv6 Packet with Extension Headers
(containing a TCP segment)

the upper-layer data carried by the IPv6 packet consist of a TCP header followed by a block of application data.

The **Hop-by-Hop Options header** carries optional information that, if present, must be examined by every router along the path. The header consists of the following fields:

- **Next Header (8 bits):** Identifies the type of header immediately following this header.
- **Header Extension Length (8 bits):** Length of this header in 64-bit units, not including the first 64 bits.
- **Options:** Contains one or more options. Each option consists of three subfields: a tag, indicating the option type; a length; and a value.

Only one option has so far been defined: the Jumbo Payload option, used to send IPv6 packets with payloads longer than $2^{16} - 1 = 65,535$ octets. The Option Data field of this option is 32 bits long and gives the length of the packet in octets, excluding the IPv6 header. For such packets, the Payload Length field in the IPv6 header must be set to zero, and there must be no Fragment header. With this option, IPv6 supports packet sizes up to more than 4 billion octets. This facilitates the transmission of large video packets and enables IPv6 to make the best use of available capacity over any transmission medium.

The **Routing header** contains a list of one or more intermediate nodes to be visited on the way to a packet's destination. All routing headers start with a 32-bit block consisting of four 8-bit fields, followed by routing data specific to a given routing type. The four 8-bit fields are Next Header, Header Extension Length, and

- **Routing Type:** Identifies a particular Routing header variant. If a router does not recognize the Routing Type value, it must discard the packet.
- **Segments Left:** Number of explicitly listed intermediate nodes still to be visited before reaching the final destination.

In addition to this general header definition, the IPv6 specification defines the Type 0 Routing header. When using the Type 0 Routing header, the source node does not place the ultimate destination address in the IPv6 header. Instead, that address is the last address listed in the Routing header, and the IPv6 header contains the destination address of the first desired router on the path. The Routing header will not be examined until the packet reaches the node identified in the IPv6 header. At that point, the IPv6 and Routing header contents are updated and the packet is forwarded. The update consists of placing the next address to be visited in the IPv6 header and decrementing the Segments Left field in the Routing header.

IPv6 requires an IPv6 node to reverse routes in a packet it receives containing a Routing header, to return a packet to the sender.

The **Fragment header** is used by a source when fragmentation is required. In IPv6, fragmentation may only be performed by source nodes, not by routers along a packet's delivery path. To take full advantage of the internetworking environment, a node must perform a path discovery algorithm that enables it to learn the smallest maximum transmission unit (MTU) supported by any subnetwork on the path.

In other words, the path discovery algorithm enables a node to learn the MTU of the "bottleneck" subnetwork on the path. With this knowledge, the source node will fragment, as required, for each given destination address. Otherwise the source must limit all packets to 1280 octets, which is the minimum MTU that must be supported by each subnetwork.

In addition to the Next Header field, the fragment header includes the following fields:

- **Fragment Offset (13 bits):** Indicates where in the original packet the payload of this fragment belongs. It is measured in 64-bit units. This implies that fragments (other than the last fragment) must contain a data field that is a multiple of 64 bits long.
- **Res (2 bits):** Reserved for future use.
- **M Flag (1 bit):** 1 = more fragments; 0 = last fragment.
- **Identification (32 bits):** Intended to identify uniquely the original packet. The identifier must be unique for the packet's source address and destination address for the time during which the packet will remain in the internet. All fragments with the same identifier, source address, and destination address are reassembled to form the original packet.

The **Destination Options header** carries optional information that, if present, is examined only by the packet's destination node. The format of this header is the same as that of the Hop-by-Hop Options header.

CHAPTER 7

WEB SECURITY

7.1 Web Security Considerations

Web Security Threats
Web Traffic Security Approaches

7.2 Secure Socket Layer and Transport Layer Security

SSL Architecture
SSL Record Protocol
Change Cipher Spec Protocol
Alert Protocol
Handshake Protocol
Cryptographic Computations
Transport Layer Security

7.3 Secure Electronic Transaction

SET Overview
Dual Signature
Payment Processing

7.4 Recommended Reading and Web Sites

7.5 Key Terms, Review Questions, and Problems

Key Terms
Review Questions
Problems

Use your mentality
Wake up to reality

—From the song "I've Got You under My Skin"
by Cole Porter

irtually all businesses, most government agencies, and many individuals now have Web sites. The number of individuals and companies with Internet access is expanding rapidly, and all of these have graphical Web browsers. As a result, businesses are enthusiastic about setting up facilities on the Web for electronic commerce. But the reality is that the Internet and the Web are extremely vulnerable to compromises of various sorts. As businesses wake up to this reality, the demand for secure Web services grows.

The topic of Web security is a broad one and can easily fill a book (several are recommended at the end of this chapter). In this chapter, we begin with a discussion of the general requirements for Web security and then focus on two standardized schemes that are becoming increasingly important as part of Web commerce: SSL/TLS and SET.

7.1 WEB SECURITY CONSIDERATIONS

The World Wide Web is fundamentally a client/server application running over the Internet and TCP/IP intranets. As such, the security tools and approaches discussed so far in this book are relevant to the issue of Web security. But, as pointed out in [GARF97], the Web presents new challenges not generally appreciated in the context of computer and network security:

- The Internet is two way. Unlike traditional publishing environments, even electronic publishing systems involving teletext, voice response, or fax-back, the Web is vulnerable to attacks on the Web servers over the Internet.
- The Web is increasingly serving as a highly visible outlet for corporate and product information and as the platform for business transactions. Reputations can be damaged and money can be lost if the Web servers are subverted.
- Although Web browsers are very easy to use, Web servers are relatively easy to configure and manage, and Web content is increasingly easy to develop, the underlying software is extraordinarily complex. This complex software may hide many potential security flaws. The short history of the Web is filled with examples of new and upgraded systems, properly installed, that are vulnerable to a variety of security attacks.

Table 7.1   A Comparison of Threats on the Web [RUBI97]

	Threats	Consequences	Countermeasures
Integrity	• Modification of user data • Trojan horse browser • Modification of memory • Modification of message traffic in transit	• Loss of information • Compromise of machine • Vulnerability to all other threats	Cryptographic checksums
Confidentiality	• Eavesdropping on the Net • Theft of info from server • Theft of data from client • Info about network configuration • Info about which client talks to server	• Loss of information • Loss of privacy	Encryption, Web proxies
Denial of Service	• Killing of user threads • Flooding machine with bogus threats • Filling up disk or memory • Isolating machine by DNS attacks	• Disruptive • Annoying • Prevent user from getting work done	Difficult to prevent
Authentication	• Impersonation of legitimate users • Data forgery	• Misrepresentation of user • Belief that false information is valid	Cryptographic techniques

- A Web server can be exploited as a launching pad into the corporation's or agency's entire computer complex. Once the Web server is subverted, an attacker may be able to gain access to data and systems not part of the Web itself but connected to the server at the local site.
- Casual and untrained (in security matters) users are common clients for Web-based services. Such users are not necessarily aware of the security risks that exist and do not have the tools or knowledge to take effective countermeasures.

Web Security Threats

Table 7.1 provides a summary of the types of security threats faced in using the Web. One way to group these threats is in terms of passive and active attacks. Passive attacks include eavesdropping on network traffic between browser and server and gaining access to information on a Web site that is supposed to be restricted. Active attacks include impersonating another user, altering messages in transit between client and server, and altering information on a Web site.

Another way to classify Web security threats is in terms of the location of the threat: Web server, Web browser, and network traffic between browser and server. Issues of server and browser security fall into the category of computer system secu-

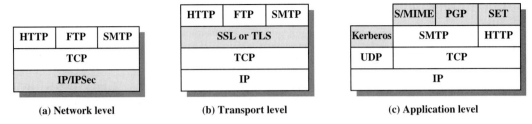

Figure 7.1   Relative Location of Security Facilities in the TCP/IP Protocol Stack

rity; Part Four of this book addresses the issue of system security in general but is also applicable to Web system security. Issues of traffic security fall into the category of network security and are addressed in this chapter.

Web Traffic Security Approaches

A number of approaches to providing Web security are possible. The various approaches that have been considered are similar in the services they provide and, to some extent, in the mechanisms that they use, but they differ with respect to their scope of applicability and their relative location within the TCP/IP protocol stack.

Figure 7.1 illustrates this difference. One way to provide Web security is to use IP Security (Figure 7.1a). The advantage of using IPSec is that it is transparent to end users and applications and provides a general-purpose solution. Further, IPSec includes a filtering capability so that only selected traffic need incur the overhead of IPSec processing.

Another relatively general-purpose solution is to implement security just above TCP (Figure 7.1b). The foremost example of this approach is the Secure Sockets Layer (SSL) and the follow-on Internet standard known as Transport Layer Security (TLS). At this level, there are two implementation choices. For full generality, SSL (or TLS) could be provided as part of the underlying protocol suite and therefore be transparent to applications. Alternatively, SSL can be embedded in specific packages. For example, Netscape and Microsoft Explorer browsers come equipped with SSL, and most Web servers have implemented the protocol.

Application-specific security services are embedded within the particular application. Figure 7.1c shows examples of this architecture. The advantage of this approach is that the service can be tailored to the specific needs of a given application. In the context of Web security, an important example of this approach is Secure Electronic Transaction (SET).[1]

The remainder of this chapter is devoted to a discussion of SSL/TLS and SET.

---

[1]Figure 7.1c shows SET on top of HTTP; this is a common implementation. In some implementations, SET makes use of TCP directly.

7.2 SECURE SOCKET LAYER AND TRANSPORT LAYER SECURITY

Netscape originated SSL. Version 3 of the protocol was designed with public review and input from industry and was published as an Internet draft document. Subsequently, when a consensus was reached to submit the protocol for Internet standardization, the TLS working group was formed within IETF to develop a common standard. This first published version of TLS can be viewed as essentially an SSLv3.1 and is very close to and backward compatible with SSLv3.

The bulk of this section is devoted to a discussion of SSLv3. At the end of the section, the principal differences between SSLv3 and TLS are described.

SSL Architecture

SSL is designed to make use of TCP to provide a reliable end-to-end secure service. SSL is not a single protocol but rather two layers of protocols, as illustrated in Figure 7.2.

The SSL Record Protocol provides basic security services to various higher-layer protocols. In particular, the Hypertext Transfer Protocol (HTTP), which provides the transfer service for Web client/server interaction, can operate on top of SSL. Three higher-layer protocols are defined as part of SSL: the Handshake Protocol, The Change Cipher Spec Protocol, and the Alert Protocol. These SSL-specific protocols are used in the management of SSL exchanges and are examined later in this section.

Two important SSL concepts are the SSL session and the SSL connection, which are defined in the specification as follows:

- **Connection:** A connection is a transport (in the OSI layering model definition) that provides a suitable type of service. For SSL, such connections are peer-to-peer relationships. The connections are transient. Every connection is associated with one session.

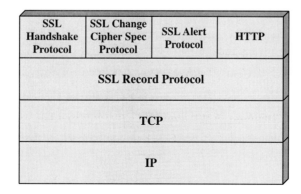

Figure 7.2 SSL Protocol Stack

- **Session:** An SSL session is an association between a client and a server. Sessions are created by the Handshake Protocol. Sessions define a set of cryptographic security parameters, which can be shared among multiple connections. Sessions are used to avoid the expensive negotiation of new security parameters for each connection.

Between any pair of parties (applications such as HTTP on client and server), there may be multiple secure connections. In theory, there may also be multiple simultaneous sessions between parties, but this feature is not used in practice.

There are actually a number of states associated with each session. Once a session is established, there is a current operating state for both read and write (i.e., receive and send). In addition, during the Handshake Protocol, pending read and write states are created. Upon successful conclusion of the Handshake Protocol, the pending states become the current states.

A session state is defined by the following parameters (definitions taken from the SSL specification):

- **Session identifier:** An arbitrary byte sequence chosen by the server to identify an active or resumable session state.
- **Peer certificate:** An X509.v3 certificate of the peer. This element of the state may be null.
- **Compression method:** The algorithm used to compress data prior to encryption.
- **Cipher spec:** Specifies the bulk data encryption algorithm (such as null, DES, etc.) and a hash algorithm (such as MD5 or SHA-1) used for MAC calculation. It also defines cryptographic attributes such as the hash_size.
- **Master secret:** 48-byte secret shared between the client and server.
- **Is resumable:** A flag indicating whether the session can be used to initiate new connections.

A connection state is defined by the following parameters:

- **Server and client random:** Byte sequences that are chosen by the server and client for each connection.
- **Server write MAC secret:** The secret key used in MAC operations on data sent by the server.
- **Client write MAC secret:** The secret key used in MAC operations on data sent by the client.
- **Server write key:** The conventional encryption key for data encrypted by the server and decrypted by the client.
- **Client write key:** The conventional encryption key for data encrypted by the client and decrypted by the server.
- **Initialization vectors:** When a block cipher in CBC mode is used, an initialization vector (IV) is maintained for each key. This field is first initialized by the SSL Handshake Protocol. Thereafter the final ciphertext block from each record is preserved for use as the IV with the following record.
- **Sequence numbers:** Each party maintains separate sequence numbers for transmitted and received messages for each connection. When a party sends

or receives a change cipher spec message, the appropriate sequence number is set to zero. Sequence numbers may not exceed $2^{64} - 1$.

SSL Record Protocol

The SSL Record Protocol provides two services for SSL connections:

- **Confidentiality:** The Handshake Protocol defines a shared secret key that is used for conventional encryption of SSL payloads.
- **Message Integrity:** The Handshake Protocol also defines a shared secret key that is used to form a message authentication code (MAC).

Figure 7.3 indicates the overall operation of the SSL Record Protocol. The Record Protocol takes an application message to be transmitted, fragments the data into manageable blocks, optionally compresses the data, applies a MAC, encrypts, adds a header, and transmits the resulting unit in a TCP segment. Received data are decrypted, verified, decompressed, and reassembled and then delivered to higher-level users.

The first step is **fragmentation**. Each upper-layer message is fragmented into blocks of 2^{14} bytes (16384 bytes) or less. Next, **compression** is optionally applied. Compression must be lossless and may not increase the content length by more than 1024 bytes.[2] In SLLv3 (as well as the current version of TLS), no compression algorithm is specified, so the default compression algorithm is null.

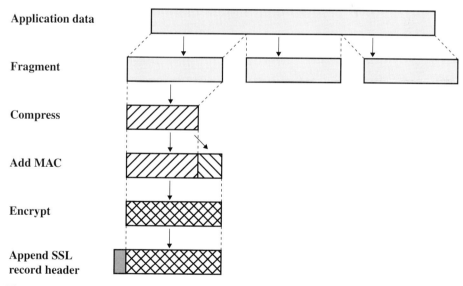

Figure 7.3 SSL Record Protocol Operation

---

[2]Of course, one hopes that compression shrinks rather than expands the data. However, for very short blocks, it is possible, because of formatting conventions, that the compression algorithm will actually provide output that is longer than the input.

The next step in processing is to compute a **message authentication code** over the compressed data. For this purpose, a shared secret key is used. The calculation is defined as:

hash(MAC_write_secret || pad_2 ||

        hash(MAC_write_secret || pad_1 || seq_num || SSLCompressed.type ||

        SSLCompressed.length || SSLCompressed.fragment))

where

||	= concatenation
MAC_write_secret	= shared secret key
hash	= cryptographic hash algorithm; either MD5 or SHA-1
pad_1	= the byte 0x36 (0011 0110) repeated 48 times (384 bits) for MD5 and 40 times (320 bits) for SHA-1
pad_2	= the byte 0x5C (0101 1100) repeated 48 times for MD5 and 40 times for SHA-1
seq_num	= the sequence number for this message
SSLCompressed.type	= the higher-level protocol used to process this fragment
SSLCompressed.length	= the length of the compressed fragment
SSLCompressed.fragment	= the compressed fragment (if compression is not used, the plaintext fragment)

Note that this is very similar to the HMAC algorithm defined in Chapter 3. The difference is that the two pads are concatenated in SSLv3 and are XORed in HMAC. The SSLv3 MAC algorithm is based on the original Internet draft for HMAC, which used concatenation. The final version of HMAC, defined in RFC 2104, uses the XOR.

Next, the compressed message plus the MAC are **encrypted** using symmetric encryption. Encryption may not increase the content length by more than 1024 bytes, so that the total length may not exceed $2^{14} + 2048$. The following encryption algorithms are permitted:

Block Cipher		Stream Cipher	
Algorithm	**Key Size**	**Algorithm**	**Key Size**
IDEA	128	RC4-40	40
RC2-40	40	RC4-128	128
DES-40	40		
DES	56		
3DES	168		
Fortezza	80		

Fortezza can be used in a smart card encryption scheme.

For stream encryption, the compressed message plus the MAC are encrypted. Note that the MAC is computed before encryption takes place and that the MAC is then encrypted along with the plaintext or compressed plaintext.

For block encryption, padding may be added after the MAC prior to encryption. The padding is in the form of a number of padding bytes followed by a one-byte indication of the length of the padding. The total amount of padding is the smallest amount such that the total size of the data to be encrypted (plaintext plus MAC plus padding) is a multiple of the cipher's block length. An example is a plaintext (or compressed text if compression is used) of 58 bytes, with a MAC of 20 bytes (using SHA-1), that is encrypted using a block length of 8 bytes (e.g., DES). With the padding.length byte, this yields a total of 79 bytes. To make the total an integer multiple of 8, one byte of padding is added.

The final step of SSL Record Protocol processing is to prepend a header, consisting of the following fields:

- **Content Type (8 bits):** The higher layer protocol used to process the enclosed fragment.
- **Major Version (8 bits):** Indicates major version of SSL in use. For SSLv3, the value is 3.
- **Minor Version (8 bits):** Indicates minor version in use. For SSLv3, the value is 0.
- **Compressed Length (16 bits):** The length in bytes of the plaintext fragment (or compressed fragment if compression is used). The maximum value is $2^{14} + 2048$.

The content types that have been defined are change_cipher_spec, alert, handshake, and application_data. The first three are the SSL-specific protocols, discussed next. Note that no distinction is made among the various applications (e.g., HTTP) that might use SSL; the content of the data created by such applications is opaque to SSL.

Figure 7.4 illustrates the SSL record format.

Change Cipher Spec Protocol

The Change Cipher Spec Protocol is one of the three SSL-specific protocols that use the SSL Record Protocol, and it is the simplest. This protocol consists of a single message (Figure 7.5a), which consists of a single byte with the value 1. The sole purpose of this message is to cause the pending state to be copied into the current state, which updates the cipher suite to be used on this connection.

Alert Protocol

The Alert Protocol is used to convey SSL-related alerts to the peer entity. As with other applications that use SSL, alert messages are compressed and encrypted, as specified by the current state.

Each message in this protocol consists of two bytes (Figure 7.5b). The first byte takes the value warning(1) or fatal(2) to convey the severity of the message. If the level is fatal, SSL immediately terminates the connection. Other connections on the same session may continue, but no new connections on this session may be

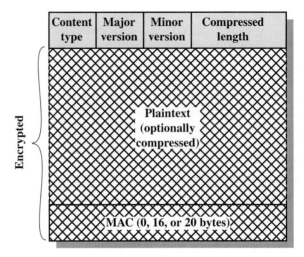

Figure 7.4 SSL Record Format

established. The second byte contains a code that indicates the specific alert. First, we list those alerts that are always fatal (definitions from the SSL specification):

- **unexpected_message:** An inappropriate message was received.
- **bad_record_mac:** An incorrect MAC was received.
- **decompression_failure:** The decompression function received improper input (e.g., unable to decompress or decompress to greater than maximum allowable length).
- **handshake_failure:** Sender was unable to negotiate an acceptable set of security parameters given the options available.
- **illegal_parameter:** A field in a handshake message was out of range or inconsistent with other fields.

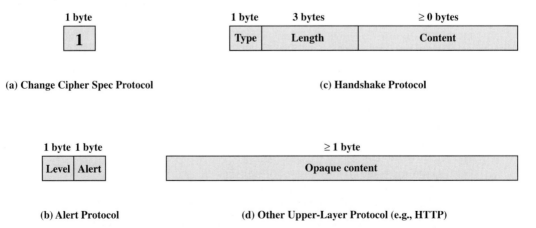

Figure 7.5 SSL Record Protocol Payload

The remainder of the alerts are the following:

- **close_notify:** Notifies the recipient that the sender will not send any more messages on this connection. Each party is required to send a close_notify alert before closing the write side of a connection.
- **no_certificate:** May be sent in response to a certificate request if no appropriate certificate is available.
- **bad_certificate:** A received certificate was corrupt (e.g., contained a signature that did not verify).
- **unsupported_certificate:** The type of the received certificate is not supported.
- **certificate_revoked:** A certificate has been revoked by its signer.
- **certificate_expired:** A certificate has expired.
- **certificate_unknown:** Some other unspecified issue arose in processing the certificate, rendering it unacceptable.

Handshake Protocol

The most complex part of SSL is the Handshake Protocol. This protocol allows the server and client to authenticate each other and to negotiate an encryption and MAC algorithm and cryptographic keys to be used to protect data sent in an SSL record. The Handshake Protocol is used before any application data is transmitted.

The Handshake Protocol consists of a series of messages exchanged by client and server. All of these have the format shown in Figure 7.5c. Each message has three fields:

- **Type (1 byte):** Indicates one of 10 messages. Table 7.2 lists the defined message types.
- **Length (3 bytes):** The length of the message in bytes.
- **Content ($\geq$ 1 byte):** The parameters associated with this message; these are listed in Table 7.2.

Figure 7.6 shows the initial exchange needed to establish a logical connection between client and server. The exchange can be viewed as having four phases.

Table 7.2 SSL Handshake Protocol Message Types

Message Type	Parameters
hello_request	null
client_hello	version, random, session id, cipher suite, compression method
server_hello	version, random, session id, cipher suite, compression method
certificate	chain of X.509v3 certificates
server_key_exchange	parameters, signature
certificate_request	type, authorities
server_done	null
certificate_verify	signature
client_key_exchange	parameters, signature
finished	hash value

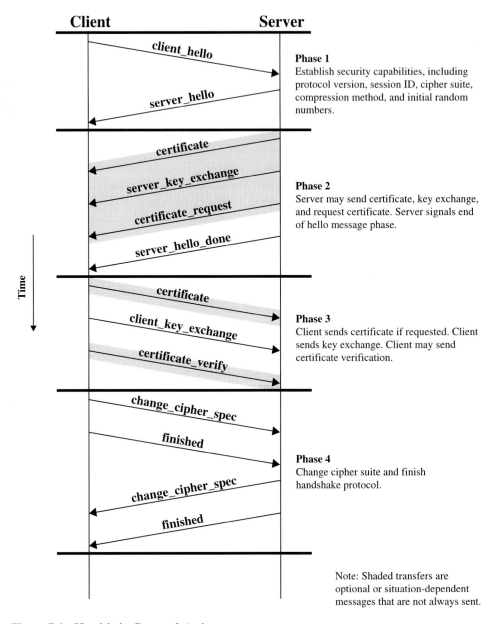

Figure 7.6 Handshake Protocol Action

Phase 1. Establish Security Capabilities

This phase is used to initiate a logical connection and to establish the security capabilities that will be associated with it. The exchange is initiated by the client, which sends a **client_hello message** with the following parameters:

- **Version:** The highest SSL version understood by the client.

- **Random:** A client-generated random structure, consisting of a 32-bit timestamp and 28 bytes generated by a secure random number generator. These values serve as nonces and are used during key exchange to prevent replay attacks.
- **Session ID:** A variable-length session identifier. A nonzero value indicates that the client wishes to update the parameters of an existing connection or create a new connection on this session. A zero value indicates that the client wishes to establish a new connection on a new session.
- **CipherSuite:** This is a list that contains the combinations of cryptographic algorithms supported by the client, in decreasing order of preference. Each element of the list (each cipher suite) defines both a key exchange algorithm and a CipherSpec; these are discussed subsequently.
- **Compression Method:** This is a list of the compression methods the client supports.

After sending the client_hello message, the client waits for the **server_hello message**, which contains the same parameters as the client_hello message. For the server_hello message, the following conventions apply. The Version field contains the lower of the version suggested by the client and the highest supported by the server. The Random field is generated by the server and is independent of the client's Random field. If the SessionID field of the client was nonzero, the same value is used by the server; otherwise the server's SessionID field contains the value for a new session. The CipherSuite field contains the single cipher suite selected by the server from those proposed by the client. The Compression field contains the compression method selected by the server from those proposed by the client.

The first element of the Cipher Suite parameter is the key exchange method (i.e., the means by which the cryptographic keys for conventional encryption and MAC are exchanged). The following key exchange methods are supported:

- **RSA:** The secret key is encrypted with the receiver's RSA public key. A public-key certificate for the receiver's key must be made available.
- **Fixed Diffie-Hellman:** This is a Diffie-Hellman key exchange in which the server's certificate contains the Diffie-Hellman public parameters signed by the certificate authority (CA). That is, the public-key certificate contains the Diffie-Hellman public-key parameters. The client provides its Diffie-Hellman public key parameters either in a certificate, if client authentication is required, or in a key exchange message. This method results in a fixed secret key between two peers, based on the Diffie-Hellman calculation using the fixed public keys.
- **Ephemeral Diffie-Hellman:** This technique is used to create ephemeral (temporary, one-time) secret keys. In this case, the Diffie-Hellman public keys are exchanged, signed using the sender's private RSA or DSS key. The receiver can use the corresponding public key to verify the signature. Certificates are used to authenticate the public keys. This would appear to be the most secure of the three Diffie-Hellman options because it results in a temporary, authenticated key.
- **Anonymous Diffie-Hellman:** The base Diffie-Hellman algorithm is used, with no authentication. That is, each side sends its public Diffie-Hellman para-

meters to the other, with no authentication. This approach is vulnerable to man-in-the-middle attacks, in which the attacker conducts anonymous Diffie-Hellman with both parties.

- **Fortezza:** The technique defined for the Fortezza scheme.

Following the definition of a key exchange method is the CipherSpec, which includes the following fields:

- **CipherAlgorithm:** Any of the algorithms mentioned earlier: RC4, RC2, DES, 3DES, DES40, IDEA, Fortezza
- **MACAlgorithm:** MD5 or SHA-1
- **CipherType:** Stream or Block
- **IsExportable:** True or False
- **HashSize:** 0, 16 (for MD5), or 20 (for SHA-1) bytes
- **Key Material:** A sequence of bytes that contain data used in generating the write keys
- **IV Size:** The size of the Initialization Value for Cipher Block Chaining (CBC) encryption

Phase 2. Server Authentication and Key Exchange

The server begins this phase by sending its certificate, if it needs to be authenticated; the message contains one or a chain of X.509 certificates. The **certificate message** is required for any agreed-on key exchange method except anonymous Diffie-Hellman. Note that if fixed Diffie-Hellman is used, this certificate message functions as the server's key exchange message because it contains the server's public Diffie-Hellman parameters.

Next, a **server_key_exchange message** may be sent if it is required. It is not required in two instances: (1) The server has sent a certificate with fixed Diffie-Hellman parameters, or (2) RSA key exchange is to be used. The server_key_exchange message is needed for the following:

- **Anonymous Diffie-Hellman:** The message content consists of the two global Diffie-Hellman values (a prime number and a primitive root of that number) plus the server's public Diffie-Hellman key (see Figure 3.10).
- **Ephemeral Diffie-Hellman:** The message content includes the three Diffie-Hellman parameters provided for anonymous Diffie-Hellman, plus a signature of those parameters.
- **RSA key exchange, in which the server is using RSA but has a signature-only RSA key:** Accordingly, the client cannot simply send a secret key encrypted with the server's public key. Instead, the server must create a temporary RSA public/private key pair and use the server_key_exchange message to send the public key. The message content includes the two parameters of the temporary RSA public key (exponent and modulus; see Figure 3.8) plus a signature of those parameters.
- **Fortezza**

Some further details about the signatures are warranted. As usual, a signature is created by taking the hash of a message and encrypting it with the sender's private key. In this case the hash is defined as

$$\text{hash(ClientHello.random} \parallel \text{ServerHello.random} \parallel \text{ServerParams)}$$

So the hash covers not only the Diffie-Hellman or RSA parameters, but also the two nonces from the initial hello messages. This ensures against replay attacks and misrepresentation. In the case of a DSS signature, the hash is performed using the SHA-1 algorithm. In the case of an RSA signature, both an MD5 and an SHA-1 hash are calculated, and the concatenation of the two hashes (36 bytes) is encrypted with the server's private key.

Next, a nonanonymous server (server not using anonymous Diffie-Hellman) can request a certificate from the client. The **certificate_request message** includes two parameters: certificate_type and certificate_authorities. The certificate type indicates the public-key algorithm and its use:

- RSA, signature only
- DSS, signature only
- RSA for fixed Diffie-Hellman; in this case the signature is used only for authentication, by sending a certificate signed with RSA
- DSS for fixed Diffie-Hellman; again, used only for authentication
- RSA for ephemeral Diffie-Hellman
- DSS for ephemeral Diffie-Hellman
- Fortezza

The second parameter in the certificate_request message is a list of the distinguished names of acceptable certificate authorities.

The final message in Phase 2, and one that is always required, is the **server_done message**, which is sent by the server to indicate the end of the server hello and associated messages. After sending this message, the server will wait for a client response. This message has no parameters.

Phase 3. Client Authentication and Key Exchange

Upon receipt of the server_done message, the client should verify that the server provided a valid certificate if required and check that the server_hello parameters are acceptable. If all is satisfactory, the client sends one or more messages back to the server.

If the server has requested a certificate, the client begins this phase by sending a **certificate message**. If no suitable certificate is available, the client sends a no_certificate alert instead.

Next is the **client_key_exchange message**, which must be sent in this phase. The content of the message depends on the type of key exchange, as follows:

- **RSA:** The client generates a 48-byte *pre-master secret* and encrypts with the public key from the server's certificate or temporary RSA key from a server_key_exchange message. Its use to compute a *master secret* is explained later.

- **Ephemeral or Anonymous Diffie-Hellman:** The client's public Diffie-Hellman parameters are sent.
- **Fixed Diffie-Hellman:** The client's public Diffie-Hellman parameters were sent in a certificate message, so the content of this message is null.
- **Fortezza:** The client's Fortezza parameters are sent.

Finally, in this phase, the client may send a **certificate_verify message** to provide explicit verification of a client certificate. This message is only sent following any client certificate that has signing capability (i.e., all certificates except those containing fixed Diffie-Hellman parameters). This message signs a hash code based on the preceding messages, defined as follows:

CertificateVerify.signature.md5_hash

   MD5(master_secret || pad_2 || MD5(handshake_messages || master_secret || pad_1));

Certificate.signature.sha_hash

   SHA(master_secret || pad_2 || SHA(handshake_messages || master_secret || pad_1));

where pad_1 and pad_2 are the values defined earlier for the MAC, handshake_ messages refers to all Handshake Protocol messages sent or received starting at client_hello but not including this message, and master_secret is the calculated secret whose construction is explained later in this section. If the user's private key is DSS, then it is used to encrypt the SHA-1 hash. If the user's private key is RSA, it is used to encrypt the concatenation of the MD5 and SHA-1 hashes. In either case, the purpose is to verify the client's ownership of the private key for the client certificate. Even if someone is misusing the client's certificate, he or she would be unable to send this message.

Phase 4. Finish

This phase completes the setting up of a secure connection. The client sends a **change_cipher_spec message** and copies the pending CipherSpec into the current CipherSpec. Note that this message is not considered part of the Handshake Protocol but is sent using the Change Cipher Spec Protocol. The client then immediately sends the **finished message** under the new algorithms, keys, and secrets. The finished message verifies that the key exchange and authentication processes were successful. The content of the finished message is the concatenation of two hash values:

MD5(master_secret || pad2 || MD5(handshake_messages || Sender || master_secret || pad1))

SHA(master_secret || pad2 || SHA(handshake_messages || Sender || master_secret || pad1))

where Sender is a code that identifies that the sender is the client and handshake_ messages is all of the data from all handshake messages up to but not including this message.

In response to these two messages, the server sends its own change_cipher_spec message, transfers the pending to the current CipherSpec, and sends its finished message. At this point the handshake is complete and the client and server may begin to exchange application layer data.

Cryptographic Computations

Two further items are of interest: the creation of a shared master secret by means of the key exchange, and the generation of cryptographic parameters from the master secret.

Master Secret Creation

The shared master secret is a one-time 48-byte value (384 bits) generated for this session by means of secure key exchange. The creation is in two stages. First, a pre_master_secret is exchanged. Second, the master_secret is calculated by both parties. For pre_master_secret exchange, there are two possibilities:

- **RSA:** A 48-byte pre_master_secret is generated by the client, encrypted with the server's public RSA key, and sent to the server. The server decrypts the ciphertext using its private key to recover the pre_master_secret.
- **Diffie-Hellman:** Both client and server generate a Diffie-Hellman public key. After these are exchanged, each side performs the Diffie-Hellman calculation to create the shared pre_master_secret.

Both sides now compute the master_secret as follows:

$$master\_secret = MD5(pre\_master\_secret \parallel SHA('A' \parallel pre\_master\_secret \parallel$$
$$ClientHello.random \parallel ServerHello.random)) \parallel$$
$$MD5(pre\_master\_secret \parallel SHA('BB' \parallel pre\_master\_secret \parallel$$
$$ClientHello.random \parallel ServerHello.random)) \parallel$$
$$MD5(pre\_master\_secret \parallel SHA('CCC' \parallel pre\_master\_secret \parallel$$
$$ClientHello.random \parallel ServerHello.random))$$

where ClientHello.random and ServerHello.random are the two nonce values exchanged in the initial hello messages.

Generation of Cryptographic Parameters

CipherSpecs require a client write MAC secret, a server write MAC secret, a client write key, a server write key, a client write IV, and a server write IV, which are generated from the master secret in that order. These parameters are generated from the master secret by hashing the master secret into a sequence of secure bytes of sufficient length for all needed parameters.

The generation of the key material from the master secret uses the same format for generation of the master secret from the pre-master secret:

$$\text{key\_block} = \text{MD5}(\text{master\_secret} \,\|\, \text{SHA}(\text{'A'} \,\|\, \text{master\_secret} \,\|\,$$
$$\text{ServerHello.random} \,\|\, \text{ClientHello.random})) \,\|\,$$
$$\text{MD5}(\text{master\_secret} \,\|\, \text{SHA}(\text{'BB'} \,\|\, \text{master\_secret} \,\|\,$$
$$\text{ServerHello.random} \,\|\, \text{ClientHello.random})) \,\|\,$$
$$\text{MD5}(\text{master\_secret} \,\|\, \text{SHA}(\text{'CCC'} \,\|\, \text{master\_secret} \,\|\,$$
$$\text{ServerHello.random} \,\|\, \text{ClientHello.random})) \,\|\, \ldots$$

until enough output has been generated. The result of this algorithmic structure is a pseudorandom function. We can view the master_secret as the pseudorandom seed value to the function. The client and server random numbers can be viewed as salt values to complicate cryptanalysis (see Chapter 9 for a discussion of the use of salt values).

Transport Layer Security

TLS is an IETF standardization initiative whose goal is to produce an Internet standard version of SSL. TLS is defined as a Proposed Internet Standard in RFC 2246. RFC 2246 is very similar to SSLv3. In this section, we highlight the differences.

Version Number

The TLS Record Format is the same as that of the SSL Record Format (Figure 7.4), and the fields in the header have the same meanings. The one difference is in version values. For the current version of TLS, the Major Version is 3 and the Minor Version is 1.

Message Authentication Code

There are two differences between the SSLv3 and TLS MAC schemes: the actual algorithm and the scope of the MAC calculation. TLS makes use of the HMAC algorithm defined in RFC 2104. Recall from Chapter 3 that HMAC is defined as follows:

$$\text{HMAC}_K(M) = \text{H}[(K^+ \oplus \text{opad}) \,\|\, \text{H}[(K^+ \oplus \text{ipad}) \,\|\, M]]$$

where

H = embedded hash function (for TLS, either MD5 or SHA-1)

M = message input to HMAC

K^+ = secret key padded with zeros on the left so that the result is equal to the block length of the hash code (for MD5 and SHA-1, block length = 512 bits)

ipad = 00110110 (36 in hexadecimal) repeated 64 times (512 bits)

opad = 01011100 (5C in hexadecimal) repeated 64 times (512 bits)

SSLv3 uses the same algorithm, except that the padding bytes are concatenated with the secret key rather than being XORed with the secret key padded to the block length. The level of security should be about the same in both cases.

For TLS, the MAC calculation encompasses the fields indicated in the following expression:

HMAC_hash(MAC_write_secret, seq_num || TLSCompressed.type ||

TLSCompressed.version || TLSCompressed.length || TLSCompressed.fragment))

The MAC calculation covers all of the fields covered by the SSLv3 calculation, plus the field TLSCompressed.version, which is the version of the protocol being employed.

Pseudorandom Function

TLS makes use of a pseudorandom function referred to as PRF to expand secrets into blocks of data for purposes of key generation or validation. The objective is to make use of a relatively small shared secret value but to generate longer blocks of data in a way that is secure from the kinds of attacks made on hash functions and MACs. The PRF is based on the following data expansion function (Figure 7.7):

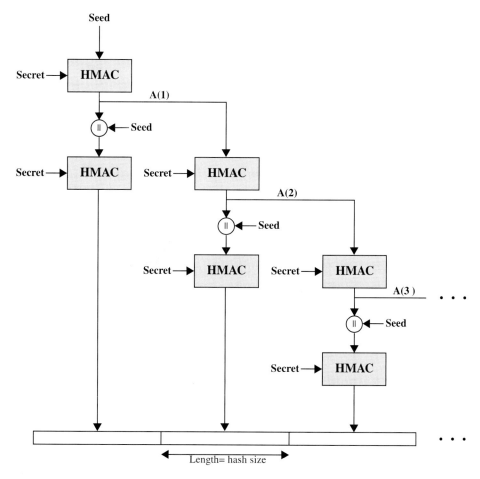

Figure 7.7 TLS Function P_hash (secret, seed)

$$P\_hash(secret, seed) = HMAC\_hash(secret, A(1) \parallel seed) \parallel$$
$$HMAC\_hash(secret, A(2) \parallel seed) \parallel$$
$$HMAC\_hash(secret, A(3) \parallel seed) \parallel \ldots$$

where $A()$ is defined as

$$A(0) = seed$$
$$A(i) = HMAC\_hash(secret, A(i-1))$$

The data expansion function makes use of the HMAC algorithm, with either MD5 or SHA-1 as the underlying hash function. As can be seen, P_hash can be iterated as many times as necessary to produce the required quantity of data. For example, if P_SHA-1 was used to generate 64 bytes of data, it would have to be iterated four times, producing 80 bytes of data, of which the last 16 would be discarded. In this case, P_MD5 would also have to be iterated four times, producing exactly 64 bytes of data. Note that each iteration involves two executions of HMAC, each of which in turn involves two executions of the underlying hash algorithm.

To make PRF as secure as possible, it uses two hash algorithms in a way that should guarantee its security if either algorithm remains secure. PRF is defined as

$$PRF(secret, label, seed) = P\_MD5(S1, label \parallel seed) \oplus P\_SHA\text{-}1(S2, label \parallel seed)$$

PRF takes as input a secret value, an identifying label, and a seed value and produces an output of arbitrary length. The output is created by splitting the secret value into two halves (S1 and S2) and performing P_hash on each half, using MD5 on one half and SHA-1 on the other half. The two results are exclusive-ORed to produce the output; for this purpose, P_MD5 will generally have to be iterated more times than P_SHA-1 to produce an equal amount of data for input to the exclusive-OR function.

Alert Codes

TLS supports all of the alert codes defined in SSLv3 with the exception of no_certificate. A number of additional codes are defined in TLS; of these, the following are always fatal:

- **decryption_failed:** A ciphertext decrypted in an invalid way; either it was not an even multiple of the block length or its padding values, when checked, were incorrect.
- **record_overflow:** A TLS record was received with a payload (ciphertext) whose length exceeds $2^{14} + 2048$ bytes, or the ciphertext decrypted to a length of greater than $2^{14} + 1024$ bytes.
- **unknown_ca:** A valid certificate chain or partial chain was received, but the certificate was not accepted because the CA certificate could not be located or could not be matched with a known, trusted CA.
- **access_denied:** A valid certificate was received, but when access control was applied, the sender decided not to proceed with the negotiation.

- **decode_error:** A message could not be decoded because a field was out of its specified range or the length of the message was incorrect.
- **export_restriction:** A negotiation not in compliance with export restrictions on key length was detected.
- **protocol_version:** The protocol version the client attempted to negotiate is recognized but not supported.
- **insufficient_security:** Returned instead of handshake_failure when a negotiation has failed specifically because the server requires ciphers more secure than those supported by the client.
- **internal_error:** An internal error unrelated to the peer or the correctness of the protocol makes it impossible to continue.

The remainder of the new alerts are the following:

- **decrypt_error:** A handshake cryptographic operation failed, including being unable to verify a signature, decrypt a key exchange, or validate a finished message.
- **user_canceled:** This handshake is being canceled for some reason unrelated to a protocol failure.
- **no_renegotiation:** Sent by a client in response to a hello request or by the server in response to a client hello after initial handshaking. Either of these messages would normally result in renegotiation, but this alert indicates that the sender is not able to renegotiate. This message is always a warning.

Cipher Suites

There are several small differences between the cipher suites available under SSLv3 and under TLS:

- **Key Exchange:** TLS supports all of the key exchange techniques of SSLv3 with the exception of Fortezza.
- **Symmetric Encryption Algorithms:** TLS includes all of the symmetric encryption algorithms found in SSLv3, with the exception of Fortezza.

Client Certificate Types

TLS defines the following certificate types to be requested in a certificate_request message: rsa_sign, dss_sign, rsa_fixed_dh, and dss_fixed_dh. These are all defined in SSLv3. In addition, SSLv3 includes rsa_ephemeral_dh, dss_ephemeral_dh, and fortezza_kea. Ephemeral Diffie-Hellman involves signing the Diffie-Hellman parameters with either RSA or DSS; for TLS, the rsa_sign and dss_sign types are used for that function; a separate signing type is not needed to sign Diffie-Hellman parameters. TLS does not include the Fortezza scheme.

Certificate_Verify and Finished Messages

In the TLS certificate_verify message, the MD5 and SHA-1 hashes are calculated only over handshake_messages. Recall that for SSLv3, the hash calculation also included the master secret and pads. These extra fields were felt to add no additional security.

As with the finished message in SSLv3, the finished message in TLS is a hash based on the shared master_secret, the previous handshake messages, and a label that identifies client or server. The calculation is somewhat different. For TLS, we have

PRF(master_secret, finished_label, MD5(handshake_messages) $\|$ SHA-1(handshake_messages))

where finished_label is the string "client finished" for the client and "server finished" for the server.

Cryptographic Computations

The pre_master_secret for TLS is calculated in the same way as in SSLv3. As in SSLv3, the master_secret in TLS is calculated as a hash function of the pre_master_secret and the two hello random numbers. The form of the TLS calculation is different from that of SSLv3 and is defined as follows:

master_secret =
    PRF(pre_master_secret, "master secret", ClientHello.random $\|$ ServerHello.random)

The algorithm is performed until 48 bytes of pseudorandom output are produced. The calculation of the key block material (MAC secret keys, session encryption keys, and IVs) is defined as follows:

key_block =
    PRF(master_secret, "key expansion",
        SecurityParameters.server_random $\|$ SecurityParameters.client_random)

until enough output has been generated. As with SSLv3, the key_block is a function of the master_secret and the client and server random numbers, but for TLS the actual algorithm is different.

Padding

In SSL, the padding added prior to encryption of user data is the minimum amount required so that the total size of the data to be encrypted is a multiple of the cipher's block length. In TLS, the padding can be any amount that results in a total that is a multiple of the cipher's block length, up to a maximum of 255 bytes. For example, if the plaintext (or compressed text if compression is used) plus MAC plus padding.length byte is 79 bytes long, then the padding length, in bytes, can be 1, 9, 17, and so on, up to 249. A variable padding length may be used to frustrate attacks based on an analysis of the lengths of exchanged messages.

7.3 SECURE ELECTRONIC TRANSACTION

SET is an open encryption and security specification designed to protect credit card transactions on the Internet. The current version, SETv1, emerged from a call for security standards by MasterCard and Visa in February 1996. A wide range of companies were involved in developing the initial specification, including IBM, Microsoft, Netscape, RSA, Terisa, and Verisign. Beginning in 1996, there have been numerous tests of the concept, and by 1998 the first wave of SET-compliant products was available.

SET is not itself a payment system. Rather it is a set of security protocols and formats that enables users to employ the existing credit card payment infrastructure on an open network, such as the Internet, in a secure fashion. In essence, SET provides three services:

- Provides a secure communications channel among all parties involved in a transaction
- Provides trust by the use of X.509v3 digital certificates
- Ensures privacy because the information is only available to parties in a transaction when and where necessary

SET is a complex specification defined in three books issued in May of 1997:

- **Book 1:** Business Description (80 pages)
- **Book 2:** Programmer's Guide (629 pages)
- **Book 3:** Formal Protocol Definition (262 pages)

This is a total of 971 pages of specification. In contrast, the SSLv3 specification is 63 pages long and the TLS specification is 80 pages long. Accordingly, only a summary of this many-faceted specification is provided in this section.

SET Overview

A good way to begin our discussion of SET is to look at the business requirements for SET, its key features, and the participants in SET transactions.

Requirements

Book 1 of the SET specification lists the following business requirements for secure payment processing with credit cards over the Internet and other networks:

- **Provide confidentiality of payment and ordering information:** It is necessary to assure cardholders that this information is safe and accessible only to the intended recipient. Confidentiality also reduces the risk of fraud by either party to the transaction or by malicious third parties. SET uses encryption to provide confidentiality.
- **Ensure the integrity of all transmitted data:** That is, ensure that no changes in content occur during transmission of SET messages. Digital signatures are used to provide integrity.
- **Provide authentication that a cardholder is a legitimate user of a credit card account:** A mechanism that links a cardholder to a specific account number reduces the incidence of fraud and the overall cost of payment processing. Digital signatures and certificates are used to verify that a cardholder is a legitimate user of a valid account.

- **Provide authentication that a merchant can accept credit card transactions through its relationship with a financial institution:** This is the complement to the preceding requirement. Cardholders need to be able to identify merchants with whom they can conduct secure transactions. Again, digital signatures and certificates are used.

- **Ensure the use of the best security practices and system design techniques to protect all legitimate parties in an electronic commerce transaction:** SET is a well-tested specification based on highly secure cryptographic algorithms and protocols.

- **Create a protocol that neither depends on transport security mechanisms nor prevents their use:** SET can securely operate over a "raw" TCP/IP stack. However, SET does not interfere with the use of other security mechanisms, such as IPSec and SSL/TLS.

- **Facilitate and encourage interoperability among software and network providers:** The SET protocols and formats are independent of hardware platform, operating system, and Web software.

Key Features of SET

To meet the requirements just outlined, SET incorporates the following features:

- **Confidentiality of information:** Cardholder account and payment information is secured as it travels across the network. An interesting and important feature of SET is that it prevents the merchant from learning the cardholder's credit card number; this is only provided to the issuing bank. Conventional encryption by DES is used to provide confidentiality.

- **Integrity of data:** Payment information sent from cardholders to merchants includes order information, personal data, and payment instructions. SET guarantees that these message contents are not altered in transit. RSA digital signatures, using SHA-1 hash codes, provide message integrity. Certain messages are also protected by HMAC using SHA-1.

- **Cardholder account authentication:** SET enables merchants to verify that a cardholder is a legitimate user of a valid card account number. SET uses X.509v3 digital certificates with RSA signatures for this purpose.

- **Merchant authentication:** SET enables cardholders to verify that a merchant has a relationship with a financial institution allowing it to accept payment cards. SET uses X.509v3 digital certificates with RSA signatures for this purpose.

Note that unlike IPSec and SSL/TLS, SET provides only one choice for each cryptographic algorithm. This makes sense, because SET is a single application with a single set of requirements, whereas IPSec and SSL/TLS are intended to support a range of applications.

SET Participants

Figure 7.8 indicates the participants in the SET system, which include the following:

- **Cardholder:** In the electronic environment, consumers and corporate purchasers interact with merchants from personal computers over the Internet. A cardholder is an authorized holder of a payment card (e.g., MasterCard, Visa) that has been issued by an issuer.

- **Merchant:** A merchant is a person or organization that has goods or services to sell to the cardholder. Typically, these goods and services are offered via a Web site or by electronic mail. A merchant that accepts payment cards must have a relationship with an acquirer.

- **Issuer:** This is a financial institution, such as a bank, that provides the cardholder with the payment card. Typically, accounts are applied for and opened by mail or in person. Ultimately, it is the issuer that is responsible for the payment of the debt of the cardholder.

- **Acquirer:** This is a financial institution that establishes an account with a merchant and processes payment card authorizations and payments. Merchants will usually accept more than one credit card brand but do not want to deal with multiple bankcard associations or with multiple individual issuers. The acquirer provides authorization to the merchant that a given card account is active and that the proposed purchase does not exceed the credit limit. The acquirer also provides electronic transfer of payments to the merchant's account. Subsequently, the acquirer is reimbursed by the issuer over some sort of payment network for electronic funds transfer.

- **Payment gateway:** This is a function operated by the acquirer or a designated third party that processes merchant payment messages. The payment gateway interfaces between SET and the existing bankcard payment networks for autho-

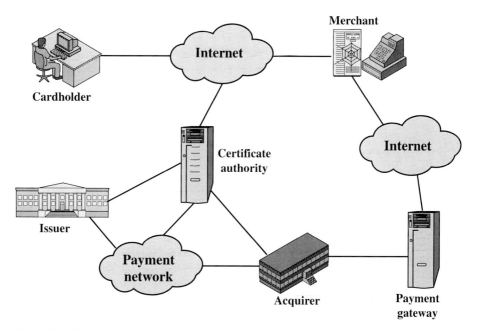

Figure 7.8   Secure Electronic Commerce Components

rization and payment functions. The merchant exchanges SET messages with the payment gateway over the Internet, while the payment gateway has some direct or network connection to the acquirer's financial processing system.

- **Certification authority (CA):** This is an entity that is trusted to issue X.509v3 public-key certificates for cardholders, merchants, and payment gateways. The success of SET will depend on the existence of a CA infrastructure available for this purpose. As was discussed in previous chapters, a hierarchy of CAs is used, so that participants need not be directly certified by a root authority.

We now briefly describe the sequence of events that are required for a transaction. We will then look at some of the cryptographic details.

1. **The customer opens an account.** The customer obtains a credit card account, such as MasterCard or Visa, with a bank that supports electronic payment and SET.

2. **The customer receives a certificate.** After suitable verification of identity, the customer receives an X.509v3 digital certificate, which is signed by the bank. The certificate verifies the customer's RSA public key and its expiration date. It also establishes a relationship, guaranteed by the bank, between the customer's key pair and his or her credit card.

3. **Merchants have their own certificates.** A merchant who accepts a certain brand of card must be in possession of two certificates for two public keys owned by the merchant: one for signing messages, and one for key exchange. The merchant also needs a copy of the payment gateway's public-key certificate.

4. **The customer places an order.** This is a process that may involve the customer first browsing through the merchant's Web site to select items and determine the price. The customer then sends a list of the items to be purchased to the merchant, who returns an order form containing the list of items, their price, a total price, and an order number.

5. **The merchant is verified.** In addition to the order form, the merchant sends a copy of its certificate, so that the customer can verify that he or she is dealing with a valid store.

6. **The order and payment are sent.** The customer sends both a order and payment information to the merchant, along with the customer's certificate. The order confirms the purchase of the items in the order form. The payment contains credit card details. The payment information is encrypted in such a way that it cannot be read by the merchant. The customer's certificate enables the merchant to verify the customer.

7. **The merchant requests payment authorization.** The merchant sends the payment information to the payment gateway, requesting authorization that the customer's available credit is sufficient for this purchase.

8. **The merchant confirms the order.** The merchant sends confirmation of the order to the customer.

9. **The merchant provides the goods or service.** The merchant ships the goods or provides the service to the customer.

10. **The merchant requests payment.** This request is sent to the payment gateway, which handles all of the payment processing.

Dual Signature

Before looking at the details of the SET protocol, let us discuss an important innovation introduced in SET: the dual signature. The purpose of the dual signature is to link two messages that are intended for two different recipients. In this case, the customer want to send the order information (OI) to the merchant and the payment information (PI) to the bank. The merchant does not need to know the customer's credit card number, and the bank does not need to know the details of the customer's order. The customer is afforded extra protection in terms of privacy by keeping these two items separate. However, the two items must be linked in a way that can be used to resolve disputes if necessary. The link is needed so that the customer can prove that this payment is intended for this order and not for some other goods or service.

To see the need for the link, suppose that the customers send the merchant two messages—a signed OI and a signed PI—and the merchant passes the PI on to the bank. If the merchant can capture another OI from this customer, the merchant could claim that this OI goes with the PI rather than the original OI. The linkage prevents this.

Figure 7.9 shows the use of a dual signature to meet the requirement of the preceding paragraph. The customer takes the hash (using SHA-1) of the PI and the hash of the OI. These two hashes are then concatenated and the hash of the result is taken. Finally, the customer encrypts the final hash with his or her private signature key, creating the dual signature. The operation can be summarized as

$$DS = E_{KR_c}[H(H(PI) \parallel H(OI))]$$

where KR_c is the customer's private signature key. Now suppose that the merchant is in possession of the dual signature (DS), the OI, and the message digest for the PI (PIMD). The merchant also has the public key of the customer, taken from the customer's certificate. Then the merchant can compute the following two quantities:

$$H(PIMD \parallel H(OI)) \text{ and } D_{KU_c}[DS]$$

where KU_c is the customer's public signature key. If these two quantities are equal, then the merchant has verified the signature. Similarly, if the bank is in possession of DS, PI, the message digest for OI (OIMD), and the customer's public key, then the bank can compute the following:

$$H(H(PI) \parallel OIMD) \text{ and } D_{KU_c}[DS]$$

Again, if these two quantities are equal, then the bank has verified the signature. In summary,

1. The merchant has received OI and verified the signature.
2. The bank has received PI and verified the signature.
3. The customer has linked the OI and PI and can prove the linkage.

For example, suppose the merchant wishes to substitute another OI in this transaction, to its advantage. It would then have to find another OI whose hash

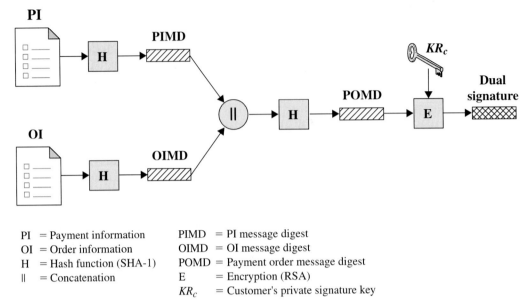

PI = Payment information PIMD = PI message digest
OI = Order information   OIMD = OI message digest
H = Hash function (SHA-1) POMD = Payment order message digest
‖ = Concatenation   E   = Encryption (RSA)
           KR_c = Customer's private signature key

Figure 7.9 Construction of Dual Signature

matches the existing OIMD. With SHA-1, this is deemed not to be feasible. Thus, the merchant cannot link another OI with this PI.

Payment Processing

Table 7.3 lists the transaction types supported by SET. In what follows we look in some detail at the following transactions:

- Purchase request
- Payment authorization
- Payment capture

Purchase Request

Before the Purchase Request exchange begins, the cardholder has completed browsing, selecting, and ordering. The end of this preliminary phase occurs when the merchant sends a completed order form to the customer. All of the preceding occurs without the use of SET.

The purchase request exchange consists of four messages: Initiate Request, Initiate Response, Purchase Request, and Purchase Response.

In order to send SET messages to the merchant, the cardholder must have a copy of the certificates of the merchant and the payment gateway. The customer requests the certificates in the **Initiate Request** message, sent to the merchant. This message includes the brand of the credit card that the customer is using. The message also includes an ID assigned to this request/response pair by the customer and a nonce used to ensure timeliness.

Table 7.3 SET Transaction Types

Cardholder registration	Cardholders must register with a CA before they can send SET messages to merchants.
Merchant registration	Merchants must register with a CA before they can exchange SET messages with customers and payment gateways.
Purchase request	Message from customer to merchant containing OI for merchant and PI for bank.
Payment authorization	Exchange between merchant and payment gateway to authorize a given amount for a purchase on a given credit card account.
Payment capture	Allows the merchant to request payment from the payment gateway.
Certificate inquiry and status	If the CA is unable to complete the processing of a certificate request quickly, it will send a reply to the cardholder or merchant indicating that the requester should check back later. The cardholder or merchant sends the *Certificate Inquiry* message to determine the status of the certificate request and to receive the certificate if the request has been approved.
Purchase inquiry	Allows the cardholder to check the status of the processing of an order after the purchase response has been received. Note that this message does not include information such as the status of back-ordered goods but does indicate the status of authorization, capture, and credit processing.
Authorization reversal	Allows a merchant to correct previous authorization requests. If the order will not be completed, the merchant reverses the entire authorization. If part of the order will not be completed (such as when goods are back ordered), the merchant reverses part of the amount of the authorization.
Capture reversal	Allows a merchant to correct errors in capture requests such as transaction amounts that were entered incorrectly by a clerk.
Credit	Allows a merchant to issue a credit to a cardholder's account such as when goods are returned or were damaged during shipping. Note that the SET *Credit* message is always initiated by the merchant, not the cardholder. All communications between the cardholder and merchant that result in a credit being processed happen outside of SET.
Credit reversal	Allows a merchant to correct a previously request credit.
Payment gateway certificate request	Allows a merchant to query the payment gateway and receive a copy of the gateway's current key exchange and signature certificates.
Batch administration	Allows a merchant to communicate information to the payment gateway regarding merchant batches.
Error message	Indicates that a responder rejects a message because it fails format or content verification tests.

The merchant generates a response and signs it with its private signature key. The response includes the nonce from the customer, another nonce for the customer to return in the next message, and a transaction ID for this purchase transaction. In addition to the signed response, the **Initiate Response** message includes the merchant's signature certificate and the payment gateway's key exchange certificate.

The cardholder verifies the merchant and gateway certificates by means of their respective CA signatures and then creates the OI and PI. The transaction ID assigned by the merchant is placed in both the OI and PI. The OI does not contain explicit order data such as the number and price of items. Rather, it contains an order reference generated in the exchange between merchant and customer during the shopping phase before the first SET message. Next, the cardholder prepares the **Purchase Request** message (Figure 7.10). For this purpose, the cardholder generates a one-time symmetric encryption key, K_s. The message includes the following:

1. **Purchase-related information.** This information will be forwarded to the payment gateway by the merchant and consists of
   - The PI
   - The dual signature, calculated over the PI and OI, signed with the customer's private signature key
   - The OI message digest (OIMD)

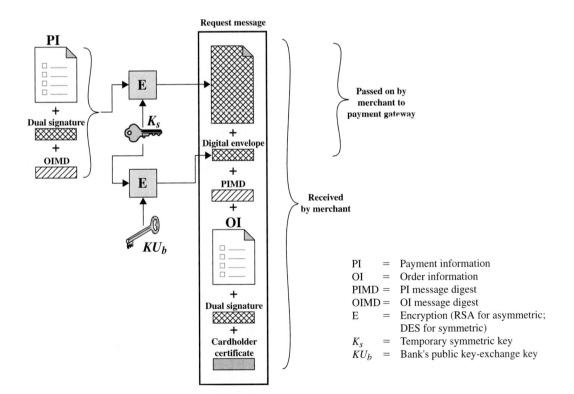

Figure 7.10 Cardholder Sends Purchase Request

The OIMD is needed for the payment gateway to verify the dual signature, as explained previously. All of these items are encrypted with K_s. The final item is

○ The digital envelope. This is formed by encrypting K_s with the payment gateway's public key-exchange key. It is called a digital envelope because this envelope must be opened (decrypted) before the other items listed previously can be read.

The value of K_s is not made available to the merchant. Therefore, the merchant cannot read any of this payment-related information.

2. **Order-related information.** This information is needed by the merchant and consists of

○ The OI

○ The dual signature, calculated over the PI and OI, signed with the customer's private signature key

○ The PI message digest (PIMD)

The PIMD is needed for the merchant to verify the dual signature. Note that the OI is sent in the clear.

3. **Cardholder certificate.** This contains the cardholder's public signature key. It is needed by the merchant and by the payment gateway.

When the merchant receives the Purchase Request message, it performs the following actions (Figure 7.11):

1. Verifies the cardholder certificates by means of its CA signatures.
2. Verifies the dual signature using the customer's public signature key. This ensures that the order has not been tampered with in transit and that it was signed using the cardholder's private signature key.
3. Processes the order and forwards the payment information to the payment gateway for authorization (described later).
4. Sends a purchase response to the cardholder.

The **Purchase Response** message includes a response block that acknowledges the order and references the corresponding transaction number. This block is signed by the merchant using its private signature key. The block and its signature are sent to the customer, along with the merchant's signature certificate.

When the cardholder software receives the purchase response message, it verifies the merchant's certificate and then verifies the signature on the response block. Finally, it takes some action based on the response, such as displaying a message to the user or updating a database with the status of the order.

Payment Authorization

During the processing of an order from a cardholder, the merchant authorizes the transaction with the payment gateway. The payment authorization ensures that the transaction was approved by the issuer. This authorization guarantees that the merchant will receive payment; the merchant can therefore provide the services or goods to the customer. The payment authorization exchange consists of two messages: Authorization Request and Authorization response.

Request message

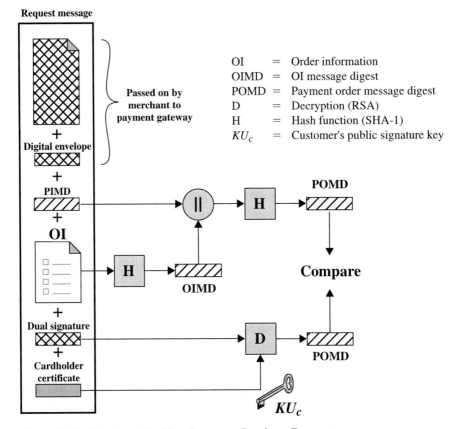

OI	= Order information
OIMD	= OI message digest
POMD	= Payment order message digest
D	= Decryption (RSA)
H	= Hash function (SHA-1)
KU_c	= Customer's public signature key

Figure 7.11 Merchant Verifies Customer Purchase Request

The merchant sends an **Authorization Request** message to the payment gateway consisting of the following:

1. **Purchase-related information.** This information was obtained from the customer and consists of the following:
   - The PI
   - The dual signature, calculated over the PI and OI, signed with the customer's private signature key
   - The OI message digest (OIMD)
   - The digital envelope

2. **Authorization-related information.** This information is generated by the merchant and consists of
   - An authorization block that includes the transaction ID, signed with the merchant's private signature key and encrypted with a one-time symmetric key generated by the merchant
   - A digital envelope. This is formed by encrypting the one-time key with the payment gateway's public key-exchange key.

3. **Certificates.** The merchant includes the cardholder's signature key certificate (used to verify the dual signature), the merchant's signature key certificate (used to verify the merchant's signature), and the merchant's key-exchange certificate (needed in the payment gateway's response).

The payment gateway performs the following tasks:

1. Verifies all certificates
2. Decrypts the digital envelope of the authorization block to obtain the symmetric key and then decrypts the authorization block
3. Verifies the merchant's signature on the authorization block
4. Decrypts the digital envelope of the payment block to obtain the symmetric key and then decrypts the payment block
5. Verifies the dual signature on the payment block
6. Verifies that the transaction ID received from the merchant matches that in the PI received (indirectly) from the customer
7. Requests and receives an authorization from the issuer

Having obtained authorization from the issuer, the payment gateway returns an **Authorization Response** message to the merchant. It includes the following elements:

1. **Authorization-related information.** Includes an authorization block, signed with the gateway's private signature key and encrypted with a one-time symmetric key generated by the gateway. Also includes a digital envelope that contains the one-time key encrypted with the merchants public key-exchange key.
2. **Capture token information.** This information will be used to effect payment later. This block is of the same form as (1), namely, a signed, encrypted capture token together with a digital envelope. This token is not processed by the merchant. Rather, it must be returned, as is, with a payment request.
3. **Certificate.** The gateway's signature key certificate.

With the authorization from the gateway, the merchant can provide the goods or service to the customer.

Payment Capture

To obtain payment, the merchant engages the payment gateway in a payment capture transaction, consisting of a capture request and a capture response message.

For the **Capture Request** message, the merchant generates, signs, and encrypts a capture request block, which includes the payment amount and the transaction ID. The message also includes the encrypted capture token received earlier (in the Authorization Response) for this transaction, as well as the merchant's signature key and key-exchange key certificates.

When the payment gateway receives the capture request message, it decrypts and verifies the capture request block and decrypts and verifies the capture token block. It then checks for consistency between the capture request and capture token. It then creates a clearing request that is sent to the issuer over the private payment network. This request causes funds to be transferred to the merchant's account.

The gateway then notifies the merchant of payment in a **Capture Response** message. The message includes a capture response block that the gateway signs and encrypts. The message also includes the gateway's signature key certificate. The merchant software stores the capture response to be used for reconciliation with payment received from the acquirer.

7.4 RECOMMENDED READING AND WEB SITES

[RESC01] is a good detailed treatment of SSL and TLS.

The best-detailed overview of SET is in Book 1 of the specification, available at the MasterCard SET Web site. Another excellent overview is [MACG97]. [DREW99] is also a good source.

DREW99 Drew, G. *Using SET for Secure Electronic Commerce.* Upper Saddle River, NJ: Prentice Hall, 1999.

MACG97 Macgregor, R.; Ezvan, C.; Liguori, L.; and Han, J. *Secure Electronic Transactions: Credit Card Payment on the Web in Theory and Practice.* IBM RedBook SG24-4978-00, 1997. Available at www.redbooks.ibm.com.

RESC01 Rescorla, E. *SSL and TLS: Designing and Building Secure Systems.* Reading, MA: Addison-Wesley, 2001.

Recommended Web sites:

- **Netscape's SSL Page:** Contains the SSL specification
- **Transport Layer Security Charter:** Latest RFCs and Internet drafts for TLS
- **MasterCard SET Site:** Latest SET documents, glossary of terms, and application information
- **SETCo:** Latest SET documents, glossary of terms, and other information

7.5 KEY TERMS, REVIEW QUESTIONS, AND PROBLEMS

Key Terms

acquirer	issuer	Secure Electronic Transaction (SET)
cardholder	merchant	Secure Socket Layer (SSL)
certification authority (CA)	payment gateway	Transport Layer Security (TLS)
dual signature		

Review Questions

7.1   What are the advantages of each of the three approaches shown in Figure 7.1?

7.2   What protocols comprise SSL?

7.3   What is the difference between and SSL connection and an SSL session?

7.4   List and briefly define the parameters that define an SSL session state.

7.5   List and briefly define the parameters that define an SSL session connection.

7.6   What services are provided by the SSL Record Protocol?

7.7   What steps are involved in the SSL Record Protocol transmission?

7.8   List and briefly define the principal categories of SET participants.

7.9   What is a dual signature and what is its purpose?

Problems

7.1   In SSL and TLS, why is there a separate Change Cipher Spec Protocol, rather than including a change_cipher_spec message in the Handshake Protocol?

7.2   Consider the following threats to Web security and describe how each is countered by a particular feature of SSL.

    a. Brute-Force Cryptanalytic Attack: An exhaustive search of the key space for a conventional encryption algorithm.

    b. Known Plaintext Dictionary Attack: Many messages will contain predictable plaintext, such as the HTTP GET command. An attacker constructs a dictionary containing every possible encryption of the known-plaintext message. When an encrypted message is intercepted, the attacker takes the portion containing the encrypted known plaintext and looks up the ciphertext in the dictionary. The ciphertext should match against an entry that was encrypted with the same secret key. If there are several matchcs, each of these can be tried against the full ciphertext to determine the right one. This attack is especially effective against small key sizes (e.g., 40-bit keys).

    c. Replay Attack: Earlier SSL handshake messages are replayed.

    d. Man-in-the-Middle Attack: An attacker interposes during key exchange, acting as the client to the server and as the server to the client.

    e. Password Sniffing: Passwords in HTTP or other application traffic are eavesdropped.

    f. IP Spoofing: Uses forged IP addresses to fool a host into accepting bogus data.

    g. IP Hijacking: An active, authenticated connection between two hosts is disrupted and the attacker takes the place of one of the hosts.

    h. SYN Flooding: An attacker sends TCP SYN messages to request a connection but does not respond to the final message to establish the connection fully. The attacked TCP module typically leaves the "half-open connection" around for a few minutes. Repeated SYN messages can clog the TCP module.

7.3   Based on what you have learned in this chapter, is it possible in SSL for the receiver to reorder SSL record blocks that arrive out of order? If so, explain how it can be done. If not, why not?

CHAPTER 8

NETWORK MANAGEMENT SECURITY

8.1 Basic Concepts of SNMP

    Network Management Architecture
    Network Management Protocol Architecture
    Proxies
    SNMPv2

8.2 SNMPv1 Community Facility

    Communities and Community Names
    Authentication Service
    Access Policy
    Proxy Service

8.3 SNMPv3

    SNMP Architecture
    Message Processing and the User Security Model
    View-Based Access Control

8.4 Recommended Reading and Web Sites

8.5 Key Terms, Review Questions, and Problems

    Key Terms
    Review Questions
    Problems

The control of a large force is the same in principle as the control of a few men; it is merely a question of dividing up their numbers..

—The Art of War, Sun Tzu

Networks and distributed processing systems are of critical and growing importance in business, government, and other organizations. Within a given organization, the trend is toward larger, more complex networks supporting more applications and more users. As these networks grow in scale, two facts become painfully evident:

- The network and its associated resources and distributed applications become indispensable to the organization.
- More things can go wrong, disabling the network or a portion of the network or degrading performance to an unacceptable level.

A large network cannot be put together and managed by human effort alone. The complexity of such a system dictates the use of automated network management tools. If the network includes equipment from multiple vendors, the need for such tools is increased, and the difficulty of supplying such tools is also increased. In response to this need, standards that deal with network management have been developed, covering services, protocols, and management information bases. By far, the most widely used such standard is the Simple Network Management Protocol (SNMP).

Since its publication in 1988, SNMP has found use in a growing number of networks and in increasingly complex environments. As the use of SNMP spread, new functionality was needed to accommodate new demands. Also, the importance of providing a security capability as part of network management became increasingly apparent. To provide enhanced functionality, version 2 of SNMP[1] was defined. Security enhancements were promulgated in SNMPv3.

This chapter describes the rudimentary security facility available in SNMPv1 and the much more extensive set of security features provided by SNMPv3.

8.1 BASIC CONCEPTS OF SNMP

This section provides an overview of the basic framework for SNMP.

---

[1]Version 2 is denoted as SNMPv2. To distinguish the original version from the new version, the original version is now generally referred to as SNMPv1.

Network Management Architecture

A network management system is a collection of tools for network monitoring and control that is integrated in the following senses:

- A single operator interface with a powerful but user-friendly set of commands for performing most or all network management tasks.
- A minimal amount of separate equipment. That is, most of the hardware and software required for network management is incorporated into the existing user equipment.

A network management system consists of incremental hardware and software additions implemented among existing network components. The software used in accomplishing the network management tasks resides in the host computers and communications processors (e.g., front-end processors, terminal cluster controllers). A network management system is designed to view the entire network as a unified architecture, with addresses and labels assigned to each point and the specific attributes of each element and link known to the system. The active elements of the network provide regular feedback of status information to the network control center.

The model of network management that is used for SNMP includes the following key elements:

- Management station
- Management agent
- Management information base
- Network management protocol

The **management station** is typically a stand-alone device, but may be a capability implemented on a shared system. In either case, the management station serves as the interface for the human network manager into the network management system. The management station will have, at minimum,

- A set of management applications for data analysis, fault recovery, and so on
- An interface by which the network manager may monitor and control the network
- The capability of translating the network manager's requirements into the actual monitoring and control of remote elements in the network
- A database of information extracted from the MIBs of all the managed entities in the network

Only the last two elements are the subject of SNMP standardization.

The other active element in the network management system is the **management agent**. Key platforms, such as hosts, bridges, routers, and hubs, may be equipped with SNMP so that they may be managed from a management station. The management agent responds to requests for information from a management station, responds to requests for actions from the management station, and may asynchronously provide the management station with important but unsolicited information.

To manage resources in the network, each resource is represented as an object. An object is, essentially, a data variable that represents one aspect of the managed agent. The collection of objects is referred to as a **management information base** (MIB). The MIB functions as a collection of access points at the agent for the management station. These objects are standardized across systems of a particular class (e.g., bridges all support the same management objects). A management station performs the monitoring function by retrieving the value of MIB objects. A management station can cause an action to take place at an agent or can change the configuration settings of an agent by modifying the value of specific objects.

The management station and agents are linked by a **network management protocol**. The protocol used for the management of TCP/IP networks is the Simple Network Management Protocol (SNMP). This protocol includes the following key capabilities:

- **Get:** Enables the management station to retrieve the value of objects at the agent
- **Set:** Enables the management station to set the value of objects at the agent
- **Notify:** Enables an agent to notify the management station of significant events

Network Management Protocol Architecture

In 1988, the specification for SNMP was issued and rapidly became the dominant network management standard. A number of vendors offer stand-alone network management workstations based on SNMP, and most vendors of bridges, routers, workstations, and PCs offer SNMP agent packages that allow their products to be managed by an SNMP management station.

As the name suggests, SNMP is a simple tool for network management. It defines a limited, easily implemented management information base (MIB) of scalar variables and two-dimensional tables, and it defines a streamlined protocol to enable a manager to get and set MIB variables and to enable an agent to issue unsolicited notifications, called *traps*. This simplicity is the strength of SNMP. SNMP is easily implemented and consumes modest processor and network resources. Also, the structures of the protocol and the MIB are sufficiently straightforward that it is not difficult to achieve interoperability among management stations and agent software from a mix of vendors.

The three foundation specifications are:

- **Structure and Identification of Management Information for TCP/IP-Based Networks (RFC 1155):** Describes how managed objects contained in the MIB are defined
- **Management Information Base for Network Management of TCP/IP-based Internets: MIB-II (RFC 1213):** Describes the managed objects contained in the MIB
- **Simple Network Management Protocol (RFC 1157):** Defines the protocol used to manage these objects

SNMP was designed to be an application-level protocol that is part of the TCP/IP protocol suite. It is intended to operate over the User Datagram Protocol (UDP), defined in RFC 768. For a stand-alone management station, a manager process controls access to the central MIB at the management station and provides an interface to the network manager. The manager process achieves network management by using SNMP, which is implemented on top of UDP, IP, and the relevant network-dependent protocols (e.g., Ethernet, FDDI, X.25).

Each agent must also implement SNMP, UDP, and IP. In addition, there is an agent process that interprets the SNMP messages and controls the agent's MIB. For an agent device that supports other applications, such as FTP, TCP as well as UDP is required.

Figure 8.1 illustrates the protocol context of SNMP. From a management station, three types of SNMP messages are issued on behalf of a management applications: GetRequest, GetNextRequest, and SetRequest. The first two are two variations of the get function. All three messages are acknowledged by the agent in the form of a GetResponse message, which is passed up to the management application. In addition, an agent may issue a trap message in response to an event that affects the MIB and the underlying managed resources.

Because SNMP relies on UDP, which is a connectionless protocol, SNMP is itself connectionless. No ongoing connections are maintained between a management station and its agents. Instead, each exchange is a separate transaction between a management station and an agent.

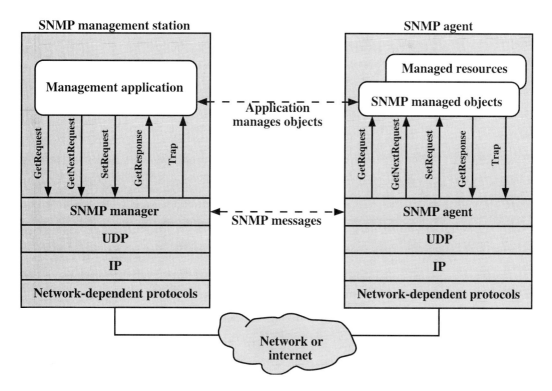

Figure 8.1   The Role of SNMP

Proxies

In SNMPv1 all agents, as well as management stations, must support UDP and IP. This limits direct management to such devices and excludes other devices, such as some bridges and modems, that do not support any part of the TCP/IP protocol suite. Further, there may be numerous small systems (personal computers, workstations, programmable controllers) that do implement TCP/IP to support their applications, but for which it is not desirable to add the additional burden of SNMP, agent logic, and MIB maintenance.

To accommodate devices that do not implement SNMP, the concept of proxy was developed. In this scheme an SNMP agent acts as a proxy for one or more other devices; that is, the SNMP agent acts on behalf of the proxied devices.

Figure 8.2 indicates the type of protocol architecture that is often involved. The management station sends queries concerning a device to its proxy agent. The proxy agent converts each query into the management protocol that is used by the device. When the agent receives a reply to a query, it passes that reply back to the management station. Similarly, if an event notification of some sort from the device is transmitted to the proxy, the proxy sends that on to the management station in the form of a trap message.

SNMPv2 allows the use of not only the TCP/IP protocol suite but others as well. In particular, SNMPv2 is intended to run on the OSI protocol suite. Thus, SNMPv2 can be used to manage a greater variety of networked configurations. With respect to proxies, any device that does not implement SNMPv2 can only be managed by means of proxy. This even includes SNMPv1 devices. That is, if a device implements the agent software for SNMPv1, it can be reached from an SNMPv2 manager only by a proxy device that implements the SNMPv2 agent and the SNMPv1 manager software.

The cases described in the preceding paragraph are referred to as foreign proxy relationships in SNMPv2. In addition, SNMPv2 supports a native proxy relationship in which the proxied device does support SNMPv2. In this case, an SNMPv2 manager communicates with an SNMPv2 node acting as an agent. This node then acts as a manager to reach the proxied device, which acts as an SNMPv2 agent. The reason for supporting this type of indirection is to enable users to configure hierarchical, decentralized network management systems, as discussed later.

SNMPv2

The strength of SNMP is its simplicity. SNMP provides a basic set of network management tools in a package that is easy to implement and easy to configure. However, as users have come to rely more and more on SNMP to manage ever-expanding networks with ever-growing workloads, its deficiencies have become all too apparent. These deficiencies fall into three categories:

- Lack of support for distributed network management
- Functional deficiencies
- Security deficiencies

The first two categories of deficiencies are addressed in SNMPv2, which was issued in 1993, with a revised version issued in 1996 (currently RFCs 1901, 1904

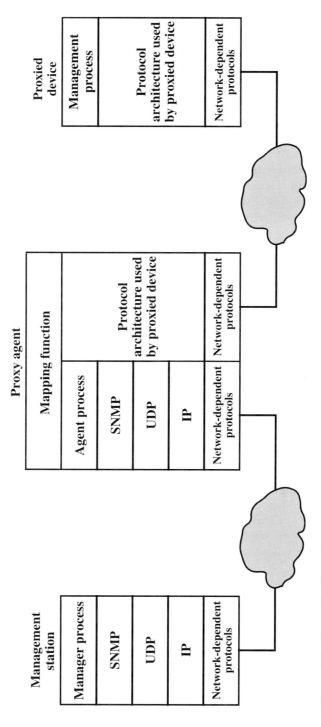

Figure 8.2 Proxy Configuration

255

through 1908, 2578, and 2579). SNMPv2 quickly gained support, and a number of vendors announced products within months of the issuance of the standard. The security deficiencies have been address in SNMPv3.

In the remainder of this subsection, we briefly summarize the new features provided by SNMPv2. The security features of SNMPv1 and SNMPv3 are examined in detail in Sections 8.2 and 8.3, respectively.

Distributed Network Management

In a traditional centralized network management scheme, one host in the configuration has the role of a network management station; there may be one or two other management stations in a backup role. The remainder of the devices on the network contains agent software and a MIB, to allow monitoring and control from the management station. As networks grow in size and traffic load, such a centralized system is unworkable. Too much burden is placed on the management station, and there is too much traffic, with reports from every single agent having to wend their way across the entire network to headquarters. In such circumstances, a decentralized, distributed approach works best (e.g., Figure 8.3). In a decentralized network management scheme, there may be multiple top-level management stations, which might be referred to as management servers. Each such server might directly manage a portion of the total pool of agents. However, for many of the agents, the management server delegates responsibility to an intermediate manager. The intermediate manager plays the role of manager to monitor and control the agents under its responsibility. It also plays an agent role to provide information and accept control from a higher-level management server. This type of architecture spreads the processing burden and reduces total network traffic.

SNMPv2 supports either a highly centralized network management strategy or a distributed one. In the latter case, some systems operate both in the role of manager and of agent. In its agent role, such a system will accept commands from a superior management system. Some of those commands relate to the local MIB at the agent. Other commands require the agent to act as a proxy for remote devices. In this case, the proxy agent assumes the role of manager to access information at a remote agent and then assumes the role of an agent to pass that information on to a superior manager.

Functional Enhancements

Table 8.1 suggests the functional enhancements that have been made in SNMPv2. Both protocols are defined in terms of a set of commands that are communicated as protocol data units (PDUs). In the case of SNMPv1, there are five commands. A manager issues the Get command to an agent to retrieve values of objects in the MIB. The GetNext command exploits the fact that objects in a MIB are arranged in a tree structure. When an object is named in a GetNext command, the agent finds the next object in the tree and returns its value. GetNext is useful because it allows a manager to "walk" a tree at an agent when it does not know the exact set of objects supported by that agent. The Set command enables a manager to update values at an agent; it is also used for creating and deleting rows in tables. An agent uses the GetResponse command to respond to a manager command. Finally, the Trap command enables an agent to send information to a manager with-

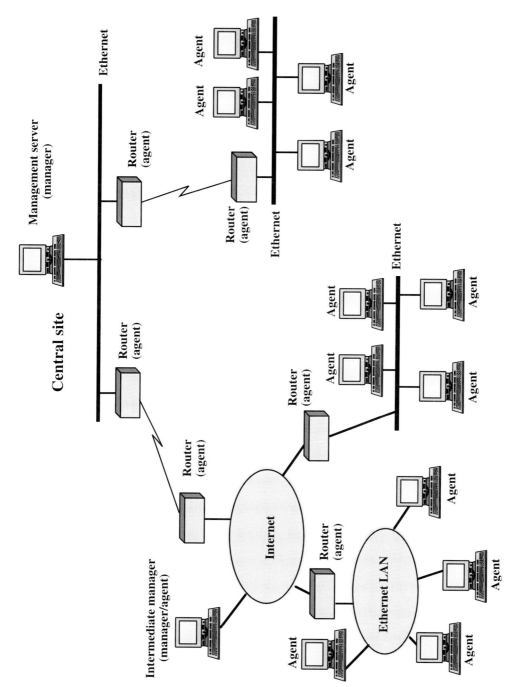

Figure 8.3 Example Distributed Network Management Configuration

257

Table 8.1 Comparison of SNMPv1 and SNMPv2 Protocol Data Units (PDUs)

SNMPv1 PDU	SNMPv2 PDU	Direction	Description
GetRequest	GetRequest	Manager to agent	Request value for each listed object
GetNextRequest	GetNextRequest	Manager to agent	Request next value for each listed object
—	GetBulkRequest	Manager to agent	Request multiple values
SetRequest	SetRequest	Manager to agent	Set value for each listed object
—	InformRequest	Manager to manager	Transmit unsolicited information
GetResponse	Response	Agent to manager or Manager to manager (SNMPv2)	Respond to manager request
Trap	SNMPv2-Trap	Agent to manager	Transmit unsolicited information

out waiting for a management request. For example, an agent could be configured to send a Trap when a link fails or when traffic exceeds a threshold.

SNMPv2 includes all of the commands found in SNMPv1 plus two new ones. The most important of these is the Inform command. This command is sent by one management station to another and, like the trap, includes information relating to conditions or events at the sender. The advantage of the Inform command is that it can be used to construct a configuration in which multiple managers cooperate to share management responsibility in a large network.

The other new command, GetBulk, allows a manager to retrieve a large block of data at one time. In particular, the GetBulk command is designed for the transmission of entire tables with one command.

A final difference: The Get command is atomic in the case of SNMPv1 but not in the case of SNMPv2. If an SNMPv1 Get command contains a list of objects for which values are requested, and at least one of the objects does not exist at the agent, then the entire command is rejected. For SNMPv2, partial results may be returned. The nonatomic Get command allows for more efficient use of network capacity by the manager.

8.2 SNMPv1 COMMUNITY FACILITY

SNMPv1, as defined in RFC 1157, provides only a rudimentary security facility based on the concept of community. This facility gives a certain level of security but is open to various attacks [CERT02, JIAN02].

Communities and Community Names

Like other distributed applications, network management involves the interaction of a number of application entities supported by an application protocol. In the case of SNMP network management, the application entities are the manager applications and the agent applications that use SNMP.

SNMP network management has several characteristics not typical of all distributed applications. The application involves a one-to-many relationship between a manager and a set of agents: The manager is able to get and set objects in the agents and is able to received traps from the agents. Thus, from an operational or control point of view, the manager "manages" a number of agents. There may be a number of managers, each of which manages all or a subset of the agents in the configuration. These subsets may overlap.

We also need to be able to view SNMP network management as a one-to-many relationship between an agent and a set of managers. Each agent controls its own local MIB and must be able to control the use of that MIB by a number of managers. There are three aspects of this control:

- **Authentication service:** The agent may wish to limit access to the MIB to authorized managers.
- **Access policy:** The agent may wish to give different access privileges to different managers.
- **Proxy service:** An agent may act as proxy to other agents. This may involve implementing the authentication service and/or access policy for the other agents on the proxy system.

All of these aspects relate to security concerns. In an environment in which responsibility for network components is split, such as among a number of administrative entities, agents need to protect themselves and their MIBs from unwanted/unauthorized access. SNMP, as defined in RFC 1157, provides only a primitive and limited capability for such security, namely the concept of a community.

An **SNMP community** is a relationship between an SNMP agent and a set of SNMP managers that defines authentication, access control, and proxy characteristics. The community concept is a local one, defined at the agent. The agent establishes one community for each desired combination of authentication, access control, and proxy characteristics. Each community is given a unique (within this agent) community name, and the managers within that community are provided with and must employ the community name in all get and set operations. The agent may establish a number of communities, with overlapping manager membership.

Because communities are defined locally at the agent, different agents may use the same name. This identity of names is irrelevant and does not indicate any similarity between the defined communities. Thus, a manager must keep track of the community name or names that are associated with each of the agents that it wishes to access.

Authentication Service

The purpose of the SNMPv1 authentication service is to assure the recipient that an SNMPv1 message is from the source that it claims to be from. SNMPv1 only provides for a trivial scheme for authentication. Every message (get or put request) from a manager to an agent includes a community name. This name functions as a password, and the message is assumed to be authentic if the sender knows the password.

With this limited form of authentication, many network managers are reluctant to allow anything other than network monitoring; that is, get and trap operations. Network control, via a set operation, is clearly a more sensitive area. The community name could be used to trigger an authentication procedure, with the name functioning simply as an initial password-screening device. The authentication procedure could involve the use of encryption/decryption for more secure authentication functions. This is beyond the scope of RFC 1157.

Access Policy

By defining a community, an agent limits access to its MIB to a selected set of managers. By the use of more than one community, the agent can provide different categories of MIB access to different managers. There are two aspects to this access control:

- **SNMP MIB view:** A subset of the objects within an MIB. Different MIB views may be defined for each community. The set of objects in a view need not belong to a single sub-tree of the MIB.
- **SNMP access mode:** An element of the set {READ-ONLY, READ-WRITE}. An access mode is defined for each community.

The combination of an MIB view and access mode is referred to as an **SNMP community profile**. Thus, a community profile consists of a defined subset of the MIB at the agent, plus an access mode for those objects. The SNMP access mode is applied uniformly to all of the objects in the MIB view. Thus, if the access mode READ-ONLY is selected, it applies to all of the objects in the view and limits managers; access of this view to read-only operations.

A community profile is associated with each community defined by an agent; the combination of an SNMP community and an SNMP community profile is referred to as an **SNMP access policy**. Figure 8.4 illustrates the various concepts just introduced.

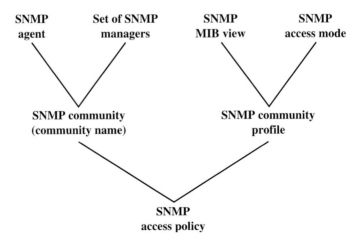

Figure 8.4 SNMPv1 Administrative Concepts

Proxy Service

The community concept is also useful in supporting the proxy service. Recall that a proxy is an SNMP agent that acts on behalf of other devices. Typically, the other devices are foreign, in the sense that they do not support TCP/IP and SNMP. In some cases, the proxied system may support SNMP but the proxy is used to minimize the interaction between the proxied device and network management systems.

For each device that the proxy system represents, it maintains an SNMP access policy. Thus, the proxy knows which MIB objects can be used to manage the proxied system (the MIB view) and their access mode.

8.3 SNMPv3

In 1998, the IETF SNMPv3 working group produced a set of Proposed Internet standards, currently RFCs 2570 through 2576. This document set defines a framework for incorporating security features into an overall capability that includes either SNMPv1 or SNMPv2 functionality. In addition, the documents define a specific set of capabilities for network security and access control.

It is important to realize that SNMPv3 is not a stand-alone replacement for SNMPv1 and/or SNMPv2. SNMPv3 defines a security capability to be used in conjunction with SNMPv2 (preferred) or SNMPv1. In addition, RFC 2571 describes an architecture within which all current and future versions of SNMP fit. RFC 2575 describes an access control facility, which is intended to operate independently of the core SNMPv3 capability. In this section, we take a broad view and provide a survey of the capabilities defined in RFCs 2570 through 2576.

Figure 8.5 indicates the relationship among the different versions of SNMP by means of the formats involved. Information is exchanged between a management

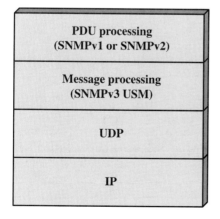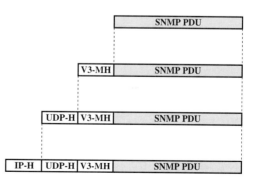

IP-H   = IP header
UDP-H = UDP header
V3-MH = SNMPv3 message header
PDU   = Protocol data unit

Figure 8.5 SNMP Protocol Architecture

station and an agent in the form of an SNMP message. Security-related processing occurs at the message level; for example, SNMPv3 specifies a User Security Model (USM) that makes use of fields in the message header. The payload of an SNMP message is either an SNMPv1 or an SNMPv2 protocol data unit (PDU). A PDU indicates a type of management action (e.g., get or set a managed object) and a list of variable names related to that action.

RFCs 2570 through 2576 describe an overall architecture plus specific message structures and security features, but do not define a new SNMP PDU format. Thus, the existing SNMPv1 or SNMPv2 PDU format must be used within the new architecture. An implementation referred to as SNMPv3 consists of the security and architectural features defined in RFCs 2570 through 2576 plus the PDU format and functionality defined in the SNMPv2 documents. This is expressed in RFC 2570 as follows: "SNMPv3 can be thought of as SNMPv2 with additional security and administration capabilities."

The remainder of this section is organized as follows. First, we provide a brief introduction to the basic SNMP architecture defined in RFC 2571. Next, we describe the confidentiality and authentication facilities provided by the SNMPv3 User Security Model (USM) are described. Finally, we discuss access control and the view-based access control model (VACM).

SNMP Architecture

The SNMP architecture, as envisioned by RFC 2571, consists of a distributed, interacting collection of SNMP entities. Each entity implements a portion of the SNMP capability and may act as an agent node, a manager node, or a combination of the two. Each SNMP entity consists of a collection of modules that interact with each other to provide services. These interactions can be modeled as a set of abstract primitives and parameters.

The RFC 2571 architecture reflects a key design requirement for SNMPv3: Design a modular architecture that will (1) allow implementation over a wide range of operational environments, some of which need minimal, inexpensive functionality and some of which may support additional features for managing large networks; (2) make it possible to move portions of the architecture forward in the standards track even if consensus has not been reached on all pieces; and (3) accommodate alternative security models

SNMP Entity

Each SNMP entity includes a single SNMP engine. An SNMP engine implements functions for sending and receiving messages, authenticating and encrypting/decrypting messages, and controlling access to managed objects. These functions are provided as services to one or more applications that are configured with the SNMP engine to form an SNMP entity.

Both the SNMP engine and the applications it supports are defined as a collection of discrete modules. This architecture provides several advantages. First the role of an SNMP entity is determined by which modules are implemented in that entity. A certain set of modules is required for an SNMP agent, while a different (though overlapping) set of modules is required for an SNMP manager. Second, the modular structure of the specification lends itself to defining different versions of each module. This in turn makes it possible to (1) define alternative or enhanced capabilities for certain aspects of SNMP without needing to go to a new version of the entire standard (e.g., SNMPv4), and (2) clearly specify coexistence and transition strategies (RFC 2576).

To get a better understanding of the role of each module and its relationship to other modules, it is best to look at their use in traditional SNMP managers and agents. The term *traditional*, equivalent to *pure*, is used to emphasize the fact that a given implementation need not be a pure manager or agent but may have modules that allow the entity to perform both management and agent tasks.

Figure 8.6, based on a figure in RFC 2571, is a block diagram of a **traditional SNMP manager**. A traditional SNMP manager interacts with SNMP agents by issuing commands (get, set) and by receiving trap messages; the manager may also interact with other managers by issuing Inform Request PDUs, which provide alerts, and by receiving Inform Response PDUs, which acknowledge Inform Requests. In SNMPv3 terminology, a traditional SNMP manager includes three categories of

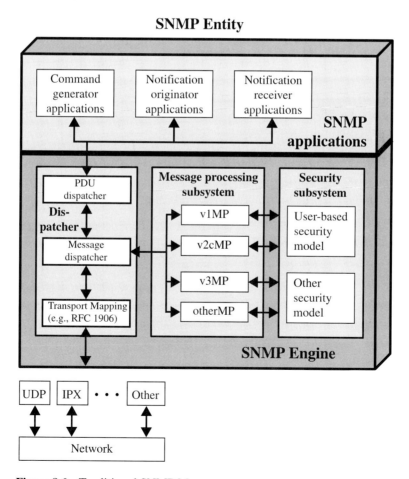

Figure 8.6 Traditional SNMP Manager

applications. The Command Generator Applications monitor and manipulate management data at remote agents; they make use of SNMPv1 and/or SNMPv2 PDUs, including Get, GetNext, GetBulk, and Set. A Notification Originator Application initiates asynchronous messages; in the case of a traditional manager, the InformRequest PDU is used for this application. A Notification Receiver Application processes incoming asynchronous messages; these include InformRequest, SNMPv2-Trap, and SNMPv1 Trap PDUs. In the case of an incoming InformRequest PDU, the Notification Receiver Application will respond with a Response PDU.

All of the applications just described make use of the services provided by the SNMP engine for this entity. The SNMP engine performs two overall functions:

- It accepts outgoing PDUs from SNMP applications; performs the necessary processing, including inserting authentication codes and encrypting; and then encapsulates the PDUs into messages for transmission.
- It accepts incoming SNMP messages from the transport layer; performs the necessary processing, including authentication and decryption; and then extracts the PDUs from the messages and passes these on to the appropriate SNMP application.

In a traditional manager, the SNMP engine contains a Dispatcher, a Message Processing Subsystem, and a Security Subsystem. The Dispatcher is a simple traffic manager. For outgoing PDUs, the Dispatcher accepts PDUs from applications and performs the following functions. For each PDU, the Dispatcher determines the type of message processing required (i.e., for SNMPv1, SNMPv2c, or SNMPv3) and passes the PDU on to the appropriate message processing module in the Message Processing Subsystem. Subsequently, the Message Processing Subsystem returns a message containing that PDU and including the appropriate message headers. The Dispatcher then maps this message onto a transport layer for transmission.

For incoming messages, the Dispatcher accepts messages from the transport layer and performs the following functions. The Dispatcher routes each message to the appropriate message processing module. Subsequently, the Message Processing Subsystem returns the PDU contained in the message. The Dispatcher then passes this PDU to the appropriate application.

The Message Processing Subsystem accepts outgoing PDUs from the Dispatcher and prepares these for transmission by wrapping them in the appropriate message header and returning them to the Dispatcher. The Message Processing Subsystem also accepts incoming messages from the Dispatcher, processes each message header, and returns the enclosed PDU to the Dispatcher. An implementation of the Message Processing Subsystem may support a single message format corresponding to a single version of SNMP (SNMPv1, SNMPv2c, SNMPv3), or it may contain a number of modules, each supporting a different version of SNMP.

The Security Subsystem performs authentication and encryption functions. Each outgoing message is passed to the Security Subsystem from the Message Processing Subsystem. Depending on the services required, the Security Subsystem may encrypt the enclosed PDU and possibly some fields in the message header, and it may generate an authentication code and insert it into the message header. The processed message is then returned to the Message Processing Subsystem. Similarly, each incoming message is passed to the Security Subsystem from the Message Processing Subsystem. If required, the Security Subsystem checks the authentication code and performs decryption. It then returns the processed message to the Message Processing Subsystem. An implementation of the Security Subsystem may support one or more distinct security models. So far, the only defined security model is the User-Based Security Model (USM) for SNMPv3, specified in RFC 2574.

Figure 8.7, based on a figure in RFC 2571, is a block diagram of a **traditional SNMP agent**. The traditional agent may contain three types of applications. Command Responder Applications provide access to management data. These applications respond to incoming requests by retrieving and/or setting managed objects and then issuing a Response PDU. A Notification Originator Application initiates asynchronous messages; in the case of a traditional agent, the SNMPv2-Trap or SNMPv1 Trap PDU is used for this application. A Proxy Forwarder Application forwards messages between entities.

The SNMP engine for a traditional agent has all of the components found in the SNMP engine for a traditional manager, plus an Access Control Subsystem. This subsystem provides authorization services to control access to MIBs for the reading and setting of management objects. These services are performed on the basis of the

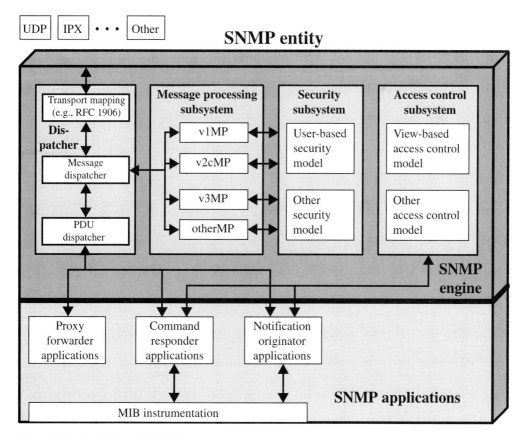

Figure 8.7 Traditional SNMP Agent

contents of PDUs. An implementation of the Security Subsystem may support one or more distinct access control models. So far, the only defined security model is the View-Based Access Control Model (VACM), specified in RFC 2575.

Note that security-related functions are organized into two separate subsystems: security and access control. This is an excellent example of good modular design, because the two subsystems perform quite distinct functions and therefore it makes sense to allow standardization of these two areas to proceed independently. The Security Subsystem is concerned with privacy and authentication and operates on SNMP messages. The Access Control Subsystem is concerned with authorized access to management information and operates on SNMP PDUs.

Terminology

Table 8.2 briefly defines some terms that are introduced in RFC 2571. Associated with each SNMP entity is a unique snmpEngineID. For purposes of access

Table 8.2 SNMPv3 Terminology

snmpEngineId
Unique and unambiguous identifier of an SNMP engine, as well as the SNMP entity that corresponds to that engine. It is defined by a textual convention, with a syntax of Octet String.

contextEngineID
Uniquely identifies an SNMP entity that may realize an instance of a context with a particular contextName.

contextName
Identifies a particular context within an SNMP engine. It is passed as a parameter to the Dispatcher and Access Control Subsystem.

scopedPDU
A block of data consisting of a contextEngineID, a contextName, and an SNMP PDU. It is passed as a parameter to/from the Security Subsystem.

snmpMessageProcessingModel
Unique identifier of a message processing model of the Message Processing Subsystem. Possible values include SNMPv1, SNMPv2c, and SNMPv3. It is defined by a textual convention, with a syntax of Integer.

snmpSecurityModel
Unique identifier of a security model of the Security Subsystem. Possible values include SNMPv1, SNMPv2c, and USM. It is defined by a textual convention, with a syntax of Integer.

snmpSecurityLevel
A level of security at which SNMP messages can be sent or with which operations are being processed, expressed in terms of whether or not authentication and/or privacy are provided. The alternative values are noAuthnoPriv, authNoPriv, and authPriv. It is defined by a textual convention, with a syntax of Integer.

principal
The entity on whose behalf services are provided or processing takes place. A principal can be an individual acting in a particular role; a set of individuals, with each acting in a particular role; an application or set of applications; and combinations thereof.

securityName
A human-readable string representing a principal. It is passed as a parameter in all of the SNMP primitives (Dispatcher, Message Processing, Security, Access Control).

control, each SNMP entity is considered to manage a number of contexts of managed information, each of which has a contextName that is unique within that entity. To emphasize that there is a single manager of contexts within an entity, each entity has a unique contextEngineID associated with it; because there is a one-to-one correspondence between the context engine and the SNMP engine at this entity, the contextEngineID is identical in value to the snmpEngineID. Access control is governed by the specific context for which access is attempted and the identity of the user requesting access; this latter identity is expressed as a principal, which may be an individual or an application or a group of individuals or applications.

Other terms of importance relate to the processing of messages. The snmpMessageProcessingModel determines the message format and the SNMP version for message processing. The snmpSecurityModel determines which security model is to be used. The snmpSecurityLevel determines which security services are requested for this specific operation. The user may request just authentication, or authentication plus privacy (encryption), or neither.

SNMPv3 Applications

The services between modules in an SNMP entity are defined in the RFCs in terms of primitives and parameters. A primitive specifies the function to be performed, and the parameters are used to pass data and control information. We can think of these primitives and parameters as a formalized way of defining SNMP services. The actual form of a primitive is implementation dependent; an example is a procedure call. In the discussion that follows, it may be useful to refer to Figure 8.8, based on a figure in RFC 2571, to see how all of these primitives fit together. Figure 8.8a shows the sequence of events in which a Command Generator or Notification Originator application requests that a PDU be sent, and subsequently how the matching response is returned to that application; these events occur at a manager. Figure 8.8b shows the corresponding events at an agent. The figure shows how an incoming message results in the dispatch of the enclosed PDU to an application, and how that application's response results in an outgoing message. Note that some of the arrows in the diagram are labeled with a primitive name, representing a call. Unlabeled arrows represents the return from a call, and the shading indicates the matching between call and return.

RFC 2573 defines, in general terms, the procedures followed by each type of application when generating PDUs for transmission or processing incoming PDUs. In all cases, the procedures are defined in terms of interaction with the Dispatcher by means of the Dispatcher primitives.

A **command generator application** makes use of the sendPdu and processResponsePdu Dispatcher primitives. The sendPdu provides the Dispatcher with information about the intended destination, security parameters, and the actual PDU to be sent. The Dispatcher then invokes the Message Processing Model, which in turn invokes the Security Model, to prepare the message. The Dispatcher hands the prepared message over to the transport layer (e.g., UDP) for transmission. If message preparation fails, the return primitive value of the sendPdu, set by the Dispatcher, is an error indication. If message preparation succeeds, the Dispatcher assigns a sendPduHandle identifier to this PDU and returns that value to the command generator. The command generator stores the sendPduHandle so that it can match the subsequent response PDU to the original request.

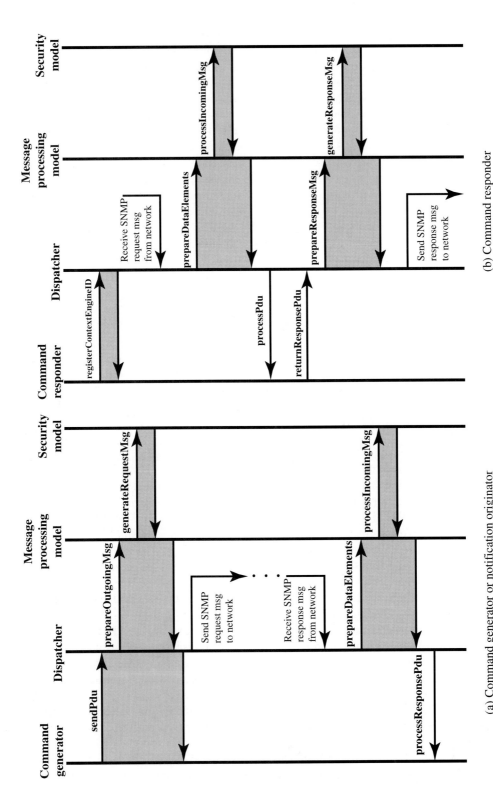

(a) Command generator or notification originator

(b) Command responder

Figure 8.8 SNMPv3 Flow

268

The Dispatcher delivers each incoming response PDU to the correct command generator application, using the processResponsePdu primitive.

A **command responder application** makes use of four Dispatcher primitives (registerContextEngineID, unregisterContextEngineID, processPdu, returnResponse-Pdu) and one Access Control Subsystem primitive (isAccessAllowed).

The registerContextEngineID primitive enables a command responder application to associate itself with an SNMP engine for the purpose of processing certain PDU types for a context engine. Once a command responder has registered, all asynchronously received messages containing the registered combination of contextEngineID and pduType supported are sent to the command responder that registered to support that combination. A command responder can disassociate from an SNMP engine using the unregisterContextEngineID primitive.

The Dispatcher delivers each incoming request PDU to the correct command responder application, using the processPdu primitive. The command responder then performs the following steps:

- The command responder examines the contents of the request PDU. The operation type must match one of the types previously registered by this application.
- The command responder determines if access is allowed for performing the management operation requested in this PDU. For this purpose, the isAccess-Allowed primitive is called.
- The securityModel parameter indicates which security model the Access Control Subsystem is to use in responding to this call. The Access Control Subsystem determines if the requesting principal (securityName) at this security level (securityLevel) has permission to request the management operation (viewType) on the management object (variableName) in this context (contextName).
- If access is permitted, the command responder performs the management operation and prepares a response PDU. If access fails, the command responder prepares the appropriate response PDU to signal that failure.
- The command responder calls the Dispatcher with a returnResponsePdu primitive to send the response PDU.

A **notification generator application** follows the same general procedures used for a command generator application. If an Inform Request PDU is to be sent, both the sendPdu and processResponsePdu primitives are used, in the same fashion as for command generator applications. If a trap PDU is to be sent, only the sendPdu primitive is used.

A **notification receiver application** follows a subset of the general procedures as for a command responder application. The notification receiver must first register to receive Inform and/or trap PDUs. Both types of PDUs are received by means of a processPdu primitive. For an Inform PDU, a returnResponsePdu primitive is used to respond.

A **proxy forwarder application** makes use of Dispatcher primitives to forward SNMP messages. The proxy forwarder handles four basic types of messages:

- Messages containing PDU types from a command generator application. The proxy forwarder determines either the target SNMP engine or an SNMP engine that is closer, or downstream, to the target and sends the appropriate request PDU.
- Messages containing PDU types from a notification originator application. The proxy forwarder determines which SNMP engines should receive the notification and sends the appropriate notification PDU or PDUs.
- Messages containing a Response PDU type. The proxy forwarder determines which previously forwarded request or notification, if any, is matched by this response, and sends the appropriate response PDU.
- Messages containing a report indication. Report PDUs are SNMPv3 engine-to-engine communications. The proxy forwarder determines which previously forwarded request or notification, if any, is matched by this report indication and forwards the report indication back to the initiator of the request or notification.

Message Processing and the User Security Model

Message processing involves a general-purpose message processing model and a specific security model; this relationship is shown in Figure 8.8.

Message Processing Model

RFC 2572 defines a general-purpose message processing model. This model is responsible for accepting PDUs from the Dispatcher, encapsulating them in messages, and invoking the USM to insert security-related parameters in the message header. The message processing model also accepts incoming messages, invokes the USM to process the security-related parameters in the message header, and delivers the encapsulated PDU to the Dispatcher.

Figure 8.9 illustrates the message structure. The first five fields are generated by the message processing model on outgoing messages and processed by the message processing model on incoming messages. The next six fields show security parameters used by USM. Finally, the PDU, together with the contextEngineID and contextName, constitutes a *scoped PDU*, used for PDU processing.

The first five fields are as follows:

- **msgVersion:** Set to snmpv3(3).
- **msgID:** A unique identifier used between two SNMP entities to coordinate request and response messages, and by the message processor to coordinate the processing of the message by different subsystem models within the architecture. The range of this ID is 0 through $2^{31} - 1$.
- **msgMaxSize:** Conveys the maximum size of a message in octets supported by the sender of the message, with a range of 484 through $2^{31} - 1$. This is the maximum segment size that the sender can accept from another SNMP engine (whether a response or some other message type).
- **msgFlags:** An octet string containing three flags in the least significant three bits: reportableFlag, privFlag, authFlag. If reportableFlag = 1, then a Report PDU must be returned to the sender under those conditions that can cause the

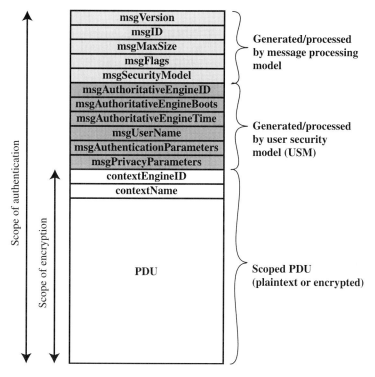

Figure 8.9   SNMPv3 Message Format with USM

generation of a Report PDU; when the flag is zero, a Report PDU may not be sent. The reportableFlag is set to 1 by the sender in all messages containing a request (Get, Set) or an Inform, and set to 0 for messages containing a Response, a Trap, or a Report PDU. The reportableFlag is a secondary aid in determining when to send a Report. It is only used in cases in which the PDU portion of the message cannot be decoded (e.g., when decryption fails due to incorrect key). The privFlag and authFlag are set by the sender to indicate the security level that was applied to the message. For privFlag = 1, encryption was applied and for privFlag = 0, authentication was applied. All combinations are allowed except (privFlag = 1 AND authFlag = 0); that is, encryption without authentication is not allowed.

- **msgSecurityModel:** An identifier in the range of 0 through $2^{31} - 1$ that indicates which security model was used by the sender to prepare this message and therefore which security model the receiver must use to process this message. Reserved values include 1 for SNMPv1, 2 for SNMPv2c (SNMPv2 with the SNMPv1 community facility), and 3 for SNMPv3.

User Security Model

RFC 2574 defines the User Security Model (USM). USM provides authentication and privacy services for SNMP. Specifically, USM is designed to secure against the following principal threats:

- **Modification of information:** An entity could alter an in-transit message generated by an authorized entity in such a way as to cause unauthorized management operations, including the setting of object values. The essence of this threat is that an unauthorized entity could change any management parameter, including those related to configuration, operations, and accounting.
- **Masquerade:** Management operations that are not authorized for some entity may be attempted by that entity by assuming the identity of an authorized entity.
- **Message stream modification:** SNMP is designed to operate over a connectionless transport protocol. There is a threat that SNMP messages could be re-ordered, delayed, or replayed (duplicated) to cause unauthorized management operations. For example, a message to reboot a device could be copied and replayed later.
- **Disclosure:** An entity could observe exchanges between a manager and an agent and thereby learn the values of managed objects and learn of notifiable events. For example, the observation of a set command that changes passwords would enable an attacker to learn the new passwords.

USM is not intended to secure against the following two threats:

- **Denial of service:** An attacker may prevent exchanges between a manager and an agent.
- **Traffic analysis:** An attacker may observe the general pattern of traffic between managers and agents.

The lack of a counter to the denial-of-service threat may be justified on two grounds: First, denial-of-service attacks are in many cases indistinguishable from the type of network failures with which any viable network management application must cope as a matter of course; and second, a denial-of-service attack is likely to disrupt all types of exchanges and is a matter for an overall security facility, not one embedded in a network management protocol. As to traffic analysis, many network management traffic patterns are predictable (e.g., entities may be managed via SNMP commands issued on a regular basis by one or a few management stations) and therefore there is no significant advantage to protecting against observing these traffic patterns.

Cryptographic Functions

Two cryptographic functions are defined for USM: authentication and encryption. To support these functions, an SNMP engine requires two values: a privacy key (privKey) and an authentication key (authKey). Separate values of these two keys are maintained for the following users:

- **Local users:** Any principal at this SNMP engine for which management operations are authorized
- **Remote users:** Any principal at a remote SNMP engine for which communication is desired

These values are user attributes stored for each relevant user. The values of privKey and authKey are not accessible via SNMP.

USM allows the use of one of two alternative authentication protocols: HMAC-MD5-96 and HMAC-SHA-96. HMAC, described in Chapter 3, uses a secure hash function and a secret key to produce a message authentication code. For HMAC-MD5-96, HMAC is used with MD5 as the underlying hash function. A 16-octet (128-bit) authKey is used as input to the HMAC algorithm. The algorithm produces a 128-bit output, which is truncated to 12 octets (96 bits). For HMAC-SHA-96, the underling hash function is SHA-1. The authKey is 20 octets in length. The algorithm produces a 20-octet output, which is again truncated to 12 octets.

USM uses the cipher block chaining (CBC) mode of the Data Encryption Standard (DES) for encryption. A 16-octet privKey is provided as input to the encryption protocol. The first 8 octets (64 bits) of this privKey are used as a DES key. Because DES only requires a 56-bit key, the least significant bit of each octet is ignored. For CBC mode, a 64-bit initialization vector (IV) is required. The last 8 octets of the privKey contain a value that is used to generate this IV.

Authoritative and Nonauthoritative Engines

In any message transmission, one of the two entities, transmitter or receiver, is designated as the authoritative SNMP engine, according to the following rules:

- When an SNMP message contains a payload that expects a response (for example, a Get, GetNext, GetBulk, Set, or Inform PDU), then the receiver of such messages is authoritative.
- When an SNMP message contains a payload that does not expect a response (for example, an SNMPv2-Trap, Response, or Report PDU), then the sender of such a message is authoritative.

Thus, for messages sent on behalf of a Command Generator and for Inform messages from a Notification Originator, the receiver is authoritative. For messages sent on behalf of a Command Responder or for Trap messages from a Notification Originator, the sender is authoritative. This designation serves two purposes:

- The timeliness of a message is determined with respect to a clock maintained by the authoritative engine. When an authoritative engine sends a message (Trap, Response, Report), it contains the current value of its clock, so that the nonauthoritative recipient can synchronize on that clock. When a nonauthoritative engine sends a message (Get, GetNext, GetBulk, Set, Inform), it includes its current estimate of the time value at the destination, allowing the destination to assess the message's timeliness.
- A key localization process, described later, enables a single principal to own keys stored in multiple engines; these keys are localized to the authoritative engine in such a way that the principal is responsible for a single key but avoids the security risk of storing multiple copies of the same key in a distributed network.

It makes sense to designate the receiver of Command Generator and Inform PDUs as the authoritative engine, and therefore responsible for checking message timeliness. If a response or trap is delayed or replayed, little harm should occur. However, Command Generator and, to some extent, Inform PDUs result in management operations, such as reading or setting MIB objects. Thus, it is important to guarantee that such PDUs are not delayed or replayed, which could cause undesired effects.

USM Message Parameters

When an outgoing message is passed to the USM by the Message Processor, the USM fills in the security-related parameters in the message header. When an incoming message is passed to the USM by the Message Processor, the USM processes the values contained in those fields. The security-related parameters are the following:

- **msgAuthoritativeEngineID:** The snmpEngineID of the authoritative SNMP engine involved in the exchange of this message. Thus, this value refers to the source for a Trap, Response, or Report, and to the destination for a Get, GetNext, GetBulk, Set, or Inform.
- **msgAuthoritativeEngineBoots:** The snmpEngineBoots value of the authoritative SNMP engine involved in the exchange of this message. The object snmpEngineBoots is an integer in the range 0 through $2^{31} - 1$ that represents the number of times that this SNMP engine has initialized or reinitialized itself since its initial configuration.
- **msgAuthoritativeEngineTime:** The snmpEngineTime value of the authoritative SNMP engine involved in the exchange of this message. The object snmpEngineTime is an integer in the range 0 through $2^{31} - 1$ that represents the number of seconds since this authoritative SNMP engine last incremented the snmpEngineBoots object. Each authoritative SNMP engine is responsible for incrementing its own snmpEngineTime value once per second. A nonauthoritative engine is responsible for incrementing its notion of snmpEngineTime for each remote authoritative engine with which it communicates.
- **msgUserName:** The user (principal) on whose behalf the message is being exchanged.
- **msgAuthenticationParameters:** Null if authentication is not being used for this exchange. Otherwise, this is an authentication parameter. For the current definition of USM, the authentication parameter is an HMAC message authentication code.
- **msgPrivacyParameters:** Null if privacy is not being used for this exchange. Otherwise, this is a privacy parameter. For the current definition of USM, the privacy parameter is a value used to form the initial value (IV) in the DES CBC algorithm.

Figure 8.10 summarizes the operation of USM. For message transmission, encryption is performed first, if needed. The scoped PDU is encrypted and placed in the message payload, and the msgPrivacyParameters value is set to the value needed to generate the IV. Then authentication is performed, if needed. The entire message, including the scoped PDU is input to HMAC, and the resulting authentication code is placed in msgAuthenticationParameters. For incoming messages,

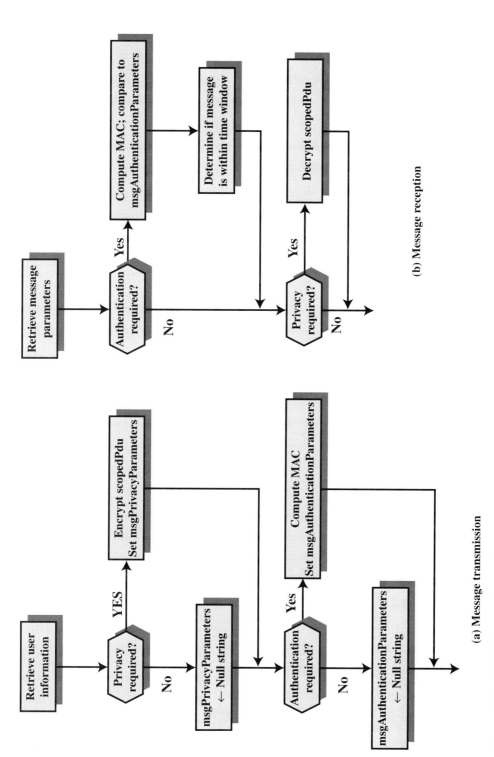

(b) Message reception

(a) Message transmission

Figure 8.10 USM Message Processing

275

authentication is performed first if needed. USM first checks the incoming MAC against a MAC that it calculated; if the two values match, then the message is assumed to be authentic (comes from the alleged source and has not been altered in transmission). Then USM checks whether the message is within a valid time window, as explained later. If the message is not timely, it is discarded as not authentic. Finally, if the scoped PDU has been encrypted, USM performs a decryption and returns the plaintext.

USM Timeliness Mechanisms

USM includes a set of timeliness mechanisms to guard against message delay and message replay. Each SNMP engine that can ever act in the capacity of an authoritative engine must maintain two objects, snmpEngineBoots and snmpEngineTime, that refer to its local time. When an SNMP engine is first installed, these two object values are set to 0. Thereafter, snmpEngineTime is incremented once per second. If snmpEngineTime ever reaches its maximum value ($2^{31} - 1$), snmpEngineBoots is incremented, as if the system had rebooted, and snmpEngineTime is set to 0 and begins incrementing again. Using a synchronization mechanism, a nonauthoritative engine maintains an estimate of the time values for each authoritative engine with which it communicates. These estimated values are placed in each outgoing message and enable the receiving authoritative engine to determine whether or not the incoming message is timely.

The synchronization mechanism works in the following fashion. A nonauthoritative engine keeps a local copy of three variables for each authoritative SNMP engine that is known to this engine:

- **snmpEngineBoots:** The most recent value of snmpEngineBoots for the remote authoritative engine.
- **snmpEngineTime:** This engine's notion of snmpEngineTime for the remote authoritative engine. This value is synchronized to the remote authoritative engine by the synchronization process described later. Between synchronization events, this value is logically incremented once per second to maintain a loose synchronization with the remote authoritative engine.
- **latestReceivedEngineTime:** The highest value of msgAuthoritativeEngineTime that has been received by this engine from the remote authoritative engine; this value is updated whenever a larger value of msgAuthoritativeEngineTime is received. The purpose of this variable is to protect against a replay message attack that would prevent the nonauthoritative SNMP engine's notion of snmpEngineTime from advancing.

One set of these three variables is maintained for each remote authoritative engine known to this engine. Logically, the values are maintained in some sort of cache, indexed by the unique snmpEngineID of each remote authoritative engine.

To enable nonauthoritative engines to maintain time synchronization, each authoritative engine inserts its current boot and time values, as well as its value of snmpEngineID, in each outgoing Response, Report, or Trap message in the fields msgAuthoritativeEngineBoots, msgAuthoritativeEngineTime, and msgAuthoritativeEngineID. If the message is authentic, and if the message is within the time window, then the receiving nonauthoritative engine updates is local variables (snmpEngine-Boots, snmpEngineTime, and latestReceivedEngineTime) for that remote engine according to the following rules:

1. An update occurs if at least one of the two following conditions is true:
   ○ (msgAuthoritativeEngineBoots > snmpEngineBoots) OR
   ○ [(msgAuthoritativeEngineBoots = snmpEngineBoots) AND
   ○ (msgAuthoritativeEngineTime > latestReceivedEngineTime)]

   The first condition says that an update should occur if the boot value from the authoritative engine has increased since the last update. The second condition says that if the boot value has not increased, then an update should occur if the incoming engine time is greater than the latest received engine time. The incoming engine time will be less than the latest received engine time if two incoming messages arrive out of order, which can happen, or if a replay attack is underway; in either case, the receiving engine will not perform an update.

2. If an update is called for, then the following changes are made:
   ○ set snmpEngineBoots to the value of msgAuthoritativeEngineBoots
   ○ set snmpEngineTime to the value of msgAuthoritativeEngineTime
   ○ set latestReceivedEngineTime to the value of msgAuthoritativeEngineTime

   If we turn the logic around, we see that if msgAuthoritativeEngineBoots < snmpEngineBoots, then no update occurs. Such a message is considered not authentic and must be ignored. If msgAuthoritativeEngineBoots = snmpEngineBoots but msgAuthoritativeEngineTime < latestReceivedEngineTime, then again no update occurs. In this case, the message may be authentic, but it may be misordered, in which case an update of snmpEngineTime is not warranted.

   Note that synchronization is only employed if the authentication service is in use for this message and the message has been determined to be authentic via HMAC. This restriction is essential because the scope of authentication includes msgAuthoritativeEngineID, msgAuthoritativeEngineBoots, and msgAuthoritative-EngineTime, thus assuring that these values are valid.

   SNMPv3 dictates that a message must be received within a reasonable time window, to avoid delay and replay attacks. The time window should be chosen to be as small as possible given the accuracy of the clocks involved, round-trip communication delays, and the frequency with which clocks are synchronized. If the time window is set too small, authentic messages will be rejected as unauthentic. On the other hand, a large time window increases the vulnerability to malicious delays of messages.

   We consider the more important case of an authoritative receiver; timeliness testing by a nonauthoritative receiver differs slightly. With each incoming message that has been authenticated and whose msgAuthoritativeEngineID is the same as the value of snmpEngineID for this engine, the engine compares the values of msgAuthoritativeEngineBoots and msgAuthoritativeEngineTime from the incoming message with the values of snmpEngineBoots and snmpEngineTime that this engine maintains for itself. The incoming message is considered outside the time window if any one of the following conditions is true:

- snmpEngineBoots = $2^{31} - 1$ OR
- msgAuthoritativeEngineBoots $\neq$ snmpEngineBoots OR
- the value of msgAuthoritativeEngineTime differs from that of snmpEngineTime by more than $\pm$ 150 seconds

The first condition says that if snmpEngineBoots is latched at its maximum value, no incoming message can be considered authentic. The second condition says that a message must have a boot time equal to the local engine's boot time; for example, if the local engine has rebooted and the remote engine has not synchronized with the local engine since the reboot, the messages from that remote engine are considered not authentic. The final condition says that the time on the incoming message must be greater than the local time minus 150 seconds and less than the local time plus 150 seconds.

If a message is considered to be outside the time window, then the message is considered not authentic, and an error indication (notInTimeWindow) is returned to the calling module.

Again, as with synchronization, timeliness checking is only done if the authentication service is in use and the message is authentic, assuring the validity of the message header fields.

Key Localization

A requirement for the use of the authentication and privacy services of SNMPv3 is that, for any communication between a principal on a nonauthoritative engine and a remote authoritative engine, a secret authentication key and a secret privacy key must be shared. These keys enable a user at a nonauthoritative engine (typically a management system) to employ authentication and privacy with remote authoritative systems that the user manages (typically, agent systems). RFC 2574 provides guidelines for the creation, update, and management of these keys.

To simplify the key management burden on principals, each principal is only required to maintain a single authentication key and a single encryption key. These keys are not stored in a MIB and are not accessible via SNMP. In this subsection we look first at the technique for generating these keys from a password. Then we look at the concept of key localization, which enables a principal to share a unique authentication and encryption key with each remote engine while only maintaining a single authentication and encryption key locally. These two techniques were first proposed in [BLUM97a].

A user requires a 16-octet privacy key and an authentication key of length either 16 or 20 octets. For keys owned by human users, it is desirable that the user be able to employ a human-readable password rather than a bit-string key. Accordingly, RFC 2574 defines an algorithm for mapping from the user password to a 16- or 20-octet key. USM places no restriction on the password itself, but local management policies should dictate that users employ passwords that are not easily guessed.

Password to key generation is performed as follows:

- Take the user's password as input and produce a string of length 2^{20} octets (1,048,576 octets) by repeating the password value as many times as necessary, truncating the last value if necessary, to form the string digest0. For example, an 8-character password (2^3 octets) would be concatenated with itself 2^{17} times to form digest0.
- If a 16-octet key is desired, take the MD5 hash of digest0 to form digest1. If a 20-octet key is desired, take the SHA-1 hash of digest0 to form digest1. The output is the user's key.

One advantage of this technique is that it greatly slows down a brute-force dictionary attack, in which an adversary tries many different potential passwords, generating the key from each one, and then tests whether the resulting key works with the authentication or encryption data available to him or her. For example, if an attacker intercepts an authenticated message, the attacker could try generating the HMAC value with different possible user keys. If a match occurs, the attacker can assume that the password has been discovered. The two-step process just outlined significantly increases the amount of time such an attack will take.

Another advantage of this technique is that it decouples the user's keys from any particular network management system (NMS). No NMS need store values of user keys. Instead, when needed, a user key is generated from that user's password. [BLUM97b] lists the following considerations that motivate the use of a password approach that is independent of NSM:

- If a key is to be stored rather than generated from a password, one alternative is to maintain a centralized repository of secret keys. But this adversely affects overall reliability and can make troubleshooting impossible if the repository itself is not accessible when needed.
- On the other hand, if duplicate repositories are maintained, this endangers overall security by providing potential breakers with more targets to attack.
- If either centralized or multiple duplicate repositories are used, they must be maintained in secure locations. This may reduce the opportunity for "forward camp" establishment during firefighting (i.e., troubleshooting when unpredictable segments of the network are inoperative and/or inaccessible for an unpredictable length of time).

A single password could be used to generate a single key for both authentication and encryption. A more secure scheme is to use two passwords, one to generate an authentication key and one to generate a distinct encryption key.

A localized key is defined in RFC 2574 as a secret key shared between a user and one authoritative SNMP engine. The objective is that the user need only maintain a single key (or two keys if both authentication and privacy are required) and therefore need only remember one password (or two). The actual secrets shared between a particular user and each authoritative SNMP engine are different. The process by which a single user key is converted into multiple unique keys, one for each remote SNMP engine, is referred to as key localization. [BLUM97a] gives a motivation for this strategy, which we summarize here.

We can define the following goals for key management:

- Every SNMP agent system in a distributed network has its own unique key for every user authorized to manage it. If multiple users are authorized as managers, the agent has a unique authentication key and a unique encryption key for each user. Thus, if the key for one user is compromised, the keys for other users are not compromised.
- The keys for a user on different agents are different. Thus, if an agent is compromised, only the user keys for that agent are compromised and not the user keys in use for other agents.
- Network management can be performed from any point on the network, regardless of the availability of a preconfigured network management system (NMS). This allows a user to perform management functions from any management station. This capability is provided by the password-to-key algorithm described previously.

We can also define the following as things to avoid:

- A user has to remember (or otherwise manage) a large number of keys, a number that grows with the addition of new managed agents.
- An adversary who learns a key for one agent is now able to impersonate any other agent to any user, or any user to any other agent.

To address the preceding goals and considerations, a single user key is mapped by means of a nonreversible one-way function (i.e., a secure hash function) into different localized keys for different authenticated engines (different agents). The procedure is as follows:

- Form the string digest2 by concatenating digest1 (described previously), the authoritative engine's snmpEngineID value, and digest1.
- If a 16-octet key is desired, take the MD5 hash of digest2. If a 20-octet key is desired, take the SHA-1 hash of digest2. The output is the user's localized key.

The resulting localized key can then be configured on the agent's system in some secure fashion. Because of the one-way nature of MD5 and SHA-1, it is infeasible for an adversary to learn a user key even if the adversary manages to discover a localized key.

Figure 8.11 summarizes the key localization process.

View–Based Access Control

Access control is a security function performed at the PDU level. An access control document defines mechanisms for determining whether access to a managed object in a local MIB by a remote principal should be allowed. Conceivable, multiple

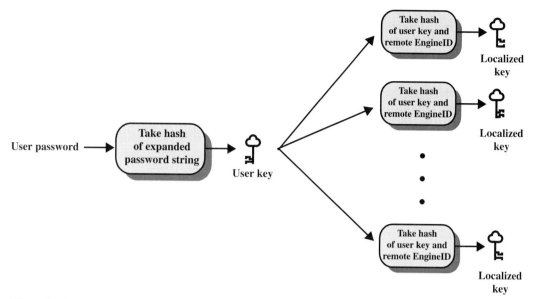

Figure 8.11   Key Localization

access control mechanisms could be defined. The SNMPv3 documents define the view-based access control (VACM) model. VACM itself makes use of a MIB that defines the access control policy for this agent and makes it possible for remote configuration to be used.

VACM has two important characteristics:

- VACM determines whether access to a managed object in a local MIB by a remote principal should be allowed.
- VACM makes use of a MIB that
  - ○ defines the access control policy for this agent
  - ○ makes it possible for remote configuration to be used

Elements of the VACM Model

RFC 2575 defines five elements that make up the VACM: groups, security level, contexts, MIB views, and access policy.

A **group** is defined as a set of zero or more <securityModel, securityName> tuples on whose behalf SNMP management objects can be accessed. A security-Name refers to a principal, and access rights for all principals in a given group are identical. A unique groupName is associated with each group. The group concept is a useful tool for categorizing managers with respect to access rights. For example, all top-level managers may have one set of access rights, while intermediate-level managers may have a different set of access rights.

Any given combination of securityModel and securityName can belong to at most one group. That is, for this agent, a given principal whose communications are protected by a given securityModel can only be included in one group.

The access rights for a group may differ depending on the **security level** of the message that contains the request. For example, an agent may allow read-only access for a request communicated in an unauthenticated message but may require authentication for write access. Further, for certain sensitive objects, the agent may require that the request and its response be communicated using the privacy service.

A **MIB context** is a named subset of the object instances in the local MIB. Contexts provide a useful way of aggregating objects into collections with different access policies.

The context is a concept that relates to access control. When a management station interacts with an agent to access management information at the agent, then the interaction is between a management principal and the agent's SNMP engine, and the access control privileges are expressed in a MIB view that applies to this principal and this context. Contexts have the following key characteristics:

- An SNMP entity, uniquely identified by a contextEngineID, may maintain more than one context.

- An object or an object instance may appear in more than one context.

- When multiple contexts exist, to identify an individual object instance, its contextName and contextEngineID must be identified in addition to its object type and its instance.

It is often the case that we would like to restrict the access of a particular group to a subset of the managed objects at an agent. To achieve this objective, access to a context is by means of a **MIB view**, which defines a specific set of managed objects (and optionally specific object instances). VACM makes use of a powerful and flexible technique for defining MIB views, based on the concepts of view subtrees and view families. The MIB view is defined in terms of a collection, or family, of subtrees, with each subtree being included in or excluded from the view.

The managed objects in a local database are organized into a hierarchy, or tree, based on the object identifiers of the objects. This local database comprises a subset of all object types defined according to the Internet-standard Structure of Management Information (SMI) and includes object instances whose identifiers conform to the SMI conventions.

SNMPv3 includes the concept of a subtree. A subtree is simply a node in the MIB's naming hierarchy plus all of its subordinate elements. More formally, a subtree may be defined as the set of all objects and object instances that have a common ASN.1 OBJECT IDENTIFIER prefix to their names. The longest common prefix of all of the instances in the subtree is the object identifier of the parent node of that subtree.

Associated with each entry in vacmAccessTable are three MIB views, one each for read, write, and notify access. Each MIB view consists of a set of view subtrees. Each view subtree in the MIB view is specified as being included or excluded.

That is, the MIB view either includes or excludes all object instances contained in that subtree. In addition, a view mask is defined in order to reduce the amount of configuration information required when fine-grained access control is required (e.g., access control at the object instance level).

VACM enables an SNMP engine to be configured to enforce a particular set of access rights, which constitutes an **access policy**. Access determination depends on the following factors:

- The **principal** making the access request. The VACM makes it possible for an agent to allow different access privileges for different users. For example, a manager system responsible for network-wide configuration may have broad authority to alter items in the local MIB, while an intermediate-level manager with monitoring responsibility may have read-only access and may further be limited to accessing only a subset of the local MIB. As was discussed, principals are assigned to groups and access policy is specified with respect to groups.

- The **security level** by which the request was communicated in an SNMP message. Typically, an agent will require the use of authentication for messages containing a set request (write operation).

- The **security model** used for processing the request message. If multiple security models are implemented at an agent, the agent may be configured to provide different levels of access to requests communicated by messages processed by different security models. For example, certain items may be accessible if the request message comes through USM, but not accessible if the Security Model is SNMPv1.

- The **MIB context** for the request.

- The specific **object instance** for which access is requested. Some objects hold more critical or sensitive information than others, and therefore the access policy must depend on the specific object instance requested.

- The **type of access** requested (read, write, notify). Read, write, and notify are distinct management operations, and different access control policies may apply for each of these operations.

Access Control Processing

An SNMP application invokes VACM via the isAccessAllowed primitive, with the input parameters securityModel, securityName, securityLevel, vicwType, context-Name, and variableName. All of these parameters are needed to make the access control decision. Put another way, the Access Control Subsystem is defined in such a way as to provide a very flexible tool for configuring access control at the agent, by breaking down the components of the access control decision into six separate variables.

Figure 8.12, adapted from a figure in RFC 2575, provides a useful way of looking at the input variables and shows how the various tables in the VACM MIB come into play in making the access control decision.

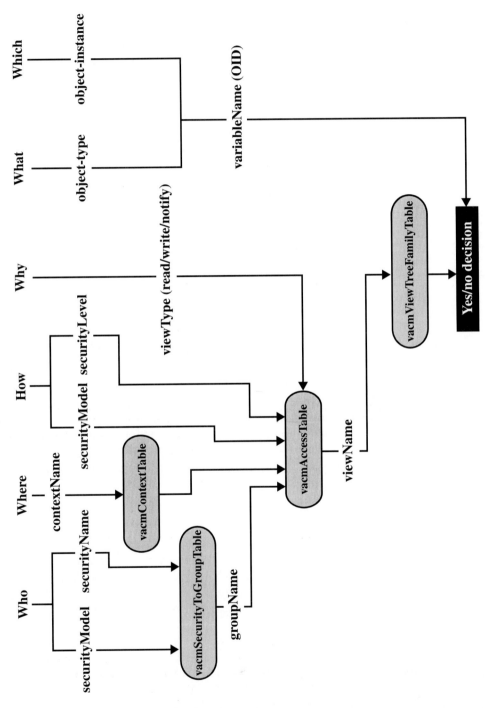

Figure 8.12 VACM Logic

284

- **who:** The combination of securityModel and securityName define the *who* of this operation; it identifies a given principal whose communications are protected by a given securityModel. This combination belongs to at most one group at this SNMP engine. The vacmSecurityToGroupTable provides the groupName, given the securityModel and securityName.
- **where:** The contextName specifies *where* the desired management object is to be found. The vacmContextTable contains a list of the recognized contextNames.
- **how:** The combination of securityModel and securityLevel defines *how* the incoming request or Inform PDU was protected. The combination of who, where, and how identifies zero or one entries in vacmAccessTable.
- **why:** The viewType specifies *why* access is requested: for a read, write, or notify operation. The selected entry in vacmAccessTable contains one MIB viewName for each of these three types of operation, and viewType is used to select a specific viewName. This viewName selects the appropriate MIB view from vacmViewTreeFamilyTable.
- **what:** The variableName is an object identifier whose prefix identifies a specific object type and whose suffix identifies a specific object instance. The object type indicates *what* type of management information is requested.
- **which:** The object instance indicates *which* specific item of information is requested.

Finally, the variableName is compared to the retrieved MIB view. If the variableName matches an element included in the MIB view, then access is granted.

Motivation

The concepts that make up VACM appear to result in a rather complex definition of access control. The motivations for introducing these concepts are to clarify the relationships involved in accessing management information and to minimize the storage and processing requirements at the agent. To understand these motivations, consider the following. In SNMPv1, the community concept is used to represent the following security-related information:

- The identity of the requesting entity (management station)
- The identity of the performing entity (agent acting for itself or for a proxied entity)
- The identity of the location of the management information to be accessed (agent or proxied entity)
- Authentication information
- Access control information (authorization to perform required operation)
- MIB view information

By lumping all of these concepts into a single variable, flexibility and functionality are lost. VACM provides the same set of security-related information using distinct variables for each item. This is a substantial improvement over SNMPv1. It uncouples various concepts so that values can be assigned to each one separately.

8.4 RECOMMENDED READING AND WEB SITES

[STAL99] provides a comprehensive and detailed examination of SNMP, SNMPv2, and SNMPv3; the book also provides an overview of network management technology.

STAL99 Stallings, W. *SNMP, SNMPv2, SNMPv3, and RMON 1 and 2.* Reading, MA: Addison-Wesley, 1999.

Recommended Web sites:

- **IETF SNMPv3 working group:** Maintains the most recent copies of SNMPv3-related RFCs and Internet draft documents, plus a schedule of past and future work.
- **SNMPv3 Web site:** Maintained by the Technical University of Braunschweig. It provides links to the RFCs and Internet drafts, copies of clarifications and proposed changes posted by the working group, and links to vendors with SNMPv3 implementations.
- **The Simple Web site:** Maintained by the University of Twente. It is a good source of information on SNMP, including pointers to many public-domain implementations and lists of books and articles.

8.5 KEY TERMS, REVIEW QUESTIONS, AND PROBLEMS

Key Terms

access policy	management information	proxy
agent	base (MIB)	Simple Network Management
community	management station	Protocol (SNMP)
community name	message processing model	user security model (USM)
key localization	network management	view-based access control
		model (VACM)

Review Questions

8.1 In what sense is a network management architecture considered integrated?
8.2 What are the key elements of the SNMP model?
8.3 What is a MIB?
8.4 What basic capabilities or commands are provided in SNMPv1?
8.5 What is the function of an SNMP proxy?
8.6 Briefly explain the SNMPv1 concept of community.
8.7 What is the relationship among SNMPv1, SNMPv2, and SNMPv3?
8.8 What threats is USM designed to counter?
8.9 What is the difference between an authoritative and a nonauthoritative engine?
8.10 What is key localization?
8.11 List and briefly define the elements that comprise VACM.

Problems

8.1 SNMPv1 defines a data type referred to as gauge and includes the following explanation of the semantics of this type:

> This application-wide type represents a non-negative integer, which may increase or decrease, but which latches at a maximum value. This standard specifies a maximum value of $2^{32} - 1$ (4294967295 decimal) for gauges.

Unfortunately, the word *latch* is not defined, and this has resulted in two different interpretations. The SNMPv2 standard cleared up the ambiguity with the following definition:

> The value of a Gauge has its maximum value whenever the information being modeled is greater than or equal to that maximum value; if the information being modeled subsequently decreases below the maximum value, the Gauge also decreases.

a. What is the alternative interpretation?

b. Discuss the pros and cons of the two interpretations.

8.2 In SNMPv1, any object in a MIB is defined has having a MIB Access Category, which can be assigned the one of the following values: read-only, read-write, write-only, and not-accessible. A read is accomplished with a get or trap operation, and a write is accomplished with a set operation. For write-only, the object may be available for get and trap operations, but this is implementation dependent. The MIB Access Category specifies the maximum access that may be allowed for an object, but in the SNMPv1 community facility, the Access Mode may further restrict this access for a given community profile. In the following table, fill in each entry to show the access allowed.

MIB Access Category	SNMP Access Mode	
	READ-ONLY	READ-WRITE
read-only		
read-write		
write-only		
not-accessible		

8.3 **a.** RFC 2574 states that for a nonauthoritative engine, the values of msgAuthoritativeEngineBoots and msgAuthoritativeEngineTime in an outgoing message header are set only if the message is to be authenticated by the authoritative receiver. Why does this restriction make sense?

b. However, for a Response message from an authoritative engine, the values of msgAuthoritativeEngineBoots and msgAuthoritativeEngineTime in the outgoing message header are always set. Why might this be so?

8.4 RFC 2574 specifies that clock synchronization (updating local clock based on incoming values) occurs before time window verification (check that incoming message is timely). This means that a nonauthoritative engine may update its notion of the authoritative engine's clock if the received message is authentic even if the message is not within the time window. Since the publication of the RFC, there has been an ongoing dispute about this on the SNMPv3 mailing list, but as of this writing, it appears that the wording in the standard will not change. It is instructive to look at the implications of this. Given the following definitions:

> MAEB = msgAuthoritativeEngineBoots
> MAET = msgAuthoritativeEngineTime
> SEB = local notion of snmpEngineBoots for the remote authoritative engine
> SET = local notion of snmpEngineTime for the remote authoritative engine
> LRET = latestReceivedEngineTime

Then suppose a nonauthoritative engine receives a message so that

$$(MAEB = SEB) \text{ AND } [LRET < MAET < (SET - 150)]$$

Then the conditions are right for a clock update, so it gets done:

$$SET := MAET; \quad LRET := MAET$$

Now, when we come to the time window check, we have

$$(MAEB = SEB) \text{ AND } (MAET = SET)$$

so we declare that the message is timely. Suppose, however, that we had done the time window check first. Would we have declared the message timely or untimely?

8.5 In the original published version of the USM specification (RFC 2274), discussing the clock synchronization and time window verification procedures, the following comment is made: "Note that this procedure does not allow for automatic time synchronization if the nonauthoritative SNMP engine has a real out-of-sync situation whereby the authoritative SNMP engine is more than 150 seconds behind the nonauthoritative SNMP engine." This statement was dropped from the revised version (RFC 2574) after this author pointed out to the working group that the statement is not always true. Using the example in Problem 8.4, show that the statement is not always true.

8.6 SNMPv3 assumes that there is some secure means of delivering localized keys to authenticated (agent) systems. This secure delivery is beyond the scope of SNMPv3; it may be manual or by some other secure protocol. Once an initial key (or pair of keys for authentication and privacy) is delivered to an agent, SNMPv3 provides a mechanism for securely updating keys. It is desirable that keys be changed from time to time to enhance security. A user, on his or her own, could initiate the key change process by request and supply a new password. Alternatively, the network management system (NMS) could initiate the process by requesting a new password. In either case, the user key at the NMS is updated. The NMS can then calculate a localized key for each communicating agent. The NMS must then securely communicate to each agent to cause that agent to update its localized key. Obviously, the NMS cannot simply send the key in plaintext over the network. Two options present themselves:

- Encrypt the new key using the old key as the encryption key.
- Use some sort of one-way function to produce a value from the old key. Exclusive-OR (XOR) this value with the new key and send the result to the agent. The agent can then XOR the incoming result with same function applied to the old key to produce the new key.

SNMPv3 uses a variant of the second method. What is the advantage of this approach over the first one?

8.7 The SNMPv3 approach involves the use of a KeyChange object in the target system's MIB. A remote principal or NMS sets this object, which is then automatically used by the agent to update the corresponding key. The algorithm is in two phases, one of which takes place at the requestor engine and one of which takes place at the remote agent engine.

The process begins when a requestor wishes to update an existing key keyOld to a new value keyNew. The requestor performs the following steps:

1. Generate a value *random* either from a pseudorandom number generator or a true random number generator.

2. Compute

$$digest = Hash(keyOld \,\|\, random)$$

where Hash is either MD5 or SHA-1, depending on whether a 16-octet or 20-octet key is desired and the symbol ‖ represents concatenation.

3. Compute

$$delta = digest \oplus keyNew$$
$$protocolKeyChange = (random \parallel delta)$$

where $\oplus$ is the exclusive-OR operation.

4. The value protocolKeyChange is then sent to the agent in a Set command to update a KeyChange object instance in agent's MIB.

What must the agent do with the incoming value to update the key?

8.8 A simpler procedure than that outlined in the preceding problem would be to XOR the keyOld with keyNew and transmit that value. The receiver then takes the XOR of the received value and keyOld to produce keyNew. Because the attacker does not know keyOld, the attacker cannot deduce the value of keyNew. What are advantages to using the random number and the secure one-way hash function of Problem 8.7 compared to this approach?

PART THREE   System Security

Part Three looks at system-level security issues, including the threat of and countermeasures for intruders and viruses and the use of firewalls and trusted systems.

CHAPTER 9   INTRUDERS

Chapter 9 examines a variety of information access and service threats presented by hackers that exploit vulnerabilities in network-based computing systems. The chapter begins with a discussion of the types of attacks that can be made by unauthorized users, or intruders, and analyzes various approaches to prevention and detection. This chapter also covers the related issue of password management.

CHAPTER 10   MALICIOUS SOFTWARE

Chapter 10 examines software threats to systems, with a special emphasis on viruses and worms. The chapter begins with a survey of various types of malicious software, with a more detailed look at the nature of viruses and worms. The remainder of the chapter looks at countermeasures.

CHAPTER 11   FIREWALLS

A standard approach to the protection of local computer assets from external threats is the use of a firewall. Chapter 11 discusses the principles of firewall design and looks at specific techniques. This chapter also covers the related issue of trusted systems.

CHAPTER 9

INTRUDERS

9.1 Intruders

Intrusion Techniques

9.2 Intrusion Detection

Audit Records
Statistical Anomaly Detection
Rule-Based Intrusion Detection
The Base-Rate Fallacy
Distributed Intrusion Detection
Honeypots
Intrusion Detection Exchange Format

9.3 Password Management

Password Protection
Password Selection Strategies

9.4 Recommended Reading and Web Sites

9.5 Key Terms, Review Questions, and Problems

Key Terms
Review Questions
Problems

Appendix 9A   The Base-Rate Fallacy

Conditional Probability and Independence
Bayes' Theorem
The Base-Rate Fallacy Demonstrated

They agreed that Graham should set the test for Charles Mabledene. It was neither more nor less than that Dragon should get Stern's code. If he had the 'in' at Utting which he claimed to have this should be possible, only loyalty to Moscow Centre would prevent it. If he got the key to the code he would prove his loyalty to London Central beyond a doubt.

— ***Talking to Strange Men,*** **Ruth Rendell**

A significant security problem for networked systems is hostile, or at least unwanted, trespass by users or software. User trespass can take the form of unauthorized logon to a machine or, in the case of an authorized user, acquisition of privileges or performance of actions beyond those that have been authorized. Software trespass can take the form of a virus, worm, or Trojan horse.

All these attacks relate to network security because system entry can be achieved by means of a network. However, these attacks are not confined to network-based attacks. A user with access to a local terminal may attempt trespass without using an intermediate network. A virus or Trojan horse may be introduced into a system by means of a diskette. Only the worm is a uniquely network phenomenon. Thus, system trespass is an area in which the concerns of network security and computer security overlap.

Because the focus of this book is network security, we do not attempt a comprehensive analysis of either the attacks or the security countermeasures related to system trespass. Instead, in this part we present a broad overview of these concerns.

This chapter covers with the subject of intruders. First, we examine the nature of the attack and then look at strategies intended for prevention and, failing that, detection. Next we examine the related topic of password management.

9.1   INTRUDERS

One of the two most publicized threats to security is the intruder (the other is viruses), generally referred to as a hacker or cracker. In an important early study of intrusion, Anderson [ANDE80] identified three classes of intruders:

- **Masquerader:** An individual who is not authorized to use the computer and who penetrates a system's access controls to exploit a legitimate user's account
- **Misfeasor:** A legitimate user who accesses data, programs, or resources for which such access is not authorized, or who is authorized for such access but misuses his or her privileges
- **Clandestine user:** An individual who seizes supervisory control of the system and uses this control to evade auditing and access controls or to suppress audit collection

The masquerader is likely to be an outsider; the misfeasor generally is an insider; and the clandestine user can be either an outsider or an insider.

Intruder attacks range from the benign to the serious. At the benign end of the scale, there are many people who simply wish to explore internets and see what is out there. At the serious end are individuals who are attempting to read privileged data, perform unauthorized modifications to data, or disrupt the system.

The intruder threat has been well publicized, particularly because of the famous "Wily Hacker" incident of 1986–1987, documented by Cliff Stoll [STOL88, 89]. In 1990 there was a nationwide crackdown on illicit computer hackers, with arrests, criminal charges, one dramatic show trial, several guilty pleas, and confiscation of massive amounts of data and computer equipment [STER92]. Many people believed that the problem had been brought under control.

In fact, the problem has not been brought under control. To cite one example, a group at Bell Labs [BELL92, BELL93] has reported persistent and frequent attacks on its computer complex via the Internet over an extended period and from a variety of sources. At the time of these reports, the Bell group was experiencing the following:

- Attempts to copy the password file (discussed later) at a rate exceeding once every other day
- Suspicious remote procedure call (RPC) requests at a rate exceeding once per week
- Attempts to connect to nonexistent "bait" machines at least every two weeks

Benign intruders might be tolerable, although they do consume resources and may slow performance for legitimate users. However, there is no way in advance to know whether an intruder will be benign or malign. Consequently, even for systems with no particularly sensitive resources, there is a motivation to control this problem.

An example that dramatically illustrates the threat occurred at Texas A&M University [SAFF93]. In August 1992, the computer center there was notified that one of its machines was being used to attack computers at another location via the Internet. By monitoring activity, the computer center personnel learned that there were several outside intruders involved, who were running password-cracking routines on various computers (the site consists of a total of 12,000 interconnected machines). The center disconnected affected machines, plugged known security holes, and resumed normal operation. A few days later, one of the local system managers detected that the intruder attack had resumed. It turned out that the attack was far more sophisticated than had been originally believed. Files were found containing hundreds of captured passwords, including some on major and supposedly secure servers. In addition, one local machine had been set up as a hacker bulletin board, which the hackers used to contact each other and to discuss techniques and progress.

An analysis of this attack revealed that there were actually two levels of hackers. The high level were sophisticated users with a thorough knowledge of the technology; the low level were the "foot soldiers" who merely used the supplied cracking programs with little understanding of how they worked. This teamwork combined the two most serious weapons in the intruder armory: sophisticated knowledge of how to intrude and a willingness to spend countless hours "turning doorknobs" to probe for weaknesses.

One of the results of the growing awareness of the intruder problem has been the establishment of a number of computer emergency response teams (CERTs). These cooperative ventures collect information about system vulnerabilities and disseminate it to systems managers. Unfortunately, hackers can also gain access to CERT reports. In the Texas A&M incident, later analysis showed that the hackers had developed programs to test the attacked machines for virtually every vulnerability that had been announced by CERT. If even one machine had failed to respond promptly to a CERT advisory, it was wide open to such attacks.

In addition to running password-cracking programs, the intruders attempted to modify login software to enable them to capture passwords of users logging on to systems. This made it possible for them to build up an impressive collection of compromised passwords, which was made available on the bulletin board set up on one of the victim's own machines.

In this section we look at the techniques used for intrusion. Then we examine ways to detect intrusion. Finally, we look at password-based approaches to intrusion prevention.

Intrusion Techniques

The objective of the intruder is to gain access to a system or to increase the range of privileges accessible on a system. Generally, this requires the intruder to acquire information that should have been protected. In most cases, this information is in the form of a user password. With knowledge of some other user's password, an intruder can log in to a system and exercise all the privileges accorded to the legitimate user.

Typically, a system must maintain a file that associates a password with each authorized user. If such a file is stored with no protection, then it is an easy matter to gain access to it and learn passwords. The password file can be protected in one of two ways:

- **One-way encryption:** The system stores only an encrypted form of the user's password. When the user presents a password, the system encrypts that password and compares it with the stored value. In practice, the system usually performs a one-way transformation (not reversible) in which the password is used to generate a key for the encryption function and in which a fixed-length output is produced.
- **Access control:** Access to the password file is limited to one or a very few accounts.

If one or both of these countermeasures are in place, some effort is needed for a potential intruder to learn passwords. On the basis of a survey of the literature and interviews with a number of password crackers, [ALVA90] reports the following techniques for learning passwords:

1. Try default passwords used with standard accounts that are shipped with the system. Many administrators do not bother to change these defaults.
2. Exhaustively try all short passwords (those of one to three characters).

3. Try words in the system's online dictionary or a list of likely passwords. Examples of the latter are readily available on hacker bulletin boards.
4. Collect information about users, such as their full names, the names of their spouse and children, pictures in their office, and books in their office that are related to hobbies.
5. Try users' phone numbers, Social Security numbers, and room numbers.
6. Try all legitimate license plate numbers for this state.
7. Use a Trojan horse (described in Section 9.2) to bypass restrictions on access.
8. Tap the line between a remote user and the host system.

The first six methods are various ways of guessing a password. If an intruder has to verify the guess by attempting to log in, it is a tedious and easily countered means of attack. For example, a system can simply reject any login after three password attempts, thus requiring the intruder to reconnect to the host to try again. Under these circumstances, it is not practical to try more than a handful of passwords. However, the intruder is unlikely to try such crude methods. For example, if an intruder can gain access with a low level of privileges to an encrypted password file, then the strategy would be to capture that file and then use the encryption mechanism of that particular system at leisure until a valid password that provided greater privileges was discovered.

Guessing attacks are feasible, and indeed highly effective, when a large number of guesses can be attempted automatically and each guess verified, without the guessing process being detectable. Later in this chapter, we have much to say about thwarting guessing attacks.

The seventh method of attack listed earlier, the Trojan horse, can be particularly difficult to counter. An example of a program that bypasses access controls was cited in [ALVA90]. A low-privilege user produced a game program and invited the system operator to use it in his or her spare time. The program did indeed play a game, but in the background it also contained code to copy the password file, which was unencrypted but access protected, into the user's file. Because the game was running under the operator's high-privilege mode, it was able to gain access to the password file.

The eighth attack listed, line tapping, is a matter of physical security. It can be countered with link encryption techniques, discussed in Chapter 2.

We turn now to a discussion of the two principal countermeasures: detection and prevention. Detection is concerned with learning of an attack, either before or after its success. Prevention is a challenging security goal and an uphill battle at all times. The difficulty stems from the fact that the defender must attempt to thwart all possible attacks, whereas the attacker is free to try to find the weakest link in the defense chain and attack at that point.

9.2 INTRUSION DETECTION

Inevitably, the best intrusion prevention system will fail. A system's second line of defense is intrusion detection, and this has been the focus of much research in recent years. This interest is motivated by a number of considerations, including the following:

1. If an intrusion is detected quickly enough, the intruder can be identified and ejected from the system before any damage is done or any data are compromised. Even if the detection is not sufficiently timely to preempt the intruder, the sooner that the intrusion is detected, the less the amount of damage and the more quickly that recovery can be achieved.

2. An effective intrusion detection system can serve as a deterrent, so acting to prevent intrusions.

3. Intrusion detection enables the collection of information about intrusion techniques that can be used to strengthen the intrusion prevention facility.

Intrusion detection is based on the assumption that the behavior of the intruder differs from that of a legitimate user in ways that can be quantified. Of course, we cannot expect that there will be a crisp, exact distinction between an attack by an intruder and the normal use of resources by an authorized user. Rather, we must expect that there will be some overlap.

Figure 9.1 suggests, in very abstract terms, the nature of the task confronting the designer of an intrusion detection system. Although the typical behavior of an intruder differs from the typical behavior of an authorized user, there is an overlap in these behaviors. Thus, a loose interpretation of intruder behavior, which will catch more intruders, will also lead to a number of "false positives," or authorized users identified as intruders. On the other hand, an attempt to limit false positives by a tight interpretation of intruder behavior will lead to an increase in false negatives, or intruders not identified as intruders. Thus, there is an element of compromise and art in the practice of intrusion detection.

In Anderson's study [ANDE80], it was postulated that one could, with reasonable confidence, distinguish between a masquerader and a legitimate user. Pat-

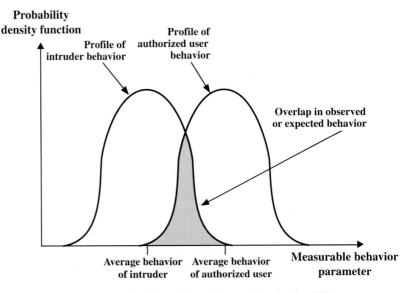

Figure 9.1   Profiles of Behavior of Intruders and Authorized Users

terns of legitimate user behavior can be established by observing past history, and significant deviation from such patterns can be detected. Anderson suggests that the task of detecting a misfeasor (legitimate user performing in an unauthorized fashion) is more difficult, in that the distinction between abnormal and normal behavior may be small. Anderson concluded that such violations would be undetectable solely through the search for anomalous behavior. However, misfeasor behavior might nevertheless be detectable by intelligent definition of the class of conditions that suggest unauthorized use. Finally, the detection of the clandestine user was felt to be beyond the scope of purely automated techniques. These observations, which were made in 1980, remain true today.

[PORR92] identifies the following approaches to intrusion detection:

1. **Statistical anomaly detection:** Involves the collection of data relating to the behavior of legitimate users over a period of time. Then statistical tests are applied to observed behavior to determine with a high level of confidence whether that behavior is not legitimate user behavior.
   a. Threshold detection: This approach involves defining thresholds, independent of user, for the frequency of occurrence of various events.
   b. Profile based: A profile of the activity of each user is developed and used to detect changes in the behavior of individual accounts.
2. **Rule-Based Detection:** Involves an attempt to define a set of rules that can be used to decide that a given behavior is that of an intruder.
   a. Anomaly detection: Rules are developed to detect deviation from previous usage patterns.
   b. Penetration identification: An expert system approach that searches for suspicious behavior.

In a nutshell, statistical approaches attempt to define normal, or expected, behavior, whereas rule-based approaches attempt to define proper behavior.

In terms of the types of attackers listed earlier, statistical anomaly detection is effective against masqueraders, who are unlikely to mimic the behavior patterns of the accounts they appropriate. On the other hand, such techniques may be unable to deal with misfeasors. For such attacks, rule-based approaches may be able to recognize events and sequences that, in context, reveal penetration. In practice, a system may exhibit a combination of both approaches to be effective against a broad range of attacks.

Audit Records

A fundamental tool for intrusion detection is the audit record. Some record of ongoing activity by users must be maintained as input to an intrusion detection system. Basically, two plans are used:

- **Native audit records:** Virtually all multiuser operating systems include accounting software that collects information on user activity. The advantage of using this information is that no additional collection software is needed. The disadvantage is that the native audit records may not contain the needed information or may not contain it in a convenient form.

- **Detection-specific audit records:** A collection facility can be implemented that generates audit records containing only that information required by the intrusion detection system. One advantage of such an approach is that it could be made vendor independent and ported to a variety of systems. The disadvantage is the extra overhead involved in having, in effect, two accounting packages running on a machine.

A good example of detection-specific audit records is one developed by Dorothy Denning [DENN87]. Each audit record contains the following fields:

- **Subject:** Initiators of actions. A subject is typically a terminal user but might also be a process acting on behalf of users or groups of users. All activity arises through commands issued by subjects. Subjects may be grouped into different access classes, and these classes may overlap.
- **Action:** Operation performed by the subject on or with an object; for example, login, read, perform I/O, execute.
- **Object:** Receptors of actions. Examples include files, programs, messages, records, terminals, printers, and user- or program-created structures. When a subject is the recipient of an action, such as electronic mail, then that subject is considered an object. Objects may be grouped by type. Object granularity may vary by object type and by environment. For example, database actions may be audited for the database as a whole or at the record level.
- **Exception-Condition:** Denotes which, if any, exception condition is raised on return.
- **Resource-Usage:** A list of quantitative elements in which each element gives the amount used of some resource (e.g., number of lines printed or displayed, number of records read or written, processor time, I/O units used, session elapsed time).
- **Time-stamp:** Unique time-and-date stamp identifying when the action took place.

Most user operations are made up of a number of elementary actions. For example, a file copy involves the execution of the user command, which includes doing access validation and setting up the copy, plus the read from one file, plus the write to another file. Consider the command

```
COPY GAME.EXE TO <Library>GAME.EXE
```

issued by Smith to copy an executable file GAME from the current directory to the <Library> directory. The following audit records may be generated:

Smith	execute	<Library>COPY.EXE	0	CPU = 00002	11058721678

Smith	read	<Smith>GAME.EXE	0	RECORDS = 0	11058721679

Smith	execute	<Library>COPY.EXE	write-viol	RECORDS = 0	11058721680

In this case, the copy is aborted because Smith does not have write permission to <Library>.

The decomposition of a user operation into elementary actions has three advantages:

1. Because objects are the protectable entities in a system, the use of elementary actions enables an audit of all behavior affecting an object. Thus, the system can detect attempted subversions of access controls (by noting an abnormality in the number of exception conditions returned) and can detect successful subversions by noting an abnormality in the set of objects accessible to the subject.

2. Single-object, single-action audit records simplify the model and the implementation.

3. Because of the simple, uniform structure of the detection-specific audit records, it may be relatively easy to obtain this information or at least part of it by a straightforward mapping from existing native audit records to the detection-specific audit records.

Statistical Anomaly Detection

As was mentioned, statistical anomaly detection techniques fall into two broad categories: threshold detection and profile-based systems. Threshold detection involves counting the number of occurrences of a specific event type over an interval of time. If the count surpasses what is considered a reasonable number that one might expect to occur, then intrusion is assumed.

Threshold analysis, by itself, is a crude and ineffective detector of even moderately sophisticated attacks. Both the threshold and the time interval must be determined. Because of the variability across users, such thresholds are likely to generate either a lot of false positives or a lot of false negatives. However, simple threshold detectors may be useful in conjunction with more sophisticated techniques.

Profile-based anomaly detection focuses on characterizing the past behavior of individual users or related groups of users and then detecting significant deviations. A profile may consist of a set of parameters, so that deviation on just a single parameter may not be sufficient in itself to signal an alert.

The foundation of this approach is an analysis of audit records. The audit records provide input to the intrusion detection function in two ways. First, the designer must decide on a number of quantitative metrics that can be used to measure user behavior. An analysis of audit records over a period of time can be used to determine the activity profile of the average user. Thus, the audit records serve to define typical behavior. Second, current audit records are the input used to detect intrusion. That is, the intrusion detection model analyzes incoming audit records to determine deviation from average behavior.

Examples of metrics that are useful for profile-based intrusion detection are the following:

- **Counter:** A nonnegative integer that may be incremented but not decremented until it is reset by management action. Typically, a count of certain event types is kept over a particular period of time. Examples include the number of logins by a single user during an hour, the number of times a given command is executed during a single user session, and the number of password failures during a minute.

- **Gauge:** A nonnegative integer that may be incremented or decremented. Typically, a gauge is used to measure the current value of some entity. Examples include the number of logical connections assigned to a user application and the number of outgoing messages queued for a user process.
- **Interval timer:** The length of time between two related events. An example is the length of time between successive logins to an account.
- **Resource utilization:** Quantity of resources consumed during a specified period. Examples include the number of pages printed during a user session and total time consumed by a program execution.

Given these general metrics, various tests can be performed to determine whether current activity fits within acceptable limits. [DENN87] lists the following approaches that may be taken:

- Mean and standard deviation
- Multivariate
- Markov process
- Time series
- Operational

The simplest statistical test is to measure the **mean and standard deviation** of a parameter over some historical period. This gives a reflection of the average behavior and its variability. The use of mean and standard deviation is applicable to a wide variety of counters, timers, and resource measures. But these measures, by themselves, are typically too crude for intrusion detection purposes.

A **multivariate** model is based on correlations between two or more variables. Intruder behavior may be characterized with greater confidence by considering such correlations (for example, processor time and resource usage, or login frequency and session elapsed time).

A **Markov process** model is used to establish transition probabilities among various states. As an example, this model might be used to look at transitions between certain commands.

A **time series** model focuses on time intervals, looking for sequences of events that happen too rapidly or too slowly. A variety of statistical tests can be applied to characterize abnormal timing.

Finally, an **operational model** is based on a judgment of what is considered abnormal, rather than an automated analysis of past audit records. Typically, fixed limits are defined and intrusion is suspected for an observation that is outside the limits. This type of approach works best where intruder behavior can be deduced from certain types of activities. For example, a large number of login attempts over a short period suggests an attempted intrusion.

As an example of the use of these various metrics and models, Table 9.1 shows various measures considered or tested for the Stanford Research Institute (SRI) intrusion detection system (IDES) [DENN87, JAVI91, LUNT88].

Table 9.1 Measures That May Be Used for Intrusion Detection

Measure	Model	Type of Intrusion Detected
Login and Session Activity		
Login frequency by day and time	Mean and standard deviation	Intruders may be likely to log in during off-hours.
Frequency of login at different locations	Mean and standard deviation	Intruders may log in from a location that a particular user rarely or never uses.
Time since last login	Operational	Break-in on a "dead" account.
Elapsed time per session	Mean and standard deviation	Significant deviations might indicate masquerader.
Quantity of output to location	Mean and standard deviation	Excessive amounts of data transmitted to remote locations could signify leakage of sensitive data.
Session resource utilization	Mean and standard deviation	Unusual processor or I/O levels could signal an intruder.
Password failures at login	Operational	Attempted break-in by password guessing.
Failures to login from specified terminals	Operational	Attempted break-in.
Command or Program Execution Activity		
Execution frequency	Mean and standard deviation	May detect intruders, who are likely to use different commands, or a successful penetration by a legitimate user, who has gained access to privileged commands.
Program resource utilization	Mean and standard deviation	An abnormal value might suggest injection of a virus or Trojan horse, which performs side-effects that increase I/O or processor utilization.
Execution denials	Operational model	May detect penetration attempt by individual user who seeks higher privileges.
File Access Activity		
Read, write, create, delete frequency	Mean and standard deviation	Abnormalities for read and write access for individual users may signify masquerading or browsing.
Records read, written	Mean and standard deviation	Abnormality could signify an attempt to obtain sensitive data by inference and aggregation.
Failure count for read, write, create, delete	Operational	May detect users who persistently attempt to access unauthorized files.
File resource exhaustion counter	Operational	

The main advantage of the use of statistical profiles is that a prior knowledge of security flaws is not required. The detector program learns what is "normal" behavior and then looks for deviations. The approach is not based on system-dependent characteristics and vulnerabilities. Thus, it should be readily portable among a variety of systems.

Rule-Based Intrusion Detection

Rule-based techniques detect intrusion by observing events in the system and applying a set of rules that lead to a decision regarding whether a given pattern of activity is or is not suspicious. In very general terms, we can characterize all approaches as focusing on either anomaly detection or penetration identification, although there is some overlap in these approaches.

Rule-based anomaly detection is similar in terms of its approach and strengths to statistical anomaly detection. With the rule-based approach, historical audit records are analyzed to identify usage patterns and to generate automatically rules that describe those patterns. Rules may represent past behavior patterns of users, programs, privileges, time slots, terminals, and so on. Current behavior is then observed, and each transaction is matched against the set of rules to determine if it conforms to any historically observed pattern of behavior.

As with statistical anomaly detection, rule-based anomaly detection does not require knowledge of security vulnerabilities within the system. Rather, the scheme is based on observing past behavior and, in effect, assuming that the future will be like the past. In order for this approach to be effective, a rather large database of rules will be needed. For example, a scheme described in [VACC89] contains anywhere from 10^4 to 10^6 rules.

Rule-based penetration identification takes a very different approach to intrusion detection, one based on expert system technology. The key feature of such systems is the use of rules for identifying known penetrations or penetrations that would exploit known weaknesses. Rules can also be defined that identify suspicious behavior, even when the behavior is within the bounds of established patterns of usage. Typically, the rules used in these systems are specific to the machine and operating system. Also, such rules are generated by "experts" rather than by means of an automated analysis of audit records. The normal procedure is to interview system administrators and security analysts to collect a suite of known penetration scenarios and key events that threaten the security of the target system.[1] Thus, the strength of the approach depends on the skill of those involved in setting up the rules.

A simple example of the type of rules that can be used is found in NIDX, an early system that used heuristic rules that can be used to assign degrees of suspicion to activities [BAUE88]. Example heuristics are the following:

1. Users should not read files in other users' personal directories.
2. Users must not write other users' files.

---

[1]Such interviews may even extend to reformed or unreformed crackers who will share their expertise for a fee [FREE93].

3. Users who log in after hours often access the same files they used earlier.
4. Users do not generally open disk devices directly but rely on higher-level operating system utilities.
5. Users should not be logged in more than once to the same system.
6. Users do not make copies of system programs.

The penetration identification scheme used in IDES is representative of the strategy followed. Audit records are examined as they are generated, and they are matched against the rule base. If a match is found, then the user's *suspicion rating* is increased. If enough rules are matched, then the rating will pass a threshold that results in the reporting of an anomaly.

The IDES approach is based on an examination of audit records. A weakness of this plan is its lack of flexibility. For a given penetration scenario, there may be a number of alternative audit record sequences that could be produced, each varying from the others slightly or in subtle ways. It may be difficult to pin down all these variations in explicit rules. Another method is to develop a higher-level model independent of specific audit records. An example of this is a state transition model known as USTAT [ILGU93]. USTAT deals in general actions rather than the detailed specific actions recorded by the UNIX auditing mechanism. USTAT is implemented on a SunOS system that provides audit records on 239 events. Of these, only 28 are used by a preprocessor, which maps these onto 10 general actions (Table 9.2). Using just these actions and the parameters that are invoked with each action, a state transition diagram is developed that characterizes suspicious activity.

Table 9.2 USTAT Actions versus SunOS Event Types

USTAT Action	SunOS Event Type
Read	open_r, open_rc, open_rtc, open_rwc, open_rwtc, open_rt, open_rw, open_rwt
Write	truncate, ftruncate, creat, open_rtc, open_rwc, open_rwtc, open_rt, open_rw, open_rwt, open_w, open_wt, open_wc, open_wct
Create	mkdir, creat, open_rc, open_rtc, open_rwc, open_rwtc, open_wc, open_wtc, mknod
Delete	rmdir, unlink
Execute	exec, execve
Exit	exit
Modify_Owner	chown, fchown
Modify_Perm	chmod, fchmod
Rename	rename
Hardlink	link

Because a number of different auditable events map into a smaller number of actions, the rule-creation process is simpler. Furthermore, the state transition diagram model is easily modified to accommodate newly learned intrusion behaviors.

The Base–Rate Fallacy

To be of practical use, an intrusion detection system should detect a substantial percentage of intrusions while keeping the false alarm rate at an acceptable level. If only a modest percentage of actual intrusions are detected, the system provides a false sense of security. On the other hand, if the system frequently triggers an alert when there is no intrusion (a false alarm), then either system managers will begin to ignore the alarms, or much time will be wasted analyzing the false alarms.

Unfortunately, because of the nature of the probabilities involved, it is very difficult to meet the standard of high rate of detections with a low rate of false alarms. In general, if the actual numbers of intrusions is low compared to the number of legitimate uses of a system, then the false alarm rate will be high unless the test is extremely discriminating. A study of existing intrusion detection systems, reported in [AXEL00], indicated that current systems have not overcome the problem of the base-rate fallacy. See Appendix 9A for a brief background on the mathematics of this problem.

Distributed Intrusion Detection

Until recently, work on intrusion detection systems focused on single-system stand-alone facilities. The typical organization, however, needs to defend a distributed collection of hosts supported by a LAN or internetwork. Although it is possible to mount a defense by using stand-alone intrusion detection systems on each host, a more effective defense can be achieved by coordination and cooperation among intrusion detection systems across the network.

Porras points out the following major issues in the design of a distributed intrusion detection system [PORR92]:

- A distributed intrusion detection system may need to deal with different audit record formats. In a heterogeneous environment, different systems will employ different native audit collection systems and, if using intrusion detection, may employ different formats for security-related audit records.
- One or more nodes in the network will serve as collection and analysis points for the data from the systems on the network. Thus, either raw audit data or summary data must be transmitted across the network. Therefore, there is a requirement to assure the integrity and confidentiality of these data. Integrity is required to prevent an intruder from masking his or her activities by altering the transmitted audit information. Confidentiality is required because the transmitted audit information could be valuable.
- Either a centralized or decentralized architecture can be used. With a centralized architecture, there is a single central point of collection and analysis of all audit data. This eases the task of correlating incoming reports but creates a potential bottleneck and single point of failure. With a decentralized architecture, there are more than one analysis centers, but these must coordinate their activities and exchange information.

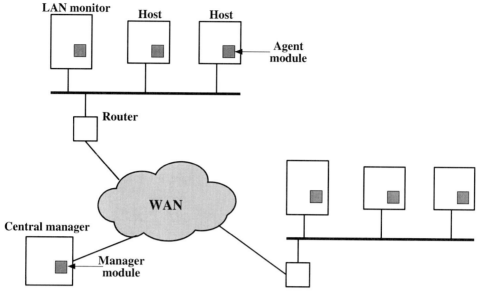

Figure 9.2 Architecture for Distributed Intrusion Detection

A good example of a distributed intrusion detection system is one developed at the University of California at Davis [HEBE92, SNAP91]. Figure 9.2 shows the overall architecture, which consists of three main components:

- **Host agent module:** An audit collection module operating as a background process on a monitored system. Its purpose is to collect data on security-related events on the host and transmit these to the central manager.
- **LAN monitor agent module:** Operates in the same fashion as a host agent module except that it analyzes LAN traffic and reports the results to the central manager.
- **Central manager module:** Receives reports from LAN monitor and host agents and processes and correlates these reports to detect intrusion.

The scheme is designed to be independent of any operating system or system auditing implementation. Figure 9.3 [SNAP91] shows the general approach that is taken. The agent captures each audit record produced by the native audit collection system. A filter is applied that retains only those records that are of security interest. These records are then reformatted into a standardized format referred to as the host audit record (HAR). Next, a template-driven logic module analyzes the records for suspicious activity. At the lowest level, the agent scans for notable events that are of interest independent of any past events. Examples include failed file accesses, accessing system files, and changing a file's access control. At the next higher level, the agent looks for sequences of events, such as known attack patterns (signatures). Finally, the agent looks for anomalous behavior of an individual user based on a historical profile of that user, such as number of programs executed, number of files accessed, and the like.

When suspicious activity is detected, an alert is sent to the central manager. The central manager includes an expert system that can draw inferences from received data. The manager may also query individual systems for copies of HARs to correlate with those from other agents.

The LAN monitor agent also supplies information to the central manager. The LAN monitor agent audits host-host connections, services used, and volume of traffic. It searches for significant events, such as sudden changes in network load, the use of security-related services, and network activities such as *rlogin*.

The architecture depicted in Figures 9.2 and 9.3 is quite general and flexible. It offers a foundation for a machine-independent approach that can expand from stand-alone intrusion detection to a system that is able to correlate activity from a number of sites and networks to detect suspicious activity that would otherwise remain undetected.

Honeypots

A relatively recent innovation in intrusion detection technology is the honeypot. Honeypots are decoy systems that are designed to lure a potential attacker away from critical systems. Honeypots are designed to

- divert an attacker from accessing critical systems
- collect information about the attacker's activity
- encourage the attacker to stay on the system long enough for administrators to respond

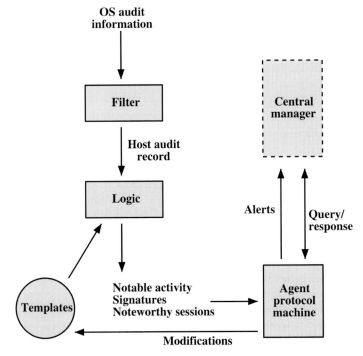

Figure 9.3 Agent Architecture

These systems are filled with fabricated information designed to appear valuable but that a legitimate user of the system wouldn't access. Thus, any access to the honeypot is suspect. The system is instrumented with sensitive monitors and event loggers that detect these accesses and collect information about the attacker's activities. Because any attack against the honeypot is made to seem successful, administrators have time to mobilize and log and track the attacker without ever exposing productive systems.

Initial efforts involved a single honeypot computer with IP addresses designed to attract hackers. More recent research has focused on building entire honeypot networks that emulate an enterprise, possibly with actual or simulated traffic and data. Once hackers are within the network, administrators can observe their behavior in detail and figure out defenses.

Intrusion Detection Exchange Format

To facilitate the development of distributed intrusion detection systems that can function across a wide range of platforms and environments, standards are needed to support interoperability. Such standards are the focus of the IETF Intrusion Detection Working Group. The purpose of the working group is to define data formats and exchange procedures for sharing information of interest to intrusion detection and response systems, and to management systems that may need to interact with them. The outputs of this working group include the following:

1. A requirements document, which describes the high-level functional requirements for communication between intrusion detection systems and requirements for communication between intrusion detection systems and with management systems, including the rationale for those requirements. Scenarios will be used to illustrate the requirements.
2. A common intrusion language specification, which describes data formats that satisfy the requirements.
3. A framework document, which identifies existing protocols best used for communication between intrusion detection systems, and describes how the devised data formats relate to them.

As of this writing, all of these documents are in an Internet-draft document stage.

9.3 PASSWORD MANAGEMENT

Password Protection

The front line of defense against intruders is the password system. Virtually all multiuser systems require that a user provide not only a name or identifier (ID) but also a password. The password serves to authenticate the ID of the individual logging on to the system. In turn, the ID provides security in the following ways:

- The ID determines whether the user is authorized to gain access to a system. In some systems, only those who already have an ID filed on the system are allowed to gain access.

- The ID determines the privileges accorded to the user. A few users may have supervisory or "superuser" status that enables them to read files and perform functions that are especially protected by the operating system. Some systems have guest or anonymous accounts, and users of these accounts have more limited privileges than others.
- The ID is used in what is referred to as discretionary access control. For example, by listing the IDs of the other users, a user may grant permission to them to read files owned by that user.

The Vulnerability of Passwords

To understand the nature of the threat to password-based systems, let us consider a scheme that is widely used on UNIX, in which passwords are never stored in the clear. Rather, the following procedure is employed (Figure 9.4a). Each user selects a password of up to eight printable characters in length. This is converted into a 56-bit value (using 7-bit ASCII) that serves as the key input to an encryption routine. The encryption routine, known as crypt(3), is based on DES. The DES algorithm is modified using a 12-bit "salt" value. Typically, this value is related to the time at which the password is assigned to the user. The modified DES algorithm is exercised with a data input consisting of a 64-bit block of zeros. The output of the algorithm then serves as input for a second encryption. This process is repeated for a total of 25 encryptions. The resulting 64-bit output is then translated into an 11-character sequence. The ciphertext password is then stored, together with a plaintext copy of the salt, in the password file for the corresponding user ID.

The salt serves three purposes:

- It prevents duplicate passwords from being visible in the password file. Even if two users choose the same password, those passwords will be assigned at different times. Hence, the "extended" passwords of the two users will differ.
- It effectively increases the length of the password without requiring the user to remember two additional characters. Hence, the number of possible passwords is increased by a factor of 4096, increasing the difficulty of guessing a password.
- It prevents the use of a hardware implementation of DES, which would ease the difficulty of a brute-force guessing attack.

When a user attempts to log on to a UNIX system, the user provides an ID and a password. The operating system uses the ID to index into the password file and retrieve the plaintext salt and the encrypted password. The salt and user-supplied password are used as input to the encryption routine. If the result matches the stored value, the password is accepted.

The encryption routine is designed to discourage guessing attacks. Software implementations of DES are slow compared to hardware versions, and the use of 25 iterations multiplies the time required by 25. However, since the original design of this algorithm, two changes have occurred. First, newer implementations of the algorithm itself have resulted in speedups. For example, the Internet worm described in Chapter 10 was able to do online password guessing of a few hundred

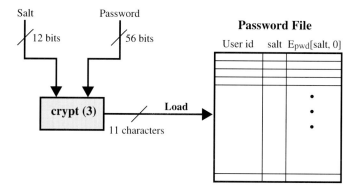

(a) Loading a new password

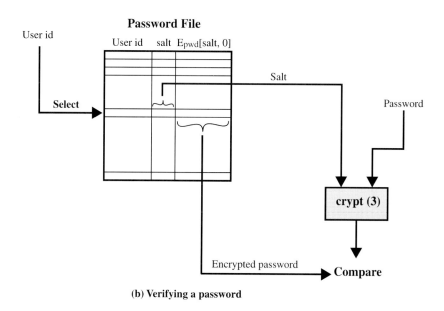

(b) Verifying a password

Figure 9.4 UNIX Password Scheme

passwords in a reasonably short time by using a more efficient encryption algorithm than the standard one stored on the UNIX systems that it attacked. Second, hardware performance continues to increase, so that any software algorithm executes more quickly.

Thus, there are two threats to the UNIX password scheme. First, a user can gain access on a machine using a guest account or by some other means and then run a password guessing program, called a password cracker, on that machine. The attacker should be able to check hundreds and perhaps thousands of possible pass-

Table 9.3 Observed Password Lengths [SPAF92a]

Length	Number	Fraction of Total
1	55	.004
2	87	.006
3	212	.02
4	449	.03
5	1260	.09
6	3035	.22
7	2917	.21
8	5772	.42
Total	13787	1.0

words with little resource consumption. In addition, if an opponent is able to obtain a copy of the password file, then a cracker program can be run on another machine at leisure. This enables the opponent to run through many thousands of possible passwords in a reasonable period.

As an example, a password cracker was reported on the Internet in August 1993 [MADS93]. Using a Thinking Machines Corporation parallel computer, a performance of 1560 encryptions per second per vector unit was achieved. With four vector units per processing node (a standard configuration), this works out to 800,000 encryptions per second on a 128-node machine (which is a modest size) and 6.4 million encryptions per second on a 1024-node machine.

Even these stupendous guessing rates do not yet make it feasible for an attacker to use a dumb brute-force technique of trying all possible combinations of characters to discover a password. Instead, password crackers rely on the fact that some people choose easily guessable passwords.

Some users, when permitted to choose their own password, pick one that is absurdly short. The results of one study at Purdue University are shown in Table 9.3. The study observed password change choices on 54 machines, representing approximately 7000 user accounts. Almost 3% of the passwords were three characters or fewer in length. An attacker could begin the attack by exhaustively testing all possible passwords of length 3 or fewer. A simple remedy is for the system to reject any password choice of fewer than, say, six characters or even to require that all passwords be exactly eight characters in length. Most users would not complain about such a restriction.

Password length is only part of the problem. Many people, when permitted to choose their own password, pick a password that is guessable, such as their own name, their street name, a common dictionary word, and so forth. This makes the job of password cracking straightforward. The cracker simply has to test the password file against lists of likely passwords. Because many people use guessable passwords, such a strategy should succeed on virtually all systems.

One demonstration of the effectiveness of guessing is reported in [KLEI90]. From a variety of sources, the author collected UNIX password files, containing nearly 14,000 encrypted passwords. The result, which the author rightly characterizes as frightening, is shown in Table 9.4. In all, nearly one-fourth of the passwords were guessed. The following strategy was used:

1. Try the user's name, initials, account name, and other relevant personal information. In all, 130 different permutations for each user were tried.
2. Try words from various dictionaries. The author compiled a dictionary of over 60,000 words, including the online dictionary on the system itself, and various other lists as shown.
3. Try various permutations on the words from step 2. This included making the first letter uppercase or a control character, making the entire word uppercase, reversing the word, changing the letter "o" to the digit "zero", and so on. These permutations added another 1 million words to the list.
4. Try various capitalization permutations on the words from step 2 that were not considered in step 3. This added almost 2 million additional words to the list.

Thus, the test involved in the neighborhood of 3 million words. Using the fastest Thinking Machines implementation listed earlier, the time to encrypt all these words

Table 9.4   Passwords Cracked from a Sample Set of 13,797 Accounts [KLEI90]

Type of Password	Search Size	Number of Matches	Percentage of Passwords Matched	Cost/Benefit Ratio[a]
User/account name	130	368	2.7%	2.830
Character sequences	866	22	0.2%	0.025
Numbers	427	9	0.1%	0.021
Chinese	392	56	0.4%	0.143
Place names	628	82	0.6%	0.131
Common names	2239	548	4.0%	0.245
Female names	4280	161	1.2%	0.038
Male names	2866	140	1.0%	0.049
Uncommon names	4955	130	0.9%	0.026
Myths & legends	1246	66	0.5%	0.053
Shakespearean	473	11	0.1%	0.023
Sports terms	238	32	0.2%	0.134
Science fiction	691	59	0.4%	0.085
Movies and actors	99	12	0.1%	0.121
Cartoons	92	9	0.1%	0.098
Famous people	290	55	0.4%	0.190
Phrases and patterns	933	253	1.8%	0.271
Surnames	33	9	0.1%	0.273
Biology	58	1	0.0%	0.017
System dictionary	19683	1027	7.4%	0.052
Machine names	9018	132	1.0%	0.015
Mnemonics	14	2	0.0%	0.143
King James Bible	7525	83	0.6%	0.011
Miscellaneous words	3212	54	0.4%	0.017
Yiddish words	56	0	0.0%	0.000
Asteroids	2407	19	0.1%	0.007
TOTAL	62727	3340	24.2%	0.053

[a]Computed as the number of matches divided by the search size. The more words that need to be tested for a match, the lower the cost/benefit ratio.

for all possible salt values is under an hour. Keep in mind that such a thorough search could produce a success rate of about 25%, whereas even a single hit may be enough to gain a wide range of privileges on a system.

Access Control

One way to thwart a password attack is to deny the opponent access to the password file. If the encrypted password portion of the file is accessible only by a privileged user, then the opponent cannot read it without already knowing the password of a privileged user. [SPAF92a] points out several flaws in this strategy:

- Many systems, including most UNIX systems, are susceptible to unanticipated break-ins. Once an attacker has gained access by some means, he or she may wish to obtain a collection of passwords in order to use different accounts for different logon sessions to decrease the risk of detection. Or a user with an account may desire another user's account to access privileged data or to sabotage the system.
- An accident of protection might render the password file readable, thus compromising all the accounts.
- Some of the users have accounts on other machines in other protection domains, and they use the same password. Thus, if the passwords could be read by anyone on one machine, a machine in another location might be compromised.

Thus, a more effective strategy would be to force users to select passwords that are difficult to guess.

Password Selection Strategies

The lesson from the two experiments just described (Tables 9.3 and 9.4) is that, left to their own devices, many users choose a password that is too short or too easy to guess. At the other extreme, if users are assigned passwords consisting of eight randomly selected printable characters, password cracking is effectively impossible. But it would be almost as impossible for most users to remember their passwords. Fortunately, even if we limit the password universe to strings of characters that are reasonably memorable, the size of the universe is still too large to permit practical cracking. Our goal, then, is to eliminate guessable passwords while allowing the user to select a password that is memorable. Four basic techniques are in use:

- User education
- Computer-generated passwords
- Reactive password checking
- Proactive password checking

Users can be told the importance of using hard-to-guess passwords and can be provided with guidelines for selecting strong passwords. This **user education** strategy is unlikely to succeed at most installations, particularly where there is a large user population or a lot of turnover. Many users will simply ignore the guidelines. Others may not be good judges of what is a strong password. For example, many users (mistakenly) believe that reversing a word or capitalizing the last letter makes a password unguessable.

Computer-generated passwords also have problems. If the passwords are quite random in nature, users will not be able to remember them. Even if the password is pronounceable, the user may have difficulty remembering it and so be tempted to write it down. In general, computer-generated password schemes have a history of poor acceptance by users. FIPS PUB 181 defines one of the best-designed automated password generators. The standard includes not only a description of the approach but also a complete listing of the C source code of the algorithm. The algorithm generates words by forming pronounceable syllables and concatenating them to form a word. A random number generator produces a random stream of characters used to construct the syllables and words.

A **reactive password checking** strategy is one in which the system periodically runs its own password cracker to find guessable passwords. The system cancels any passwords that are guessed and notifies the user. This tactic has a number of drawbacks. First, it is resource intensive if the job is done right. Because a determined opponent who is able to steal a password file can devote full CPU time to the task for hours or even days, an effective reactive password checker is at a distinct disadvantage. Furthermore, any existing passwords remain vulnerable until the reactive password checker finds them.

The most promising approach to improved password security is a **proactive password checker**. In this scheme, a user is allowed to select his or her own password. However, at the time of selection, the system checks to see if the password is allowable and, if not, rejects it. Such checkers are based on the philosophy that, with sufficient guidance from the system, users can select memorable passwords from a fairly large password space that are not likely to be guessed in a dictionary attack.

The trick with a proactive password checker is to strike a balance between user acceptability and strength. If the system rejects too many passwords, users will complain that it is too hard to select a password. If the system uses some simple algorithm to define what is acceptable, this provides guidance to password crackers to refine their guessing technique. In the remainder of this subsection, we look at possible approaches to proactive password checking.

The first approach is a simple system for rule enforcement. For example, the following rules could be enforced:

- All passwords must be at least eight characters long
- In the first eight characters, the passwords must include at least one each of uppercase, lowercase, numeric digits, and punctuation marks

These rules could be coupled with advice to the user. Although this approach is superior to simply educating users, it may not be sufficient to thwart password crackers. This scheme alerts crackers as to which passwords *not* to try but may still make it possible to do password cracking.

Another possible procedure is simply to compile a large dictionary of possible "bad" passwords. When a user selects a password, the system checks to make sure that it is not on the disapproved list. There are two problems with this approach:

- **Space**: The dictionary must be very large to be effective. For example, the dictionary used in the Purdue study [SPAF92a] occupies more than 30 megabytes of storage.
- **Time:** The time required to search a large dictionary may itself be large. In addition, to check for likely permutations of dictionary words, either those words most be included in the dictionary, making it truly huge, or each search must also involve considerable processing.

Two techniques for developing an effective and efficient proactive password checker that is based on rejecting words on a list show promise. One of these develops a Markov model for the generation of guessable passwords [DAVI93]. Figure 9.5 shows a simplified version of such a model. This model shows a language consisting of an alphabet of three characters. The state of the system at any time is the identity of the most recent letter. The value on the transition from one state to another represents the probability that one letter follows another. Thus, the probability that the next letter is b, given that the current letter is a, is 0.5.

In general, a Markov model is a quadruple $[m, A, \mathbf{T}, k]$, where m is the number of states in the model, A is the state space, $\mathbf{T}$ is the matrix of transition probabilities, and k is the order of the model. For a kth-order model, the probability of

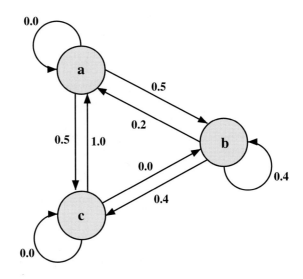

$M = \{3, \{a, b, c\}, \mathbf{T}, 1\}$ where

$$\mathbf{T} = \begin{bmatrix} 0.0 & 0.5 & 0.5 \\ 0.2 & 0.4 & 0.4 \\ 1.0 & 0.0 & 0.0 \end{bmatrix}$$

e.g., string probably from this language: **abbcacaba**

e.g., string probably not from this language: **aacccbaaa**

Figure 9.5   An Example Markov Model

making a transition to a particular letter depends on the previous k letters that have been generated. Figure 9.5 shows a simple first-order model.

The authors report on the development and use of a second-order model. To begin, a dictionary of guessable passwords is constructed. Then the transition matrix is calculated as follows:

1. Determine the frequency matrix $\mathbf{f}$, where $\mathbf{f}(i, j, k)$ is the number of occurrences of the trigram consisting of the ith, jth, and kth character. For example, the password *parsnips* yields the trigrams par, ars, rsn, sni, nip, and ips.
2. For each bigram ij, calculate $\mathbf{f}(i, j, \infty)$ as the total number of trigrams beginning with ij. For example, $\mathbf{f}(a, b, \infty)$ would be the total number of trigrams of the form aba, abb, abc, and so on.
3. Compute the entries of $\mathbf{T}$ as follows:

$$\mathbf{T}(i, j, k) = \frac{\mathbf{f}(i, j, k)}{\mathbf{f}(i, j, \infty)}$$

The result is a model that reflects the structure of the words in the dictionary. With this model, the question "Is this a bad password?" is transformed into the question "Was this string (password) generated by this Markov model?" For a given password, the transition probabilities of all its trigrams can be looked up. Some standard statistical tests can then be used to determine if the password is likely or unlikely for that model. Passwords that are likely to be generated by the model are rejected. The authors report good results for a second-order model. Their system catches virtually all the passwords in their dictionary and does not exclude so many potentially good passwords as to be user unfriendly.

A quite different approach has been reported by Spafford [SPAF92a, SPAF92b]. It is based on the use of a Bloom filter [BLOO70]. To begin, we explain the operation of the Bloom filter. A Bloom filter of order k consists of a set of k independent hash functions $H_1(x), H_2(x), \ldots, H_k(x)$, where each function maps a password into a hash value in the range 0 to $N - 1$. That is,

$$H_i(X_j) = y \qquad 1 \le i \le k; \qquad 1 \le j \le D; \qquad 0 \le y \le N - 1$$

where

$$X_j = j\text{th word in password dictionary}$$
$$D = \text{number of words in password dictionary}$$

The following procedure is then applied to the dictionary:

1. A hash table of N bits is defined, with all bits initially set to 0.
2. For each password, its k hash values are calculated, and the corresponding bits in the hash table are set to 1. Thus, if $H_i(X_j) = 67$ for some (i, j), then the sixty-seventh bit of the hash table is set to 1; if the bit already has the value 1, it remains at 1.

When a new password is presented to the checker, its k hash values are calculated. If all the corresponding bits of the hash table are equal to 1, then the password is rejected. All passwords in the dictionary will be rejected. But there will also be some "false positives" (that is, passwords that are not in the dictionary but that produce a match in the hash table). To see this, consider a scheme with two hash functions. Suppose that the passwords *undertaker* and *hulkhogan* are in the dictionary, but *xG%#jj98* is not. Further suppose that

$$H_1(\text{undertaker}) = 25 \qquad H_1(\text{hulkhogan}) = 83 \qquad H_1(\text{xG\%\#jj98}) = 665$$

$$H_2(\text{undertaker}) = 998 \qquad H_2(\text{hulkhogan}) = 665 \qquad H_2(\text{xG\%\#jj98}) = 998$$

If the password xG%#jj98 is presented to the system, it will be rejected even though it is not in the dictionary. If there are too many such false positives, it will be difficult for users to select passwords. Therefore, we would like to design the hash scheme to minimize false positives. It can be shown that the probability of a false positive can be approximated by

$$P \approx (1 - e^{kD/N})^k = (1 - e^{k/R})^k$$

or, equivalently,

$$R \approx \frac{-k}{\ln(1 - P^{1/k})}$$

where

k = number of hash functions
N = number of bits in hash table
D = number of words in dictionary
R = N/D, ratio of hash table size (bits) to dictionary size (words)

Figure 9.6 plots P as a function of R for various values of k. Suppose we have a dictionary of 1 million words and we wish to have a 0.01 probability of rejecting a password not in the dictionary. If we choose six hash functions, the required ratio is $R = 9.6$. Therefore, we need a hash table of 9.6×10^6 bits or about 1.2 MBytes of storage. In contrast, storage of the entire dictionary would require on the order of 8 MBytes. Thus, we achieve a compression of almost a factor of 7. Furthermore, password checking involves the straightforward calculation of six hash functions and is independent of the size of the dictionary, whereas with the use of the full dictionary, there is substantial searching.[2]

---

[2]Both the Markov model and the Bloom filter involve the use of probabilistic techniques. In the case of the Markov model, there is a small probability that some passwords in the dictionary will not be caught and a small probability that some passwords not in the dictionary will be rejected. In the case of the Bloom filter, there is a small probability that some passwords not in the dictionary will be rejected.

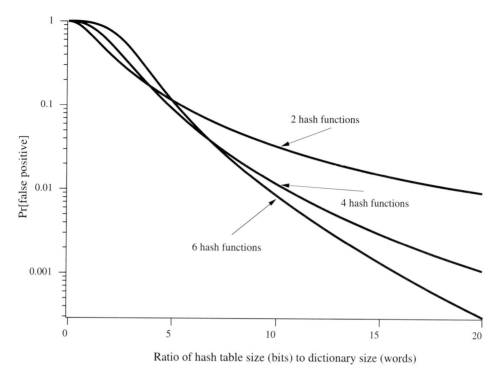

Figure 9.6   Performance of Bloom Filter

9.4   RECOMMENDED READING AND WEB SITES

Two thorough treatments of intrusion detection are [BACE00] and [PROC01]. A more concise but very worthwhile treatment is [BACE01]. Two short but useful survey articles on the subject are [KENT00] and [MCHU00]. [HONE01] is the definitive account on honeypots and provides a detailed analysis of the tools and methods of hackers.

BACE00   Bace, R. *Intrusion Detection.* Indianapolis, IN: Macmillan Technical Publishing, 2000.

BACE01   Bace, R., and Mell, P. *Intrusion Detection Systems.* NIST Special Publication SP 800-31, November 2000.

HONE01   The Honeynet Project. *Know Your Enemy: Revealing the Security Tools, Tactics, and Motives of the Blackhat Community.* Reading, MA: Addison-Wesley, 2001.

KENT00   Kent, S. "On the Trail of Intrusions into Information Systems." *IEEE Spectrum,* December 2000.

MCHU00   McHugh, J.; Christie, A.; and Allen, J. "The Role of Intrusion Detection Systems." *IEEE Software,* September/October 2000.

PROC01   Proctor, P. *The Practical Intrusion Detection Handbook.* Upper Saddle River, NJ: Prentice Hall, 2001.

Recommended Web sites:

- **CERT Coordination Center:** The organization that grew from the computer emergency response team formed by the Defense Advanced Research Projects Agency. Site provides good information on Internet security threats, vulnerabilities, and attack statistics.
- **Honeypot Project:** A research project studying the techniques of predatory hackers and developing honeypot products.
- **Intrusion Detection Working Group:** Includes all of the documents generated by this group.

9.5   KEY TERMS, REVIEW QUESTIONS, AND PROBLEMS

Key Terms

audit record	intruder	password
Bayes' theorem	intrusion detection	rule-based intrusion detection
base-rate fallacy	intrusion detection exchange	salt
honeypot	format	statistical anomaly detection

Review Questions

9.1   List and briefly define three classes of intruders.

9.2   What are two common techniques used to protect a password file?

9.3   What are three benefits that can be provided by an intrusion detection system?

9.4   What is the difference between statistical anomaly detection and rule-based intrusion detection?

9.5   What metrics are useful for profile-based intrusion detection?

9.6   What is the difference between rule-based anomaly detection and rule-based penetration identification?

9.7   What is a honeypot?

9.8   What is a salt in the context of UNIX password management?

9.9   List and briefly define four techniques used to avoid guessable passwords.

Problems

9.1   A taxicab was involved in a fatal hit-and-run accident at night. Two cab companies, the Green and the Blue, operate in the city. You are told that

- 85% of the cabs in the city are Green and 15% are Blue
- A witness identified the cab as Blue

The court tested the reliability of the witness under the same circumstances that existed on the night of the accident and concluded that the witness was correct in identifying the color of the cab 80% of the time. What is the probability that the cab involved in the incident was Blue rather than Green?

9.2 Assume that passwords are selected from four-character combinations of 26 alphabetic characters. Assume that an adversary is able to attempt passwords at a rate of one per second.

    a. Assuming no feedback to the adversary until each attempt has been completed, what is the expected time to discover the correct password?

    b. Assuming feedback to the adversary flagging an error as each incorrect character is entered, what is the expected time to discover the correct password?

9.3 Assume that source elements of length k is mapped in some uniform fashion into a target elements of length p. If each digit can take on one of r values, then the number of source elements is r^k and the number of target elements is the smaller number r^p. A particular source element x_i is mapped to a particular target element y_j.

    a. What is the probability that the correct source element can be selected by an adversary on one try?

    b. What is the probability that a different source element x_k ($x_i \neq x_k$) that results in the same target element, y_j, could be produced by an adversary?

    c. What is the probability that the correct target element can be produced by an adversary on one try?

9.4 A phonetic password generator picks two segments randomly for each six-letter password. The form of each segment is CVC (consonant, vowel, consonant), where V = <a,e,i,o,u> and C = $\overline{V}$.

    a. What is the total password population?

    b. What is the probability of an adversary guessing a password correctly?

9.5 Assume that passwords are limited to the use of the 95 printable ASCII characters and that all passwords are 10 characters in length. Assume a password cracker with an encryption rate of 6.4 million encryptions per second. How long will it take to test exhaustively all possible passwords on a UNIX system?

9.6 Because of the known risks of the UNIX password system, the SunOS-4.0 documentation recommends that the password file be removed and replaced with a publicly readable file called /etc/publickey. An entry in the file for user A consists of a user's identifier ID_A, the user's public key, KU_a, and the corresponding private key KR_a. This private key is encrypted using DES with a key derived from the user's login password P_a. When A logs in the system decrypts $E_{P_a}[KR_a]$ to obtain KR_a.

    a. The system then verifies that P_a was correctly supplied. How?

    b. How can an opponent attack this system?

9.7 The encryption scheme used for UNIX passwords is one way; it is not possible to reverse it. Therefore, would it be accurate to say that this is, in fact, a hash code rather than an encryption of the password?

9.8 It was stated that the inclusion of the salt in the UNIX password scheme increases the difficulty of guessing by a factor of 4096. But the salt is stored in plaintext in the same entry as the corresponding ciphertext password. Therefore, those two characters are known to the attacker and need not be guessed. Why is it asserted that the salt increases security?

9.9 Assuming that you have successfully answered the preceding problem and understand the significance of the salt, here is another question. Wouldn't it be possible to thwart completely all password crackers by dramatically increasing the salt size to, say, 24 or 48 bits?

9.10 Consider the Bloom filter discussed in Section 9.3. Define k = number of hash functions; N = number of bits in hash table; and D = number of words in dictionary.

a. Show that the expected number of bits in the hash table that are equal to zero is expressed as

$$\phi = \left(1 - \frac{k}{N}\right)^D$$

b. Show that the probability that an input word, not in the dictionary, will be falsely accepted as being in the dictionary is

$$P = (1 - \phi)^k$$

c. Show that the preceding expression can be approximated as

$$P \approx (1 - e^{-kD/N})^k$$

APPENDIX 9A   THE BASE-RATE FALLACY

We begin with a review of important results from probability theory, then demonstrate the base-rate fallacy.

Conditional Probability and Independence

We often want to know a probability that is conditional on some event. The effect of the condition is to remove some of the outcomes from the sample space. For example, what is the probability of getting a sum of 8 on the roll of two dice, if we know that the face of at least one die is an even number? We can reason as follows. Because one die is even and the sum is even, the second die must show an even number. Thus, there are three equally likely successful outcomes: $(2, 6)$, $(4, 4)$ and $(6, 2)$, out of a total set of possibilities of [36 − (number of events with both faces odd)] = $36 - 3 \times 3 = 27$. The resulting probability is $3/27 = 1/9$.

Formally, the **conditional probability** of an event A assuming the event B has occurred, denoted by $\Pr[A|B]$, is defined as the ratio

$$\Pr[A|B] = \frac{\Pr[AB]}{\Pr[B]}$$

where we assume $\Pr[B]$ is not zero.

In our example, $A = \{$sum of 8$\}$ and $B = \{$at least one die even$\}$. The quantity $\Pr[AB]$ encompasses all of those outcomes in which the sum is 8 and at least one die is even. As we have seen, there are three such outcomes. Thus, $\Pr[AB] = 3/36 = 1/12$. A moment's thought should convince you that $\Pr[B] = 3/4$. We can now calculate

$$\Pr[A|B] = \frac{1/12}{3/4} = \frac{1}{9}$$

This agrees with our previous reasoning.

Two events A and B are called **independent** if $\Pr[AB] = \Pr[A]\Pr[B]$. It can easily be seen that if A and B are independent, $\Pr[A|B] = \Pr[A]$ and $\Pr[B|A] = \Pr[B]$.

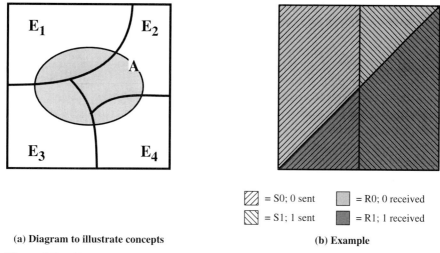

= S0; 0 sent   = R0; 0 received

= S1; 1 sent   = R1; 1 received

(a) Diagram to illustrate concepts   **(b) Example**

Figure 9.7   Illustration of Total Probability and Bayes' Theorem

Bayes' Theorem

One of the most important results from probability theory is known as Bayes' theorem. First we need to state the total probability formula. Given a set of mutually exclusive events $E_1, E_2, \ldots E_n$, such that the union of these events covers all possible outcomes and, and given an arbitrary event A, then it can be shown that

$$\Pr[A] = \sum_{i=1}^{n} \Pr[A \mid E_i]\Pr[E_i] \tag{9.1}$$

Bayes' theorem may be stated as follows:

$$\Pr[E_i \mid A] = \frac{\Pr[A \mid E_i]\mathrm{P}[E_i]}{\Pr[A]} = \frac{\Pr[A \mid E_i]\mathrm{P}[E_i]}{\sum_{j=1}^{n} \Pr[A \mid E_j]\Pr[E_j]} \tag{9.2}$$

Figure 9.7a illustrates the concepts of total probability and Bayes' theorem.

Bayes' theorem is used to calculate "posterior odds," that is, the probability that something really is the case, given evidence in favor of it. For example, suppose we are transmitting a sequence of zerocs and ones over a noisy transmission line. Let S0 and S1 be the events a zero is sent at a given time and a one is sent, respectively, and R0 and R1 be the events that a zero is received and a one is received. Suppose we know the probabilities of the source, namely $\Pr[S1] = p$ and $\Pr[S0] = 1 - p$. Now the line is observed to determine how frequently an error occurs when a one is sent and when a zero is sent, and the following probabilities are calculated: $\Pr[R0 \mid S1] = p_a$ and $\Pr[R1 \mid S0] = p_b$. If a zero is received, we can then calculate the conditional probability of an error, namely the conditional probability that a one was sent given that a zero was received, using Bayes' theorem:

$$Pr[S1|R0] = \frac{Pr[R0|S1]Pr[S1]}{Pr[R0|S1]Pr[S1] + Pr[R0|S0]Pr[S0]} = \frac{p_a p}{p_a p + (1 - p_b)(1 - p)}$$

Figure 9.7b illustrates the preceding equation. In the figure, the sample space is represented by a unit square. Half of the square corresponds to SO and half to S1, so Pr[SO[= Pr[S1] = 0.5. Similarly, half of the square corresponds to RO and half to R1, so Pr[R0] = Pr[R1] = 0.5. Within the area representing S0, $\frac{1}{4}$ of that area corresponds to R1, so Pr[R1/S0] = 0.25. Other conditional probabilities are similarly evident.

The Base-Rate Fallacy Demonstrated

Consider the following situation. A patient has a test for some disease that comes back positive (indicating he has the disease). You are told that

- the accuracy of the test is 87% (i.e., if a patient has the disease, 87% of the time, the test yields the correct result, and if the patient does not have the disease, 87% of the time, the test yields the correct result)
- the incidence of the disease in the population is 1%

Given that the test is positive, how probable is it that the patient does not have the disease? That is, what is the probability that this is a false alarm? We need Bayes' theorem to get the correct answer:

$$Pr[well/positive] = \frac{Pr[positive/well]Pr[well]}{Pr[positive/disease]Pr[disease] + Pr[positive/well]Pr[well]}$$

$$= \frac{(0.13)(0.99)}{(0.87)(0.01) + (0.13)(0.99)} = 0.937$$

Thus, in the vast majority of cases, when a disease condition is detected, it is a false alarm.

This problem, used in a study [PIAT91], was presented to a number of people. Most subjects gave the answer 13%. The vast majority, including many physicians, gave a number below 50%. Many physicians who guessed wrong lamented, "If you are right, there is no point in making clinical tests!" The reason most people get it wrong is that they do not take into account the basic rate of incidence (the base rate) when intuitively solving the problem. This error is known as the *base-rate fallacy*.

How could this problem be fixed? Suppose we could drive both of the correct result rates to 99%. That is, suppose we have Pr[positive/disease] = 0.99 and Pr[negative/well] = 0.99. Plugging these numbers into the Equation (9.2), we get Pr[well/positive] = 0.01. Thus, if we can accurately detect disease and accurately detect lack of disease at a level of 99%, then the rate of false alarms, will be only 1%. However, now suppose that the incidence of the disease in the population is only 1/10000 = 0.0001. We then end up with a rate of false alarms of 99%. In actual situations, [AXEL00] found that the probabilities associated with intrusion detection systems were such that the false alarm rate was unsatisfactory.

CHAPTER 10

MALICIOUS SOFTWARE

10.1 Viruses and Related Threats

Malicious Programs
The Nature of Viruses
Types of Viruses
Macro Viruses
E-mail Viruses
Worms

10.2 Virus Countermeasures

Antivirus Approaches
Advanced Antivirus Techniques
Behavior-Blocking Software

10.3 Recommended Reading and Web Site

10.4 Key Terms, Review Questions, and Problems

Key Terms
Review Questions
Problems

What is the concept of defense: The parrying of a blow. What is its characteristic feature: Awaiting the blow.

—On War, **Carl Von Clausewitz**

T his chapter examines malicious software, especially viruses and worms.

10.1 VIRUSES AND RELATED THREATS

Perhaps the most sophisticated types of threats to computer systems are presented by programs that exploit vulnerabilities in computing systems. In this context, we are concerned with application programs as well as utility programs, such as editors and compilers.

We begin this section with an overview of the spectrum of such software threats. The remainder of the section is devoted to viruses and worms, first looking at their nature and then at countermeasures.

Malicious Programs

Figure 10.1 provides an overall taxonomy of software threats, or malicious programs. These threats can be divided into two categories: those that need a host program, and those that are independent. The former are essentially fragments of programs that cannot exist independently of some actual application program, utility, or system program. The latter are self-contained programs that can be scheduled and run by the operating system.

We can also differentiate between those software threats that do not replicate and those that do. The former are fragments of programs that are to be activated when the host program is invoked to perform a specific function. The latter consist of either a program fragment (virus) or an independent program (worm, bacterium) that, when executed, may produce one or more copies of itself to be activated later on the same system or some other system.

Although the taxonomy of Figure 10.1 is useful in organizing the information we are discussing, it is not the whole picture. In particular, logic bombs or Trojan horses may be part of a virus or worm. In the remainder of this subsection, we briefly survey each of these examples of malicious software, with the exception of viruses and worms, which are covered in more detail later in this section.

Trap doors

A trap door is a secret entry point into a program that allows someone that is aware of the trapdoor to gain access without going through the usual security access procedures. Trap doors have been used legitimately for many years by programmers to debug and test programs. This usually is done when the programmer is developing an application that has an authentication procedure, or a long setup, requiring the user to enter many different values to run the application. To debug the program, the developer may wish to gain special privileges or to avoid all the necessary setup and authentication. The programmer may also want to ensure that there is a method of activating the program should something be wrong with the authentication procedure that is being built into the application. The trap door is code that recognizes some special sequence of input or is triggered by being run from a certain user ID or by an unlikely sequence of events.

Trap doors become threats when they are used by unscrupulous programmers to gain unauthorized access. The trap door was the basic idea for the vulnerability portrayed in the movie *War Games*. Another example is that during the development of Multics, penetration tests were conducted by an Air Force "tiger team" (simulating adversaries). One tactic employed was to send a bogus operating system update to a site running Multics. The update contained a Trojan horse (described later) that could be activated by a trap door and that allowed the tiger team to gain access. The threat was so well implemented that the Multics developers could not find it, even after they were informed of its presence [ENGE80].

It is difficult to implement operating system controls for trap doors. Security measures must focus on the program development and software update activities.

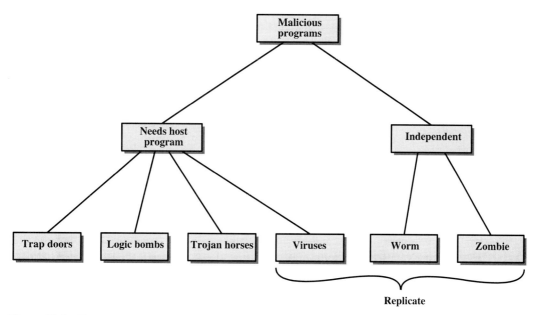

Figure 10.1   Taxonomy of Malicious Programs

Logic Bomb

One of the oldest types of program threat, predating viruses and worms, is the logic bomb. The logic bomb is code embedded in some legitimate program that is set to "explode" when certain conditions are met. Examples of conditions that can be used as triggers for a logic bomb are the presence or absence of certain files, a particular day of the week or date, or a particular user running the application. Once triggered, a bomb may alter or delete data or entire files, cause a machine halt, or do some other damage. A striking example of how logic bombs can be employed was the case of Tim Lloyd, who was convicted of setting a logic bomb that cost his employer, Omega Engineering, more than $10 million, derailed its corporate growth strategy, and eventually led to the layoff of 80 workers [GAUD00]. Ultimately, Lloyd was sentenced to 41 months in prison and ordered to pay $2 million in restitution.

Trojan Horses

A Trojan horse is a useful, or apparently useful, program or command procedure containing hidden code that, when invoked, performs some unwanted or harmful function.

Trojan horse programs can be used to accomplish functions indirectly that an unauthorized user could not accomplish directly. For example, to gain access to the files of another user on a shared system, a user could create a Trojan horse program that, when executed, changed the invoking user's file permissions so that the files are readable by any user. The author could then induce users to run the program by placing it in a common directory and naming it such that it appears to be a useful utility. An example is a program that ostensibly produces a listing of the user's files in a desirable format. After another user has run the program, the author can then access the information in the user's files. An example of a Trojan horse program that would be difficult to detect is a compiler that has been modified to insert additional code into certain programs as they are compiled, such as a system login program [THOM84]. The code creates a trap door in the login program that permits the author to log on to the system using a special password. This Trojan horse can never be discovered by reading the source code of the login program.

Another common motivation for the Trojan horse is data destruction. The program appears to be performing a useful function (e.g., a calculator program), but it may also be quietly deleting the user's files. For example, a CBS executive was victimized by a Trojan horse that destroyed all information contained in his computer's memory [TIME90]. The Trojan horse was implanted in a graphics routine offered on an electronic bulletin board system.

Zombie

A zombie is a program that secretly takes over another Internet-attached computer and then uses that computer to launch attacks that are difficult to trace to the zombie's creator. Zombies are used in denial-of-service attacks, typically against targeted Web sites. The zombie is planted on hundreds of computers belonging to unsuspecting third parties, and then used to overwhelm the target Web site by launching an overwhelming onslaught of Internet traffic.

The Nature of Viruses

A virus is a program that can "infect" other programs by modifying them; the modification includes a copy of the virus program, which can then go on to infect other programs.

Biological viruses are tiny scraps of genetic code—DNA or RNA—that can take over the machinery of a living cell and trick it into making thousands of flawless replicas of the original virus. Like its biological counterpart, a computer virus carries in its instructional code the recipe for making perfect copies of itself. Lodged in a host computer, the typical virus takes temporary control of the computer's disk operating system. Then, whenever the infected computer comes into contact with an uninfected piece of software, a fresh copy of the virus passes into the new program. Thus, the infection can be spread from computer to computer by unsuspecting users who either swap disks or send programs to one another over a network. In a network environment, the ability to access applications and system services on other computers provides a perfect culture for the spread of a virus.

A virus can do anything that other programs do. The only difference is that it attaches itself to another program and executes secretly when the host program is run. Once a virus is executing, it can perform any function, such as erasing files and programs.

During its lifetime, a typical virus goes through the following four phases:

- **Dormant phase:** The virus is idle. The virus will eventually be activated by some event, such as a date, the presence of another program or file, or the capacity of the disk exceeding some limit. Not all viruses have this stage.

- **Propagation phase:** The virus places an identical copy of itself into other programs or into certain system areas on the disk. Each infected program will now contain a clone of the virus, which will itself enter a propagation phase.

- **Triggering phase:** The virus is activated to perform the function for which it was intended. As with the dormant phase, the triggering phase can be caused by a variety of system events, including a count of the number of times that this copy of the virus has made copies of itself.

- **Execution phase:** The function is performed. The function may be harmless, such as a message on the screen, or damaging, such as the destruction of programs and data files.

Most viruses carry out their work in a manner that is specific to a particular operating system and, in some cases, specific to a particular hardware platform. Thus, they are designed to take advantage of the details and weaknesses of particular systems.

Virus Structure

A virus can be prepended or postpended to an executable program, or it can be embedded in some other fashion. The key to its operation is that the infected

```
                    program V :=

        {goto main;
                1234567;

                    subroutine infect-executable :=
                        {loop:
                        file := get-random-executable-file;
                        if (first-line-of-file = 1234567)
                                then goto loop
                                else prepend V to file; }

                    subroutine do-damage :=
                        {whatever damage is to be done}

                    subroutine trigger-pulled :=
                        {return true if some condition holds}

        main:       main-program :=
                        {infect-executable;
                        if trigger-pulled then do-damage;
                        goto next;}

        next:

        }
```

Figure 10.2   A Simple Virus

program, when invoked, will first execute the virus code and then execute the original code of the program.

A very general depiction of virus structure is shown in Figure 10.2 (based on [COHE94]). In this case, the virus code, V, is prepended to infected programs, and it is assumed that the entry point to the program, when invoked, is the first line of the program.

An infected program begins with the virus code and works as follows. The first line of code is a jump to the main virus program. The second line is a special marker that is used by the virus to determine whether or not a potential victim program has already been infected with this virus. When the program is invoked, control is immediately transferred to the main virus program. The virus program first seeks out uninfected executable files and infects them. Next, the virus may perform some action, usually detrimental to the system. This action could be performed every time the program is invoked, or it could be a logic bomb that triggers only under certain conditions. Finally, the virus transfers control to the original program. If the infection phase of the program is reasonably rapid, a user is unlikely to notice any difference between the execution of an infected and uninfected program.

A virus such as the one just described is easily detected because an infected version of a program is longer than the corresponding uninfected one. A way to thwart such a simple means of detecting a virus is to compress the executable file so that both the infected and uninfected versions are of identical length. Figure 10.3

```
        program CV :=

{goto main;
    01234567;

        subroutine infect-executable :=
                {loop:
                        file := get-random-executable-file;
                if (first-line-of-file = 01234567) then goto loop;
    (1)     compress file;
    (2)     prepend CV to file;
                }

main: main-program :=
                {if ask-permission then infect-executable;
    (3)     uncompress rest-of-file;
    (4)     run uncompressed file;}
                }
```

Figure 10.3 Logic for a Compression Virus

[COHE94] shows in general terms the logic required. The key lines in this virus are numbered, and Figure 10.4 [COHE94] illustrates the operation. We assume that program P_1 is infected with the virus CV. When this program is invoked, control passes to its virus, which performs the following steps:

1. For each uninfected file P_2 that is found, the virus first compresses that file to produce P_2', which is shorter than the original program by the size of the virus.
2. A copy of the virus is prepended to the compressed program.

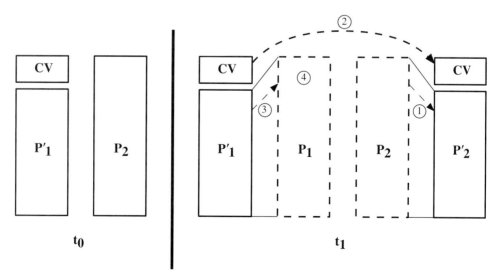

Figure 10.4 A Compression Virus

3. The compressed version of the original infected program, P_1', is uncompressed.

4. The uncompressed original program is executed.

In this example, the virus does nothing other than propagate. As in the previous example, the virus may include a logic bomb.

Initial Infection

Once a virus has gained entry to a system by infecting a single program, it is in a position to infect some or all other executable files on that system when the infected program executes. Thus, viral infection can be completely prevented by preventing the virus from gaining entry in the first place. Unfortunately, prevention is extraordinarily difficult because a virus can be part of any program outside a system. Thus, unless one is content to take an absolutely bare piece of iron and write all one's own system and application programs, one is vulnerable.

Most viral infections initiate with a disk from which programs are copied onto a machine. Many of these are disks that have games or simple but handy utilities that employees obtain for their home computers and then bring in and put on an office machine. Some, incredibly, are present on disks that come shrink-wrapped from the manufacturer of an application. Only a small fraction of infections begin across a network connection. Again, typically, an employee will download a game or apparently useful utility only to discover later that it contains a virus.

Types of Viruses

There has been a continuous arms race between virus writers and writers of antivirus software since viruses first appeared. As effective countermeasures have been developed for existing types of viruses, new types have been developed. [STEP93] suggests the following categories as being among the most significant types of viruses:

- **Parasitic virus:** The traditional and still most common form of virus. A parasitic virus attaches itself to executable files and replicates, when the infected program is executed, by finding other executable files to infect.
- **Memory-resident virus:** Lodges in main memory as part of a resident system program. From that point on, the virus infects every program that executes.
- **Boot sector virus:** Infects a master boot record or boot record and spreads when a system is booted from the disk containing the virus.
- **Stealth virus:** A form of virus explicitly designed to hide itself from detection by antivirus software.
- **Polymorphic virus:** A virus that mutates with every infection, making detection by the "signature" of the virus impossible.

One example of a **stealth virus** was discussed earlier: a virus that uses compression so that the infected program is exactly the same length as an uninfected version. Far more sophisticated techniques are possible. For example, a virus can place intercept logic in disk I/O routines, so that when there is an attempt to read suspected portions of the disk using these routines, the virus will present back the original, uninfected program. Thus, *stealth* is not a term that applies to a virus as such but, rather, is a technique used by a virus to evade detection.

A **polymorphic virus** creates copies during replication that are functionally equivalent but have distinctly different bit patterns. As with a stealth virus, the purpose is to defeat programs that scan for viruses. In this case, the "signature" of the virus will vary with each copy. To achieve this variation, the virus may randomly insert superfluous instructions or interchange the order of independent instructions. A more effective approach is to use encryption. A portion of the virus, generally called a *mutation engine*, creates a random encryption key to encrypt the remainder of the virus. The key is stored with the virus, and the mutation engine itself is altered. When an infected program is invoked, the virus uses the stored random key to decrypt the virus. When the virus replicates, a different random key is selected.

Another weapon in the virus writers' armory is the virus-creation toolkit. Such a toolkit enables a relative novice to create quickly a number of different viruses. Although viruses created with toolkits tend to be less sophisticated than viruses designed from scratch, the sheer number of new viruses that can be generated creates a problem for antivirus schemes.

Macro Viruses

In recent years, the number of viruses encountered at corporate sites has risen dramatically. Virtually all of this increase is due to the proliferation of one of the newest types of virus: the macro virus. According to the National Computer Security Agency (www.ncsa.com), macro viruses now make up two-thirds of all computer viruses.

Macro viruses are particularly threatening for a number of reasons:

1. A macro virus is platform independent. Virtually all of the macro viruses infect Microsoft Word documents. Any hardware platform and operating system that supports Word can be infected.

2. Macro viruses infect documents, not executable portions of code. Most of the information introduced onto a computer system is in the form of a document rather than a program.

3. Macro viruses are easily spread. A very common method is by electronic mail.

Macro viruses take advantage of a feature found in Word and other office applications such as Microsoft Excel, namely the macro. In essence, a macro is an executable program embedded in a word processing document or other type of file. Typically, users employ macros to automate repetitive tasks and thereby save keystrokes. The macro language is usually some form of the Basic programming language. A user might define a sequence of keystrokes in a macro and set it up so that the macro is invoked when a function key or special short combination of keys is input.

What makes it possible to create a macro virus is the autoexecuting macro. This is a macro that is automatically invoked, without explicit user input. Common autoexecute events are opening a file, closing a file, and starting an application.

Once a macro is running, it can copy itself to other documents, delete files, and cause other sorts of damage to the user's system. In Microsoft Word, there are three types of autoexecuting macros:

- **Autoexecute:** If a macro named AutoExec is in the "normal.dot" template or in a global template stored in Word's startup directory, it is executed whenever Word is started.
- **Automacro:** An automacro executes when a defined event occurs, such as opening or closing a document, creating a new document, or quitting Word.
- **Command macro:** If a macro in a global macro file or a macro attached to a document has the name of an existing Word command, it is executed whenever the user invokes that command (e.g., File Save).

A common technique for spreading a macro virus is as follows. An automacro or command macro is attached to a Word document that is introduced into a system by e-mail or disk transfer. At some point after the document is opened, the macro executes. The macro copies itself to the global macro file. When the next session of Word opens, the infected global macro is active. When this macro executes, it can replicate itself and cause damage.

Successive releases of Word provide increased protection against macro viruses. For example, Microsoft offers an optional Macro Virus Protection tool that detects suspicious Word files and alerts the customer to the potential risk of opening a file with macros. Various antivirus product vendors have also developed tools to detect and correct macro viruses. As in other types of viruses, the arms race continues in the field of macro viruses.

E-mail Viruses

A more recent development in malicious software is the e-mail virus. The first rapidly spreading e-mail viruses, such as Melissa, made use of a Microsoft Word macro embedded in an attachment. If the recipient opens the e-mail attachment, the Word macro is activated. Then

1. The e-mail virus sends itself to everyone on the mailing list in the user's e-mail package.
2. The virus does local damage.

At the end of 1999, a more powerful version of the e-mail virus appeared. This newer version can be activated merely by opening an e-mail that contains the virus rather than opening an attachment. The virus uses the Visual Basic scripting language supported by the e-mail package.

Thus we see a new generation of malware that arrives via e-mail and uses e-mail software features to replicate itself across the Internet. The virus propagates itself as soon as activated (either by opening an e-mail attachment of by opening the e-mail) to all of the e-mail addresses known to the infected host. As a result, whereas viruses used to take months or years to propagate, they now do so in hours. This makes it very difficult for antivirus software to respond before much damage is done. Ultimately, a greater degree of security must be built into Internet utility and application software on PCs to counter the growing threat.

Worms

An e-mail virus has some of the characteristics of a worm, because it propagates itself from system to system. However, we can still classify it as a virus because it requires a human to move it forward. A worm actively seeks out more machines to infect and each machine that is infected serves as an automated launching pad for attacks on other machines.

Network worm programs use network connections to spread from system to system. Once active within a system, a network worm can behave as a computer virus or bacteria, or it could implant Trojan horse programs or perform any number of disruptive or destructive actions.

To replicate itself, a network worm uses some sort of network vehicle. Examples include

- **Electronic mail facility:** A worm mails a copy of itself to other systems.
- **Remote execution capability:** A worm executes a copy of itself on another system.
- **Remote login capability:** A worm logs onto a remote system as a user and then uses commands to copy itself from one system to the other.

The new copy of the worm program is then run on the remote system where, in addition to any functions that it performs at that system, it continues to spread in the same fashion.

A network worm exhibits the same characteristics as a computer virus: a dormant phase, a propagation phase, a triggering phase, and an execution phase. The propagation phase generally performs the following functions:

1. Search for other systems to infect by cxamining host tables or similar repositories of remote system addresses.
2. Establish a connection with a remote system.
3. Copy itself to the remote system and cause the copy to be run.

The network worm may also attempt to determine whether a system has previously been infected before copying itself to the system. In a multiprogramming system, it may also disguise its presence by naming itself as a system process or using some other name that may not be noticed by a system operator.

As with viruses, network worms are difficult to counter. However, both network security and single-system security measures, if properly designed and implemented, minimize the threat of worms.

The Morris Worm

Until the current generation of worms, the best known was the worm released onto the Internet by Robert Morris in 1998. The Morris worm was designed to spread on UNIX systems and used a number of different techniques for propagation. When a copy began execution, its first task was to discover other hosts known to this host that would allow entry from this host. The worm performed this task by examining a variety of lists and tables, including system tables that declared which other machines were trusted by this host, users' mail forwarding files, tables by which users gave themselves permission for access to remote accounts, and from a program that reported the status of network connections. For each discovered host, the worm tried a number of methods for gaining access:

1. It attempted to log on to a remote host as a legitimate user. In this method, the worm first attempted to crack the local password file, and then used the discovered passwords and corresponding user IDs. The assumption was that many users would use the same password on different systems. To obtain the passwords, the worm ran a password-cracking program that tried:
   (a) Each user's account name and simple permutations of it.
   (b) A list of 432 built-in passwords that Morris thought to be likely candidates.
   (c) All the words in the local system directory.
2. It exploited a bug in the finger protocol, which reports the whereabouts of a remote user.
3. It exploited a trapdoor in the debug option of the remote process that receives and sends mail.

If any of these attacks succeeded, the worm achieved communication with the operating system command interpreter. It then sent this interpreter a short boot-strap program, issued a command to execute that program, and then logged off. The bootstrap program then called back the parent program and downloaded the remainder of the worm. The new worm was then executed.

Recent Worm Attacks

The contemporary era of worm threats began with the release of the Code Red worm in July of 2001. Code Red exploits a security hole in the Microsoft Internet Information Server (IIS) to penetrate and spread. It also disables the system file checker in Windows. The worm probes random IP addresses to spread to other hosts. During a certain period of time, it only spreads. It then initiates a denial-of-service attack against a government Web site by flooding the site with packets from numerous hosts. The worm then suspends activities and reactivates periodically. In the second wave of attack, Code Red infected nearly 360,000 servers in 14 hours. In addition to the havoc it causes at the targeted server, Code Red can consume enormous amounts of Internet capacity, disrupting service.

Code Red II is a variant that targets Microsoft IISs. In addition, this newer worm installs a backdoor allowing a hacker to direct activities of victim computers.

In late 2001, a more versatile worm appeared, known as Nimda. Nimda spreads by multiple mechanisms:

- from client to client via e-mail
- from client to client via open network shares
- from Web server to client via browsing of compromised Web sites
- from client to Web server via active scanning for and exploitation of various Microsoft IIS 4.0 / 5.0 directory traversal vulnerabilities

- from client to Web server via scanning for the back doors left behind by the "Code Red II" worms

The worm modifies Web documents (e.g., .htm, .html, and .asp files) and certain executable files found on the systems it infects, and creates numerous copies of itself under various filenames.

10.2 VIRUS COUNTERMEASURES

Antivirus Approaches

The ideal solution to the threat of viruses is prevention: Do not allow a virus to get into the system in the first place. This goal is, in general, impossible to achieve, although prevention can reduce the number of successful viral attacks. The next best approach is to be able to do the following:

- **Detection:** Once the infection has occurred, determine that it has occurred and locate the virus.
- **Identification:** Once detection has been achieved, identify the specific virus that has infected a program.
- **Removal:** Once the specific virus has been identified, remove all traces of the virus from the infected program and restore it to its original state. Remove the virus from all infected systems so that the disease cannot spread further.

If detection succeeds but either identification or removal is not possible, then the alternative is to discard the infected program and reload a clean backup version.

Advances in virus and antivirus technology go hand in hand. Early viruses were relatively simple code fragments and could be identified and purged with relatively simple antivirus software packages. As the virus arms race has evolved, both viruses and, necessarily, antivirus software have grown more complex and sophisticated.

[STEP93] identifies four generations of antivirus software:

- First generation: simple scanners
- Second generation: heuristic scanners
- Third generation: activity traps
- Fourth generation: full-featured protection

A **first-generation** scanner requires a virus signature to identify a virus. The virus may contain "wildcards" but has essentially the same structure and bit pattern in all copies. Such signature-specific scanners are limited to the detection of known viruses. Another type of first-generation scanner maintains a record of the length of programs and looks for changes in length.

A **second-generation** scanner does not rely on a specific signature. Rather, the scanner uses heuristic rules to search for probable virus infection. One class of such scanners looks for fragments of code that are often associated with viruses.

For example, a scanner may look for the beginning of an encryption loop used in a polymorphic virus and discover the encryption key. Once the key is discovered, the scanner can decrypt the virus to identify it, then remove the infection and return the program to service.

Another second-generation approach is integrity checking. A checksum can be appended to each program. If a virus infects the program without changing the checksum, then an integrity check will catch the change. To counter a virus that is sophisticated enough to change the checksum when it infects a program, an encrypted hash function can be used. The encryption key is stored separately from the program so that the virus cannot generate a new hash code and encrypt that. By using a hash function rather than a simpler checksum, the virus is prevented from adjusting the program to produce the same hash code as before.

Third-generation programs are memory-resident programs that identify a virus by its actions rather than its structure in an infected program. Such programs have the advantage that it is not necessary to develop signatures and heuristics for a wide array of viruses. Rather, it is necessary only to identify the small set of actions that indicate an infection is being attempted and then to intervene.

Fourth-generation products are packages consisting of a variety of antivirus techniques used in conjunction. These include scanning and activity trap components. In addition, such a package includes access control capability, which limits the ability of viruses to penetrate a system and then limits the ability of a virus to update files in order to pass on the infection.

The arms race continues. With fourth-generation packages, a more comprehensive defense strategy is employed, broadening the scope of defense to more general-purpose computer security measures.

Advanced Antivirus Techniques

More sophisticated antivirus approaches and products continue to appear. In this subsection, we highlight two of the most important.

Generic Decryption

Generic decryption (GD) technology enables the antivirus program to detect easily even the most complex polymorphic viruses, while maintaining fast scanning speeds [NACH97]. Recall that when a file containing a polymorphic virus is executed, the virus must decrypt itself to activate. In order to detect such a structure, executable files are run through a GD scanner, which contains the following elements:

- **CPU emulator:** A software-based virtual computer. Instructions in an executable file are interpreted by the emulator rather than executed on the underlying processor. The emulator includes software versions of all registers and other processor hardware, so that the underlying processor is unaffected by programs interpreted on the emulator.
- **Virus signature scanner:** A module that scans the target code looking for known virus signatures.
- **Emulation control module:** Controls the execution of the target code.

At the start of each simulation, the emulator begins interpreting instructions in the target code, one at a time. Thus, if the code includes a decryption routine that decrypts and hence exposes the virus, that code is interpreted. In effect, the virus does the work for the antivirus program by exposing the virus. Periodically, the control module interrupts interpretation to scan the target code for virus signatures.

During interpretation, the target code can cause no damage to the actual personal computer environment, because it is being interpreted in a completely controlled environment.

The most difficult design issue with a GD scanner is to determine how long to run each interpretation. Typically, virus elements are activated soon after a program begins executing, but this need not be the case. The longer the scanner emulates a particular program, the more likely it is to catch any hidden viruses. However, the antivirus program can take up only a limited amount of time and resources before users complain.

Digital Immune System

The digital immune system is a comprehensive approach to virus protection developed by IBM [KEPH97a, KEPH97b]. The motivation for this development has been the rising threat of Internet-based virus propagation. We first say a few words about this threat and then summarize IBM's approach.

Traditionally, the virus threat was characterized by the relatively slow spread of new viruses and new mutations. Antivirus software was typically updated on a monthly basis, and this was sufficient to control the problem. Also traditionally, the Internet played a comparatively small role in the spread of viruses. But as [CHES97] points out, two major trends in Internet technology have had an increasing impact on the rate of virus propagation in recent years:

- **Integrated mail systems:** Systems such as Lotus Notes and Microsoft Outlook make it very simple to send anything to anyone and to work with objects that are received.
- **Mobile-program systems:** Capabilities such as Java and ActiveX allow programs to move on their own from one system to another.

In response to the threat posed by these Internet-based capabilities, IBM has developed a prototype digital immune system. This system expands on the use of program emulation discussed in the preceding subsection and provides a general-purpose emulation and virus-detection system. The objective of this system is to provide rapid response time so that viruses can be stamped out almost as soon as they are introduced. When a new virus enters an organization, the immune system automatically captures it, analyzes it, adds detection and shielding for it, removes it, and passes information about that virus to systems running IBM AntiVirus so that it can be detected before it is allowed to run elsewhere.

Figure 10.5 illustrates the typical steps in digital immune system operation:

1. A monitoring program on each PC uses a variety of heuristics based on system behavior, suspicious changes to programs, or family signature to infer that a virus may be present. The monitoring program forwards a copy of any program thought to be infected to an administrative machine within the organization.

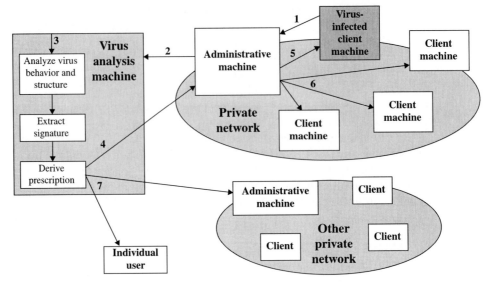

Figure 10.5 Digital Immune System

2. The administrative machine encrypts the sample and sends it to a central virus analysis machine.
3. This machine creates an environment in which the infected program can be safely run for analysis. Techniques used for this purpose include emulation, or the creation of a protected environment within which the suspect program can be executed and monitored. The virus analysis machine then produces a prescription for identifying and removing the virus.
4. The resulting prescription is sent back to the administrative machine.
5. The administrative machine forwards the prescription to the infected client.
6. The prescription is also forwarded to other clients in the organization.
7. Subscribers around the world receive regular antivirus updates that protect them from the new virus.

The success of the digital immune system depends on the ability of the virus analysis machine to detect new and innovative virus strains. By constantly analyzing and monitoring the viruses found in the wild, it should be possible continually to update the digital immune software to keep up with the threat.

Behavior-Blocking Software

Unlike heuristics or fingerprint-based scanners, behavior-blocking software integrates with the operating system of a host computer and monitors program behavior in real-time for malicious actions. The behavior blocking software then blocks potentially malicious actions before they have a chance to affect the system. Monitored behaviors can include

- Attempts to open, view, delete, and/or modify files
- Attempts to format disk drives and other unrecoverable disk operations
- Modifications to the logic of executable files, scripts of macros
- Modification of critical system settings, such as start-up settings
- Scripting of e-mail and instant messaging clients to send executable content
- Initiation of network communications

If the behavior blocker detects that a program is initiating would-be malicious behaviors as it runs, it can block these behaviors in real-time and/or terminate the offending software. This gives it a fundamental advantage over such established antivirus detection techniques such as fingerprinting or heuristics. While there are literally trillions of different ways to obfuscate and rearrange the instructions of a virus or worm, many of which will evade detection by a fingerprint scanner or heuristic, eventually malicious code must make a well-defined request to the operating system. Given that the behavior blocker can intercept all such requests, it can identify and block malicious actions regardless of how obfuscated the program logic appears to be.

The ability to watch software as it runs in real time clearly confers a huge benefit to the behavior blocker; however, it also has drawbacks. Since the malicious code must actually run on the target machine before all its behaviors can be identified, it can cause a great deal of harm to the system before it has been detected and blocked by the behavior blocking system. For instance, a new virus might shuffle a number of seemingly unimportant files around the hard drive before infecting a single file and being blocked. Even though the actual infection was blocked, the user may be unable to locate their files, causing a loss to productivity or possibly worse.

10.3 RECOMMENDED READING AND WEB SITE

For a thorough understanding of viruses, the book to read is [HARL01]. Good overview articles on viruses and worms are [CASS01], [FORR97], [KEPH97], and [NACH97]. [MEIN01] provides a good treatment of the Code Red worm.

CASS01   Cass, S. "Anatomy of Malice." *IEEE Spectrum*, November 2001.

FORR97   Forrest, S.; Hofmeyr, S.; and Somayaji, A. "Computer Immunology." *Communications of the ACM*, October 1997.

HARL01   Harley, D.; Slade, R.; and Gattiker, U. *Viruses Revealed*. New York: Osborne/McGraw-Hill, 2001.

KEPH97   Kephart, J.; Sorkin, G.; Chess, D.; and White, S. "Fighting Computer Viruses." *Scientific American*, November 1997.

MEIN01   Meinel, C. "Code Red for the Web." *Scientific American*, October 2001.

NACH97   Nachenberg, C. "Computer Virus-Antivirus Coevolution." *Communications of the ACM*, January 1997.

Recommended Web site:

- **AntiVirus On-line:** IBM's site on virus information; one of the best.

10.4 KEY TERMS, REVIEW QUESTIONS, AND PROBLEMS

Key Terms

digital immune system	malicious software (malware)	trojan horse
e-mail virus	polymorphic virus	virus
logic bomb	stealth virus	worm
macro virus	trap door	zombie

Review Questions

10.1 Briefly define each type of malware shown in Figure 10.1.

10.2 What is the role of compression in the operation of a virus?

10.3 What is the role of encryption in the operation of a virus?

10.4 What are typical phases of operation of a virus or worm?

10.5 In general terms, how does a worm propagate?

10.6 What is a digital immune system?

10.7 How does behavior-blocking software work?

Problems

10.1 There is a flaw in the virus program of Figure 10.2. What is it?

10.2 The question arises as to whether it is possible to develop a program that can analyze a piece of software to determine if it is a virus. Consider that we have a program D that is supposed to be able to do that. That is, for any program P, if we run D(P), the result returned is TRUE (P is a virus) or FALSE (P is not a virus). Now consider the following program:

```
Program CV :=
  { ...
  main-program :=
        {if D(CV) then goto next:
              else infect-executable;
        }
next:
  }
```

In the preceding program, infect-executable is a module that scans memory for executable programs and replicates itself in those programs. Determine if D can correctly decide whether CV is a virus.

CHAPTER 11

FIREWALLS

11.1 Firewall Design Principles

Firewall Characteristics
Types of Firewalls
Firewall Configurations

11.2 Trusted Systems

Data Access Control
The Concept of Trusted Systems
Trojan Horse Defense

11.3 Recommended Reading and Web Site

11.4 Key Terms, Review Questions, and Problems

Key Terms
Review Questions
Problems

The function of a strong position is to make the forces holding it practically unassailable.

—*On War*, **Carl Von Clausewitz**

On the day that you take up your command, block the frontier passes, destroy the official tallies, and stop the passage of all emissaries.

The Art of War, **Sun Tzu**

Firewalls can be an effective means of protecting a local system or network of systems from network-based security threats while at the same time affording access to the outside world via wide area networks and the Internet.

We begin this chapter with an overview of the functionality and design principles of firewalls. Next, we address the issue of the security of the firewall itself and, in particular, the concept of a trusted system, or secure operating system.

11.1 FIREWALL DESIGN PRINCIPLES

Information systems in corporations, government agencies, and other organizations have undergone a steady evolution:

- Centralized data processing system, with a central mainframe supporting a number of directly connected terminals
- Local area networks (LANs) interconnecting PCs and terminals to each other and the mainframe
- Premises network, consisting of a number of LANs, interconnecting PCs, servers, and perhaps a mainframe or two
- Enterprise-wide network, consisting of multiple, geographically distributed premises networks interconnected by a private wide area network (WAN)
- Internet connectivity, in which the various premises networks all hook into the Internet and may or may not also be connected by a private WAN

Internet connectivity is no longer an option for most organizations. The information and services available are essential to the organization. Moreover, individual users within the organization want and need Internet access, and if this is not provided via their LAN, they will use dial-up capability from their PC to an Internet service provider (ISP). However, while Internet access provides benefits to the organization, it enables the outside world to reach and interact with local network assets. This creates a threat to the organization. While it is possible to equip each workstation and server on the premises network with strong security features, such as intrusion protection, this is not a practical approach. Consider a network with hundreds or even thousands of systems, running a mix of various versions of UNIX, plus Windows. When a security flaw is discovered, each potentially affected system must be upgraded to fix that flaw. The alternative, increasingly accepted, is the firewall. The firewall is inserted between the premises network and the Internet to establish a controlled link and to erect an outer security wall or perimeter. The aim of this perimeter is to protect the premises network from Internet-based attacks and to provide a single choke point where security and audit can be imposed. The firewall may be a single computer system or a set of two or more systems that cooperate to perform the firewall function.

In this section, we look first at the general characteristics of firewalls. Then we look at the types of firewalls currently in common use. Finally, we examine some of the most common firewall configurations.

Firewall Characteristics

[BELL94] lists the following design goals for a firewall:

1. **All traffic from inside to outside, and vice versa, must pass through the firewall.** This is achieved by physically blocking all access to the local network except via the firewall. Various configurations are possible, as explained later in this section.

2. **Only authorized traffic, as defined by the local security policy, will be allowed to pass.** Various types of firewalls are used, which implement various types of security policies, as explained later in this section.

3. **The firewall itself is immune to penetration.** This implies that use of a trusted system with a secure operating system. This topic is discussed in Section 11.2.

[SMIT97] lists four general techniques that firewalls use to control access and enforce the site's security policy. Originally, firewalls focused primarily on service control, but they have since evolved to provide all four:

- **Service control:** Determines the types of Internet services that can be accessed, inbound or outbound. The firewall may filter traffic on the basis of IP address and TCP port number; may provide proxy software that receives and interprets each service request before passing it on; or may host the server software itself, such as a Web or mail service.

- **Direction control:** Determines the direction in which particular service requests may be initiated and allowed to flow through the firewall.

- **User control:** Controls access to a service according to which user is attempting to access it. This feature is typically applied to users inside the firewall perimeter (local users). It may also be applied to incoming traffic from external users; the latter requires some form of secure authentication technology, such as is provided in IPSec (Chapter 6).

- **Behavior control:** Controls how particular services are used. For example, the firewall may filter e-mail to eliminate spam, or it may enable external access to only a portion of the information on a local Web server.

Before proceeding to the details of firewall types and configurations, it is best to summarize what one can expect from a firewall. The following capabilities are within the scope of a firewall:

1. A firewall defines a single choke point that keeps unauthorized users out of the protected network, prohibits potentially vulnerable services from entering or leaving the network, and provides protection from various kinds of IP spoofing and routing attacks. The use of a single choke point simplifies security management because security capabilities are consolidated on a single system or set of systems.

2. A firewall provides a location for monitoring security-related events. Audits and alarms can be implemented on the firewall system.

3. A firewall is a convenient platform for several Internet functions that are not security related. These include a network address translator, which maps local addresses to Internet addresses, and a network management function that audits or logs Internet usage.

4. A firewall can serve as the platform for IPSec. Using the tunnel mode capability described in Chapter 6, the firewall can be used to implement virtual private networks.

Firewalls have their limitations, including the following:

1. The firewall cannot protect against attacks that bypass the firewall. Internal systems may have dial-out capability to connect to an ISP. An internal LAN may support a modem pool that provides dial-in capability for traveling employees and telecommuters.

2. The firewall does not protect against internal threats, such as a disgruntled employee or an employee who unwittingly cooperates with an external attacker.

3. The firewall cannot protect against the transfer of virus-infected programs or files. Because of the variety of operating systems and applications supported inside the perimeter, it would be impractical and perhaps impossible for the firewall to scan all incoming files, e-mail, and messages for viruses.

Types of Firewalls

Figure 11.1 illustrates the three common types of firewalls: packet filters, application-level gateways, and circuit-level gateways. We examine each of these in turn.

Packet-Filtering Router

A packet-filtering router applies a set of rules to each incoming IP packet and then forwards or discards the packet. The router is typically configured to filter packets going in both directions (from and to the internal network). Filtering rules are based on information contained in a network packet:

- **Source IP address:** The IP address of the system that originated the IP packet (e.g., 192.168.1.1)

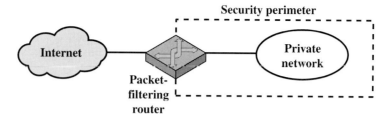

(a) Packet-filtering router

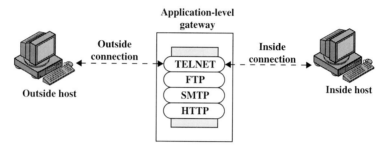

(b) Application-level gateway

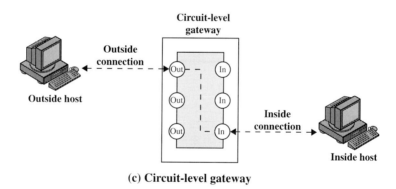

(c) Circuit-level gateway

Figure 11.1   Firewall Types

- **Destination IP address:** The IP address of the system the IP packet is trying to reach (e.g., 192.168.1.2)
- **Source and destination transport-level address:** The transport level (e.g., TCP or UDP) port number, which defines applications such as SNMP or TELNET
- **IP protocol field:** Defines the transport protocol
- **Interface:** For a router with three or more ports, which interface of the router the packet came from or which interface of the router the packet is destined for

The packet filter is typically set up as a list of rules based on matches to fields in the IP or TCP header. If there is a match to one of the rules, that rule is invoked to determine whether to forward or discard the packet. If there is no match to any rule, then a default action is taken. Two default policies are possible:

- **Default = discard:** That which is not expressly permitted is prohibited.
- **Default = forward:** That which is not expressly prohibited is permitted.

The default discard policy is the more conservative. Initially, everything is blocked, and services must be added on a case-by-case basis. This policy is more visible to users, who are more likely to see the firewall as a hindrance. The default forward policy increases ease of use for end users but provides reduced security; the security administrator must, in essence, react to each new security threat as it becomes known.

Table 11.1, from [BELL94], gives some examples of packet-filtering rule sets. In each set, the rules are applied top to bottom. The "*" in a field is a wildcard designator that matches everything. We assume that the default = discard policy is in force.

Table 11.1 Packet-Filtering Examples

A

action	ourhost	port	theirhost	port	comment
block	*	*	SPIGOT	*	we don't trust these people
allow	OUR-GW	25	*	*	connection to our SMTP port

B

action	ourhost	port	theirhost	port	comment
block	*	*	*	*	default

C

action	ourhost	port	theirhost	port	comment
allow	*	*	*	25	connection to their SMTP port

D

action	src	port	dest	port	flags	comment
allow	{our hosts}	*	*	25		our packets to their SMTP port
allow	*	25	*	*	ACK	their replies

E

action	src	port	dest	port	flags	comment
allow	{our hosts}	*	*	*		our outgoing calls
allow	*	*	*	*	ACK	replies to our calls
allow	*	*	*	>1024		traffic to nonservers

A. Inbound mail is allowed (port 25 is for SMTP incoming), but only to a gateway host. However, mail from a particular external host, SPIGOT, is blocked because that host has a history of sending massive files in e-mail messages.

B. This is an explicit statement of the default policy. All rule sets include this rule implicitly as the last rule.

C. This rule set is intended to specify that any inside host can send mail to the outside. A TCP packet with a destination port of 25 is routed to the SMTP server on the destination machine. The problem with this rule is that the use of port 25 for SMTP receipt is only a default; an outside machine could be configured to have some other application linked to port 25. As this rule is written, an attacker could gain access to internal machines by sending packets with a TCP source port number of 25.

D. This rule set achieves the intended result that was not achieved in C. The rules take advantage of a feature of TCP connections. Once a connection is set up, the ACK flag of a TCP segment is set to acknowledge segments sent from the other side. Thus, this rule set states that it allows IP packets where the source IP address is one of a list of designated internal hosts and the destination TCP port number is 25. It also allows incoming packets with a source port number of 25 that include the ACK flag in the TCP segment. Note that we explicitly designate source and destination systems to define these rules explicitly.

E. This rule set is one approach to handling FTP connections. With FTP, two TCP connections are used: a control connection to set up the file transfer and a data connection for the actual file transfer. The data connection uses a different port number that is dynamically assigned for thc transfer. Most servers, and hence most attack targets, live on low-numbered ports; most outgoing calls tend to use a higher-numbered port, typically above 1023. Thus, this rule set allows

- Packets that originate internally
- Reply packets to a connection initiated by an internal machine
- Packets destined for a high-numbered port on an internal machine

This scheme requires that the systems be configured so that only the appropriate port numbers are in use.

Rule set E points out the difficulty in dealing with applications at the packet-filtering level. Another way to deal with FTP and similar applications is an application-level gateway, described later in this section.

One advantage of a packet-filtering router is its simplicity. Also, packet filters typically are transparent to users and are very fast. [WACK02] lists the following weaknesses of packet filter firewalls:

- Because packet filter firewalls do not examine upper-layer data, they cannot prevent attacks that employ application-specific vulnerabilities or functions. For example, a packet filter firewall cannot block specific application commands; if a packet filter firewall allows a given application, all functions available within that application will be permitted.

- Because of the limited information available to the firewall, the logging functionality present in packet filter firewalls is limited. Packet filter logs normally contain the same information used to make access control decisions (source address, destination address, and traffic type).
- Most packet filter firewalls do not support advanced user authentication schemes. Once again, this limitation is mostly due to the lack of upper-layer functionality by the firewall.
- They are generally vulnerable to attacks and exploits that take advantage of problems within the TCP/IP specification and protocol stack, such as *network layer address spoofing.*

  Many packet filter firewalls cannot detect a network packet in which the OSI Layer 3 addressing information has been altered. Spoofing attacks are generally employed by intruders to bypass the security controls implemented in a firewall platform.
- Finally, due to the small number of variables used in access control decisions, packet filter firewalls are susceptible to security breaches caused by improper configurations. In other words, it is easy to accidentally configure a packet filter firewall to allow traffic types, sources, and destinations that should be denied based on an organization's information security policy.

Some of the attacks that can be made on packet-filtering routers and the appropriate countermeasures are the following:

- **IP address spoofing:** The intruder transmits packets from the outside with a source IP address field containing an address of an internal host. The attacker hopes that the use of a spoofed address will allow penetration of systems that employ simple source address security, in which packets from specific trusted internal hosts are accepted. The countermeasure is to discard packets with an inside source address if the packet arrives on an external interface.
- **Source routing attacks:** The source station specifies the route that a packet should take as it crosses the Internet, in the hopes that this will bypass security measures that do not analyze the source routing information. The countermeasure is to discard all packets that use this option.
- **Tiny fragment attacks:** The intruder uses the IP fragmentation option to create extremely small fragments and force the TCP header information into a separate packet fragment. This attack is designed to circumvent filtering rules that depend on TCP header information. The attacker hopes that only the first fragment is examined by the filtering router and that the remaining fragments are passed through. A tiny fragment attack can be defeated by discarding all packets where the protocol type is TCP and the IP Fragment Offset is equal to 1.

Stateful Inspection Firewalls

A traditional packet filter makes filtering decisions on an individual packet basis and does not take into consideration any higher layer context. To understand what is meant by context and why a traditional packet filter is limited with regard to context, a little background is needed. Most standardized applications that run on top of TCP follow a client/server model. For example, for the Simple Mail Transfer Protocol (SMTP), e-mail is transmitted from a client system to a server system. The client system generates new e-mail messages, typically from user input. The server system accepts incoming e-mail messages and places them in the appropriate user mailboxes. SMTP operates by setting up a TCP connection between client and server, in which the TCP server port number, which identifies the SMTP server application, is 25. The TCP port number for the SMTP client is a number between 1024 and 16383 that is generated by the SMTP client.

In general, when an application that uses TCP creates a session with a remote host, it creates a TCP connection in which the TCP port number for the remote (server) application is a number less than 1024 and the TCP port number for the local (client) application is a number between 1024 and 16383. The numbers less than 1024 are the "well-known" port numbers and are assigned permanently to particular applications (e.g., 25 for server SMTP). The numbers between 1024 and 16383 are generated dynamically and have temporary significance only for the lifetime of a TCP connection.

A simple packet-filtering firewall must permit inbound network traffic on all these high-numbered ports for TCP-based traffic to occur. This creates a vulnerability that can be exploited by unauthorized users.

A stateful inspection packet filter tightens up the rules for TCP traffic by creating a directory of outbound TCP connections, as shown in Table 11.2. There is an entry for each currently established connection. The packet filter will now allow incoming traffic to high-numbered ports only for those packets that fit the profile of one of the entries in this directory.

Table 11.2 Example Stateful Firewall Connection State Table [WACK02]

Source Address	Source Port	Destination Address	Destination Port	Connection State
192.168.1.100	1030	210.9.88.29	80	Established
192.168.1.102	1031	216.32.42.123	80	Established
192.168.1.101	1033	173.66.32.122	25	Established
192.168.1.106	1035	177.231.32.12	79	Established
223.43.21.231	1990	192.168.1.6	80	Established
219.22.123.32	2112	192.168.1.6	80	Established
210.99.212.18	3321	192.168.1.6	80	Established
24.102.32.23	1025	192.168.1.6	80	Established
223.212.212	1046	192.168.1.6	80	Established

Application-Level Gateway

An application-level gateway, also called a proxy server, acts as a relay of application-level traffic (Figure 11.1b). The user contacts the gateway using a TCP/IP application, such as Telnet or FTP, and the gateway asks the user for the name of the remote host to be accessed. When the user responds and provides a valid user ID and authentication information, the gateway contacts the application on the remote host and relays TCP segments containing the application data between the two endpoints. If the gateway does not implement the proxy code for a specific application, the service is not supported and cannot be forwarded across the firewall. Further, the gateway can be configured to support only specific features of an application that the network administrator considers acceptable while denying all other features.

Application-level gateways tend to be more secure than packet filters. Rather than trying to deal with the numerous possible combinations that are to be allowed and forbidden at the TCP and IP level, the application-level gateway need only scrutinize a few allowable applications. In addition, it is easy to log and audit all incoming traffic at the application level.

A prime disadvantage of this type of gateway is the additional processing overhead on each connection. In effect, there are two spliced connections between the end users, with the gateway at the splice point, and the gateway must examine and forward all traffic in both directions.

Circuit-Level Gateway

A third type of firewall is the circuit-level gateway (Figure 11.1c). This can be a stand-alone system or it can be a specialized function performed by an application-level gateway for certain applications. A circuit-level gateway does not permit an end-to-end TCP connection; rather, the gateway sets up two TCP connections, one between itself and a TCP user on an inner host and one between itself and a TCP user on an outside host. Once the two connections are established, the gateway typically relays TCP segments from one connection to the other without examining the contents. The security function consists of determining which connections will be allowed.

A typical use of circuit-level gateways is a situation in which the system administrator trusts the internal users. The gateway can be configured to support application-level or proxy service on inbound connections and circuit-level functions for outbound connections. In this configuration, the gateway can incur the processing overhead of examining incoming application data for forbidden functions but does not incur that overhead on outgoing data.

An example of a circuit-level gateway implementation is the SOCKS package [KOBL92]; version 5 of SOCKS is defined in RFC 1928. The RFC defines SOCKS in the following fashion:

> The protocol described here is designed to provide a framework for client-server applications in both the TCP and UDP domains to conveniently and securely use the services of a network firewall. The protocol is conceptually a "shim-layer" between the application layer and the transport layer, and as such does not provide network-layer gateway services, such as forwarding of ICMP messages.

SOCKS consists of the following components:

- The SOCKS server, which runs on a UNIX-based firewall.
- The SOCKS client library, which runs on internal hosts protected by the firewall.
- SOCKS-ified versions of several standard client programs such as FTP and TELNET. The implementation of the SOCKS protocol typically involves the recompilation or relinking of TCP-based client applications to use the appropriate encapsulation routines in the SOCKS library.

When a TCP-based client wishes to establish a connection to an object that is reachable only via a firewall (such determination is left up to the implementation), it must open a TCP connection to the appropriate SOCKS port on the SOCKS server system. The SOCKS service is located on TCP port 1080. If the connection request succeeds, the client enters a negotiation for the authentication method to be used, authenticates with the chosen method, and then sends a relay request. The SOCKS server evaluates the request and either establishes the appropriate connection or denies it. UDP exchanges are handled in a similar fashion. In essence, a TCP connection is opened to authenticate a user to send and receive UDP segments, and the UDP segments are forwarded as long as the TCP connection is open.

Bastion Host

A bastion host is a system identified by the firewall administrator as a critical strong point in the network's security. Typically, the bastion host serves as a platform for an application-level or circuit-level gateway. Common characteristics of a bastion host are as follows:

- The bastion host hardware platform executes a secure version of its operating system, making it a trusted system.
- Only the services that the network administrator considers essential are installed on the bastion host. These include proxy applications such as Telnet, DNS, FTP, SMTP, and user authentication.
- The bastion host may require additional authentication before a user is allowed access to the proxy services. In addition, each proxy service may require its own authentication before granting user access.
- Each proxy is configured to support only a subset of the standard application's command set.
- Each proxy is configured to allow access only to specific host systems. This means that the limited command/feature set may be applied only to a subset of systems on the protected network.
- Each proxy maintains detailed audit information by logging all traffic, each connection, and the duration of each connection. The audit log is an essential tool for discovering and terminating intruder attacks.
- Each proxy module is a very small software package specifically designed for network security. Because of its relative simplicity, it is easier to check such modules for security flaws. For example, a typical UNIX mail application may contain over 20,000 lines of code, while a mail proxy may contain fewer than 1000.

- Each proxy is independent of other proxies on the bastion host. If there is a problem with the operation of any proxy, or if a future vulnerability is discovered, it can be uninstalled without affecting the operation of the other proxy applications. Also, if the user population requires support for a new service, the network administrator can easily install the required proxy on the bastion host.
- A proxy generally performs no disk access other than to read its initial configuration file. This makes it difficult for an intruder to install Trojan horse sniffers or other dangerous files on the bastion host.
- Each proxy runs as a nonprivileged user in a private and secured directory on the bastion host.

Firewall Configurations

In addition to the use of a simple configuration consisting of a single system, such as a single packet-filtering router or a single gateway (Figure 11.1), more complex configurations are possible and indeed more common. Figure 11.2 illustrates three common firewall configurations. We examine each of these in turn.

In the **screened host firewall, single-homed bastion** configuration (Figure 11.2a), the firewall consists of two systems: a packet-filtering router and a bastion host. Typically, the router is configured so that

1. For traffic from the Internet, only IP packets destined for the bastion host are allowed in.
2. For traffic from the internal network, only IP packets from the bastion host are allowed out.

The bastion host performs authentication and proxy functions. This configuration has greater security than simply a packet-filtering router or an application-level gateway alone, for two reasons. First, this configuration implements both packet-level and application-level filtering, allowing for considerable flexibility in defining security policy. Second, an intruder must generally penetrate two separate systems before the security of the internal network is compromised.

This configuration also affords flexibility in providing direct Internet access. For example, the internal network may include a public information server, such as a Web server, for which a high level of security is not required. In that case, the router can be configured to allow direct traffic between the information server and the Internet.

In the single-homed configuration just described, if the packet-filtering router is completely compromised, traffic could flow directly through the router between the Internet and other hosts on the private network. The **screened host firewall, dual-homed bastion** configuration physically prevents such a security breach (Figure 11.2b). The advantages of dual layers of security that were present in the previous configuration are present here as well. Again, an information server or other hosts can be allowed direct communication with the router if this is in accord with the security policy.

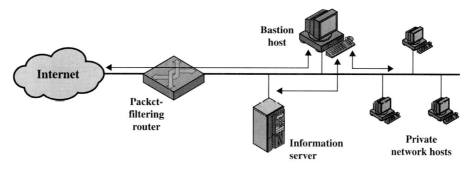

(a) Screened host firewall system (single-homed bastion host)

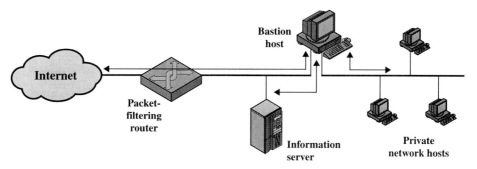

(b) Screened host firewall system (dual-homed bastion host)

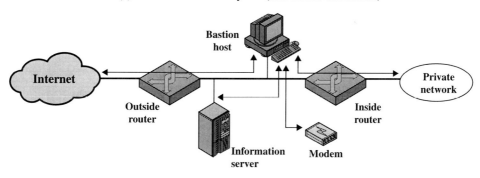

(c) Screened-subnet firewall system

Figure 11.2 Firewall Configurations

The **screened subnet firewall** configuration of Figure 11.2c is the most secure of those we have considered. In this configuration, two packet-filtering routers are used, one between the bastion host and the Internet and one between the bastion host and the internal network. This configuration creates an isolated subnetwork, which may consist of simply the bastion host but may also include one or more information servers and modems for dial-in capability. Typically, both the Internet and the internal network have access to hosts on the screened subnet, but traffic across the screened subnet is blocked. This configuration offers several advantages:

- There are now three levels of defense to thwart intruders.
- The outside router advertises only the existence of the screened subnet to the Internet; therefore, the internal network is invisible to the Internet.
- Similarly, the inside router advertises only the existence of the screened subnet to the internal network; therefore, the systems on the inside network cannot construct direct routes to the Internet.

11.2 TRUSTED SYSTEMS

One way to enhance the ability of a system to defend against intruders and malicious programs is to implement trusted system technology. This section provides a brief overview of this topic. We begin by looking at some basic concepts of data access control.

Data Access Control

Following successful logon, the user has been granted access to one or a set of hosts and applications. This is generally not sufficient for a system that includes sensitive data in its database. Through the user access control procedure, a user can be identified to the system. Associated with each user, there can be a profile that specifies permissible operations and file accesses. The operating system can then enforce rules based on the user profile. The database management system, however, must control access to specific records or even portions of records. For example, it may be permissible for anyone in administration to obtain a list of company personnel, but only selected individuals may have access to salary information. The issue is more than just one of level of detail. Whereas the operating system may grant a user permission to access a file or use an application, following which there are no further security checks, the database management system must make a decision on each individual access attempt. That decision will depend not only on the user's identity but also on the specific parts of the data being accessed and even on the information already divulged to the user.

A general model of access control as exercised by an file or database management system is that of an **access matrix** (Figure 11.3a). The basic elements of the model are as follows:

- **Subject:** An entity capable of accessing objects. Generally, the concept of subject equates with that of process. Any user or application actually gains access to an object by means of a process that represents that user or application.
- **Object:** Anything to which access is controlled. Examples include files, portions of files, programs, and segments of memory.

- **Access right:** The way in which an object is accessed by a subject. Examples are read, write, and execute.

One axis of the matrix consists of identified subjects that may attempt data access. Typically, this list will consist of individual users or user groups, although access could be controlled for terminals, hosts, or applications instead of or in addition to users. The other axis lists the objects that may be accessed. At the greatest level of detail, objects may be individual data fields. More aggregate groupings, such as records, files, or even the entire database, may also be objects in the matrix. Each entry in the matrix indicates the access rights of that subject for that object.

In practice, an access matrix is usually sparse and is implemented by decomposition in one of two ways. The matrix may be decomposed by columns, yielding **access control lists** (Figure 11.3b). Thus, for each object, an access control list lists users and their permitted access rights. The access control list may contain a default, or public, entry. This allows users that are not explicitly listed as having special rights to have a default set of rights. Elements of the list may include individual users as well as groups of users.

	Program1	...	SegmentA	SegmentB
Process1	Read Execute		Read Write	
Process2				Read
⋮				

(a) Access matrix

Access control list for Program1:
Process1 (Read, Execute)

Access control list for SegmentA:
Process1 (Read, Write)

Access control list for SegmentB:
Process2 (Read)

(b) Access control list

Capability list for Process1:
Program1 (Read, Execute)
SegmentA (Read, Write)

Capability list for Process2:
SegmentB (Read)

(c) Capability list

Figure 11.3 Access Control Structure

Decomposition by rows yields **capability tickets** (Figure 11.3c). A capability ticket specifies authorized objects and operations for a user. Each user has a number of tickets and may be authorized to loan or give them to others. Because tickets may be dispersed around the system, they present a greater security problem than access control lists. In particular, the ticket must be unforgeable. One way to accomplish this is to have the operating system hold all tickets on behalf of users. These tickets would have to be held in a region of memory inaccessible to users.

The Concept of Trusted Systems

Much of what we have discussed so far has been concerned with protecting a given message or item from passive or active attack by a given user. A somewhat different but widely applicable requirement is to protect data or resources on the basis of levels of security. This is commonly found in the military, where information is categorized as unclassified (U), confidential (C), secret (S), top secret (TS), or beyond. This concept is equally applicable in other areas, where information can be organized into gross categories and users can be granted clearances to access certain categories of data. For example, the highest level of security might be for strategic corporate planning documents and data, accessible by only corporate officers and their staff; next might come sensitive financial and personnel data, accessible only by administration personnel, corporate officers, and so on.

When multiple categories or levels of data are defined, the requirement is referred to as **multilevel security**. The general statement of the requirement for multilevel security is that a subject at a high level may not convey information to a subject at a lower or noncomparable level unless that flow accurately reflects the will of an authorized user. For implementation purposes, this requirement is in two parts and is simply stated. A multilevel secure system must enforce:

- **No read up:** A subject can only read an object of less or equal security level. This is referred to in the literature as the **Simple Security Property**.
- **No write down:** A subject can only write into an object of greater or equal security level. This is referred to in the literature as the ***-Property**[1] (pronounced *star property*).

These two rules, if properly enforced, provide multilevel security. For a data processing system, the approach that has been taken, and has been the object of much research and development, is based on the *reference monitor* concept. This approach is depicted in Figure 11.4. The reference monitor is a controlling element in the hardware and operating system of a computer that regulates the access of subjects

---

[1]The "*" does not stand for anything. No one could think of an appropriate name for the property during the writing of the first report on the model. The asterisk was a dummy character entered in the draft so that a text editor could rapidly find and replace all instances of its use once the property was named. No name was ever devised, and so the report was published with the "*" intact.

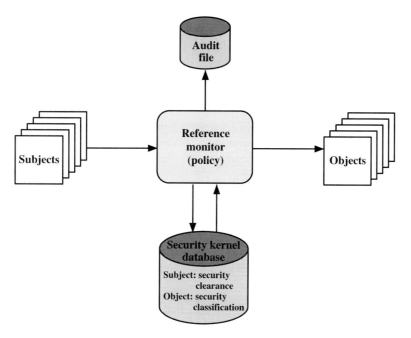

Figure 11.4 Reference Monitor Concept

to objects on the basis of security parameters of the subject and object. The reference monitor has access to a file, known as the *security kernel database*, that lists the access privileges (security clearance) of each subject and the protection attributes (classification level) of each object. The reference monitor enforces the security rules (no read up, no write down) and has the following properties:

- **Complete mediation:** The security rules are enforced on every access, not just, for example, when a file is opened.
- **Isolation:** The reference monitor and database are protected from unauthorized modification.
- **Verifiability:** The reference monitor's correctness must be provable. That is, it must be possible to demonstrate mathematically that the reference monitor enforces the security rules and provides complete mediation and isolation.

These are stiff requirements. The requirement for complete mediation means that every access to data within main memory and on disk and tape must be mediated. Pure software implementations impose too high a performance penalty to be practical; the solution must be at least partly in hardware. The requirement for isolation means that it must not be possible for an attacker, no matter how clever, to change the logic of the reference monitor or the contents of the security kernel database. Finally, the requirement for mathematical proof is formidable for something as complex as a general-purpose computer. A system that can provide such verification is referred to as a **trusted system**.

A final element illustrated in Figure 11.4 is an audit file. Important security events, such as detected security violations and authorized changes to the security kernel database, are stored in the audit file.

In an effort to meet its own needs and as a service to the public, the U.S. Department of Defense in 1981 established the Computer Security Center within the National Security Agency (NSA) with the goal of encouraging the widespread availability of trusted computer systems. This goal is realized through the center's Commercial Product Evaluation Program. In essence, the center attempts to evaluate commercially available products as meeting the security requirements just outlined. The center classifies evaluated products according to the range of security features that they provide. These evaluations are needed for Department of Defense procurements but are published and freely available. Hence, they can serve as guidance to commercial customers for the purchase of commercially available, off-the-shelf equipment.

Trojan Horse Defense

One way to secure against Trojan horse attacks is the use of a secure, trusted operating system. Figure 11.5 illustrates an example. In this case, a Trojan horse is used to get around the standard security mechanism used by most file management and operating systems: the access control list. In this example, a user named Bob interacts through a program with a data file containing the critically sensitive character string "CPE170KS." User Bob has created the file with read/write permission provided only to programs executing on his own behalf: that is, only processes that are owned by Bob may access the file.

The Trojan horse attack begins when a hostile user, named Alice, gains legitimate access to the system and installs both a Trojan horse program and a private file to be used in the attack as a "back pocket." Alice gives read/write permission to herself for this file and gives Bob write-only permission (Figure 11.5a). Alice now induces Bob to invoke the Trojan horse program, perhaps by advertising it as a useful utility. When the program detects that it is being executed by Bob, it reads the sensitive character string from Bob's file and copies it into Alice's back-pocket file (Figure 11.5b). Both the read and write operations satisfy the constraints imposed by access control lists. Alice then has only to access Bob's file at a later time to learn the value of the string.

Now consider the use of a secure operating system in this scenario (Figure 11.5c). Security levels are assigned to subjects at logon on the basis of criteria such as the terminal from which the computer is being accessed and the user involved, as identified by password/ID. In this example, there are two security levels, sensitive and public, ordered so that sensitive is higher than public. Processes owned by Bob and Bob's data file are assigned the security level sensitive. Alice's file and processes are restricted to public. If Bob invokes the Trojan horse program (Figure 11.5d), that program acquires Bob's security level. It is therefore able, under the simple security property, to observe the sensitive character string. When the program attempts to store the string in a public file (the back-pocket file), however, the *-Property is

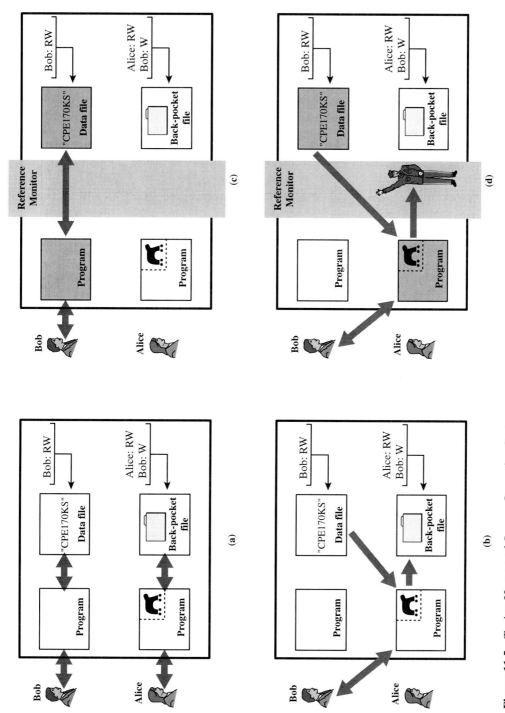

Figure 11.5 Trojan Horse and Secure Operating System

violated and the attempt is disallowed by the reference monitor. Thus, the attempt to write into the back-pocket file is denied even though the access control list permits it: The security policy takes precedence over the access control list mechanism.

11.3 RECOMMENDED READING AND WEB SITE

A classic treatment of firewalls, still well worth reading, is [CHAP95]. Another classic, recently updated, is [CHES00]. [LODI98], [OPPL97], and [BELL94] are good overview articles on the subject. [WACK02] is an excellent overview of firewall technology and firewall policies.

[GASS88] provides a comprehensive study of trusted computer systems. [PFLE97] and [GOLL99] also provide coverage.

BELL94   Bellovin, S., and Cheswick, W. "Network Firewalls." *IEEE Communications Magazine*, September 1994.

CHAP95   Chapman, D., and Zwicky, E. *Building Internet Firewalls*. Sebastopol, CA: O'Reilly, 1995.

CHES00   Cheswick, W., and Bellovin, S. *Firewalls and Internet Security: Repelling the Wily Hacker*. Reading, MA: Addison-Wesley, 2000.

GASS88   Gasser, M. *Building a Secure Computer System*. New York: Van Nostrand Reinhold, 1988.

GOLL99   Gollmann, D. *Computer Security*. New York: Wiley, 1999.

LODI98   Lodin, S., and Schuba, C. "Firewalls Fend Off Invasions from the Net." *IEEE Spectrum*, February 1998.

OPPL97   Oppliger, R. "Internet Security: Firewalls and Beyond." *Communications of the ACM*, May 1997.

PFLE97   Pfleeger, C. *Security in Computing*. Upper Saddle River, NJ: Prentice Hall, 1997.

WACK02   Wack, J.; Cutler, K.; and Pole, J. *Guidelines on Firewalls and Firewall Policy*. NIST Special Publication SP 800-41, January 2002.

Recommended Web site:

- **Firewall.com:** Numerous links to firewall references and software resources

11.4 KEY TERMS, REVIEW QUESTIONS, AND PROBLEMS

Key Terms

access control list (ACL)	capability ticket	packet-filtering router
access matrix	circuit-level gateway	reference monitor
access right	firewall	stateful inspection firewall
application-level gateway	multilevel security	subject
bastion host	object	trusted system

Review Questions

11.1 List three design goals for a firewall.

11.2 List four techniques used by firewalls to control access and enforce a security policy.

11.3 What information is used by a typical packet-filtering router?

11.4 What are some weaknesses of a packet-filtering router?

11.5 What is the difference between a packet-filtering router and a stateful inspection firewall?

11.6 What is an application-level gateway?

11.7 What is a circuit-level gateway?

11.8 What are the differences among the three configurations of Figure 11.2?

11.9 In the context of access control, what is the difference between a subject and an object?

11.10 What is the difference between an access control list and a capability ticket?

11.11 What are the two rules that a reference monitor enforces?

11.12 What properties are required of a reference monitor?

Problems

11.1 The necessity of the "no read up" rule for a multilevel secure system is fairly obvious. What is the importance of the "no write down" rule?

11.2 In Figure 11.5 one link of the Trojan horse copy-and-observe-later chain is broken. There are two other possible angles of attack by Drake: Drake logging on and attempting to read the string directly, and Drake assigning a security level of sensitive to the back-pocket file. Does the reference monitor prevent these attacks?

APPENDIX A

STANDARDS CITED IN THIS BOOK

There are some dogs who wouldn't debase what are to them sacred forms. A very fine, very serious German Shepherd I worked with, for instance, grumbled noisily at other dogs when they didn't obey. When training him to retrieve, at one point I set the dumbbell on its end for the fun of it. He glared disapprovingly at the dumbbell and at me, then pushed it carefully back into its proper position before picking it up and returning with it, rather sullenly.

—Adam's Task: Calling Animals by Name, *Vicki Hearne*

ANSI Standards

Number	Title	Date
X9.17	Financial Institution Key Management (wholesale)	1995

Internet RFCs

Number	Title	Date
RFC 822	Standard for the Format of ARPA Internet Text Messages	1982
RFC 1321	The MD5 Message-Digest Algorithm	1992
RFC 1510	The Kerberos Network Authentication Service (V5)	1993
RFC 1636	Security in the Internet Architecture	1994
RFC 1928	SOCKS Protocol Version 5	1996
RFC 2026	The Internet Standards Process	1996
RFC 2040	The RC5, RC5-CBC, RC5-CBC-Pad, and RC5-CTS Algorithms	1996

Internet RFCs (*continued*)

Number	Title	Date
RFC 2045	MIME Part One: Format of Internet Message Bodies	1996
RFC 2046	MIME Part Two: Media Types	1996
RFC 2047	MIME Part Three: Message Header Extensions for Non-ASCII Text	1996
RFC 2048	MIME Part Four: Registration Procedures	1996
RFC 2049	MIME Part Five: Conformance Criteria and Examples	1996
RFC 2104	HMAC: Keyed-Hashing for Message Authentication	1997
RFC 2119	Key Words for Use in RFCs to Indicate Requirement Levels	1997
RFC 2246	The TLS Protocol	1999
RFC 2401	Security Architecture for the Internet Protocol	1998
RFC 2402	IP Authentication Header	1998
RFC 2406	IP Encapsulating Security Payload (ESP)	1998
RFC 2408	Internet Security Association and Key Management Protocol	1998
RFC 2459	Internet X.509 Public Key Infrastructure Certificate and CRL Profile	1999
RFC 2570	Introduction to Version 3 of the Internet-Standard Network Management Framework	1999
RFC 2571	An Architecture for Describing SNMP Management Frameworks	1999
RFC 2572	Message Processing and Dispatching for the Simple Network Management Protocol	1999
RFC 2573	SNMP Applications	1999
RFC 2574	User-Based Security Model (USM)	1999
RFC 2575	View-Based Access Control Model (VACM)	1999
RFC 2576	Coexistence between Version 1, Version 2, and Version 3 of the Internet-standard Network Management Framework	2000
RFC 2630	Cryptographic Message Syntax	1999
RFC 2632	S/MIME Version 3 Certificate Handling	1999
RFC 2633	S/MIME Version 3 Message Specification	1999
RFC 2828	Internet Security Glossary	2000
RFC 3156	MIME Security with OpenPGP	2001
RFC 3174	US Secure Hash Algorithm 1	2001

ITU-T Recommendations

Number	Title	Date
X.509	The Directory: Public-Key and Attribute Certificate Frameworks	2000
X.800	Security Architecture for Open Systems Interconnection	1991

NIST Federal Information Processing Standards

Number	Title	Date
FIPS 46–3	Data Encryption Standard (DES)	1999
FIPS 81	DES Modes of Operation	1980
FIPS 113	Computer Data Authentication	1985
FIPS 180–1	Secure Hash Standard	1995
FIPS 180–2 (draft)	Secure Hash Standard	2001
FIPS 181	Automated Password Generator	1993
FIPS 186–2	Digital Signature Standard	2000
FIPS 197	Advanced Encryption Standards	2001
SP 800–38A	Recommendation for Block Cipher Modes of Operation	2001

APPENDIX B

SOME ASPECTS OF NUMBER THEORY

B.1 Prime and Relatively Prime Numbers

      Divisors

      Prime Numbers

      Relatively Prime Numbers

B.2 Modular Arithmetic

> *The Devil said to Daniel Webster: "Set me a task I can't carry out, and I'll give you anything in the world you ask for."*
>
> *Daniel Webster: "Fair enough. Prove that for n greater than 2, the equation $a^n + b^n = c^n$ has no non-trivial solution in the integers."*
>
> *They agreed on a three-day period for the labor, and the Devil disappeared.*
>
> *At the end of three days, the Devil presented himself, haggard, jumpy, biting his lip. Daniel Webster said to him, "Well, how did you do at my task? Did you prove the theorem?'*
>
> *"Eh? No ... no, I haven't proved it."*
>
> *"Then I can have whatever I ask for? Money? The Presidency?"*
>
> *"What? Oh, that—of course. But listen! If we could just prove the following two lemmas—"*
>
> **—The Mathematical Magpie, Clifton Fadiman**

In this appendix, we provide some background on two concepts referenced in this book: prime numbers and modular arithmetic.

B.1 PRIME AND RELATIVELY PRIME NUMBERS

In this section, unless otherwise noted, we deal only with nonnegative integers. The use of negative integers would introduce no essential differences.

Divisors

We say that $b \neq 0$ divides a if $a = mb$ for some m, where a, b, and m are integers. That is, b divides a if there is no remainder on division. The notation $b|a$ is commonly used to mean b divides a. Also, if $b|a$, we say that b is a *divisor* of a. For example, the positive divisors of 24 are 1, 2, 3, 4, 6, 8, 12, and 24.

The following relations hold:

- If $a|1$, then $a = \pm 1$.
- If $a|b$ and $b|a$, then $a = \pm b$.
- Any $b \neq 0$ divides 0.
- If $b|g$ and $b|h$, then $b|(mg + nh)$ for arbitrary integers m and n.

To see this last point, note that

If $b|g$, then g is of the form $g = b \times g_1$ for some integer g_1.
If $b|h$, then h is of the form $h = b \times h_1$ for some integer h_1.

So

$$mg + nh = mbg_1 + nbh_1 = b \times (mg_1 + nh_1)$$

and therefore b divides $mg + nh$.

Prime Numbers

An integer $p > 1$ is a prime number if its only divisors are ± 1 and $\pm p$. Prime numbers play a critical role in number theory and in the techniques discussed in Chapter 3.

Any integer $a > 1$ can be factored in a unique way as

$$a = p_1^{\alpha_1} p_2^{\alpha_2} \cdots p_t^{\alpha_t}$$

where $p_1 > p_2 > \ldots > p_t$ are prime numbers and where each $\alpha_i > 0$. For example, $91 = 7 \times 13$; and $11011 = 7 \times 11^2 \times 13$.

It is useful to cast this another way. If P is the set of all prime numbers, then any positive integer can be written uniquely in the following form:

$$a = \prod_{P} p^{a_p} \qquad \text{where each } a_p \geq 0$$

The right-hand side is the product over all possible prime numbers p; for any particular value of a, most of the exponents a_p will be 0.

The value of any given positive integer can be specified by simply listing all the nonzero exponents in the foregoing formulation. Thus, the integer 12 is represented by $\{a_2 = 2, a_3 = 1\}$, and the integer 18 is represented by $\{a_2 = 1, a_3 = 2\}$. Multiplication of two numbers is equivalent to adding the corresponding exponents:

$$k = mn \qquad \rightarrow \qquad k_p = m_p + n_p \qquad \text{for all } p$$

What does it mean, in terms of these prime factors, to say that $a|b$? Any integer of the form p^k can be divided only by an integer that is of a lesser or equal power of the same prime number, p^j with $j \leq k$. Thus, we can say

$$a|b \qquad \rightarrow \qquad a_p \leq b_p \qquad \text{for all } p$$

Relatively Prime Numbers

We will use the notation $\gcd(a, b)$ to mean the **greatest common divisor** of a and b. The positive integer c is said to be the greatest common divisor of a and b if

1. c is a divisor of a and of b;
2. any divisor of a and b is a divisor of c.

An equivalent definition is the following:

$$\gcd(a, b) = \max[k, \text{ such that } k|a \text{ and } k|b]$$

Because we require that the greatest common divisor be positive, $\gcd(a, b) = \gcd(a, -b) = \gcd(-a, b) = \gcd(-a, -b)$. In general, $\gcd(a, b) = \gcd(|a|, |b|)$. For example, $\gcd(60, 24) = \gcd(60, -24) = 12$. Also, because all nonzero integers divide 0, we have $\gcd(a, 0) = |a|$.

It is easy to determine the greatest common divisor of two positive integers if we express each integer as the product of primes. For example,

$$
\begin{aligned}
300 \quad &= 2^2 \times 3^1 \times 5^2 \\
18 \quad &= 2^1 \times 3^2 \\
\gcd(18, 300) &= 2^1 \times 3^1 \times 5^0 = 6
\end{aligned}
$$

In general,

$$ k = \gcd(a, b) \quad \rightarrow \quad k_p = \min(a_p, b_p) \text{ for all } p $$

Determining the prime factors of a large number is no easy task, so the preceding relationship does not directly lead to a way of calculating the greatest common divisor.

The integers a and b are relatively prime if they have no prime factors in common, that is, if their only common factor is 1. This is equivalent to saying that a and b are relatively prime if $\gcd(a, b) = 1$. For example, 8 and 15 are relatively prime because the divisors of 8 are 1, 2, 4, and 8, and the divisors of 15 are 1, 3, 5, and 15, so 1 is the only number on both lists.

B.2 MODULAR ARITHMETIC

Given any positive integer n and any integer a, if we divide a by n, we get a quotient q and a remainder r that obey the following relationship:

$$ a = qn + r \qquad\qquad 0 \le r < n; q = \lfloor a/n \rfloor $$

where $\lfloor x \rfloor$ is the largest integer less than or equal to x. The remainder r is often referred to as a **residue**.

If a is an integer and n is a positive integer, we define $a \bmod n$ to be the remainder when a is divided by n. Thus, for any integer a, we can always write

$$ a = \lfloor a/n \rfloor \times n + (a \bmod n) $$

Two integers a and b are said to be **congruent modulo n**, if $(a \bmod n) = (b \bmod n)$. This is written $a \equiv b \bmod n$. For example, $73 \equiv 4 \bmod 23$; and $21 \equiv -9 \bmod 10$. Note that if $a \equiv 0 \bmod n$, then $n|a$.

The modulo operator has the following properties:

1. $a \equiv b \bmod n$ if $n|(a - b)$
2. $(a \bmod n) = (b \bmod n)$ implies $a \equiv b \bmod n$

3. $a \equiv b \bmod n$ implies $b \equiv a \bmod n$

4. $a \equiv b \bmod n$ and $b \equiv c \bmod n$ imply $a \equiv c \bmod n$

To demonstrate the first point, if $n|(a - b)$, then $(a - b) = kn$ for some k. So we can write $a = b + kn$. Therefore, $(a \bmod n)$ = (remainder when $b + kn$ is divided by n) = (remainder when b is divided by n) = $(b \bmod n)$. The remaining points are as easily proved.

The $(\bmod n)$ operator maps all integers into the set of integers $\{0, 1, \ldots (n - 1)\}$. This suggests the question: Can we perform arithmetic operations within the confines of this set? It turns out that we can; the technique is known as **modular arithmetic**.

Modular arithmetic exhibits the following properties:

1. $[(a \bmod n) + (b \bmod n)] \bmod n = (a + b) \bmod n$

2. $[(a \bmod n) - (b \bmod n)] \bmod n = (a - b) \bmod n$

3. $[(a \bmod n) \times (b \bmod n)] \bmod n = (a \times b) \bmod n$

We demonstrate the first property. Define $(a \bmod n) = r_a$ and $(b \bmod n) = r_b$. Then we can write $a = r_a + jn$ for some integer j and $b = r_b + kn$ for some integer k. Then

$$
\begin{aligned}
(a + b) \bmod n &= (r_a + jn + r_b + kn) \bmod n \\
&= (r_a + r_b + (k + j)n) \bmod n \\
&= (r_a + r_b) \bmod n \\
&= [(a \bmod n) + (b \bmod n)] \bmod n
\end{aligned}
$$

The remaining properties are as easily proved.

GLOSSARY

In studying the Imperium, Arrakis, and the whole culture which produced Maud'Dib, many unfamiliar terms occur. To increase understanding is a laudable goal, hence the definitions and explanations given below.

—*Dune*, Frank Herbert

Some of the terms in this glossary are from the *Glossary of Computer Security Terminology* [NIST91]. These are indicated in the glossary by an asterisk.

Asymmetric Encryption A form of cryptosystem in which encryption and decryption are performed using two different keys, one of which is referred to as the public key and one of which is referred to as the private key. Also known as public-key encryption.

Authentication* A process used to verify the integrity of transmitted data, especially a message.

Authenticator Additional information appended to a message to enable the receiver to verify that the message should be accepted as authentic. The authenticator may be functionally independent of the content of the message itself (e.g., a nonce or a source identifier) or it may be a function of the message contents (e.g., a hash value or a cryptographic checksum).

Avalanche Effect A characteristic of an encryption algorithm in which a small change in the plaintext or key gives rise to a large change in the ciphertext. For a hash code, the avalanche effect is a characteristic in which a small change in the message gives rise to a large change in the message digest.

Bacteria Program that consumes system resources by replicating itself.

Block Chaining A procedure used during symmetric block encryption that makes an output block dependent not only on the current plaintext input block and key, but also on earlier input and/or output. The effect of block chaining is that two instances of the same plaintext input block will produce different ciphertext blocks, making cryptanalysis more difficult.

Block Cipher A symmetric encryption algorithm in which a large block of plaintext bits (typically 64) is transformed as a whole into a ciphertext block of the same length.

Cipher An algorithm for encryption and decryption. A cipher replaces a piece of information (an element in plaintext) with another object, with the intent to conceal meaning. Typically, the replacement rule is governed by a secret key.

Ciphertext The output of an encryption algorithm; the encrypted form of a message or data.

Code An unvarying rule for replacing a piece of information (e.g., letter, word, phrase) with another object, not necessarily of the same sort. Generally, there is no intent to conceal meaning. Examples include the ASCII character code (each character is represented by 7 bits) and frequency-shift keying (each binary value is represented by a particular frequency).

Computationally Secure Secure because the time and/or cost of defeating the security is too high to be feasible.

Confusion A cryptographic technique that seeks to make the relationship between the statistics of the ciphertext and the value of the encryption key as complex as possible. This is achieved by the use of a complex scrambling algorithm that depends on the key and the input.

Conventional Encryption Symmetric encryption.

Covert Channel A communications channel that enables the transfer of information in a way unintended by the designers of the communications facility.

Cryptanalysis The branch of cryptology dealing with the breaking of a cipher to recover information, or forging encrypted information that will be accepted as authentic.

Cryptographic Checksum An authenticator that is a cryptographic function of both the data to be authenticated and a secret key. Also referred to as a message authentication code (MAC).

Cryptography The branch of cryptology dealing with the design of algorithms for encryption and decryption, intended to ensure the secrecy and/or authenticity of messages.

Cryptology   The study of secure communications, which encompasses both cryptography and cryptanalysis.

Decryption   The translation of encrypted text or data (called ciphertext) into original text or data (called plaintext). Also called deciphering.

Differential Cryptanalysis   A technique in which chosen plaintexts with particular XOR difference patterns are encrypted. The difference patterns of the resulting ciphertext provide information that can be used to determine the encryption key.

Diffusion   A cryptographic technique that seeks to obscure the statistical structure of the plaintext by spreading out the influence of each individual plaintext digit over many ciphertext digits.

Digital Signature   An authentication mechanism that enables the creator of a message to attach a code that acts as a signature. The signature guarantees the source and integrity of the message.

Digram   A two-letter sequence. In English and other languages, the relative frequency of various digrams in plaintext can be used in the cryptanalysis of some ciphers. Also called *digraph.*

Discretionary Access Control*   A means of restricting access to objects based on the identity of subjects and/or groups to which they belong. The controls are discretionary in the sense that a subject with a certain access permission is capable of passing on that permission (perhaps indirectly) to any other subject (unless restrained by mandatory access control).

Encryption   The conversion of plaintext or data into unintelligible form by means of a reversible translation, based on a translation table or algorithm. Also called enciphering.

Firewall   A dedicated computer that interfaces with computers outside a network and has special security precautions built into it in order to protect sensitive files on computers within the network. It is used to service outside network, especially Internet, connections and dial-in lines.

Hash Function   A function that maps a variable-length data block or message into a fixed-length value called a hash code. The function is designed in such a way that, when protected, it provides an authenticator to the data or message. Also referred to as a message digest.

Honeypot   A decoy system designed to lure a potential attacker away from critical systems. A form of intrusion detection.

Initialization Vector A random block of data that is used to begin the encryption of multiple blocks of plaintext, when a block-chaining encryption technique is used. The IV serves to foil known-plaintext attacks.

Intruder An individual who gains, or attempts to gain, unauthorized access to a computer system or to gain unauthorized privileges on that system.

Intrusion Detection System A set of automated tools designed to detect unauthorized access to a host system.

Kerberos The name given to Project Athena's code authentication service.

Key Distribution Center A system that is authorized to transmit temporary session keys to principals. Each session key is transmitted in encrypted form, using a master key that the key distribution center shares with the target principal.

Logic Bomb Logic embedded in a computer program that checks for a certain set of conditions to be present on the system. When these conditions are met, it executes some function resulting in unauthorized actions.

Mandatory Access Control A means of restricting access to objects based on fixed security attributes assigned to users and to files and other objects. The controls are mandatory in the sense that they cannot be modified by users or their programs.

Master Key A long-lasting key that is used between a key distribution center and a principal for the purpose of encoding the transmission of session keys. Typically, the master keys are distributed by noncryptographic means. Also referred to as a key-encrypting key.

Message Authentication Code (MAC) Cryptographic checksum.

Message Digest Hash function.

Multilevel Security A capability that enforces access control across multiple levels of classification of data.

Multiple Encryption Repeated use of an encryption function, with different keys, to produce a more complex mapping from plaintext to ciphertext.

Nonce An identifier or number that is used only once.

One-Way Function A function that is easily computed, but the calculation of its inverse is infeasible.

Password* A character string used to authenticate an identity. Knowledge of the password and its associated user ID is considered proof of authorization to use the capabilities associated with that user ID.

Plaintext   The input to an encryption function or the output of a decryption function.

Primitive Root   If r and n are relatively prime integers with $n > 0$. and if $\phi(n)$ is the least positive exponent m such that $r^m \equiv 1 \bmod n$, then r is called a primitive root modulo n.

Private Key   One of the two keys used in an asymmetric encryption system. For secure communication, the private key should only be known to its creator.

Pseudorandom Number Generator   A function that deterministically produces a sequence of numbers that are apparently statistically random.

Public Key   One of the two keys used in an asymmetric encryption system. The public key is made public, to be used in conjunction with a corresponding private key.

Public-Key Encryption   Asymmetric encryption.

Replay Attacks   An attack in which a service already authorized and completed is forged by another "duplicate request" in an attempt to repeat authorized commands.

RSA Algorithm   A public-key encryption algorithm based on exponentiation in modular arithmetic. It is the only algorithm generally accepted as practical and secure for public-key encryption.

Secret Key   The key used in a symmetric encryption system. Both participants must share the same key, and this key must remain secret to protect the communication.

Session Key   A temporary encryption key used between two principals.

Stream Cipher   A symmetric encryption algorithm in which ciphertext output is produced bit-by-bit or byte-by-byte from a stream of plaintext input.

Symmetric Encryption   A form of cryptosystem in which encryption and decryption are performed using the same key. Also known as conventional encryption.

Trap-Door   Secret undocumented entry point into a program, used to grant access without normal methods of access authentication.

Trap-Door One-Way Function   A function that is easily computed; the calculation of its inverse is infeasible unless certain privileged information is known.

Trojan Horse*   A computer program with an apparently or actually useful function that contains additional (hidden) functions that surreptitiously exploit the legitimate authorizations of the invoking process to the detriment of security.

Trusted System   A computer and operating system that can be verified to implement a given security policy.

Unconditionally Secure   Secure even against an opponent with unlimited time and unlimited computing resources.

Virus   Code embedded within a program that causes a copy of itself to be inserted in one or more other programs. In addition to propagation, the virus usually performs some unwanted function.

Worm   Program that can replicate itself and send copies from computer to computer across network connections. Upon arrival, the worm may be activated to replicate and propagate again. In addition to propagation, the worm usually performs some unwanted function.

REFERENCES

In matters of this kind everyone feels he is justified in writing and publishing the first thing that comes into his head when he picks up a pen, and thinks his own idea as axiomatic as the fact that two and two make four. If critics would go to the trouble of thinking about the subject for years on end and testing each conclusion against the actual history of war, as I have done, they would undoubtedly be more careful of what they wrote.

—On War, **Carl von Clausewitz**

Abbreviations

ACM   Association for Computing Machinery

IEEE   Institute of Electrical and Electronics Engineers

NIST   National Institute of Standards and Technology

ALVA90   Alvare, A. "How Crackers Crack Passwords or What Passwords to Avoid." *Proceedings, UNIX Security Workshop II*, August 1990.

ANDE80   Anderson, J. *Computer Security Threat Monitoring and Surveillance.* Fort Washington, PA: James P. Anderson Co., April 1980.

AXEL00   Axelsson, S. "The Base-Rate Fallacy and the Difficulty of Intrusion Detection." *ACM Transactions and Information and System Security*, August 2000.

BACE00   Bace, R. *Intrusion Detection.* Indianapolis, IN: Macmillan Technical Publishing, 2000.

BACE01   Bace, R., and Mell, P. *Intrusion Detection Systems.* NIST Special Publication SP 800-31, November 2000.

BAUE88   Bauer, D., and Koblentz, M. "NIDX—An Expert System for Real-Time Network Intrusion Detection." *Proceedings, Computer Networking Symposium*, April 1988.

BELL90   Bellovin, S., and Merritt, M. "Limitations of the Kerberos Authentication System." *Computer Communications Review*, October 1990.

BELL96a   Bellare, M., Canetti, R., and Krawczyk, H. "Keying Hash Functions for Message Authentication." *Proceedings, CRYPTO '96*, August 1996; published by Springer-Verlag. An expanded version is available at http://www. cse.ucsd. edu/users/mihir.

BELL96b   Bellare, M., Canetti, R., and Krawczyk, H. "The HMAC Construction." *CryptoBytes*, Spring 1996.

BERS92   Berson, T. "Differential Cryptanalysis Mod 2^{32} with Applications to MD5." *Proceedings, EUROCRYPT '92*, May 1992; published by Springer-Verlag.

BLOO70   Bloom, B. "Space/time Trade-offs in Hash Coding with Allowable Errors." *Communications of the ACM*, July 1970.

BLUM97a   Blumenthal, U.; Hein, N.; and Wijnen, B. "Key Derivation for Network Management Applications." *IEEE Network*, May/June, 1997.

BLUM97b   Blumenthal, U., and Wijnen, B. "Security Features for SNMPv3." *The Simple Times*, December 1997.

BOER93   Boer, B., and Bosselaers, A. "Collisions for the Compression Function of MD5." *Proceedings, EUROCRYPT '93*, 1993; published by Springer-Verlag.

BOSS97   Bosselaers, A., Dobbertin, H., and Preneel, B. "The RIPEMD-160 Cryptographic Hash Function." *Dr. Dobb's Journal*, January 1997.

BRYA88   Bryant, W. *Designing an Authentication System: A Dialogue in Four Scenes.* Project Athena document, February 1988. Available at http://web. mit.edu/kerberos/www/dialogue.html.

CASS01   Cass, S. "Anatomy of Malice." *IEEE Spectrum*, November 2001.

CERT02   CERT Coordination Center. "Multiple Vulnerabilities in Many Implementations of the Simple Network Management Protocol." CERT Advisory CA-2002-03, 25 June 2002. www.ccrt.org/advisorics/CA-2002-03.html.

CHAP95   Chapman, D, and Zwicky, E. *Building Internet Firewalls.* Sebastopol, CA: O'Reilly, 1995.

CHEN98   Cheng, P., et al. "A Security Architecture for the Internet Protocol." *IBM Systems Journal*, Number 1, 1998.

CHES97   Chess, D. "The Future of Viruses on the Internet." *Proceedings, Virus Bulletin International Conference*, October 1997.

CHES00   Cheswick, W., and Bellovin, S. *Firewalls and Internet Security: Repelling the Wily Hacker.* Reading, MA: Addison-Wesley, 2000.

COHE94   Cohen, F. *A Short Course on Computer Viruses.* New York: Wiley, 1994.

COME00   Comer, D. *Internetworking with TCP/IP, Volume I: Principles, Protocols and Architecture.* Upper Saddle River, NJ: Prentice Hall, 2000.

CORM01   Cormen, T.; Leiserson, C.; Rivest, R.; and Stein, C. *Introduction to Algorithms.* Cambridge, MA: MIT Press, 2001.

DAMG89   Damgard, I. "A Design Principle for Hash Functions." *Proceedings, CRYPTO '89*, 1989; published by Springer-Verlag.

DAVI89   Davies, D., and Price, W. *Security for Computer Networks.* New York: Wiley, 1989.

DAVI93 Davies, C., and Ganesan, R. "BApasswd: A New Proactive Password Checker." *Proceedings, 16th National Computer Security Conference*, September 1993.

DENN87 Denning, D. "An Intrusion-Detection Model." *IEEE Transactions on Software Engineering*, February 1987.

DIFF76 Diffie, W., and Hellman, M. "Multiuser Cryptographic Techniques." *IEEE Transactions on Information Theory*, November 1976.

DIFF88 Diffie, W. "The First Ten Years of Public-Key Cryptography." *Proceedings of the IEEE*, May 1988. Reprinted in [SIMM92].

DOBB96a Dobbertin, H. "The Status of MD5 After a Recent Attack." *Crypto-Bytes*, Summer 1996.

DOBB96b Dobbertin, H., Bosselaers, A., and Preneel, B. "RIPEMD-160: A Strengthened Version of RIPEMD." *Proceedings, Third International Workshop on Fast Software Encryption*, 1996; published by Springer-Verlag.

DORA99 Doraswamy, N., and Harkins, D. *IPSec.* Upper Saddle River, NJ: Prentice Hall, 1999.

DREW99 Drew, G. *Using SET for Secure Electronic Commerce.* Upper Saddle River, NJ: Prentice Hall, 1999.

EFF98 Electronic Frontier Foundation. *Cracking DES: Secrets of Encryption Research, Wiretap Politics, and Chip Design.* Sebastopol, CA: O'Reilly, 1998.

ENGE80 Enger, N., and Howerton, P. *Computer Security.* New York: Amacom, 1980.

FEIS73 Feistel, H. "Cryptography and Computer Privacy." *Scientific American*, May 1973.

FORD95 Ford, W. "Advances in Public-Key Certificate Standards." *ACM SIGSAC Review*, July 1995.

FORR97 Forrest, S., Hofmeyr, S., and Somayaji, A. "Computer Immunology." *Communications of the ACM*, October 1997.

FRAN01 Frankel, S. *Demystifying the IPSec Puzzle.* Boston: Artech House, 2001.

GAUD00 Gaudin, S. "The Omega Files." *Network World*, June 26, 2000.

HARL01 Harley, D., Slade, R., and Gattiker, U. *Viruses Revealed.* New York: Osborne/McGraw-Hill, 2001.

HEBE92 Heberlein, L., Mukherjee, B., and Levitt, K. "Internetwork Security Monitor: An Intrusion-Detection System for Large-Scale Networks." *Proceedings, 15th National Computer Security Conference*, October 1992.

GARD77 Gardner, M. "A New Kind of Cipher That Would Take Millions of Years to Break." *Scientific American*, August 1977.

GARF97 Garfinkel, S., and Spafford, G. *Web Security & Commerce.* Cambridge, MA: O'Reilly and Associates, 1997.

GASS88 Gasser, M. *Building a Secure Computer System.* New York: Van Nostrand Reinhold, 1988.

GOLL99 Gollmann, D. *Computer Security.* New York: Wiley, 1999.

HELD96 Held, G. *Data and Image Compression: Tools and Techniques.* New York: Wiley, 1996.

HONE01 The Honeynet Project. *Know Your Enemy: Revealing the Security Tools, Tactics, and Motives of the Blackhat Community.* Reading, MA: Addison-Wesley, 2001.

HUIT98 Huitema, C. *IPv6: The New Internet Protocol.* Upper Saddle River, NJ: Prentice Hall, 1998.

IANS90 I'Anson, C., and Mitchell, C. "Security Defects in CCITT Recommendation X.509—The Directory Authentication Framework." *Computer Communications Review*, April 1990.

ILGU93 Ilgun, K. "USTAT: A Real-Time Intrusion Detection System for UNIX." *Proceedings, 1993 IEEE Computer Society Symposium on Research in Security and Privacy*, May 1993.

JAVI91 Javitz, H., and Valdes, A. "The SRI IDES Statistical Anomaly Detector." *Proceedings, 1991 IEEE Computer Society Symposium on Research in Security and Privacy*, May 1991.

JIAN02 Jiang, G. "Multiple Vulnerabilities in SNMP." *Security and Privacy Supplement to Computer Magazine*, 2002.

JUEN85 Jueneman, R., Matyas, S., and Meyer, C. "Message Authentication." *IEEE Communications Magazine*, September 1988.

KENT00 Kent, S. "On the Trail of Intrusions into Information Systems." *IEEE Spectrum*, December 2000.

KEPH97a Kephart, J., Sorkin, G., Chess, D., and White, S. "Fighting Computer Viruses." *Scientific American*, November 1997.

KEPH97b Kephart, J., Sorkin, G., Swimmer, B., and White, S. "Blueprint for a Computer Immune System." *Proceedings, Virus Bulletin International Conference*, October 1997.

KLEI90 Klein, D. "Foiling the Cracker: A Survey of, and Improvements to, Password Security." *Proceedings, UNIX Security Workshop II*, August 1990.

KOBL92 Koblas, D., and Koblas, M. "SOCKS." *Proceedings, UNIX Security Symposium III*, September 1992.

KOHL89 Kohl, J. "The Use of Encryption in Kerberos for Network Authentication." *Proceedings, Crypto '89*, 1989; published by Springer-Verlag.

KOHL94 Kohl, J., Neuman, B., and Ts'o, T. "The Evolution of the Kerberos Authentication Service." In Brazier, F., and Johansen, D. *Distributed Open Systems.* Los Alamitos, CA: IEEE Computer Society Press, 1994. Available at http://web.mit.edu/kerberos/www/papers.html.

LAI91 Lai, X., and Massey, J. "Markov Ciphers and Differential Cryptanalysis." *Proceedings, EUROCRYPT '91*, 1991; published by Springer-Verlag.

LEUT94 Leutwyler, K. "Superhack." *Scientific American,* July 1994.

LODI98 Lodin, S., and Schuba, C. "Firewalls Fend Off Invasions from the Net." *IEEE Spectrum*, February 1998.

LUNT88 Lunt, T., and Jagannathan, R. "A Prototype Real-Time Intrusion-Detection Expert System." *Proceedings, 1988 IEEE Computer Society Symposium on Research in Security and Privacy*, April 1988.

MACG97 Macgregor, R., Ezvan, C., Liguori, L., and Han, J. *Secure Electronic Transactions: Credit Card Payment on the Web in Theory and Practice.* IBM RedBook SG24-4978-00, 1997. Available at www.redbooks.ibm.com.

MADS93 Madsen, J. "World Record in Password Checking." *Usenet, comp.security.misc newsgroup*, August 18, 1993.

MARK97 Markham, T. "Internet Security Protocol." *Dr. Dobb's Journal*, June 1997.

MCHU00 McHugh, J., Christie, A., and Allen, J. "The Role of Intrusion Detection Systems." *IEEE Software*, September/October 2000.

MEIN01 Meinel, C. "Code Red for the Web." *Scientific American*, October 2001.

MENE97 Menezes, A., Oorshcot, P., and Vanstone, S. *Handbook of Applied Cryptography.* Boca Raton, FL: CRC Press, 1997.

MERK79 Merkle, R. *Secrecy, Authentication, and Public Key Systems.* Ph.D. Thesis, Stanford University, June 1979.

MERK89 Merkle, R. "One Way Hash Functions and DES." *Proceedings, CRYPTO '89*, 1989; published by Springer-Verlag.

MEYE82 Meyer, C., and Matyas, S. *Cryptography: A New Dimension in Computer Data Security.* New York: Wiley, 1982.

MILL88 Miller, S., Neuman, B., Schiller, J., and Saltzer, J. "Kerberos Authentication and Authorization System." *Section E.2.1, Project Athena Technical Plan*, M.I.T. Project Athena, Cambridge, MA. 27 October 1988.

MILL98 Miller, S. *IPv6: The New Internet Protocol.* Upper Saddle River, NJ: Prentice Hall, 1998.

MITC90 Mitchell, C., Walker, M., and Rush, D. "CCITT/ISO Standards for Secure Message Handling." *IEEE Journal on Selected Areas in Communications*, May 1989.

MURH98 Murhammer, M., et al. *TCP/IP: Tutorial and Technical Overview.* Upper Saddle River: NJ: Prentice Hall, 1998.

NACH97 Nachenberg, C. "Computer Virus-Antivirus Coevolution." *Communications of the ACM*, January 1997.

NEED78 Needham, R., and Schroeder, M. "Using Encryption for Authentication in Large Networks of Computers." *Communications of the ACM*, December 1978.

NICH99 Nichols, R. ed. *ICSA Guide to Cryptography.* New York: McGraw-Hill, 1999.

OPPL97 Oppliger, R. "Internet Security: Firewalls and Beyond." *Communications of the ACM*, May 1997.

PFLE97 Pfleeger, C. *Security in Computing.* Upper Saddle River, NJ: Prentice Hall, 1997.

PIAT91 Piattelli-Palmarini, M. "Probability: Neither Rational nor Capricious." *Bostonia*, March 1991.

PORR92   Porras, P. *STAT: A State Transition Analysis Tool for Intrusion Detection.* Master's Thesis, University of California at Santa Barbara, July 1992.

PROC01   Proctor, P. *The Practical Intrusion Detection Handbook.* Upper Saddle River, NJ: Prentice Hall, 2001.

RESC01   Rescorla, E. *SSL and TLS: Designing and Building Secure Systems.* Reading, MA: Addison-Wesley, 2001.

RIVE78   Rivest, R., Shamir, A., and Adleman, L. "A Method for Obtaining Digital Signatures and Public Key Cryptosystems." *Communications of the ACM*, February 1978.

RIVE94   Rivest, R. "The RC5 Encryption Algorithm." *Proceedings, Second International Workshop on Fast Software Encryption*, December 1994; published by Springer-Verlag.

RIVE95   Rivest, R. "The RC5 Encryption Algorithm." *Dr. Dobb's Journal*, January 1995.

RUBI97   Rubin, A.; Geer, D.; and Ranum, M. *Web Security Sourcebook.* New York: Wiley, 1997.

SAFF93   Safford, D., Schales, D., and Hess, D. "The TAMU Security Package: An Ongoing Response to Internet Intruders in an Academic Environment." *Proceedings, UNIX Security Symposium IV*, October 1993.

SALO96   Salomaa, A. *Public-Key Cryptography.* New York: Springer-Verlag, 1996.

SCHN93   Schneier, B. "Description of a New Variable-Length Key, 64-bit Block Cipher (Blowfish)." *Proceedings, Workshop on Fast Software Encryption*, December 1993; published by Springer-Verlag.

SCHN94   Schneier, R. "The Blowfish Encryption Algorithm." *Dr. Dobb's Journal*, April 1994.

SCHN96   Schneier, B. *Applied Cryptography.* New York: Wiley, 1996.

SCHN00   Schneier, B. *Secrets and Lies: Digital Security in a Networked World.* New York: Wiley 2000.

SIMM92   Simmons, G., ed. *Contemporary Cryptology: The Science of Information Integrity.* Piscataway, NJ: IEEE Press, 1992.

SING99   Singh, S. *The Code Book: The Science of Secrecy from Ancient Egypt to Quantum Cryptography.* New York: Anchor Books, 1999.

SMIT97   Smith, R. *Internet Cryptography.* Reading, MA: Addison-Wesley, 1997.

SNAP91   Snapp, S., et al. "A System for Distributed Intrusion Detection." *Proceedings, COMPCON Spring '91*, 1991.

SPAF92a   Spafford, E. "Observing Reusable Password Choices." *Proceedings, UNIX Security Symposium III*, September 1992.

SPAF92b   Spafford, E. "OPUS: Preventing Weak Password Choices." *Computers and Security*, No. 3, 1992.

STAL99   Stallings, W. *SNMP, SNMPv2, SNMPv3, and RMON 1 and 2.* Reading, MA: Addison-Wesley, 1999.

STAL00   Stallings, W. *Data and Computer Communications, 6th edition.* Upper Saddle River, NJ: Prentice Hall, 2000.

STAL03   Stallings, W. *Cryptography and Network Security: Principles and Practice, 3rd edition.* Upper Saddle River, NJ: Prentice Hall, 2003.

STEI88   Steiner, J., Neuman, C., and Schiller, J. "Kerberos: An Authentication Service for Open Networked Systems." *Proceedings of the Winter 1988 USENIX Conference*, February 1988.

STEP93   Stephenson, P. "Preventive Medicine." *LAN Magazine*, November 1993.

STER92   Sterling, B. *The Hacker Crackdown: Law and Disorder on the Electronic Frontier.* New York: Bantam, 1992.

STEV94   Stevens, W. *TCP/IP Illustrated, Volume 1: The Protocols.* Reading, MA: Addison-Wesley, 1994.

STIN02   Stinson, D. *Cryptography: Theory and Practice.* Boca Raton, FL: CRC Press, 2002.

STOL88   Stoll, C. "Stalking the Wily Hacker." *Communications of the ACM*, May 1988.

STOL89   Stoll, C. *The Cuckoo's Egg.* New York: Doubleday, 1989.

THOM84   Thompson, K. "Reflections on Trusting Trust (Deliberate Software Bugs)." *Communications of the ACM*, August 1984.

TIME90   Time, Inc. *Computer Security, Understanding Computers Series.* Alexandria, VA: Time-Life Books, 1990.

TSUD92   Tsudik, G. "Message Authentication with One-Way Hash Functions." *Proceedings, INFOCOM '92*, May 1992.

TUNG99   Tung, B. *Kerberos: A Network Authentication System.* Reading, MA: Addison-Wesley, 1999.

VACC89   Vaccaro, H., and Liepins, G. "Detection of Anomalous Computer Session Activity." *Proceedings of the IEEE Symposium on Research in Security and Privacy*, May 1989.

WACK02   Wack, J., Cutler, K., and Pole, J. *Guidelines on Firewalls and Firewall Policy.* NIST Special Publication SP 800-41, January 2002.

ZIV77   Ziv, J., and Lempel, A. "A Universal Algorithm for Sequential Data Compression." *IEEE Transactions on Information Theory*, May 1977.

INDEX

A

Access control, 10–11, 14
  and intruders, 296
Access control lists, 357
Access matrix, 356–57
Access type, and access determination, 283
access_denied alert code, TLS, 232
Acquirer, SET, 237
Action field, audit records, 300
Active attacks, 7–9, 54, 215
  denial-of-service, 9
  masquerade, 7–8
  modification of messages, 8–9
  replay, 8
Addressing schemes, and routers, 203
Adleman, Len, 72
Adler, Mark, 159
Advanced antivirus techniques, 338–40
AES (Advanced Encryption Standard), 38–42
  encryption/decryption, 40
  encryption round, 41
  home page, 51
  overview of, 39–42
Aggressive Exchange, ISAKMP, 200–201
Alert Protocol, 217, 221–23
Anonymous Diffie-Hellman, 225–26, 228
Antivirus approaches, 337–38
AntiVirus Online, 342

Applicability statement (AS), 20
Application-level gateway, 352
Attacks, 5
  active, 7–9, 54, 215
    denial of service, 9
    masquerade, 7–8
    modification of messages, 8–9
    replay, 8
  chosen-ciphertext, 31
  chosen-plaintext, 31
  chosen-text, 31
  ciphertext-only, 30–31
  denial-of-service, 9
    and USM, 272
    and zombies, 328
  known-plaintext, 30–31
  probable-word, 30–31
  source routing, 350
  tiny fragment, 350
Audit records, 299–301
  detection-specific, 300
  fields in, 300
  native, 299
Authentication, 9–11
  data origin, 11
  Oakley Key Determination Protocol, 193
  peer entity, 11
  using conventional encryption, 54–55
Authentication applications, 87–119
  Kerberos, 88–105

Authentication applications (*cont.*)
  X.509 authentication service, 105–14
    user certificates, 106–10
Authentication Data field:
  Authentication Header (AH), 178–79
  Encapsulating Security Payload (ESP),
    183
Authentication exchange, 14
Authentication Header (AH), 172–73,
    177–82
  anti-replay service, 178–79
  Authentication Data field, 178–79
  integrity check value, 179–80
  Next Header field, 177
  Payload Length field, 177
  Reserved field, 177
  Security Parameters Index field, 177
  Sequence Number field, 177
  transport mode AH, 180–81
  tunnel mode AH, 181–82
Authentication header, IPv6, 208
Authentication Only Exchange,
    ISAKMP, 199–200
Authority key identifier, 113
Authorization Request message, 244–45
Authorization Response message, 245
Availability service, 12–13

B
bad_certificate alert, 223
bad_record_mac alert, 222
Base Exchange, ISAKMP, 199
Base-rate fallacy, 322–24
  Bayes' theorem, 323–24
  conditional probability, 322
  demonstration of, 324
  independence, 322–23
Basic constraints, certification path, 114
Basic Encoding Rules (BER), 152
Bastion host, 353–54
Behavior-blocking software, 340–41
Behavior control, firewalls, 345
Best Current Practice (BCP), 20–21
Binary transfer encoding, 147
Block cipher, 30

Block encryption, padding, 221
Bloom filter, 317–18
Blowfish, 43
  and ESP, 183
Brute-force approach, to cryptanalysis,
    32–33

C
Capability tickets, 358
Capture Request message, 245
Capture Response message, 246
Cardholder, SET, 237
CAST-128, 126, 127, 130, 133
CAST, and ESP, 183
CERT Coordination Center, 320
Certificate authority (CA), 80, 106, 225
  and SET, 238
  SET, 238
Certificate message, 226, 227
Certificate payload, ISAKMP, 198
Certificate processing:
  S/MIME, 155–56
    user agent role, 155
    Verisign certificates, 155–56
Certificate Request payload, ISAKMP,
    198
Certificate revocation list (CRL), 110,
    155
certificate_expired alert, 223
certificate_request message, 227
certificate_revoked alert, 223
Certificates, 106–10
  forward, 109
  obtaining, 107–10
  policies, 113
  policy mappings, 114
  reverse, 109
  revocation of, 110
certificate_unknown alert, 223
certificate_verify message, 228
  TLS, 233
Certification path constraints, 114
Change Cipher Spec Protocol, 217, 221,
    228
change_cipher_spec message, 228

Chosen-ciphertext attack, 31
Chosen-plaintext attack, 31
Chosen-text attack, 31
Client write key parameter, connection state, 218
Cipher block chaining (CBC) mode, 44–46, 61, 226
Cipher feedback (CFB) mode, 47, 126
Cipher spec parameter, session state, 218
CipherAlgorithm field, CipherSpec, 226
CipherSpec, 225–26, 229
CipherSuite field, client_hello message, 225
Ciphertext, and public-key encryption, 69
Ciphertext-only attack, 30–31
CipherType field, CipherSpec, 226
Circuit-level gateway, 352–53
Clandestine user, 294
Client write MAC secret parameter, connection state, 218
client_key_exchange message, 227–28
close_notify alert, 223
COAST, 23
Code Red worm/Code Red II worm, 336–37
Codebook, 44
Collision-resistant hash function, 59*fn*
Command generator application, SNMPv3, 267–69
Command responder application, SNMPv3, 269
Commercial Product Evaluation Program, National Security Agency (NSA), 360
Compression, 219
Compression algorithm, ZIP, 160–62
Compression function, 63
Compression Method field, client_hello message, 225
Compression method, session state, 218
Compression virus, logic for, 331
Computationally secure encryption schemes, 31
Computer and Network Security Reference Index, 23

Computer Emergency Response Team (CERT), 168, 296
Computer-generated passwords, 315
Computer security, 2
Computer Security Resource Center, 23
Congruent modulo *n*, 372–73
Connection state, 218–19
Content types, S/MIME, 151
Conventional encryption, authentication using, 54–58
CPU emulator, GD scanner, 338
Cryptographic algorithms:
  S/MIME, 149–51
    DSS (Digital Signature Standard), 150
    ElGamal, 150
    MD5 message digest algorithm, 150
    public-key algorithms, 150
    RSA public-key encryption algorithm, 150
    SHA-1, 150
    TripleDES (3DES), 150
Cryptography FAQ Web site, 23

D

Data access control, 356–58
  access control lists, 357
  access matrix, 356–57
  capability tickets, 358
Data compression using ZIP, 159–62
Data confidentiality, 10–11
Data integrity, 10–12, 14
Data origin authentication, 11
Data Sensitivity Level selector, 175
decode_error alert code, TLS, 233
Decompression algorithm, ZIP, 162
decompression_failure alert, 222
decrypt_error alert code, TLS, 233
Decryption algorithm, and public-key encryption, 69
decryption_failed alert code, TLS, 232
Delete payload, ISAKMP, 199
Denial-of-service attacks, 9
  and USM, 272
  and zombies, 328

Denial-of-service threats, 215
DES (Data Encryption Standard) algorithm, 32, 34–37, 64
  "DES cracker" machine, 35
  description of, 35
  strength of, 35–37
  use of term, 35*fn*
Destination Address field:
  IPv4 header, 207
  IPv6 header, 208
Destination Address selector, 175
Destination Options header, IPv6, 208, 211
Detection-specific audit records, 300
Diffie-Hellman key exchange, 75–78, 81, 126
  Anonymous Diffie-Hellman, 225–26, 228
  Ephemeral Diffie-Hellman, 225, 226, 228
  Fixed Diffie-Hellman, 225, 228
  security of, 76–77
Digital signatures, 14, 57, 78–79, 149
  and Oakley Key Determination Protocol, 193
  and public-key cryptosystems, 71
Direction control, firewalls, 345
Divisors, 370–71
DNS, 353
Dormant phase, viruses, 329
DSS (Digital Signature Standard), 78
  and S/MIME, 150
Dual signature, SET, 239–40

E
E-mail viruses, 334–35
8bit transfer encoding, 147
Electronic codebook (ECB) mode, 44
Electronic Frontier Foundation (EFF), 35–36
Electronic mail security, 121–66
  data compression using ZIP, 159–62
  Pretty Good Privacy (PGP), 122–41
    random number generation, 164–66
  Radix-64 encoding, 162–63

S/MIME, 141–59
ElGamal, 126–27
  and S/MIME, 150
Elliptic-curve cryptography (ECC), 78
Emulation control module, GD scanner, 338
Encapsulating Security Payload (ESP), 172–73, 182–87
  Authentication Data field, 183
  encryption and authentication algorithms, 183
  format, 182–83
  Next Header field, 183
  Pad Length field, 183
  Padding field, 182–83
  Payload Data field, 182–83
  Security Parameters Index field, 182
  Sequence Number field, 182
  transport mode ESP, 184, 185–86
  tunnel mode ESP, 184, 186–87
Encapsulating Security Payload header, IPv6, 208
Encipherment, 13–14
Encrypt-decrypt-encrypt (EDE) sequence, 37
Encryption algorithm, and public-key encryption, 69
Encryption/decryption, and public-key cryptosystems, 71
Encryption devices, location, 47–49
End-to-end encryption, 47–49
Enhanced security services:
  S/MIME, 156–58
    secure mailing lists, 157–58
    security labels, 157
    signed receipts, 156–57
Ephemeral Diffie-Hellman, 225, 226, 228
ESP, *See* Encapsulating Security Payload (ESP):
Event detection, 14
Exception-Condition field, audit records, 300
Exchange Type field, ISAKMP header, 194
Execution phase, viruses, 329

Exhaustive key search, average time required for, 32
Experimental RFC, 20–21
export_restriction alert code, TLS, 233
Extension headers:
  IPv6, 208–11
    Authentication header, 208
    Destination Options header, 208, 211
    Encapsulating Security Payload header, 208
    Fragment header, 208, 210–11
    Hop-by-Hop Options header, 208, 210
    order of, 208–9
    Routing header, 208, 210
Extensions, user certificate, 107

F

Feistel cipher structure, 32–34, 64
  block size, 33
  ease of analysis, 34
  fast software encryption/decryption, 34
  key size, 33
  number of rounds, 34
  round function, 34
  subkey generation algorithm, 34
Feistel, Horst, 32
Firewall.com, 362
Firewalls, 343–63
  behavior control, 345
  capabilities, 346
  characteristics of, 345–46
  configurations, 354–56
    screened host firewall, dual-homed bastion, 354–55
    screened host firewall, single-homed bastion, 354–55
    screened subnet firewall, 355–56
  design principles, 344–56
  direction control, 345
  service control, 345
  trusted systems, 356–62
    concept of, 358–60
    data access control, 356–58

    defined, 358–60
    Trojan horse defense, 360–62
  types of, 346–54
    application-level gateway, 352
    bastion host, 353–54
    circuit-level gateway, 352–53
    packet-filtering routers, 346–50
    stateful inspection firewalls, 350–51
  user control, 345
First-generation scanners, 337
Fixed Diffie-Hellman key exchange, 225, 228
Flags field:
  IPv4 header, 206–7
  ISAKMP header, 194–96
Flow Label field, IPv6 header, 208
Fortezza technique, 226, 228
Forward certificates, 109
Fourth-generation scanners, 338
Fragment header, IPv6, 208, 210–11
Fragment Offset field:
  Fragment header, 211
  IPv4 header, 207
Fragmentation, 203, 219
Front-end processor (FEP), 50
FTP, 253, 352, 353
Functions, S/MIME, 149

G

Gailly, Jean-Iup, 159
Greatest common divisor, 371–72

H

Handshake Protocol, 217, 219, 223–29
  action, 224
  certificate_request message, 227
  certificate_verify message, 228
  change_cipher_spec message, 228
  client_hello message, 224–25
  client_key_exchange message, 227–28
  Content field, 223
  initial exchange phases, 223–29
    client authentication and key exchange (phase 3), 227–28

Handshake Protocol (*cont.*)
    establish security capabilities (phase 1), 224–26
    finish (phase 4), 228–29
    server authentication and key exchange (phase 2), 226–27
    Length field, 223
    message types, 223
    server_done message, 227
    server_hello message, 225
    server_key_exchange message, 226–27
    Type field, 223
handshake_failure alert, 222
Hash payload, ISAKMP, 198
HashSize field, CipherSpec, 226
Header Checksum field, IPv4 header, 207
Header Extension field, Hop-by-Hop Options header, 210
HMAC, 66–68, 277
    algorithm, 67–68
    design objectives, 66–67
    structure, 67
Honeypot Project, 320
Hop-by-Hop Options header, IPv6, 208, 210
Hop Limit field, IPv6 header, 208
Hypertext Transfer Protocol (HTTP), 217

I
IDEA (International Data Encryption Algorithm), 42, 126–27, 130, 133
    and ESP, 183
Identification field:
    Fragment header, 211
    IPv4 header, 206
Identification payload, ISAKMP, 198
Identity Protection Exchange, ISAKMP, 199
IEEE Technical Committee on Security and Privacy, 23
IETF Security Area, 23
IETF SNMPv3 working group, 286
illegal_parameter alert, 222

Information access threats, 17
Information security, 2
Informational Exchange, ISAKMP, 201
Initialization vectors parameter, connection state, 218
Initiator Cookie field, ISAKMP header, 194
Integrity checking, 338
Internet Society, 18
Internetwork security, 3–4
Interfaces, and routers, 203
internal_error alert code, TLS, 233
International Telecommunication Union (ITU) Telecommunication Standardization Sector (ITU-T), 4
Internet:
    RFC publication process, 20
    RFC types, 20–21
    standardization process, 18–20
    standards categories, 20
    use of term, 2
Internet Architecture Board (IAB), 18, 168
Internet Engineering Steering Group (IESG), 18
Internet Engineering Task Force (IETF), 18, 171, 207
    areas, 19
Internet Header Length field, IPv4 header, 206
Internet protocol (IP), role of, 203–5
Internet security, 2
Intruders, 293–324
    and access control, 296
    clandestine user, 294
    intrusion detection, 297–309
        anomaly detection, 299
        audit records, 299–301
        base-rate fallacy, 306
        distributed intrusion detection, 306–8
        honeypots, 308–9
        intrusion detection exchange format, 309
        penetration identification, 299
        profile-based detection, 299

rule-based anomaly detection, 304
rule-based detection, 299
rule-based intrusion detection, 304–6
rule-based penetration identification, 304
statistical anomaly detection, 299,
  301–4
threshold detection, 299
intrusion techniques, 296–97
masquerader, 294
misfeasor, 294
and one-way encryption, 296
password management, 309–19
  access control, 314
  password protection, 309–14
  password selection strategies, 314–19
  password vulnerability, 310–14
"Wily Hacker" incident (1986-87), 295
Intrusion Detection Working Group, 320
IP address spoofing, and packet-filtering
  routers, 350
IP packet, use of term, 173*fn*
IP security (IPSec), 80, 105, 167–211
  applications of, 169
  architecture, 171–77
  Authentication Header (AH), 177–82
    anti-replay service, 178–79
    Authentication Data field, 178–79
    integrity check value, 179–80
    Next Header field, 177
    Payload Length field, 177
    Reserved field, 177
    Security Parameters Index field, 177
    Sequence Number field, 177
    transport mode AH, 180–81
    tunnel mode AH, 181–82
  benefits of, 169–70
  documents, 171–72
    architecture, 171
    authentication algorithm, 171
    Authentication Header (AH), 171
    Domain of Interpretation (DOI),
      172
    Encapsulating Security Payload
      (ESP), 171
    encryption algorithm, 171

key management, 171
Encapsulating Security Payload (ESP),
  182–87
  Authentication Data field, 183
  encryption and authentication algo-
    rithms, 183
  format, 182–83
  Next Header field, 183
  Pad Length field, 183
  Padding field, 182–83
  Payload Data field, 182–83
  Security Parameters Index field, 182
  Sequence Number field, 182
  transport mode ESP, 184, 185–86
  tunnel mode ESP, 184, 186–87
functional areas, 168
key management, 190–201
  automated, 190
  ISAKMP/Oakley protocol, 190–201
  manual, 190
overview of, 168–71
routing applications, 170–71
security associations (SAs), 173–75
  combining, 187–90
  IP destination address, 173
  parameters, 174
  Security Parameters Index (SPI),
    173
  security protocol identifier, 173
  selectors, 174–75
  tunnel mode, 176–77
services, 172–73
transport mode, 176
tunnel mode, 176–77
IP Security (IPSEC) Resources site, 201
IP Security Protocol (IPSEC) Charter
  site, 201
IP Security Working Group News, 201
IP spoofing, 168
IPSec Protocol selector, 175
IPv4, 205–7
  IP header, 205–6
    Destination Address field, 207
    Flags field, 206–7
    Fragment Offset field, 207
    Header Checksum field, 207

IPv4 (*cont.*)
    Identification field, 206
    Internet Header Length field, 206
    Options field, 207
    Padding field, 207
    Protocol field, 207
    Source Address field, 207
    Time to Live field, 207
    Type of Service field, 206
    Version field, 206
IPv4 Type of Service (TOS) selector, 175
IPv6, 207–11
    extension headers, 208–11
        Authentication header, 208
        Destination Options header, 208,
            211
        Encapsulating Security Payload
            header, 208
        Fragment header, 208, 210–11
        Hop-by-Hop Options header, 208,
            210
        order of, 208–9
        Routing header, 208, 210
    header, 207–8
        Destination Address field, 208
        Flow Label field, 208
        Hop Limit field, 208
        Next Header field, 208
        Payload Length field, 208
        Source Address field, 208
        Traffic Class field, 208
        Version field, 208
IPv6 Class selector, 175
IPv6 Flow Label selector, 175
Is resumable parameter, session state,
    218
ISAKMP (Internet Security Association
    and Key Management Protocol),
    194–201
    defined, 191
    exchanges, 199–201
        Aggressive Exchange, 200–201
        Authentication Only Exchange,
            199–200
        Base Exchange, 199
        Identity Protection Exchange, 199

    Informational Exchange, 201
header format, 194–96
    Exchange Type field, 194
    Flags field, 194–96
    Initiator Cookie field, 194
    Length field, 196
    Major Version field, 194
    Message ID field, 196
    Minor Version field, 194
    Next Payload field, 194
    Responder Cookie field, 194
payload types, 196–99
    Certificate payload, 198
    Certificate Request payload, 198
    Delete payload, 199
    Hash payload, 198
    Identification payload, 198
    Key Exchange payload, 198
    Nonce payload, 198
    Notification payload, 198–99
    Proposal payload, 196–98
    SA payload, 196
    Signature payload, 198
    Transform payload, 198
status messages, 199
ISAKMP/Oakley protocol:
    ISAKMP (Internet Security Associa-
        tion and Key Management Proto-
        col), defined, 191
    Oakley Key Determination Protocol,
        190–94
    defined, 190
IsExportable field, CipherSpec, 226
Issuer alternative name field, 114
Issuer name, user certificate, 107
Issuer, SET, 237
Issuer unique identifier, user certificate,
    107
IV Size field, CipherSpec, 226

K
Kerberos, 88–105
    encryption techniques, 117–19
        password-to-key transformation,
            117–18

propagating cipher block chaining mode (PCBC), 118–19
motivation, 89–90
reliability of, 90
scalability of, 90
security of, 89
transparency of, 90
use of term, 88*fn*
version 4, 90–99
  authentication dialogue, 94–97
  authentication forwarding, 101
  compared to version 5, 99–102
  double encryption, 101
  encryption system dependence, 99
  Internet protocol dependence, 99–100
  interrealm authentication, 101
  message byte ordering, 100
  multiple Kerberi, 97–99
  password attacks, 101–2
  PCBC encryption, 101
  rationale for protocol elements of, 96–97
  realms, 97–98
  session keys, 101
  technical deficiencies, 101–2
  ticket lifetime, 100–101
version 5, 99–105
  authentication dialogue, 102–3
  authentication forwarding, 101
  authentication service exchange, 102
  client/server authentication exchange, 103
  compared to version 4, 99–102
  double encryption, 101
  encryption system dependence, 99
  Internet protocol dependence, 99–100
  interrealm authentication, 101
  message byte ordering, 100
  password attacks, 102
  PCBC encryption, 101
  session keys, 101
  ticket flags, 103–5
  ticket-granting service exchange foi, 103
  ticket lifetime, 100–101
Key distribution, 49–51
Key distribution center (KDC), 50
Key exchange, and public-key cryptosystems, 71
Key Exchange payload, ISAKMP, 198
Key ID:
  private-key ring, 133
  public-key ring, 134
Key legitimacy field, 138
Key management, 79–81
Key Material field, CipherSpec, 226
Known-plaintext attack, 30–31

L
L277, 159–60
Lai, Xuejia, 42
latestReceivedEngineTime parameter, USM, 276
Lempel, Abraham, 159
Length field, ISAKMP header, 196
Link encryption, 47–49
Lloyd, Tim, 328
Logic bomb, 328

M
M Flag field, Fragment header, 211
MACAlgorithm field, CipherSpec, 226
Macro viruses, 333–34
Mailing List Agent (MLA), S/MIME, 158
Major Version field, ISAKMP header, 194
Malicious software, 325–42, *See also* Worms; Threats; Viruses
  logic bomb, 328
  threats, 326–37
  trap doors, 326–27
  Trojan horses, 328
  viruses, 326–37
    counterattacks, 337–41
    dormant phase, 329
    e-mail viruses, 334–35
    execution phase, 329

Malicious software (*cont.*)
    macro viruses, 333–34
    memory-resident virus, 332
    nature of, 329–35
    parasitic virus, 332
    polymorphic virus, 332–33
    propagation phase, 329
    stealth virus, 332–33
    structure, 329–32
    triggering phase, 329
    types of, 332–33
   worms, 335–37
    Code Red worm/Code Red II worm, 336–37
    Morris worm, 335–36
    network vehicle, 335
    Nimda, 336–37
    recent attacks, 336–37
   zombies, 328
Management agent, 251
   SNMP, 251
Management Information Base for Network Management of TCP/IP-based Internets: MIB-II (RFC 1213), 252
Management information base (MIB), 252
Management station, 251
   SNMP, 251
Markov model, for password selection, 316–18
Masquerade, 7–8
Masquerader, 294
Massey, James, 42
Master secret, 228, 229–30
Master secret parameter, session state, 218
MasterCard SET Site, 246
Maximum packet sizes, and routers, 203
MD5 message digest aigorithm, 65, 228, 280
  and S/MIME, 150
Melissa virus, 334
Memory-resident virus, 332
Merchant, SET, 237
Message authentication, 54–58

code, 55–57
  defined, 54
  one-way hash function, 57–58
  using conventional encryption, 54–58
  without message encryption, 55–58
Message authentication code (MAC), 219–21, 230–31
Message component, 131
Message ID field, ISAKMP header, 196
Message processing, SHA-1, 61–64
  append length, 62
  append padding bits, 61–62
  initialize MD buffer, 62
  output, 64
  process message in 512-bit (16-word) blocks, 63–64
Messages:
  S/MIME, 151–55
   certificates-only message, 155
   clear signing, 154
   envelopedData smime-type, 152–53
   MIME entity, securing, 152
   registration request, 154–55
   signedData smime-type, 153–54
Metrics, statistical anomaly detection, 301–3
MIB context, and access determination, 283
MIB view, 282
Microsoft, and macro viruses, 333–34
MIME (Multipurpose Internet Mail Extensions), 142–49
  application type, 146
  base64 transfer encoding, 147
  canonical form, 147, 149
  Content-Description field, 144
  Content-ID field, 144
  Content-Transfer-Encoding field, 143, 146–47
  Content-Type field, 143
  content types, 144–46
  defined, 142–49
  elements, 143
  header fields, 143–44
  message/partial subtype, 146
  message/rfc822 subtype, 146

message structure, example of, 148
message type, 146
MIME-Version field, 143
multipart/alternative subtype, 145–46
multipart/digest subtype, 146
multipart example, 147–48
multipart/mixed subtype, 145
multipart/parallel subtype, 145
multipart type, 145–46
native form, 149
quoted-printable transfer, 147
text type, 145
transfer encodings, 146–47
Minor Version field, ISAKMP header, 194
Misfeasor, 294
MIT Distribution Site for PGP, 158
MIT Kerberos Site, 115
Modification of messages, 8–9
Modular arithmetic, 372–73
congruent modulo n, 372–73
defined, 373
residue, 372
Morris, Robert, 335
Morris worm, 335–36
msgAuthenticationParameters parameter, USM, 274
msgAuthoritativeEngineBoots parameter, USM, 274, 277
msgAuthoritativeEngineID parameter, USM, 274, 277
msgAuthoritativeEngineTime parameter, USM, 274, 277
msgFlags field, 270–71
msgID field, 270
msgMaxSize field, 270
msgPrivacyParameters parameter, USM, 274
msgSecurityModel field, 270–71
msgUserName parameter, USM, 274
msgVersion field, 270
Multics, 327
Multilevel security, 358–59
Multiple Kerberi, 97–99
Multivariate model, statistical anomaly detection, 302

Mutation engine, 333

N
Name constraints, certification path, 114
National Institute of Standards and Technology (NIST), 34, 38, 61
National Security Agency (NSA), 333
Commercial Product Evaluation Program, 360
Native audit records, 299
Netscape's SSL Page, 246
Network layer address spoofing, 350
Network management architecture, 251–52
Network management protocol, 252
Network management protocol architecture, 252–53
Network management security, 249–89
SNMP (Simple Network Management Protocol), 250–86
basic concepts of, 250–58
management agent, 251
management information base (MIB), 252
management station, 251
network management architecture, 251–52
network management protocol, 252
network management protocol architecture, 252–53
proxies, 254
role of, 253
SNMPv2, 254–58
Network management system (NMS), 279–80
Network security, 2
model for, 13–17
USENET newsgroups, 23
Network vehicles, worms, 335
Network worm programs, 335
Next Header field:
Authentication Header (AH), 177
Encapsulating Security Payload (ESP), 183
Hop-by-Hop Options header, 210

Next Header field (*cont.*)
    IPv6 header, 208
Next Payload field, ISAKMP header, 194
Nimda, 336–37
NIST Secure Hashing Page, 82
No read up rule, multilevel security, 358
no-renegotiation alert code, TLS, 233
No write down rule, multilevel security, 358
no_certificate alert, 223
Nonce payload, ISAKMP, 198
Nonces, Oakley Key Determination Protocol, 193
Nonrepudiation, 10, 12
Notarization, 14
Notification generator application, SNMPv3, 269
Notification payload, ISAKMP, 198–99
Notification receiver application, SNMPv3, 269
Number theory, 369–73
    modular arithmetic, 372–73
        congruent modulo *n*, 372–73
        defined, 373
        residue, 372
    prime numbers, 370–72
        defined, 371
        divisors, 370–71
        greatest common divisor, 371–72
        relatively prime numbers, 371–72

O
Oakley Key Determination Protocol, 190–94
    cookie exchange, 192
    cookie generation requirements, 192–93
    defined, 190
    and digital signatures, 193
    example, 193–94
    features, 192–93
    nonces, 193
    and public-key encryption, 193
    and symmetric-key encryption, 193

Object field, audit records, 300
Object instance, and access determination, 283
Omega Engineering, 328
One-way authentication, 111–12
One-way encryption, and intruders, 296
One-way hash function, 57–58, 59*fn*
One-way property, 59
Operational model, statistical anomaly detection, 302
Options field:
    Hop-by-Hop Options header, 210
    IPv4 header, 207
Order, IPv6, 208–9
OSI security architecture, 4–5
Owner trust field, 138

P
Packet-filtering routers, 346–50
    attacks/countermeasures, 350
    examples, 348
    IP address spoofing, 350
    simplicity of, 349
    source routing attacks, 350
    tiny fragment attacks, 350
    weaknesses of, 349–50
Pad Length field, Encapsulating Security Payload (ESP), 183
Padding field:
    Encapsulating Security Payload (ESP), 182–83
    IPv4 header, 207
Parasitic virus, 332
Participants:
    SET, 236–38
        acquirer, 237
        cardholder, 237
        certificate authority (CA), 238
        issuer, 237
        merchant, 237
        payment gateway, 237–38
Passive attacks, 5–7, 54, 215
    detection of, 6–7
    release of message contents, 5–6
    traffic analysis, 5–6

Password management, 309–19
  access control, 314
  Bloom filter, 317–18
  Markov model, 316–18
  password protection, 309–14
  password selection strategies, 314–19
    computer-generated passwords, 315
    proactive password checking, 315
    reactive password checking, 315
    user education technique, 314–15
  password vulnerability, 310–14
Password-to-key transformation, Kerberos, 117–18
Payload Data field, Encapsulating Security Payload (ESP), 182–83
Payload Length field:
  Authentication Header (AH), 177
  IPv6 header, 208
Payload types, ISAKMP, 196–99
  Certificate payload, 198
  Certificate Request payload, 198
  Delete payload, 199
  Hash payload, 198
  Identification payload, 198
  Key Exchange payload, 198
  Nonce payload, 198
  Notification payload, 198–99
  Proposal payload, 196–98
  SA payload, 196
  Signature payload, 198
  Transform payload, 198
Payment authorization, SET, 243–45
Payment capture, SET, 245–46
Payment gateway, SET, 237–38
Payment processing, SET, 240–46
Peer certificate parameter, session state, 218
Peer entity authentication, 11
Period of validity, user certificate, 107
Permanent key, 50
PGP Home Page, 158
Plaintext, and public-key encryption, 69
Policy constraints, certification path, 114
Policy mappings, 114
Polymorphic virus, 332–33
Pre-master secret, 227, 229–30

Pretty Good Privacy (PGP), 42, 122–41
  cryptographic keys, 130–36
  defined, 122
  documentation, 124
  key rings, 133–36
    private-key ring, 133–34
    public-key ring, 134–36
  message generation, 135
  notation, 123–24
  operational description, 124–29
    authentication, 124–25
    compression, 127
    confidentiality, 125–26
    confidentiality and authentication, 126–27
    e-mail compatibility, 127–28
    segmentation and reassembly, 128
  public-key management, 136–41
    approaches to, 137–38
    revocation of public keys, 141
    trust, use of, 138–41
  random number generation, 164–66
    pseudorandom numbers, 164–66
    true random numbers, 164
  reasons for growth of, 123
  reception, 136
  session key generation, 130–31
  session key identifiers, 131–33
    message component, 131
    session key component, 133
    signature component, 131–33
  summary of services, 124
Prime numbers, 370–72
  defined, 371
  divisors, 370–71
  greatest common divisor, 371–72
  relatively prime numbers, 371–72
Principals, 13–14
  and access determination, 283
Private key, 70, 124
  private-key ring, 133
Private-key ring, 133–34
Private-key usage period, 113
Proactive password checking, 315
Probable-word attack, 30–31
Profile-based anomaly detection, 301

Profile-based anomaly detection (*cont.*)
metrics, 301–3
counter, 301–2
gauge, 302
interval timer, 302
resource utilization, 302
Propagating cipher block chaining mode (PCBC), Kerberos, 118–19
Propagation phase, viruses, 329
Proposal payload, ISAKMP, 196–98
Protocol data units (PDUs), 203, 256, 262
scoped, 270
Protocol field, IPv4 header, 207
Proxy forwarder application, SNMPv3, 269–70
Public key, 69, 70
private-key ring, 133
public-key ring, 134
Public-key algorithms, and S/MIME, 150
Public-key cryptography:
algorithms, 72–78
Diffie-Hellman key exchange, 75–78
DSS (Digital Signature Standard), 78
elliptic-curve cryptography (ECC), 78
RSA public-key encryption algorithm, 72–75
digital signatures, 78–79
key management, 79–81
Public-key cryptosystems:
applications, 70–71
digital signature, 71
encryption/decryption, 71
key exchange, 71
Public-key cyptography:
principles, 68–72
public-key cryptosystem applications, 70–71
public-key encryption structure, 68–70
requirements for, 71–72
Public-key encryption, 14*fn*
and Oakley Key Determination Protocol, 193

Public-Key Infrastructure Working Group, 115
Public-key ring, 134–36
Purchase Request message, 242–43
Purchase Response message, 243

R
RACE Integrity Primitives Evaluation (RIPE), 65
Radix-64 conversion, 128, 162–63
Random field, client_hello message, 225
RC5, 43
and ESP, 183
Reactive password checking, 315
record_overflow alert code, TLS, 232
Reference monitor concept, 358–59
Relatively prime numbers, 371–72
Release of message contents, 5–6
Reliability, and routers, 203
Replay, 8
Res field, Fragment header, 211
Reserved field, Authentication Header (AH), 177
Residue, 372
Resource-Usage field, audit records, 300
Responder Cookie field, ISAKMP header, 194
Reverse certicates, 109
Rijndael page, 51
RIPE project, 65
RIPEMD-160, 65
Rivest, Ron, 43, 72
Round function, Feistel cipher structure, 32, 34
Routers, 203–5
Routing control, 14
Routing header, IPv6, 208, 210
Routing Type field, Routing header, 210
RSA key-exchange, 226
RSA Laboratories, 82
RSA public-key encryption algorithm, 72–75, 126–27, 225–28, 233
defined, 72
example of, 74
and S/MIME, 150

S

S/MIME, 80, 105, 141–59
  certificate processing, 155–56
    user agent role, 155
    Verisign certificates, 155–56
  certificate storage and retrieval, and
    user, 155
  clear-signed data, 149
  content types, 151
  cryptographic algorithms, 149–51
    DSS (Digital Signature Standard),
      150
    ElGamal, 150
    MD5 message digest aigorithm, 150
    public-key algorithms, 150
    RSA public-key encryption algo-
      rithm, 150
    SHA-1, 150
    TripleDES (3DES), 150
  enhanced security services, 156–58
    secure mailing lists, 157–58
    security labels, 157
    signed receipts, 156–57
  enveloped data, 149
  functionality, 149–51
  functions, 149
  key generation, and user, 155
  Mailing List Agent (MLA), 158
  messages, 151–55
    certificates-only message, 155
    clear signing, 154
    envelopedData smime-type, 152–53
    MIME entity, securing, 152
    registration request, 154–55
    signedData smime-type, 153–54
  MIME (Multipurpose Internet Mail
    Extensions), 142–49
    application type, 146
    base64 transfer encoding, 147
    canonical form, 147, 149
    Content-Description field, 144
    Content-ID field, 144
    Content-Transfer-Encoding field,
      143, 146–47
    Content-Type field, 143
    content types, 144–46

    defined, 142–49
    elements, 143
    header fields, 143–44
    message/partial subtype, 146
    message/rfc822 subtype, 146
    message structure, example of, 148
    message type, 146
    MIME-Version field, 143
    multipart/alternative subtype,
      145–46
    multipart/digest subtype, 146
    multipart example, 147–48
    multipart/mixed subtype, 145
    multipart/parallel subtype, 145
    multipart type, 145–46
    native form, 149
    quoted-printable transfer, 147
    text type, 145
    transfer encodings, 146–47
  registration, and user, 155
  RFC 822, 142
  signed and enveloped data, 149
  signed data, 149
S/MIME Central site, 158
S/MIME Charter site, 158
SA payload, ISAKMP, 196
Scoped PDU, 270
Screened host firewall, dual-homed bas-
  tion, 354–55
Screened host firewall, single-homed
  bastion, 354–55
Screened subnet firewall, 355–56
Second-generation scanners, 337–38
Secret-key encryption, *See* Symmetric
  encryption:
Secret keys, 70
  public-key distribution of, 80–81
Secure Electronic Transaction (SET), 66,
  80, 216, 234–46
  Authorization Request message to,
    244–45
  Authorization Response message to,
    245
  Capture Request message, 245
  Capture Response message, 246
  dual signature, 239–40

Secure Electronic Transaction (*cont.*)
  key features, 236
  overview of, 235–38
  participants, 236–38
    acquirer, 237
    cardholder, 237
    certificate authority (CA), 238
    issuer, 237
    merchant, 237
    payment gateway, 237–38
  payment authorization, 243–45
  payment capture, 245–46
  payment processing, 240–46
  purchase request, 240–43
  Purchase Request message, 242–43
  Purchase Response message, 243
  requirements, 235–36
  sequence of events required for a trans-
    action, 238
  transaction types, 241
Secure Hash Algorithm (SHA), 61, *See
  also* SHA-1
Secure hash functions, 58–68
  comparison of, 65
  hash function requirements, 59
  HMAC, 66–68
  MD5 message digest aigorithm, 65
  RIPEMD-160 message digest aigorithm,
    65
  SHA-1, 61–64
  simple, 60–61
Secure mailing lists, 157–58
Secure Sockets Layer (SSL), 80, 216,
    217–30
  Alert Protocol, 217, 221–23
  architecture, 217–19
    connection state, 218–19
    session state, 218
    SSL connection, 217
    SSL session, 218
  Change Cipher Spec Protocol, 221
  Handshake Protocol, 223–29
  SSL Record Protocol, 219–21
Security Architecture for OSI (ITU-T Rec-
    ommendation X.800), 4, 9, 13
Security association bundle, 187

Security associations (SAs), 173–75
  combining, 187–90
    authentication plus confidentiality,
      188–89
    basic combinations, 189–90
    ESP with authentication option, 188
    iterated tunneling, 187–88
    transport adjacency, 187, 188
    transport-tunnel bundle, 188–89
  IP destination address, 173
  parameters, 174
  Security Parameters Index (SPI), 173
  security protocol identifier, 173
  selectors, 174–75
Security attacks, 5–9, *See also* Attacks
  active attacks, 7–9, 54, 215
  passive attacks, 5–7, 54, 215
Security audit trail, 14
Security kernel database, 359
Security label, 14
Security labels, 157
Security level, and access determination,
    283
Security mechanism, 5
Security mechanisms, 13–14
Security model, and access determina-
    tion, 283
Security Parameters Index field:
  Authentication Header (AH), 177
  Encapsulating Security Payload (ESP),
    182
Security recovery, 14
Security service, 5
Security services, 9–13
  access control, 10–11
  authentication, 9–11
  availability service, 12–13
  data confidentiality, 10–11
  data integrity, 10–12
  nonrepudiation, 10, 12
Security violations, 3
Segments Left field, Routing header, 210
Sequence Number field:
  Authentication Header (AH), 177
  Encapsulating Security Payload (ESP),
    182

Sequence number parameter, connection state, 218–19

Serial number, user certificate, 107

Server and client random parameter, connection state, 218

Server write key parameter, connection state, 218

Server write MAC secret parameter, connection state, 218

server_done message, 227

server_key_exchange message, 226–27

Service control, firewalls, 345

Service threats, 17

Session ID filed, client_hello message, 225

Session identifier parameter, session state, 218

Session key, 49–50

Session key component, 133

SET, 105

SETCo site, 246

7bit transfer encoding, 147

SHA-1, 64–65, 124–25, 227–28, 240, 280

  message processing, 61–64

    append length, 62

    append padding bits, 61–62

    initialize MD buffer, 62

    output, 64

    process message in 512-bit (16-word) blocks, 63–64

  and S/MIME, 150

Shamir, Adi, 72

Signature algorithm identifier, user certificate, 107

Signature component, 131–33

  key ID of sender's public keys, 133

  message digest, 131–32

    leading two octets of, 132

  timestamp, 131

Signature payload, ISAKMP, 198

Signature trust field, 138

Signature, user certificate, 107

Signed receipts, 156–57

Simple Mail Transfer Protocol (SMTP), 351, 353

Simple Network Management Protocol, *See* SNMP (Simple Network Management Protocol):

Simple Network Management Protocol (RFC 1157), 252

Simple Web site, The (University of Twente), 286

SMTP, *See* Simple Mail Transfer Protocol (SMTP):

SNMP access profile, 260

SNMP community, defined, 259

SNMP community profile, 260

SNMP (Simple Network Management Protocol), 250–86

  basic concepts of, 250–58

  management agent, 251

  management information base (MIB), 252

  management station, 251

  network management architecture, 251–52

  network management protocol, 252

  network management protocol architecture, 252–53

  proxies, 254

  role of, 253

  SNMPv1, 258–61

  SNMPv2, 254–58

  SNMPv3, 261–85

  traditional SNMP agent, 265

  traditional SNMP manager, 263–65

snmpEngineBoots parameter, USM, 276–78

snmpEngineTime parameter, USM, 276–77

SNMPv1, 258–61

  access policy, 260

  authentication service, 259–60

  communities and community names, 258–59

  proxy service, 261

  SNMP access policy, 260

  SNMP community profile, 260

SNMPv2, 254–58

  distributed network management, 256

  functional enhancements, 256–58

SNMPv3, 261–85
 applications, 267–70
 architecture, 262
 authoritative and nonauthoritative
  engines, 273–74
 command generator application,
  267–69
 command responder application, 269
 cryptographic functions, 272–73
 entity, 262–66
 key localization, 278–81
 message processing model, 270–71
 notification generator application,
  269
 notification receiver application, 269
 proxy forwarder application, 269–70
 terminology, 266–67
 User Security Model (USM), 262,
  271–72
 USM message parameters, 274–76
 USM timeliness mechanisms, 276–78
 view-based access control (VAC), 262,
  280–85
  access control processing, 283–85
  elements of the VACM model,
   281–83
  motivation, 285
SNMPv3 Web site, 286
SOCKS package, 352–53
Source Address field:
 IPv4 header, 207
 IPv6 header, 208
Source and Destination Ports selector,
 175
Source IP Address selector, 175
Source routing attacks, and packet-filter-
 ing routers, 350
SSL Record Protocol, 219–21
SSL/TLS, 105
Standard for Public-Key Cryptography
 (IEEE P1363), 78
Standards, 365–67
Standards track, 19
Stateful inspection firewalls, 350–51
 connection state table, example of,
  351

Statistical anomaly detection, 301–4, *See
  also* Profile-based anomaly detec-
  tion
 Markov process model, 302
 mean and standard deviation, 302
 metrics, 301–3
 multivariate model, 302
 operational model, 302
 time series model, 302
Stealth virus, 332–33
Stoll, Cliff, 295
Stream cipher, 30
Strong collision resistance, 59
Strong one-way hash function, 59*fn*
*Structure and Identification of Manage-
  ment Information for TCP/IP-
  Based Networks* (RFC 1155), 252
Subject alternative name field, 114
Subject directory attributes field, 114
Subject field, audit records, 300
Subject key identifier, 113
Subject name, user certificate, 107
Subject unique identifier, user certificate,
 107
Subject's public-key information, user
 certificate, 107
Subkey generation algorithm, 34
sufficient_security alert code, TLS, 233
Symmetric encryption, 28
 chosen-ciphertext attack, 31
 chosen-plaintext attack, 31
 chosen-text attack, 31
 cipher block chaining (CBC) mode,
  44–46
 cipher feedback (CFB) mode, 47
 ciphertext, 29
 ciphertext-only attack, 30–31
 computationally secure encryption
  schemes, 31
 cryptanalysis, 30–32
 cryptography, 30
 decryption algorithm, 29
 encryption algorithm, 28
 encryption devices, location of, 47–49
 Feistel cipher structure, 32–34
 key distribution, 49–51

known-plaintext attack, 30–31
plaintext, 28
principles, 28–34
probable-word attack, 30–31
requirements for secure use of, 29
secret key, 28
Symmetric encryption algorithms, 34–43
  AES (Advanced Encryption Standard), 38–42
  Blowfish, 43
  DES (Data Encryption Standard) algorithm, 34–37
  IDEA (International Data Encryption Algorithm), 42
  RC5, 43
  TripleDES (3DES), 37–38
Symmetric-key encryption, and Oakley Key Determination Protocol, 193
System security:
  firewalls, 343–63
  intruders, 293–324
  malicious software, 325–42

T
TCP/IP (Transmission Control Protocol/Internet Protocol), 4, 13, 17, 170, 207, 253, 261, 352
Technical specification (TS), 20
Telnet, 352, 353
Third-generation scanners, 338
Threats, 5, 215–16, 326–37
  authentication, 215
  comparison of, 215
  confidentiality, 215
  denial of service, 215
  information access, 17
  integrity, 215
  location of, 215–16
  service, 17
Three-key triple DES, and ESP, 183
Three-key triple IDEA, and ESP, 183
Three-way authentication, 112
3DES, *See* TripleDES (3DES)
Threshold analysis, 301

Time series model, statistical anomaly detection, 302
Time-stamp field, audit records, 300
Time to Live field, IPv4 header, 207
Timestamp:
  private-key ring, 133
  public-key ring, 134
Tiny fragment attacks, and packet-filtering routers, 350
Tom Dunigan's Security Page, 23
Traffic analysis, 5–6
  and USM, 272
Traffic Class field, IPv6 header, 208
Traffic padding, 14
Transaction types, SET, 241
Transform payload, ISAKMP, 198
Transport Layer Protocol selector, 175
Transport Layer Security Charter, 246
Transport Layer Security (TLS), 66, 216, 230–34
  alert codes, 232–33
  certificate_verify message, 233
  cipher suites, 233
  client certificate types, 233
  cryptographic computations, 234
  finished message, 233–34
  key exchanges, 233
  Message Authentication Code (MAC), 230–31
  padding, 234
  pseudorandom function, 231–32
  symmetric encryption algorithms, 233
  TLS Record Format, 230
  version number, 230
Transport mode, 176
  ESP, 184, 185–86
Trap doors, 326–27
Triggering phase, viruses, 329
TripleDES (3DES), 37–38, 126–27, 133
  and S/MIME, 150
  use of term, 35*fn*
Trojan horses, 327, 328
  defense, 360–62
Trust flag byte, contents of, 139
Trusted functionality, 14

Trusted systems, 356–62
  concept of, 358–60
  data access control, 356–58
  defined, 358–60
  Trojan horse defense, 360–62
Tunnel mode, 176–77
  ESP, 184, 186–87
Two-way authentication, 112
Type of Service field, IPv4 header, 206

U

UDP, *See* User Datagram Protocol
    (UDP):
unexpected_message alert, 222
unknown_ca alert code, TLS, 232
unsupported_certificate alert, 223
USC/ISI Kerberos Page, 115
User certificates:
  obtaining, 107–10
  revocation of, 110
User control, firewalls, 345
User Datagram Protocol (UDP), 170,
    252–53
User education technique, for password
    selection, 314–15
User ID:
  private-key ring, 133
  public-key ring, 134
User Security Model (USM), 262,
    271–72
  and cipher block chaining (CBC)
    mode, 273
  and denial-of-service attacks, 272
  and traffic analysis, 272
user_canceled alert code, TLS, 233
UserID selector, 175
USM, *See* User Security Model (USM):

V

VAC, *See* View-based access control
    (VAC):
Verisign, 115
  certificates, 155–56
Version field:
  client_hello message, 224

IPv4 header, 206
IPv6 header, 208
Version, user certificate, 107
View-based access control (VAC), 262,
    280–85
  access control processing, 283–85
  elements of the VACM model, 281–83
    access policy, 283
    group, 281
    MIB context, 282
    MIB view, 282
    security level, 282
  motivation, 285
Virtual private network, 184
Virus signature scanner, GD technology,
    338
Viruses, 2–3, 17, 326–37
  advanced antivirus techniques, 338–40
    digital immune system, 339–40
    generic decryption (GD), 338–39
  antivirus approaches, 337–38
    first-generation scanners, 337
    fourth-generation scanners, 338
    second-generation scanners, 337–38
    third-generation scanners, 338
  behavior-blocking software, 340–41
    advantages of, 341
    disavantages of, 341
    monitored behaviors, 340–41
  counterattacks, 337–41
  dormant phase, 329
  e-mail viruses, 334–35
  execution phase, 329
  macro viruses, 333–34
  memory-resident virus, 332
  nature of, 329–35
  parasitic virus, 332
  polymorphic virus, 332–33
  propagation phase, 329
  stealth virus, 332–33
  structure, 329–32
  triggering phase, 329
  types of, 332–33

W

Wales, Richard, 159

War Games, 327
Weak collision resistance, 59
Web security, 213–47
  approaches to, 216
  authentication threats, 215
  challenges of, 214–15
  confidentiality threats, 215
  cryptographic computations, 229–30
    generation of cryptographic para-
      meters, 229–30
    master secret creation, 229
  denial of service threats, 215
  integrity threats, 215
  Secure Electronic Transaction (SET),
    216, 234–46
    Authorization Request message to,
      244–45
    Authorization Response message to,
      245
    Capture Request message, 245
    Capture Response message, 246
    dual signature, 239–40
    key features, 236
    overview of, 235–38
    participants, 236–38
    payment authorization, 243–45
    payment capture, 245–46
    payment processing, 240–46
    purchase request, 240–43
    Purchase Request message,
      242–43
    Purchase Response message, 243
    requirements, 235–36
    sequence of events required for a
      transaction, 238
    transaction types, 241
  Secure Sockets Layer (SSL), 216,
    217–30
    Alert Protocol, 217, 221–23
    architecture, 217–19
    Change Cipher Spec Protocol, 221
    Handshake Protocol, 223–29
    SSL Record Protocol, 219–21
  threats, 215–16
  Transport Layer Security (TLS), 216,
    230–34
    alert codes, 232–33

    certificate_verify message, 233
    cipher suites, 233
    client certificate types, 233
    cryptographic computations, 234
    finished message, 233–34
    key exchanges, 233
    Message Authentication Code
      (MAC), 230–31
    padding, 234
    pseudorandom function, 231–32
    symmetric encryption algorithms,
      233
    version number, 230
"Wily Hacker" incident (1986–87), 295
Worms, 17, 335–37
  Code Red worm/Code Red II worm,
    336–37
  Morris worm, 335–36
  network vehicles, 335
  recent attacks, 336–37

X
x-token transfer encoding, 147
X.509 authentication service, 105–14
  authentication procedures, 110–12
    one-way authentication, 111–12
    three-way authentication, 112
    two-way authentication, 112
  user certificates, 106–10
    obtaining, 107–10
    revocation of, 110
  version 3 format, 112–14
    certificate subject and issuer attrib-
      utes, 114
    certification path constraints, 114
    key and policy information, 113–14

Z
ZIP, 128, 159–62
  compression algorithm, 160–62
    lookahead buffer, 161
    sliding history buffer, 160–61
  decompression algorithm, 162
Ziv, Jacob, 159
Zombies, 328

	Advanced Encryption Standard
	Authentication Header
	American National Standards Institute
	Cipher Block Chaining
G	Communications-Electronics Security Group
FB	Cipher Feedback
DES	Data Encryption Standard
DSA	Digital Signature Algorithm
DSS	Digital Signature Standard
ECB	Electronic Codebook
ESP	Encapsulating Security Payload
FIPS	Federal Information Processing Standard
IAB	Internet Architecture Board
IDEA	International Data Encryption Algorithm
IETF	Internet Engineering Task Force
IP	Internet Protocol
IPSec	IP Security
ISO	International Organization for Standardization
ITU	International Telecommunication Union
ITU-T	ITU Telecommunication Standardization Sector
IV	Initialization Vector
KDC	Key Distribution Center
LAN	Local Area Network
MAC	Message Authentication Code
MIC	Message Integrity Code
MIME	Multipurpose Internet Mail Extension
MD5	Message Digest, Version 5
MTU	Maximum Transmission Unit
NIST	National Institute of Standards and Technology
NSA	National Security Agency
OFB	Output Feedback
PGP	Pretty Good Privacy
PRNG	Pseudorandom Number Generator
RFC	Request for Comments
RNG	Random Number Generator
RSA	Rivest-Shamir-Adelman
SET	Secure Electronic Transaction
SHA	Secure Hash Algorithm
SHS	Secure Hash Standard
S/MIME	Secure MIME
SNMP	Simple Network Management Protocol
SNMPv3	Simple Network Management Protocol Version 3
SSL	Secure Sockets Layer
TCP	Transmission Control Protocol
TLS	Transport Layer Security
UDP	User Datagram Protocol
WAN	Wide Area Network

ACRONYMS

AES	Advanced Encryption Standard
AH	Authentication Header
ANSI	American National Standards Institute
CBC	Cipher Block Chaining
CESG	Communications-Electronics Security Group
CFB	Cipher Feedback
DES	Data Encryption Standard
DSA	Digital Signature Algorithm
DSS	Digital Signature Standard
ECB	Electronic Codebook
ESP	Encapsulating Security Payload
FIPS	Federal Information Processing Standard
IAB	Internet Architecture Board
IDEA	International Data Encryption Algorithm
IETF	Internet Engineering Task Force
IP	Internet Protocol
IPSec	IP Security
ISO	International Organization for Standardization
ITU	International Telecommunication Union
ITU-T	ITU Telecommunication Standardization Sector
IV	Initialization Vector
KDC	Key Distribution Center
LAN	Local Area Network
MAC	Message Authentication Code
MIC	Message Integrity Code
MIME	Multipurpose Internet Mail Extension
MD5	Message Digest, Version 5
MTU	Maximum Transmission Unit
NIST	National Institute of Standards and Technology
NSA	National Security Agency
OFB	Output Feedback
PGP	Pretty Good Privacy
PRNG	Pseudorandom Number Generator
RFC	Request for Comments
RNG	Random Number Generator
RSA	Rivest-Shamir-Adelman
SET	Secure Electronic Transaction
SHA	Secure Hash Algorithm
SHS	Secure Hash Standard
S/MIME	Secure MIME
SNMP	Simple Network Management Protocol
SNMPv3	Simple Network Management Protocol Version 3
SSL	Secure Sockets Layer
TCP	Transmission Control Protocol
TLS	Transport Layer Security
UDP	User Datagram Protocol
WAN	Wide Area Network